CRIMINAL JUSTICE
Readings

Edited by

THOMAS F. ADAMS
SANTA ANA COLLEGE

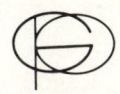

GOODYEAR PUBLISHING COMPANY, INC.
Pacific Palisades, California

**IN THE INTEREST OF JUSTICE
AND THE INDIVIDUALS INVOLVED
IN ITS ADMINISTRATION**

©1972 by
GOODYEAR PUBLISHING COMPANY, INC.

All rights reserved. No part of this book may be reproduced in any form or by any means without permission in writing from the publisher.

Library of Congress Catalog Card Number: 71-156864

ISBN: 0-87620-199-0

Y-1990-4

Current printing (last number):
10 9 8 7 6 5 4 3 2 1

Printed in the United States of America

Contents

Preface   v

SECTION ONE: THE POLICE ROLE   1

Why a Cop? Dorothy P. Humphrey   3
Are Policemen Supermen? Karl Menninger   5
Why? Richard B. Cadenasso   8
The Problems of Being a Police Officer, Richard H. Blum   9
The Patrolman, James Q. Wilson   21
A Sketch of the Policeman's "Working Personality,"
   Jerome H. Skolnick   34

SECTION TWO: POLICE SELECTION AND RETENTION   51

The Economic Aspects of Police Selection: The Oral Board,
   James H. Rankin   52
You Can't Tell by Looking, Kenneth W. Sherrill   63
Lateral Transfer, Glenn A. Marin   69
Operation: Police Manpower, James A. F. Kelly
   and Robert C. Barnum   76
*Keeping Policemen on the Job: Some Recommendations Arising from
   a Study of Men and Morale*, Richard H. Blum
   and William J. Osterloh   85
Are You Oriented to Hold Them? Thomas Reddin   92

SECTION THREE: PROFESSIONALIZATION   101

The Elusive Professionalization that Police Officers Seek,
   Walter F. Kreutzer   102
*The Working Policeman, Police "Professionalism," and the Rule
   of Law*, Jerome H. Skolnick   110

The Police: A Mission and Role, A. C. Germann — 124
Implications of Professionalism in Law Enforcement for Police-Community Relations, Louis A. Radelet — 132

SECTION FOUR: ACADEMIC PROGRESS IN LAW ENFORCEMENT — 141

Upgrading the Service, Larry D. Soderquist — 142
Law Enforcement Training and the Community College: Alternatives for Affiliation, Denny F. Pace, James D. Stinchcomb, and Jimmie C. Styles — 175
LEEP – Its Development and Potential, William E. Caldwell — 184
Federal Aid to Local Police–Trick or Treat, W. Cleon Skousen — 193

SECTION FIVE: POLICE DISCRETION — 199

"Alice" Would Have Questions Traveling in a Police Patrol Car, Dwight J. Dalbey — 200
Police Discretion, James Q. Wilson — 213
The Philosophy of Police Discretion, Thomas F. Adams — 218

SECTION SIX: CRITICAL ISSUES IN CRIMINAL JUSTICE — 233

A Justice Speaks on Law and Order, Charles E. Whittaker — 235
Bill of Rights in Spotlight during the 1960s, Harry M. Humphreys — 243
Needed: Order in the Courts, U. S. Chamber of Commerce — 257
Where the Correctional System Requires Correcting, U. S. Chamber of Commerce — 275
Current Issues in Law Enforcement, George Deukmejian — 288
Making Law and Order Work, John Lindsay — 292
Police Brutality or Public Brutality? Robert C. Byrd — 298
The Police and Society, Paul Chevigny — 303
An Open Letter on Police Review Boards, William H. Hewitt — 308
Police Brutality–Fact or Fantasy? Thomas F. Adams — 315
Lawmen Insist Only More Men Can Curb Street Crime, John Dreyfuss — 318
IMPACT–Detroit, Detroit Police Department — 322

SECTION SEVEN: COMMUNITY RELATIONS — 331

The Police Role in Community Relations, William H. Parker — 332
The Fringes of Police-Community Relations–Extremism, Nelson A. Watson — 345
Police and Politics: Speak Out on the Issues, Mark H. Furstenberg — 355
Community Indifference and the Growth of Crime, Frank D. Day — 361
Community Organizations as a Solution to Police-Community Problems, Oscar Handlin — 371

Preface

The administration of justice through our criminal justice system directly or indirectly affects everyone in our society; yet, relatively few people have any understanding of the system or the individuals who are involved in it. The average person's knowledge of criminal justice is most likely extremely limited, and his conceptions of the duties and responsibilities of the various agencies are probably misconceptions. A veil of mystery seems somehow to surround the various processes of law enforcement, prosecution, the courts, corrections, and rehabilitations—perhaps because people don't care to know unless the system touches them directly.

It is my hope that in this collection of articles the reader will find both a broad spectrum of valuable information about the criminal justice system and a variety of viewpoints. The reader is expected to use his own judgment in forming opinions about the several facets of the system. The result should be a greater understanding of the formal structure of criminal justice.

The volume is divided into seven sections: THE POLICE ROLE, POLICE SELECTION AND RETENTION, PROFESSIONALIZATION, ACADEMIC PROGRESS IN LAW ENFORCEMENT, POLICE DISCRETION, CRITICAL ISSUES IN CRIMINAL JUSTICE, COMMUNITY RELATIONS. Each section is of interest to anyone concerned with the administration of justice. These readings were selected because they are both timely and representative of the opinions of the experts, students, and interested individuals currently involved in the study and administration of the "System."

SECTION ONE

The Role of the Police

Overview

WHY A COP? Mrs. Dorothy P. Humphrey had been married to a veteran police officer 25 years when she chose to address the question from a wife's point of view.

ARE POLICEMEN SUPERMEN? Dr. Karl Menninger of the famous Menninger Clinic in Topeka, Kansas, writes about some of the psychological and social considerations of the policeman as "umpire" in the society he serves. The author seems to believe that the answer to his own question is "yes."

WHY? Richard B. Cadenasso, editor for the San Jose Peace Officers' Association and a member of that department, explains his reasons for being a police officer and he issues a challenge to those who would question him and his authority. This is a frank and honest statement of philosophy.

THE PROBLEMS OF BEING A POLICE OFFICER. Richard H. Blum discusses the personal problems of a police officer—conflict, tension, and insecurity. Some of the conflicts are centered around loyalties, temptations, use of force, and the dilemma of fear versus courage. Other conflicts involve the officer's acclimating himself to human misery and evil, making so many on-the-spot decisions, and having personal beliefs that may be out of tune with those of the society he serves.

THE PATROLMAN. James O. Wilson discusses the "order maintenance" aspect of the policeman's role, and many of the hazards and discretionary decisions involved in his job. Wilson refers to an officer as one who performs as a professional, though not belonging to a profession. The definition he presents of the "order maintenance" policeman: "... subprofessionals, working alone, exercise wide discretion in matters of utmost importance (life and death, freedom or incarceration) in an environment that is apprehensive and perhaps hostile."

A SKETCH OF THE POLICEMAN'S "WORKING PERSONALITY." This selection is from *Justice Without Trial: Law Enforcement in a Democratic Society* by Jerome H. Skolnick. An examination of the personal and emotional structure of the working policeman. Skolnick conducted exhaustive studies of the policemen and their work in two departments at opposite ends of the country which could be considered "representative" of the police community. Among other things, Skolnick discusses the social isolation of police officers.

Why a Cop?

Dorothy P. Humphrey

In December, 1964, Dick Nolan, Syndicated Columnist, after having been a judge of "best-column" entries in a regional newpaper aware contest, submitted to his readers an item entitled, "The Definition of a Cop." He admitted ignorance of the writer's identity. All entrants in the contest had been only key codes.

I am not the unknown writer of that article, but I remember it. It contained questions of who, what, when and why a policeman. The writer gave plausible answers.

The query probably responsible for my not forgetting the article was "Why." In today's society, with its turmoil of unrest, suspicion and hostility, that question looms ever larger, I'm sure, than it did in 1964.

"Why" in print is no more than a tiny, three-lettered word. We learn from experience, however, that the magnitude, scope and breadth of occurrences of human dilemmas about which it poses questions are sometimes beyond our limitations of perception or comprehension. It has been said there is an answer

Mrs. Dorothy P. Humphrey is secretary to the Richmond, California chief of police and is the wife of a 25-year veteran of the police force.

From Dorothy P. Humphrey, "Why a Cop?" *The Police Chief* 36, no. 7 (July 1969): 38-39. Reprinted by permission of the publisher.

to every question. That may be so, but I believe many answers offered by imperfect human beings could probably best be described as faulty rationalizations.

I'll try to speak of "Why a Cop." I'll admit in advance, though, that I'm not beyond my own faulty rationalizations!

My thoughts now dwell on the branches of a tree; on the twigs of a bush. Each seems to bend according to nature's laws. Are not similar laws of nature imposed on man?

A noted conductor, in presenting a masterpiece of musical composition that reveals the greatness of a composer, will remain true to the score. But even as he does, he will apply variations of the theme so that his own unique, distinctive interpretation and mastery of another's creation will be evident to those who listen.

So—even though thought, creative and emotional patterns of one person may closely parallel those of another, there are variations that omit the possibility of them being labeled identical.

I give this idea consideration in seeking answers to "Why a Cop." I can only engage in conjecture on the multitude of possibilities.

There was a time in history when man removed himself from isolated dwelling and joined with others to form a society. I believe it reasonable to assume that members of the newly formed society eventually learned there was real need for some measure of restriction on their individual and collective actions and pursuits. Before their infant society could develop and progress in an atmosphere of peace and security, controls for mutual welfare were a "must."

While it may have been difficult to determine the nature of restrictions and the extent of control needed, probably it was more difficult to determine those best qualified to act as enforcers and maintainers of the peace. It is one thing to establish rules; another to maintain them and to impartially apply them.

Human nature is fickle and illusive. Individuals may acknowledge the need for a reasonably controlled society. Even as they do, many are resentful of it. They utter cries of illogical immunity when restrictions and control are made applicable to them.

Human nature and the bend of the twig being as they are, it can pretty well be considered evident that those who first accepted responsibility for enforcement found themselves target for the resentment, condemnation and even hatred of their fellow man, for whom they were performing a requested service.

WHY A COP?

Why is any person willing to subject himself to these varying degrees of hostility? I ponder a maze of possibilities.

It could be easier for some to assume authority than to submit to it.

It could be that some, in sincerity, are their brother's "keeper," with all the intent of good will that the title implies.

It could be that some are dedicated to the fundamental principles of justice and truth; that they seek to preserve and advance these principles.

It could be that some know compassion and apply themselves to helping the *weak* and *ill* who violate the laws of society.

It could be that some need the semi-military authority and discipline of the profession, as a curb on their own activities; or as a crutch to lean on to escape responsibility for making their own life's decisions.

It could be that some are morbidly curious concerning the misfortunes of others; that they find sadistic satisfaction by vicariously involving themselves in human woes.

It could be that some seek opportunity to hide behind the guise of legal authority so they might become recipients of unlawful "pay-offs," proffered by agents of lawlessness.

It could be that some experience a "dizzy heights" surge of their egos when they are resplendent in their official attire of uniform and badge. Civilian garb would not create an illusion of romantic appeal.

It could be that some are drawn, as if magnetized, to the danger and hazards always present in law enforcement. They fancy a kind of excitement; heroic acts; martyrdom.

It could be that some merely consider the profession as a desirable way to earn a living and provide for their families.

It could be that some seek outlets for suppressed hostilities. A role of authority may offer avenues of release. To these, authority is power, not responsibility; power is righteousness; righteousness punishes sinners.

It could be that some can make come alive their ideals of humanitarianism, by exemplifying in their conduct and in their treatment of others the prevalence of good over evil; by exhibiting qualities of kindness, patience, tolerance and understanding.

I'll admit that not all possibilities offered could be considered as honorable in intent. I hope, however, they suggest reality. But . . . you know what? In my imagination, I see all the could be's placed in a pot and boiled together. Maybe the impurities would rise to the surface, to be scooped up in a ladle for discard. That which would remain might be the answer sought.

As if deduced by a chemically applied formula, the *Why* of a good cop . . . a dedicated cop . . . could be equivalent to . . . *heart!* His purpose: to suppress evil; to advance good.

Or are these merely the passé, sentimental ramblings of an "Old Timer," gleaned only from the book of practical experience and application? *It could be!*

One thing is sure. The future, with its own kinds of strife, must be inherited by the young. I can't do more than wish them good luck, good judgment and wisdom. A word of caution. Be alert in detecting the wiles and the bend of human nature.

How will the branches of our future society grow? I hope they'll be straight and true, free from the gnarls of hatred, mistrust and violence so evident as the discordant theme of this era. Variations of this theme will promise no answer. I suggest sane and harmonious digression from it, without appeasement or surrender of basic concepts of freedom inherited by all Americans—even cops.

Are Policemen Supermen?

Karl Menninger

It should not be very hard to persuade a policeman to agree that his job requires him to have the ability of a superman. As a matter of fact, in choosing his profession, he has elected to be a superman. What he has said is that he wishes to announce himself ready to act more forcefully, more wisely, more calmly, more bravely and more law-abidingly than the average man.

But can he? Is he really a superman?

In some cases he can prove it—by physical tests, for example. Furthermore, a study conducted at the Menninger Clinic a few years ago showed that our Kansas police officers, at least, are also well above the average in intelligence.

But intelligence and physique are not the only factors to be considered in the selection of competent police officers. Motives and emotions are important as well as brains and muscles. Why does an applicant want to be a police officer in the first place? What concept has he of the profession he is about to join? What ideals does he have and what sacrifices is he willing to make in order to fill his uniform with pride and competence? Does the young candidate aspire to his job because he wants to look important? Because he wants to bully people? Because he wants to have an excuse to get away from his wife a little more often? Sometimes these secret motives are the real ones.

The man who has secret inferiority feelings, the man with an over-strong, vengeful conscience, the man who lacks self-respect, the man with burning resentment against authority of any kind—such a man will become a bad police officer. He is not a superman except in authority—and he promotes public danger rather than public safety. Such individuals, given the authority of the law, become the destroyer of the law. They think that to insure respect they must inspire fear.

All of us, whether we are doctors, poets, grocery clerks, politicians, racketeers, drunkards, gangsters, scientists, priests, or police officers have within

Dr. Karl Menninger, M.D., is chairman of the Board of Trustees of The Menninger Foundation in Topeka, Kansas.
From Karl Menninger, "Are Policemen Supermen?" *The Police Chief* 32, no. 9 (September 1965): 26-27. Reprinted by permission of the publisher.

us aggressive, destructive, lawless, cruel, selfish, ruthless tendencies which are capable of coming to the surface under the right conditions.

All the things that we call civilization—the radios, bathtubs, neckties, automobiles, books, paintings, cosmetics—are really just a thick veneer over the basic biological nature of the people who drive the automobiles, use the cosmetics, read the books and listen to the radio.

I call these aggressive drives "tendencies" to indicate that while they may rarely come to full expression they are always there. Civilization is nothing more than the development of a program for controlling these aggressive impulses. We are constantly losing partial control of these tendencies and requiring help from our neighbors or our police officers or our wives.

Policemen have these destructive tendencies just like everyone else. And they must learn to master them in themselves before they can efficiently master them in others. In this respect, if in no other, a competent policeman would deserve the title of "superman."

A police officer is a personification of conscience. This may either be a conscience of ideals or a conscience of vengence. The police officer has many temptations and one of them is to use his power and authority vengefully and hence destructively instead of constructively. The possession of authority is a great burden. Few can bear it and still fewer can be trusted to employ it constructively.

One aid in the control of aggressiveness is good manners. After all, the customs and laws of the country are merely some rules about good manners. It is not good manners to take another fellow's property or to risk another fellow's life in a speeding car. It used to be, but it isn't now and it is written down in a book so it is called a law.

Good manners help. So does education. So does religion. So do work and play. It is certainly better to cut weeds than to cut throats—it takes the same kind of energy, psychological and physical. It is better to beat a golf ball around the links or to beat someone at tennis than to use this same energy in a fist fight or driving a hot-rod at 90 miles an hour.

In the list of things that can help in the control of destructive impulses I give a prominent place to the "umpire." This is my conception of the police officer of the new type—an umpire or linesman whose primary duty is not to arrest people but to enable people to avoid the necessity of being arrested.

People need policemen. People are most comfortable when they feel there are rules and regulations regarding such things as driving, for example—when these exist for a reason (the reason of safety, in this case)—and which it is not the privilege of any individual to break.

They are more comfortable when they feel that such rules and regulations are enforced by umpires who are not inverted footpads, but who are friends not of one driver, but of all drivers.

Every police officer has to remember that people are not only animals, they are also children. This is true no matter how old they are and it is one reason why the man behind the wheel of a high-powered automobile is often such a different individual from that same man as a pedestrian. A child is small and weak and knows it, but he thinks that when he grows up he will be big and strong. Then he grows up and finds he is not very big and not very strong compared to all the forces in the world. Hence, all people continue to suffer from a feeling of inferiority. And if one gives such a person who has allowed this feeling to dominate him a 160-horsepower engine that will run many times faster than the most vicious stepmother or the most irate uncle or the most domineering father—give such a grown-up child a machine like this and what does he care for little blue-coated policemen or little printed signs that say "slow" or little marks in a book that say "30 miles an hour." The child in him is always tempted to forget the rules and penalties and all the realities of social existence.

But our superman, the police officer, has to remember them and has to remember the child in every man—even in himself. And if the child or the beast in the man should become dominant, the police officer can no longer stand as a symbol, a reminder, a warning. He must act. Powered by his authority, he must oppose the irrational childishness or the ruthless beastliness of the driver. He must put himself on the side of the driver's better self, his adult self, his mature self. And the police officer should never forget there is such a self.

Even the worst man has his ideals and it is the side of these ideals, on the side of the offender's intelligence, conscience, knowledge and better judgment that the policeman must align himself. This is the part of the offender that must not be frightened by the policeman, but strengthened. It needs help from the police officer in suppressing the rebellious elements of the personality.

Some people have great difficulty, even with the very best of help, in suppressing the childishness within them. These are the habitual offenders, and they include both those who seem to have no respect for the law whatever and those who seem to respect it and try to keep it, but are always getting into trouble of some kind through "someone else's fault." The National Safety Council has said that 90 percent of the traffic accidents are caused by 10 percent of the drivers. People who have so little esteem for themselves that, consciously or unconsciously, they drive as though they were seeking to destroy themselves (not to mention others) and do it again and again—these "accident prone" people are just as sick as if they had cancer or polio or heart disease, and they need help just as badly. Many of these people would benefit more by seeing a psychiatrist than a judge.

To be a policeman does in fact require the qualities of a superman—intelligence, understanding, warmth, kindness, patience, tact and an immeasurable amount of self-control. Are these qualities appreciated by the public? Most certainly not. But let me ask you, too, if they are appreciated by the policemen themselves? When policemen come to have a higher opinion of themselves, to recognize that they are leaders in the community (the conscience of the community, as it were), umpires in the great game of semi-domesticated human beings trying to live peaceably with one another in a complicated world, they will inspire similar respect, support and admiration from the public at large.

Why?

Richard B. Cadenasso

In recent weeks, there have appeared several articles asking why anyone would want to become a "cop." In light of the fact that open warfare now rages in this country, with policemen as the prime targets, I believe that this question is a legitimate one.

As one policeman, I cannot begin to answer that question for all my brother officers. However, I would like to give my reasons for having become a policeman and for what reasons I remain in this profession.

Primarily, I believe in the American dream of freedom for all within the limits of constitutional law. Despite the fact that this country sometimes seems too timid to save itself, I believe that our system is the best that man has been able to devise to date. In my opinion, no political system prior to ours has been more responsive to human needs.

As a police officer, I don't have to wave or display a flag to demonstrate my patriotism. Just being a policeman and upholding my oath is in itself an act of patriotism. The maintenance of constitutional law is the greatest act that any man can do for this country. It is basically for this reason that I entered the police profession.

I would be the first to admit that this country is not without imperfection. It is true, that the advance of technology has placed severe strains on the present system, which in turn has led to the alienation of some people. Severe problems in fact do exist, which to many seem insurmountable. However, despite these shortcomings, I believe that our democratic process is capable of setting things straight.

Our present governmental process, in my opinion is well able to handle the gravest of problems, if only given the proper chance. Given the ingredient of "due process," a wide variety of ideas will always be available for test in the market place of government.

Radical attacks on the system employing such means as murder, bombings, rioting, and disruption of legal process are under no circumstances justifiable in a democracy. People who employ these techniques have no genuine desire for

From Richard B. Cadenasso, "Why?" *Vanguard* 8, Bulletin 19 (September 4, 1970): 2. (Published by the San Jose Peace Officers' Association.) Reprinted by permission of the author and the publisher.

justice. Criminal acts of this nature are performed by those who suffer from ego-centered motives.

In short, I became a cop to protect something that I feel deserves the fullest of protection, namely democratic process. To this end, I am prepared to lay down my life.

I never did like to see innocent people get pushed around by punks. In years past it was candidly recognized that some anti-social, non-productive leech-like elements existed in our society and no excuses were made for their behavior. These individuals, when they stepped out of line, were dealt with accordingly.

Now it seems that some of our more liberally biased contemporaries have successfully rationalized the behavior of these environmentally misshapen souls. Well, I don't buy it, sociologically speaking, a punk by any other name is still a punk.

These misfits may attempt to challenge the present system by mindless acts of violence, but are doomed to failure. Despite their cries of revolution, they scare no one. Any time they muster the courage to stop moving their mouths and want to fight it out, I and many others in this institution are more than ready for them.

I am prepared to fight for my beliefs, and if in the process a few revolutionaries go to "boot hill," *so be it.*

The Problems of Being a Police Officer

Richard H. Blum

The police comprise one of the most important occupational groups in the nation. They are important because they keep our complex society together. They keep its citizens living, working, and prospering within the framework of civilized law and acceptable social conduct. Consequently it is to the advantage of every citizen that the importance of police work be recognized, and that the performance of police work be made as efficient, sensible, and satisfying as possible.

Unfortunately there exist many hazards and problems in police work which tend to make the work itself inefficient and troublesome. These same hazards make the job difficult for the individual policeman, and can create stresses and

From Richard H. Blum, "The Problems of Being a Police Officer," *Police* 5, no. 2 (November-December 1960): 10-13 and *Police* 6, no. 2 (January-February 1961): 33-37. Reprinted by permission of the author and the publisher, Charles C Thomas.

strains in his personal life. The cause and potential cure of these occupational problems becomes the concern of the psychologist who is involved in police work.

The following discussion will be limited to personal problems which arise from the job. I will not discuss any mental health problems that individual policemen, like any other human beings, may have. I will consider only the special problems of conflict, tension, and insecurity which occur *because* a man is an officer.

Conflict is at the bottom of many emotional and mental upsets. Conflict occurs upon having two or more desires, neither of which is compatible with the other. For example: wanting to be honest and at the same time wanting to pretend to be sick in order not to perform some unpleasant task.

TYPICAL POLICE OFFICER CONFLICTS ARISING FROM THE JOB

Conflict of Loyalties

Policemen want to be loyal to brother officers in order to win their friendship and approval. Like men in any other work group, friendship ties and loyalty help people to work together, and make a man confident that he can count on another's help should some danger or trouble arise. The policeman's problem is that conflict can arise when loyalty runs afoul of administrative directives, or the law itself.

Take for example, the case of a two-man patrol car called to investigate a burglary in a liquor store. One man observes his partner take a fifth of whiskey off the shelf, and put it in his pocket. Here is the conflict, should the observing officer be loyal to his thieving partner by saying nothing about the matter? Should he apply differential standards of law enforcement by merely telling his partner, "You had better put that back, or you could get into trouble?"—or, should the observing officer enforce the law by turning his brother officer in? There is no happy solution. The conflict of loyalty versus lawfulness is always with the officer as he is faced with wanting trust, friendship and reliability, on the one hand while wanting to be lawful on the other hand. The conflict can lead to mental health problems in the policeman, shown by nervousness, sleeplessness, self-doubt, or guilt feelings.

As another example of the loyalty problem, a police department had been getting bad publicity for sloppy procedures. An outside management expert was called in, who began to interview selected men in each division to find out what was wrong. One sergeant knew very well that his superior was a lazy and inefficient supervisor, often asleep at the switch. On the other hand, the supervisor was a nice guy who had been kind to the sergeant. The outside expert asked the sergeant about his supervision. What should he say? He was in conflict, for he wanted to be loyal to his supervisor, while at the same time the sergeant knew very well that the supervisor was doing a poor job, and was responsible for some of the mess the division was in. Concealment, or the truth, was the issue. The conflict caused the sergeant many a sleepless night, but his final decision was in favor of protecting the supervisor.

Loyalty conflict is never easily solved. One lieutenant I knew decided that he would always act on the idealistic principle of honesty before loyalty. Consequently, during a grand jury investigation, he testified against several fellow supervisors whom he knew were either inefficient or dishonest. He was commended by the grand jury and the District Attorney, but it was five years before any of his fellow officers would speak to him. The anger of his colleagues was harder to take than the previous conflict of loyalty versus truthfulness. On the other hand, a sergeant I knew made the opposite decision, he decided to shield three of his men whom he knew to be drinking on duty. Loyalty came first. One of these drinking officers later wrecked a police car, seriously injuring a child in a cross-walk. Investigation revealed that the officer had been driving while intoxicated. The sergeant knew he was responsible indirectly, and became very depressed, for his conscience bothered him for not having recommended suspension of the drinking man.

Solution to these conflicts of loyalties can come only if an entire department commits itself to a principle. One man alone cannot eliminate the conflict of loyalty versus truthfulness just by resolving that he will be honest, or by being willing to withstand the anger of his fellow officers. However, if the entire police department increases its feeling of being a profession, expands its code of operating ethics to say that everyone is not only expected to put truthfulness ahead of loyalty, but will not be criticized once he does so, then the conflict can be reduced. This can happen when everyone in a department decides that they want to be proud of their profession and so instill in each other a rigorous code which does put principle above loyalty.

Conflict Coming from Temptation

Police officers, especially in larger cities, are probably more often subject to painful temptation than any other profession. The temptation, usually in the form of money or stock in trade of vice, can hardly help but appeal. One side of the conflict is the very human desire for money, gifts, or other material gains or pleasures of the flesh. The other side of the conflict is the voice of conscience which says the officer should be law-abiding. The conflict is even more difficult when the police officer is frequently exposed to citizens whom he knows are crooked, but whom he watches prosper and succeed on the basis of their racketeering, high-level thieving, or what-have-you. The more the officer is aware that crime does pay, the more he learns that justice is a fickle lady who sometimes rewards the worst, and punishes the best, the harder it is to resist temptation. Thus, the policeman himself can be tempted to seek success by the dishonesty which he sees others have so successfully employed.

The high cost of living and the officer's fixed salary also contribute to the desire of some officers to "live it up." The situation is made even worse when a police department is itself corrupt. Usually the big cities are the worst offenders in this regard. When the policeman is aware that his own fellow officers are getting ahead by being dishonest, then it is difficult to resist temptation. It becomes nearly impossible to do so when, as in some large cities, the honest policeman is punished by his own superiors for too strict enforcement of the law, while the dishonest officer is given the choice assignments as part of a department's organized corruption. The conflict still exists if the officer does participate in the corruption, for by giving in to temptation, he does not eliminate his guilty conscience or his fear of eventually being called to account for his actions.

The solution to the problem of temptation lies only partly within the individual officer's strength of character and honest will power. Much of the solution lies within the community, through the character of its citizens and the honesty of its political leaders. The individual policeman's temptation is fairly easily eliminated when the citizens of the community are not themselves criminal, do not continually tempt the police, and elect politicians who insist on honesty in the departments. If the citizens of the community will insist on honesty, and the majority do not offer temptation or condone corruption, then the police officer's conflict is much reduced.

Conflict over Fear Versus Courage

An elemental conflict arises whenever individuals are faced with danger which they should not flee. Police, more often than ordinary citizens, have the conflict of facing danger bravely, versus finding less courageous but far more comfortable safety. A case of such a conflict occurred when a foot patrolman came upon an armed robber, just as the robber was running from a grocery store. The running robber opened fire; the officer started pursuit, returning fire. He was sorely tempted to run slowly, for the policeman was a large target at close range (he weighed about 210 lbs.). The officer knew that if he ran slowly the robber would escape, thusly the officer would face less risk. Even though he wanted to slow down because of his fear, he was so intent on the pursuit that he did not. For his trouble he was wounded, but also wounded the felon.

This conflict of fear versus duty, or fear versus courage cannot be solved. However, it can be made somewhat less acute by an admission of fear, or by not having to pretend that the fear is not there. Good police training, which teaches the officer how to reduce actual risk to himself, will reduce the conflict; administrative procedures can also be worked out to provide maximum protection to the working officer by providing him with good equipment, assigning two-man patrols to high-risk areas, and so forth.

Conflict over Use of Force

This is a less frequent conflict, it occurs when a person has been raised to believe that violence is wrong, but then a police officer must use force in his work. Some policemen feel a reluctance to employ force because of their belief in its being wrong, consequently they can be in conflict over the reluctance versus the need to use force if they are to perform their job, or even to survive.

As one example you are told not to manhandle crazy people, but to bring them to the hospital with gentle understanding. On the other hand the psychotic person may be quite dangerous, and you know very well that you will have to use force to subdue him. When you bring the bruised patient into the psychiatric ward you get a stony fish-eyed glance from the nurse, who, observing the bruised patient, makes you feel like you were brutal. You end up feeling guilty about how you subdued the patient, even though there seemed to be no choice.

As another example, take the troubles the Army had during the Korean and World Wars, where up to 50 percent of the men on the line did not fire their weapons during a fire fight. They had been taught not to kill, they didn't want to draw fire, and they were afraid. As a result, they couldn't shoot. For many soldiers there was a dreadful emotional conflict over the use of force.

The same conflict can be seen in policemen, as for example, when an officer finds himself in a shooting situation for the first time. One policeman of whom I knew, had been on the force for seven years but had never been called upon to fire his weapon. One day while on foot patrol he came upon a holdup trio. They fired at him and he raised his gun to return the fire. His trigger finger was frozen, and he could not shoot. The holdup trio escaped and the officer engaged in some serious soul searching about whether or not he could ever shoot to kill.

While the moral conflict may not be solved, proper police training can help. It can help by doing what the Army now does, using human-like dummies instead of bulls-eyes as targets in pistol and rifle practice. In the case of psychiatric patients, training can be given in exactly how best to quiet a disturbed person without using excess force or violence. Part of the training problem is to give the policeman enough training that he feels confident about his own safety with violent people. Chances are that the more confident the officer feels, the more secure he is by virtue of his training, the less likely he is to use either excess force, or to fail to use as much force as the situation realistically requires.

The reverse of the reluctance to use force is an unusual, but very serious problem. It is the use of the policeman's uniform as a mask for brutality and violence. Some few individuals are only too willing to use violence, even when it is not called for in the performance of duty. They will entice citizens into argument, will lure juveniles into a fight, then will handle the situation in a brutal fashion. These men can give an entire department a bad reputation. Any conflict they have over force is resolved in favor of force, without using proper self-control.

Conflict over Human Misery and Evil

One of the most unpleasant parts of the policeman's job is that he is forced to deal with human pain, misery, and evil. At the scene of an accident, he must face death and gruesome injury without giving in to his own inclinations to get sick or run away. On a neighbor's call, he may enter a home to find a little child terribly beaten by a drunken father. The policeman must make the arrest without indulging his urge to personally punish the vicious childbeater. In such cases the policeman's first human reaction is an emotional one; to be sickened by gruesome injury, to want to run from a mangled body, to want to assault the person who has killed or injured the child, to want to shoot the killer who has shot a brother officer down in cold blood.

The problem for the policeman is that unlike other human beings he cannot allow his real emotions to be expressed; he cannot show what he feels when faced with misery or evil. Instead the requirements of his job and personal pride require that he maintain control of himself and of others, that he act with calm efficiency to help the injured, protect the public safety, or arrest a felon.

What usually happens is that the police officer learns ways of controlling himself, or of defending against his very human emotional reactions. He "gets used to" horror by paying less attention to it, he "shuts it out of his mind," by not allowing himself to think about what he has just seen, or he becomes "hard-boiled," encasing himself in a kind of emotional armour. But no matter what he does, the policeman does not escape the fact that daily he is faced with human tragedy, which he can do little to prevent or alleviate. However much the police officer may want to prevent human misery, he is powerless to do so. It is one of the greatest emotional burdens of police work. As long as policemen must face the emergencies of horror, there is no real solution. The most common partial solution is to become somewhat "hard-boiled." In doing so, however, the policeman must also try to be sure that he does not loose his inner human tenderness and sensitivity.

CONFLICT OVER DECISIONS

Another characteristic of the policeman's job is the fact that he must make immediate on-the-spot decisions. He must make up his mind "right now" without the luxury of thinking for too long, looking up information in a book, or asking a superior which course of action is best. The policeman is under real pressure; pressures which he can't avoid. The conflict occurs when some situation requires a decision which isn't easy; naturally, he would prefer not to have to commit himself to an action which may prove wrong. The wrong decision can lead to annoyances like being reprimanded by the sergeant, or it can lead to unnecessary injury or death.

Take for example, the case of the policeman pursuing an armed robber on foot in a pedestrian-crowded downtown street. The felon fires on the officer but should the officer return the fire? If he does he may endanger the lives of the fast-dispersing citizens; if he does not he may fail to make the capture, or he may himself get shot. Assume the officer decides to return the fire; assume the felon is captured but some bystander is also wounded. The town newspapers will no doubt bring pressure on the so-called "wild West" tactics of the police force.

Usually, the officer has no really excellent alternatives; most of the on-the-spot decisions he must make are like the example: a choice of evils. No wonder the policeman is in conflict from the pressure to choose one evil through a quick decision, versus his real desire to get himself off the hook by passing the buck or evading the issue.

Because the officer is always on the hot spot with having to make choice-of-evil decisions he may also develop some envious intolerance of people who don't have to stick their necks out. As a man of action the policeman can be understandably annoyed with other people who appear not to have to act or to decide in crises. The policeman, for example, can become rather impatient with the psychiatrist who "doesn't have to do anything but sit in his office and listen to people gripe," which is the way one policeman characterized the psychiatrist's work to me. This understandable impatience and intolerance of the luckier ones who don't work under such pressure can actually lead to troubles between the police profession and others with whom they must work, as for example psychiatrists, lawyers, judges and the like.

The best solution for the problem posed by the need for on-the-spot decisions is to improve police training. The job can't be changed, but the more knowledge and experience the officer can bring to the "hot spot," the better he will be able to make the right decision. Thorough training can make the policeman rightly confident of his ability to make the correct decision.

CONFLICTS IN BELIEF

Authority versus rebellion. There are certain conflicts in ideas and beliefs which are common to policemen. While these are not likely to interfere with efficiency of job performance, nor lead to real emotional upset, they are conflicts that may lead to dissatisfaction with one's job as a police officer. They may lead to irritation, confusion, or uncertainty about the profession one has chosen.

One of these problems is a conflict of admiration of the rebel versus obedience to authority. More than any other group, the police represent authority in our society. By such "authority," I mean constituted power, the right to command. To the average citizen, police are the visual signs of authority. At the same time there is, in America, a strong admiration for the rebel, the fellow who can "get away with it." There is envy of the man who can break the law, or who can laugh at authority. Because the admiration for the successful rebel is so much part of our lore, it is impossible for many people not to share it, including the policeman. As an example, the admiration for the daring initial success of the Boston Brinks robbers, which you all know is shared by many. There is envy of the way that Errol Flynn could get away with having such an underage girls friend. In the Jesse James era, you all are aware of the way in which Jesse was admired as a hero.

The consequence of this conflict between respect for authority and admiration of the rebel, is the fact that some police personnel may wonder if they are really on the right side. The officer may not be so sure that his job of being the "authority" is the right one after all. Some officers may believe that the rebel is correct. The policeman may also wonder if he wants to be the one against whom people are rebelling, for it is not pleasant to be the target of rebellion.

Conflicts in belief—How should a policeman act? At the present time, the policeman is exposed to several different philosophies about what his job is, and how he should conduct himself. It is a part of the large conflict that our society has about the policeman's approach to, and the handling of the criminal offender. What, exactly, does law-enforcement seek? Protection of the citizen, revenge on the evil-doer, prevention of crime through deterrant example, rehabilitation of the criminal? It probably seeks each, but the trouble is that these goals may be in conflict with one another. If so, the peace officer is in the middle.

The fact that rehabilitation cannot be practiced at the same time as arrest and conviction may be seen in the separation of probation from police work. A conflict can occur between peace officers and probation officers about how offenders should be treated. This can be a serious problem for both sides, one which can affect their morale and well-being. As an example, a police officer may spend considerable time and effort investigating a case, making an arrest, and preparing his reports for inclusion as evidence. His efforts to apprehend the criminal will inevitably be hard work, they may also involve physical danger to himself. Then, the court will put the offender on probation, so that the offender "beats the officer home," as the saying goes. Of course the officer cannot help but feel discouraged and frustrated; it is as though he has been hired to do the wrong duty, one that society did not actually intend for him to do. All of his efforts seemed to have been in vain.

On the other hand, the probation officer also suffers from the conflict in philosophy. He may be working very hard on the rehabilitation of an offender, a project that seems to be coming along well, when suddenly, his probationer is arrested on suspicion, and subjected to some very unfriendly interrogation. In spite of his release upon being cleared, the probationer is so discouraged by being thought of by police as "once a bum, always a bum," that he obliges them by resuming his criminal activities. The probation officer then can only blame the rehabilitation failure on the arresting policemen and their attitudes.

These problems of differing attitudes about the approach to, and the handling of offenders, are indeed serious ones for all law enforcement personnel. For example how can an officer be "understanding" with juveniles who take advantage of liberal laws, commit crimes with apparent impunity, insult the arresting officer, perhaps even hit him, and then laughingly say, "You can't touch me, I'm a juvenile." The policeman may feel obliged to be permissive with juveniles once he has received training in some ivory tower psychology course; but how can he be permissive when perhaps two 17-year-olds are shooting guns at citizens?

In point of fact, modern sociology and psychology have served in many ways to make life harder for peace officers by confusing them about their jobs and actions. Emphasis on "understanding" the criminal has been interpreted by some people as meaning that there should be no punishment for offenders, only "treatment." This is believed in spite of the fact that there are very few "treatments" known to "cure" the ordinary (not mentally-ill) criminal. Some people have gone so far as to take the scientific notion of determinism, that is, the idea that all events are caused by preceding events and present conditions, to mean that there is no free will. If this is so, then no one can be held responsible for what they do. Our entire framework of individual responsibility under the law would be out of date. Where does that leave the policeman? Confused at best.

As long as mental health notions are applied to the really sick people, either the crazy ones or the obviously neurotic ones, then the policeman can get useful information, as for example on how to recognize the mentally ill, or on handling depressed or violently ill people. On the other hand, when unclear psychological notions are applied to ordinary criminals to suggest that punishment is wrong, or that treatment of the individual is more important than protection of the community, then you have a conflict of ideas that makes law enforcement officers understandably uncertain about just what they should be doing.

For example, in Palo Alto recently, there was debate over the high speed pursuit of two juveniles who shot at the pursuing officer, and then crashed, killing an innocent driver. Review of the letter-to-the-editor column, shows a substantial number of citizens criticizing the officer for doing what his job required, i.e., pursuing a fleeing felon, and returning fire when fired upon. Some citizens write that the juveniles involved were nice kids not given a fair chance, or that the officer should not have pursued them for it would have been better to let them go. These are strong public pressures, that can only upset the policeman who did his duty. He receives criticism instead of thanks; he becomes confused by conflicting demands instead of being reassured by community agreement on what his job is.

The problems lead to the consideration of a closely related difficulty, the fact that the policeman is uncertain about how he should act. Some uncertainty is not based on any inner conflict of beliefs or motives within the officer himself, rather, it comes from society either not knowing what it wants from the police, or from various citizens acting inconsistently toward the police. The result is the policeman's uncertainty which leads towards his being discouraged, disgusted, and sometimes inefficient.

POLICE OFFICER PROBLEMS
LEADING TO UNCERTAINTY

Community Change

A community may change in its population, leaving the police with few guideposts on how to act with the new element. For example, a Negro minority group moves into a northern city, bringing with them their own customs and traditions, some of which are in conflict with the local law. Child neglect, fighting, knifings, living out of wedlock, narcotics, may all be a part of an accepted way of life for them, but not for the staid community into which they move. Just how should the policeman act? Should he enforce middle class laws on people who come from a different kind of society? If so, he tackles an almost impossible task. However, if he does not enforce those laws, then he is guilty of differential treatment, or setting up a double standard. Either way, some people in town will be displeased with the police service. While the policeman suffers from the public criticism resulting from population change, he can do nothing about it, as the problem lies in the fact that the community itself has not adjusted to its new element.

POLICE DEPARTMENT CHANGES

Another thing that leads to uncertainty and to personal distress, is the fact that police departments themselves change rather rapidly these days, both because they expand with fast growing populations, and because standards for police work are changing as fast as technical knowledge and social philosophies change. One thing that may occur is that men with seniority on the force may be passed by in promotions, in favor of the younger men with more technical training. The experienced older men can't help but be bitter, as they see less experienced youngsters get ahead of them. The older men feel betrayed, left out, discriminated against; all of this when they have worked hard and well for many years. Cliques develop within the department, and political battles take more energy than law enforcement, while the old fight the new. Morale goes to pot for all concerned.

The new men have their troubles, also; they feel frustrated when tradition or old-fashioned administrators prevent them from doing the good job they think they can do. Their skills are not applied as best they could, so they, too, become depressed and discouraged, wondering if police work was meant for them after all. The departments themselves, under so much pressure, have not had the time to coordinate experience with the new knowledge to make their changes in an efficient fashion. Again social changes have made life hard for the policeman.

PUBLIC ACCEPTANCE

Perhaps the most serious of all problems that plague the policeman is public acceptance. Here is the root of much of his uncertainty and job-caused conflict.

The public has not yet made up its mind that it really wants a policeman. As long as that is the case, the policeman has troubles. Part of the public's uncertainty is because of this American rebellion against authority, which I have noted. The public knows it *needs* policemen, but actually wanting them is another matter. Another part of the uncertainty is the fact that we haven't just one public, but we have dozens of different publics, each with its own set of standards, beliefs, and customs. For example, the Chinese, the Mexicans, the Southern Negro recently come north, the upper class set, the middle class, the working class, and etc. Because there are so many different kinds of people in America, no one can seem to reach agreement of which laws to enforce, or how to enforce them.

Another reason for the public's failure to accept the police is that in many ways we have a criminal society. Too many people want the laws to apply to the other fellow, while they are free to do what they want, whether it is being a litterbug, placing bets with a bookie, driving at 90 miles an hour, or cheating on their income tax. All of these are fairly minor offenses, as offenses go, but, too many good citizens like their bad habits enough to resent the inhibiting presence of the police. For example, you all know of John Q. Public, who needs a policeman badly enough when his store is robbed, or when there is a prowler about. Then he can't see an officer fast enough. When the officer comes, he is hero for the hour. However, on the next evening, when John Q. is drunk driving, then the arresting officer is Mr. Poison himself. What a shift from hero one minute, to brutal tyrant the next—no wonder the average policeman feels betrayed by the public who hires him. The officer can't help but be uncertain about himself, not sure if he is a public enemy, or a knight in shining armour. What the policeman needs is continuous support and respect from the public, not the continual shift from love to hate, and back again.

Part of the public acceptance problem is in the fact that the public really hasn't made up its mind about what crime is, even if there are black and white laws on the books. As long as its mind isn't made up, the public will treat its police force shabbily, giving them support one time, and a lot of resistance the next. Lynching, for example, is a crime, but the small Southern town does not accept it as such. Drunk driving is a crime, but haven't you all read newspaper articles which raise a clamor when drunk drivers lose their driver's licenses after arrest and conviction. Oral intercourse is a crime, but Kinsey tells us three out of four married couples are guilty of it; and Lord save an arresting officer who brings that charge on a prominent citizen. In Indiana, masturbation is a crime, but who can, or would, enforce that one? You see, the list is long, but the conclusion is short. The public has not yet decided what is crime and what isn't. The policeman is neither judge nor jury, but the public expects him to be both by giving him laws which cannot be enforced, or laws which should be enforced, but which he is supposed to be discreet enough to ignore. Is it no wonder that police officers become confused and depressed on the job. Their job is not clearly defined, nor can they expect to be supported when they do their job as they see it.

THE IRRITATING PRESS

One of the irritating things that contribute to the lack of public acceptance is the enjoyment that newspapers seem to take in publicizing any misbehavior on the part of police officers themselves. Because the policeman is supposed to prevent crime and not to commit it, this journalistic enthusiasm over police misconduct may be understandable, but it is certainly no help in shaping public respect. Police departments seem to be one of the favorite targets of the press. Small things are made large, any little slip gets memorialized on the front page, and given a big scandal, the papers will spend weeks in an ecstasy of editorials. Police misconduct is news, there's no getting away from it. But the effect of its being news is to constantly remind the public that their law-enforcing heroes too often have feet of clay.

The solution for this newspaper irritant is three-fold: (1) better selection of police officers so that potentially unstable or dishonest officers are not put on the force; (2) efficient and nonpolitical administration of police departments so that corruption is not allowed, and so that police department administration and appointments do not become a political football.

By taking local politics out of police appointments and management one would take away the incentive for the opposition press to use a police department as an example of the corruption or poor administration of the party in power. As an aside it is likely that removing police from politics would provide more stable and efficient police departments per se.

(3) The third part of the solution of the journalistic irritant is to develop better police department relations with the local papers. Instead of playing hide-and-seek with police reporters as some officials do, it is preferable to make the reporters feel they are getting a fair shake from the police, that they are not being denied properly public information, and that the reporter's ethical commitment not to print information given in confidence can indeed be trusted. Given better public relations with reporters and editors, one can count on a much more favorable newspaper treatment of police affairs.

If there were any easy solution to the job-caused problems that policemen suffer, of course it would have been accomplished long ago. The sad fact is, that the police, because they are one of the most important professions in our country, bear the burden of some of our most serious troubles. They are stuck with the public's own confusion about what it believes in, what it wants, and how it should behave. Instead of consistent respect which they deserve, too often the police are targets for the lunatic fringe, scapegoats for the hustling politician, of testing ground for new and unproven ideas on how to handle people. While these are general problems for most police organizations, they are also individual problems for each policeman.

For partial solutions to some of these problems, I would ask you to think about the following:

1. Endeavor to increase the professional standard of police work by setting forth high standards of training and performance which will justify the policeman's right to speak as an expert in the public forum, and which will justify his natural desire for respect as a professional person.
2. Emphasizing for all police the importance of a genuine ethical code will give every officer something to aim for in his own actions, and which will enable all officers to be pulling toward the same goals in their life work. The ethical code, for example the one supported by the California Peace Officer's Association, should clearly put loyalty to principle ahead of loyalty to any small group. This, of course, is a harsh and painful rule, but only through it can one achieve the solution of some of the most terrible conflicts which the average police officer faces.
3. It may be necessary to put pressure on our public and political leaders so that they will publically announce just what they expect their police to do, as well as what they would be expected not to do. Only through public policy can the police get clear direction so they can perform their jobs without conflict and confusion.
4. Each individual officer should realize that he has one of the most difficult jobs that any man can hold. The officer should try to face himself honestly, admitting his fears, frustrations, and weaknesses as well as his

strengths. It may be too much to expect happiness in such a difficult job, and certainly perfection is impossible. Even so, with an honest look at oneself, and one's difficulties, police work can be a source of genuine pride and personal achievement.

The Patrolman

James Q. Wilson

The patrolman's role is defined more by his responsibility for *maintaining order* than by his responsibility for enforcing the law.[1] By "order" is meant the absence of disorder, and by disorder is meant behavior that either disturbs or threatens to disturb the public peace or that involves face-to-face conflict among two or more persons. Disorder, in short, involves a dispute over what is "right" or "seemly" conduct or over who is to blame for conduct that is agreed to be wrong or unseemly. A noisy drunk, a rowdy teenager shouting or racing his car in the middle of the night, a loud radio in the apartment next door, a panhandler soliciting money from passersby, persons wearing eccentric clothes and unusual hair styles loitering in public places—all these are examples of behavior which "the public" (an onlooker, a neighbor, the community at large) may disapprove of and ask the patrolman to "put a stop to." Needless to say, the drunk, the teenager, the persons next door, the panhandler, and the hippies are likely to take a different view of the matter, to suggest that people "mind their own business," and to be irritated with the "cop" who intervenes. On the other hand, a fight, a tavern brawl, and an assault on an unfaithful lover are kinds of behavior that even the participants are not likely to condone. Thus, they may agree that the police have a right to intervene, but they are likely to disagree over who is to blame and thus against whom the police ought to act.

Some or all of these examples of disorderly behavior involve infractions of the law; any intervention by the police is at least under color of the law and in fact might be viewed as an "enforcement" of the law. A judge, examining the matter after the fact, is likely to see the issue wholly in these terms. But the patrolman does not. Though he may use the law to make an arrest, just as often he will do something else, such as tell people to "knock it off," "break it up," or "to home and sober up." In his eyes even an arrest does not always end his

From James Q. Wilson, *Varieties of Police Behavior: The Management of Law and Order in Eight Communities* (Cambridge, Mass.: Harvard University Press. 1968), pp. 16-34. Copyright © 1968 by the President and Fellows of Harvard College. Reprinted by permission of the author and the publisher.

involvement in the matter. In some sense he was involved in settling a dispute; if and how he settled it is important both to the parties involved and to the officer himself. To the patrolman, "enforcing the law" is what he does when there is no dispute—when making an arrest or issuing a summons exhausts his responsibilities. Giving a traffic ticket is the clearest case: an infraction of the law is observed and familiar, routinized steps are taken to make the offender liable to the penalties of the law. Similarly, if the patrolman comes upon a burglary in progress, catches a fleeing robber, or is involved in apprehending a person suspected of having committed a crime, he is enforcing the law. Other agencies will decide whether the suspect is in fact guilty; but *if* he is guilty, then he is to blame. Guilt is at issue in both order-maintaining and law-enforcing situations, but blame is at issue only in the former. The noisy neighbor or the knife-wielding lover may say, "Don't blame me," the fleeing robber, on the other hand, will say, "I'm not guilty."

THE MAINTENANCE OF ORDER

The problem of order, more than the problem of law enforcement, is central to the patrolman's role for several reasons. First, in at least the larger or more socially heterogeneous cities, the patrolman encounters far more problems of order maintenance than opportunities for law enforcement, except with respect to traffic laws. Table 1 shows all the radio calls to police cars made by the Syracuse Police Department during a one-week period in June 1966. About one fifth required the officer to gather information ("get a report") about an alleged crime for which no suspect was thought still to be on the scene. The patrolman's function in this case is mainly clerical—he asks routine questions, inspects the premises, and fills out a form. About a third of the calls were for services that could as easily be provided—and in many cities are—by a different government agency or by a private firm. Only about one tenth of the calls afforded, even potentially, an opportunity to perform a narrow law enforcement function by stopping a burglary in progress, catching a prowler, making an arrest of a suspect being held by another party, or investigating a suspicious car or an open window. In fact, very few of *these* will result in arrests—there will be no prowler, except in a woman's imagination, the open window will signify an owner's oversight rather than a thief's entry, the "suspicious" car will be occupied by a respectable citizen, and the burglar, if any, will be gone. Almost a third of all calls—and the vast majority of all nonservice calls—concern allegations of disorder arising out of disputes, public and private, serious and trivial. [2]

Second, the maintenance of order exposes the patrolman to physical danger, and his reaction in turn may expose the disputants to danger. Statistically, the risk of injury or death to the patrolman may not be great in order-maintenance situations but it exists and, worse, it is unpredictable, occurring, as almost every officer interviewed testified, "when you least expect it." In 1965 there were reported over 20,000 assaults on police officers, nearly 7,000 of which resulted in injury to the officer; 83 officers were killed and only 30 of these by auto

accidents.[3] There is no way to tell what proportion of these deaths and injuries occurred in the restoring of order as opposed to the pursuit and subduing of a criminal, but patrolmen almost universally contrast the random, unexpected nature of danger involved in handling, say, a domestic quarrel with the "routine" and taken-for-granted nature of danger when chasing a bank robber. Jerome Skolnick considers the preoccupation with danger an important element of the police officer's "working personality."[4] I would add that the risk of danger in

TABLE 1

Citizen complaints radioed to patrol vehicles, Syracuse Police Department, June 3-9, 1966. (This is based on a one-fifth sample of a week's calls.)

Calls		Number in Sample	Full Count (Sample Multiplied by 5)	Percent
Information gathering		69	345	22.1
Book and check	2			
Get a report	67			
Service		117	585	37.5
Accidents, illnesses, ambulance calls	42			
Animals	8			
Assist a person	1			
Drunk person	8			
Escort vehicle	3			
Fire, power line, or tree down	26			
Lost or found person or property	23			
Property damage	6			
Order maintenance		94	470	30.1
Gang disturbance	50			
Family trouble	23			
Assault, fight	9			
Investigation	8			
Neighbor trouble	4			
Law Enforcement		32	160	10.3
Burglary in progress	9			
Check a car	5			
Open door, window	8			
Prowler	6			
Make an arrest	4			
Totals		312	1,560	100.0

NOTE: Not included are internal calls—that is, those originating with another police officer (as for example, when an officer requests a check on the status of a person or vehicle or requests the wagon, and so forth)—or purely administrative calls.

order maintenance patrol work, though statistically less than the danger involved in enforcing traffic laws or apprehending felons, has a disproportionate effect on the officer partly because its unexpected nature makes him more apprehensive and partly because he tends to communicate his apprehension to the citizen.

Chasing a speeding motorist, the officer is running risks of his own choosing. Chasing a fleeing robber, he anticipates violence—weapons are drawn, gunfire is expected, and the issues are clear. But when he walks into a room where a fight is under way or stops to question a "suspicious" person, the *possibility* of danger makes the patrolman suspicious and apprehensive. To those fighting or to the person stopped, the patrolman seems "hostile" or "edgy," and if, as is often the case, the citizen has no intention of attacking the officer, he sees the patrolman as "unjustifiably" suspicious, hostile, or edgy. If the citizen then shows his resentment, the officer is likely to interpret it as animosity and thus to be even more on his guard. Both sides may be caught in an ascending spiral of antagonisms.

But most important, the order maintenance function necessarily involves the exercising of substantial discretion over matters of the greatest importance (public and private morality, honor and dishonor, life and death) in a situation that is, by definition, one of conflict and in an environment that is apprehensive and perhaps hostile.

Discretion exists both because many of the relevant laws are necessarily ambiguous and because, under the laws of many states governing arrests for certain forms of disorder, the "victim" must cooperate with the patrolman if the law is to be invoked at all. Statutes defining "disorderly conduct" or "disturbing the peace" are examples of laws that are not only ambiguous, but necessarily so. In New York State, disorderly conduct is a breach of the peace occasioned by, among other things, offensive behavior or language, disturbing other people, begging, having an "evil reputation" and "consorting with persons of like evil reputations," and "causing a crowd to collect." In California disturbing the peace includes "maliciously and wilfully" breaching the peace of a neighborhood or person by, among other things, "loud or unusual noise," "tumultuous or offensive conduct," or using "vulgar, profane, or indecent language within the presence or hearing of women or children." [5] One might object, as some have, that such statutes are vague and one might expect the courts to rule (again, as some have) all or parts of them unconstitutional for failing to specify a clear standard, but one would be hard pressed to invent a statute that would cover all possible cases of objectionable disorder in language that would leave little discretion to the officer. Most criminal laws define *acts* (murder, rape, speeding, possessing narcotics), which are held to be illegal; people may disagree as to whether the act should be illegal, as they do with respect to narcotics, for example, but there is little disagreement as to what the behavior in question consists of. Laws regarding disorderly conduct and the like assert, usually by implication, that there is a *condition* ("public order") that can be diminished by various actions. The difficulty, of course, is that public order is nowhere defined and can never be defined unambiguously because what constitutes order is a matter of opinion and convention, not a state of nature. (An unmurdered person, an unraped woman, and an unpossessed narcotic can be defined so as to be recognizable to any reasonable person.) An additional difficulty, a corollary of the first, is the impossibility of specifying, except in the extreme case, what degree of disorder is intolerable and who is to be held culpable for that degree. A suburban street is quiet and pleasant; a big city street is noisy and (to some) offensive; what degree of noise and offense, and produced by whom, constitutes "disorderly conduct"?

One could, of course, throw up his hands and say that there is no such thing as public order and thus disorderly conduct cannot be a crime. This is precisely what we have tended to do with an analogous legal situation, that pertaining to obscenity. Being unable to agree on what constitutes a decent book or picture, we—that is, the courts—have decided that, except in the undefined "extreme" case of "hard-core pornography," obscenity does not exist as a legal matter.[6] However, this reaction is unlikely in the case of disorderly conduct because such conduct can impose real costs on other persons whereas obscenity, except when it is displayed in ways such that the innocent person cannot avoid it, imposes costs, if at all, only on the person who knowingly and voluntarily consumes it.

Certain forms of disorderly or disputatious behavior can be given a relatively unambiguous legal definition—assault or battery, for example. Striking or wounding another person is legally definable because we can agree on what an unstruck or unwounded person looks like. But here another difficulty arises—the need for victim cooperation. Most crimes the patrolman is concerned with are misdemeanors, that is, any crime not a felony, which in turn is—generally speaking—a crime punishable by death or by imprisonment in a state prison, usually for one year or longer. But under the law of many states, an officer can make an arrest for a misdemeanor only when the act has been committed in his presence or upon the properly sworn complaint of a citizen in whose presence it was committed.[7] If the law, like the disorderly conduct statute or, in some states, the public intoxication statute, is ambiguous enough, the officer can always find some grounds for asserting that the offensive act was committed in his presence—he can "see" people being "disturbed" or a man being "intoxicated in a public place." But to make an arrest for an assault or a battery (misdemeanors in most states) when he has not seen the fight (as is usually the case, since most people stop fighting as soon as the police arrive), he must often obtain a sworn complaint from the victim so that the victim, in effect, makes the arrest and the officer simply takes the suspect into custody.

But it is the exception, not the rule, for the "victim" to cooperate in this way. In over half (54 percent) of the 125 cases of simple assault turned up by the household survey sponsored by the President's Crime Commission, the police were not notified at all. And in over half (57 percent) of these unreported cases, the reasons given were that the victim "did not want to harm the offender" regarded the affair as a private matter, or was afraid of reprisal.[8] In short, the victim didn't want to "get involved." A study of the files of the Oakland Police Department shows that between May 5 and May 31, 1967, there were 163 batteries reported to the police. In 85 percent of the cases, the attacker was known to his victim but in only 30.1 percent of such cases was an arrest made—in the others, the victim did not want to press charges.[9]

Even though he or she may not want to swear out a complaint, especially if this requires going downtown the next morning, the victim usually wants the police to "do something." A typical case, one which I witnessed many times, involves a wife with a black eye telling the patrolman she wants her husband, who she alleges hit her, "thrown out of the house." The officer knows he has no authority to throw husbands out of their homes and he tells her so. She is dissatisfied. He suggests she file a complaint, but she does not want her husband arrested. She may promise to make a complaint the next morning, but the patrolman knows from experience that she will probably change her mind later. If the officer does nothing about the quarrel, he is "uncooperative"; if he steps in, he is in danger of exceeding his authority. Some patrolmen develop ways of mollifying everyone, others get out as quickly as they can, but all dislike such situations and find them awkward and risky.

The difficulty of maintaining order is further exacerbated by the fact that the patrolman's discretion is exercised in an emotional, apprehensive, and perhaps hostile environment. Even though the vast majority of Americans report, in opinion polls, that they think the police are doing a good job, are properly respectful, and are honest, and even in those neighborhoods—middle-class ones, and especially white middle-class ones—where sentiments favorable to the police are most widespread,[10] police-citizen contacts in any but routine matters are likely to leave both parties dissatisfied.

The police are like various professionals, without themselves being a profession, in that they handle on a routine basis what to others are emergencies.[11] When the police arrive to look for a prowler, examine a loss, or stop a fight, the victim and suspect are agitated, fearful, even impassioned. But the police have seen it all before and they have come to distrust victim accounts (to say nothing of suspect explanations) of what happened. Instead of offering sympathy and immediately taking the victim's side, the police may seem cool, suspicious, or disinterested because they have learned that "victims" often turn out not to have been victimized at all—the "stolen" TV never existed or was lost, loaned to a boyfriend, or hidden because the payments were overdue; the "assault" was in fact a fight which the "victim" started but was unable to finish. A genuine victim, of course, is dismayed by the routine manner in which his crisis is being attended to and irritated because the police do not instantly and fully accept his version of what happened. To him, a serious matter is being mishandled or even lightly dismissed. If the police knew he was a genuine victim, they might be more sympathetic—and in fact the better officers try to develop an appropriate "bedside manner"—but they often suspect that he is not genuine or that, though genuine, he is exaggerating the incident or giving an inaccurate or incoherent account of it.

A citizen who calls an officer usually meets him for the first time and, having recounted his grievance—a missing television set or a broken jaw—rarely meets him again. If there is a suspect still on the scene, the patrolman must decide whether to make an arrest; if he does not, he usually fills out a report. In either case, he soon leaves. Unless an arrest is made—which occurs in only about 7 percent of all calls to patrolmen[12]—the client is likely to feel "nothing" has been done.

In truth, there is often little the police can do. Most crimes are crimes against property, and these are rarely solved because there are neither clues nor witnesses. Even when a suspect is identified, the police are often unable to make an arrest because, if the offense was a misdemeanor, they can only arrest when it is committed in their presence or if they have a signed complaint. Other times the police appear to do too much: they make an arrest when no grounds are evident because they sense danger, recognize a known criminal, or feel a challenge to their authority. Or if a proper arrest is made, the man may be back on the street again within a day, in which case the public may blame the police when in fact the courts have released him on bail or, if he is a juvenile, the probation department or the family court intake office has "settled" the matter with a warning.

Because the patrolman, unlike the schoolteacher or the doctor, cannot himself give a complete and visible response to the needs of his "client" and because those needs are often, to the client, of the highest importance, a citizen's evaluation of an officer—even when the latter is "getting information" or "enforcing the law" rather than maintaining order—is likely to be at best incomplete and at worst inaccurate. Furthermore, the citizen will observe that when the patrolman is not handling the citizen's momentary emergency, he is standing on a street corner, walking along the sidewalk, or driving a patrol car—apparently "doing nothing." What he is doing, of course, is waiting to be called to cope with someone else's emergency, and if he were not "doing nothing" he would not be immediately available. The citizen, forgetting this, is likely to wonder why he isn't out "looking for the man who stole my car," or whatever.

When the patrolman is working, not in a middle-class area where crime is comparatively infrequent and has mostly to do with stolen property, but in a lower-class area where it is frequent and has more to do with violence, then there is an even greater likelihood that the citizen and the patrolman will form an unfavorable impression of each other. About 70 percent of all the victims of crimes against the person uncovered in the Crime Commission's household survey had incomes under $6,000 per year (over 55 percent of the victims of crimes against property had incomes over $6,000).[13] Because most crimes against the person involve parties known or related to each other, a patrolman entering a low-income area, especially in response to a call about a crime of violence, is likely to be suspicious of the victim's story and is likely to communicate, consciously or unconsciously, that suspicion to the victim.

Thus, the tendency of the patrolman to be and act suspicious arises not simply from the danger inherent in his function but from his doubts as to the "legitimacy" of the victim. Middle-class victims who have suffered a street attack (a mugging, for example) are generally considered most legitimate; middle-class victims of burglary are seen as somewhat less legitimate (it could be an effort to make a fraudulent insurance claim); lower-class victims of theft are still less legitimate (they may have stolen the item in the first place); lower-class victims of assaults are the least legitimate (they probably brought it on themselves). A legitimate victim treated as illegitimate may become annoyed or even angered, and rightly so. But however much we may sympathize with him, we must bear in mind that it is essential for the police role to make judgments about victim legitimacy and that such judgments are in many cases based on quite reasonable empirical generalizations.

The working environment of the police is not only charged with emotion and suspicion, it is often, in the eyes of the police, hostile and uncooperative. A majority of Chicago police sergeants who completed a questionnaire in 1960 and again in 1965 felt that civilians generally did not cooperate with the police in their work, that the department did not have the respect of most Chicago citizens, that their civilian friends would criticize the department to their faces, and that most people obey the law only from fear of getting caught.[14] This view of citizens as hostile or uncooperative persisted during a period when the officers believed their department had improved greatly in quality (over half thought it poorly run in 1960; less than a fifth thought so in 1965 after five years of reform under Superintendent Orlando W. Wilson). The belief that citizens were hostile was independent of the officer's age, duty assignment, or ethnicity.[15] Finally, a majority of the respondents felt it was important that a police officer be liked by those citizens with whom he comes in contact but, as citizen respect did not rise along with departmental quality, the proportion of sergeants attaching importance to being liked fell from 79 percent in 1960 to 59 percent in 1965.[16]

In general, the police probably exaggerate the extent of citizen hostility. National opinion polls have shown that the vast majority of citizens have favorable attitudes toward the police.[17] Though Negroes are more critical of the police than whites, and higher income Negroes more critical than lower-income ones, with few exceptions both races and all classes generally approve of the police. Among men, over three-fourths of the whites at all income levels and over 60 percent of the Negroes at all income levels but the highest think the police are doing a "very good" or "pretty good" job in giving protection to the people in the neighborhood;[18] over 90 percent of the whites at all income levels and over three-fourths of the Negroes at all income levels but the highest think the police are "very good" or "pretty good" at being respectful to people like the respondent.[19]

But most police contacts are not with the general public and thus general public opinion is not most relevant. Furthermore, opinions expressed to an interviewer in a moment of calm may be quite at odds with behavior displayed in a moment of crisis; the police probably draw their conclusions about citizen attitudes from the behavior of those who are victims, suspects, or onlookers at the scene of a crime or disorder. Finally, what is true about public opinion is less important than what the police *think* is true because a misinterpretation of personal experience is harder to correct than a misreading of an opinion poll.

But in any case it is not clear that the police *are* in error; if half the victims of crime do not even notify the police, if most of those who fail to notify them give as their reason a belief that police will do nothing or a desire to protect a friend or keep the matter "private," and if the police increasingly find themselves in pitched battles with rioters and looters, then they might be pardoned for concluding that citizens are at best "uncooperative" and at worst hostile.[20]

Occupations whose members exercise, as do the police, wide discretion alone and with respect to matters of the greatest importance are typically "professions"—the medical profession, for example. The right to handle emergency situations, to be privy to "guilty information," and to make decisions involving questions of life and death or honor and dishonor is usually, as with a doctor or priest, conferred by an organized profession. The profession certifies that the member has acquired by education certain information and by apprenticeship certain arts and skills that render him competent to perform these functions and that he is willing to subject himself to the code of ethics and sense of duty of his colleagues (or, in the case of the priest, to the laws and punishments of God). Failure to perform his duties properly will, if detected, be dealt with by professional sanctions—primarily, loss of respect. Members of professions tend to govern themselves through collegial bodies, to restrict the authority of their nominal superiors, to take seriously their reputation among fellow professionals, and to encourage some of their kind to devote themselves to adding systematically to the knowledge of the profession through writing and research. The police are not in any of these senses professionals. They acquire most of their knowledge and skill on the job, not in separate academies; they are emphatically subject to the authority of their superiors; they have no serious professional society, only a union-like bargaining agent; and they do not produce, in systematic written form, new knowledge about their craft.[21]

In sum, the order-maintenance function of the patrolman defines his role and that role, which is unlike that of any other occupation, can be described as one in which *sub-professionals, working alone, exercise wide discretion in matters of utmost importance (life and death, honor and dishonor) in an environment that is apprehensive and perhaps hostile.*[22] The agents of various other governmental organizations may display one or two of these characteristics, but none or almost none display all in combination. The doctor has wide discretion over matters of life and death, but he is a professional working in a supportive environment. The teacher works alone and has considerable discretion, but he may be a professional and in any case education, though important, is not a matter of life or death. A welfare worker, though working alone among apprehensive clients, has relatively little discretion—the laws define rather precisely what payments he can authorize to a client and supervisors review his written reports and proposed family budgets.

This role places the patrolman in a special relationship to the law, a relationship that is obscured by describing what he does as "enforcing the law."

To the patrolman, the law is one resource among many that he may use to deal with disorder, but it is not the only one or even the most important; beyond that, the law is a constraint that tells him what he must *not* do. But that is peculiarly unhelpful in telling him what he should do. Thus, he approaches incidents that threaten order *not in terms of enforcing the law but in terms of "handling the situation."* The officer is expected, by colleagues as well as superiors, to "handle his beat."[23] This means keeping things under control so that there are no complaints that he is doing nothing or that he is doing too much. To handle his beat, the law provides one resource, the possibility of arrest, and a set of constraints, *but it does not supply to the patrolman a set of legal rules to be applied.* A phrase heard by interviewers countless times is "You can't go by what the book says."

This view of police work may be traced to the historical circumstances surrounding the creation of American municipal police forces. Police officers were originally "watchmen" whose task it was to walk their rounds and maintain order in the streets. To maintain order meant everything from removing obstructions on streets and keeping pigs from running loose to chasing footpads and quelling riots. Watchmen were not officers of the court charged with bringing to the bar of justice persons who had broken a law; that task was performed by constables, for a fee, and only on the basis of sworn warrants. These watchmen and later the police handled many situations that had nothing to do with enforcing the law or getting evidence and as a result they often acted under vague laws or no laws at all; a city council would later set down as written law rules that common practice had already established as binding. Throughout the nineteenth century, the fear of riot and popular uprising was usually the reason for enlarging, professionalizing, and ultimately arming the police.[24]

This role gives the patrolman an orientation quite different from that obtaining in a courtroom or assumed by the authors of legal codes. To the judge, the defense attorney, and the legal scholar, the issue is whether a given individual was legally culpable as defined by a written rule. The individualistic, rule-oriented perspective of the courtroom is at variance with the situational, order-maintenance perspective of the patrolman.[25] The patrolman senses this conflict without quite understanding it and this contributes to his unease at having his judgment tested in a courtroom.

Thus the patrolman describes his activity as "playing it by ear" and "taking each case as they come," *not* in terms of "enforcing the law" or "making exceptions to the law." Egon Bittner gives the example of a patrolman finding four men getting drunk in public; to control the situation—to prevent a disturbance that will bring a complaint, to break up the gathering, to forestall someone passing out and getting robbed—the patrolman may arrest one of the four and, having broken up the party, send the other three on their way. To him, *which* one gets arrested is not so important. To the judge, it is all-important.

To handle his beat and the situations and disputes that develop on it, the patrolman must assert his authority. To him, this means asserting his *personal* authority. As Banton points out, in a heterogeneous society where different views of proper conduct are held by various classes and subcultures, a uniform and a badge may be insufficient symbols of authority.[26] By authority the patrolman means the right to ask questions, get information, and have his orders obeyed. In a disputatious incident, the authority he personifies will not ordinarily influence the outcome unless he gets involved. To believe that a patrolman should be wholly impersonal and correct is to believe that he can control a situation by his mere presence or command; this may be true in some cases, but patrolmen do not assume it will be true in any given case. In entering a situation, he tests the participants—who is the "tough guy," who has the beef, who is blustering, who is dangerous? And he in turn is tested: how far can the policeman be used to obtain one's ends, how far can he be pushed before he responds, is he "cool" or is he unsure of himself? The patrolmen observed for this study almost always acted, and said later that they had acted, in such a way as to show immediately "who was boss." For some, their size alone was sufficient; for others, an assured and firm tone of voice was adequate; for others, shouting and pushing and cursing seemed required. (The latter were not highly regarded by their fellows as a rule, though they were rarely told to take it easy.)[27]

The felt need to "handle the situation," rather than "enforce the law" and to assert authority or "take charge" leads the officer to get involved, but "getting involved" is the antithesis of the ideal—that is, being impersonal and "correct." Patrolmen often equate being "impersonal" with being ineffective, for to be impersonal is to assume that embodying legal authority is sufficient and, in their experience, it rarely is. To get involved means to display one's personal qualities, and these qualities differ greatly among individual patrolmen. In many communities police officers are of working-class backgrounds (that is, from lower and lower-middle income families in blue-collar occupations); this means they bring to the job some of the focal concerns of working-class men—a preoccupation with maintaining self-respect, proving one's masculinity, "not taking any crap," and not being "taken in." Having to rely on personal qualities rather than on formal routines (in sociological terms, approved role behaviors) means the officer's behavior will depend crucially on how much deference he is shown, on how manageable the situation seems to be, and on what the participants in it seem to "deserve."

Many situations *are* manageable with little difficulty. On skid row, drunks frequently act as if they expect the officer to take charge, search or pat down the man stopped, and arrest or not depending on what the situation seems to warrant. Some quarreling husbands and wives welcome the arrival of the police because it ends the fight without either having to carry out threats that no one wants to carry out—neither side has its bluff called. The experienced officer senses this and plays the role expected of him—arbiter, keeper of the peace, source of ultimate authority, and so on. But if the participants are hostile or the bystanders unsympathetic, if danger is sensed, or if someone involved is suspected of having criminal tendencies (if he is a "bad actor" and not just a

32 The Role of the Police

"hothead" or "liquored up"), then the patrolman will often become suspicious, defensive, tough, harsh.

NOTES

1. The distinction between order maintenance and law enforcement is similar to distinctions made by other authors. Michael Banton notes the difference between "law officers" and "peace officers" in his *The Policeman and the Community* (London: Tavistock, 1964), pp. 6-7. Egon Bittner distinguishes between "law enforcement" and "keeping the peace" in his analysis of patrolmen handling derelicts: "The Police on Skid Row: A Study of Peace-Keeping," *American Sociological Review* 32 (October 1967): 699-715. At a higher level of generality, Eugene P. Wenninger and John P. Clark note that the police have both a value maintenance and a goal attainment function: "A Theoretical Orientation for Police Studies," in Malcom W. Klein, *Juvenile Gangs in Context* (Englewood Cliffs: Prentice-Hall, Inc., 1967), pp. 161-72. Though I employ concepts similar to those used by others, the implications of the distinction developed in this chapter are my own responsibility. The distinction may have implications larger than those relevant to the police, for it suggests that the police help perform two of the functional imperatives of any society—what Talcott Parsons calls "goal attainment" (part of which is law enforcement as here defined) and "pattern maintenance" (here, order maintenance). The relevance is suggested by Wenninger and Clark and developed somewhat in James Q. Wilson, "Dilemmas of Police Administration," *Public Administration Review* 28, no. 5 (September-October 1968): 407-17.

2. The workload of the police in dealing with noncriminal matters, especially interpersonal problems, is analyzed in Elaine Cumming, Ian Cumming, and Laura Edell, "Policeman as Philosopher, Guide and Friend," *Social Problems* 12 (Winter 1965): 276-86. The importance of order-maintenance calls in Chicago, especially those involving minor family conflicts, is discussed in Raymond I. Parnas, "The Police Response to the Domestic Disturbance," *Wisconsin Law Review* (1967), pp. 914-60. During the week studied, the Syracuse police dispatched about 7.9 operational, that is, nonadministrative, radio messages per thousand population. The message rate for the same week was somewhat higher in Oakland (11.1 per thousand population) and lower in Albany (6.4 per thousand); the distribution of messages within the various categories was about the same in all three cities.

3. Federal Bureau of Investigation, *Uniform Crime Reports,* 1965 (Washington: Government Printing Office, 1965), pp. 152-53. An even larger number of people are killed by the police. Between 1950 and 1960, an average of 240 persons per year were fatally injured by the police. The total on-duty death rate of police officers (33 per 100,000, as of 1955) was less than the comparable death rate in mining, agriculture, construction, and transportation. See Gerald D. Robin, "Justifiable Homicide by Police Officers," *Journal of Criminal Law, Criminology, and Police Science* 54 (1963): 225-31, and President's Commission on Law Enforcement and Administration of Justice, *Task Force Report: The Police* (Washington: Government Printing Office, 1967), p. 189.

4. Jerome H. Skolnick, *Justice without Trial* (New York: John Wiley & Sons, 1966), pp. 42-48.

5. New York, *Penal Law* sec. 722; California, *Penal Code,* sec. 415.

6. *See* Roth v. United States, 354 U.S. 476 (1957) and Manual Enterprises, Inc. v. Day, 370 U.S. 478 (1962).

7. *See* New York, *Code of Criminal Procedure,* sec. 177 and California, *Penal Code,* sec. 836. In Illinois, however, the police can arrest on probable cause for any offense, including a misdemeanor. *See Illinois Revised Statutes,* Chap. 38, sec. 107-2(c).

For an empirical study of the application of the misdemeanor arrest law as it exists in most states, *see* John D. O'Connell and C. Dean Larsen, "Detention, Arrest and Salt Lake City Police Practices," *Utah Law Review* 9 (Summer 1965): 593-625. A nineteenth-century Boston Police chief, who was also an author and poet of modest distinction, was able in one paragraph to describe the law of arrest as it then governed the maintenance of order of the streets: "The offenses for which persons may be legally arrested without a warrant, are, felony (crime punishable in State's Prison), assault and battery *in your presence,* persisting in disturbing the peace, and drunkenness. Simple larceny is not included in the statute, but common practice will, I think, justify an officer in taking a person charged with that crime to the Station House, for the direction of his captain. Other cases may occur, which will require much good judgment and discretion to determine what is proper." Edward H. Savage, "Advice to a Young Policeman," *Recollections of a Boston Police Officer, or, Boston by Daylight and Gaslight,* 2d ed., rev. (Boston, 1865), p. 344.

8. Philip H. Ennis, *Criminal Victimization in the United States,* A Report of a Research Study Submitted by the National Opinion Research Center to the President's Commission on Law Enforcement and Administration of Justice (Washington: Government Printing Office, 1967), pp. 42, 44.

9. The Oakland data are cited because, of the cities studied, its police keep the most careful and complete records of offenses and arrests. A crime report is prepared on every reported battery, even if the victim does not wish to prosecute. In some other cities, minor assaults are not even recorded as having occurred unless there is an arrest or a good chance of one.

10. Ennis, *Criminal Victimization,* p. 53.

11. Everett Hughes argues that one defining characteristic of a profession is the tendency of its members to treat as routine what to others is a crisis and to talk in "shocking terms" about intimate matters. *Men and Their Work* (New York: The Free Press, 1953), pp. 80-85.

12. Calculated from data in President's Commission on Law Enforcement and Administration of Justice, *Task Force Report: Science and Technology* (Washington: Government Printing Office, 1967), pp. 7-8.

13. Ennis, *Criminal Victimization,* p. 32.

14. James Q. Wilson, "Police Morale, Reform, and Citizen Respect: The Chicago Case," in David J. Bordua, ed., *The Police* (New York: John Wiley & Sons, 1967), p. 17. *See also* Skolnick, *Justice Without Trial,* pp. 9-65, and John P. Clark, "Isolation of the Police: A Comparison of the British and American Situations," *Journal of Criminal Law, Criminology and Police Science* 56 (1965): 307-19. But compare Banton, *The Policeman in the Community,* pp. 215-24. Banton's findings may result from having studied a small, fairly homogeneous American community; my study and Skolnick's were of large, heterogeneous cities. A theory relating police ethos to the conditions of community life is offered in James Q. Wilson, "The Police and Their Problems: A Theory," *Public Policy* 12 (1963): 189-216. A similar view is suggested in Jacob Chwast, "Value Conflicts in Law Enforcement," *Crime and Delinquency* 11 (1965): 151-61.

15. Wilson, "Police Morale," p. 150.

16. Ibid., p. 147.

17. Ennis, *Criminal Victimization,* p. 53.

18. Ibid., p. 55. This finding is borne out by another study in which a sample of Negro adults living in major cities was asked how they thought the police in their city treated Negroes. The percentage answering "very well" or "fairly well" was 56 percent in New York, 64 percent in Chicago, 53 percent in Atlanta, but only 31 percent in Birmingham. Gary T. Marx, *Protest and Prejudice* (New York: Harper & Row, Publishers, 1967), p. 36.

19. Ennis, *Criminal Victimization,* p. 56.

20. We can only speculate on the psychological costs to the patrolman entailed by his role. One study of ninety-three police suicides in New York City between 1934 and 1940 showed that two-thirds occurred among patrolmen; only three occurred among plainclothes detectives. That the latter group should experience only 3 percent of all the suicides may suggest that their role, defined by more consistent expectations, creates fewer psychological strains. Furthermore, a large number—40 percent—of all the suicides occurred among men who had joined between 1925 and 1927, the heyday of Tammany Hall influence in the department. Dr. Friedman conjectures that the new reform policies of Mayor Fiorella La Guardia, who came to power in 1934, produced great insecurity among these men, some of whom were unstable personalities to begin with and who got onto the force through political influence. During the Tammany era, these officers felt they were "backed up"—if

not by their nominal superiors then by their political "rabbis" or protectors. During the La Guardia era, they lost that sense of support. *See* Paul Friedman, "Suicide Among Police" in Edwin Schneidman, ed., *Essays in Self-Destruction* (New York: Science House, 1967). After the Detroit riot of 1967, the head of the police medical division reported a growing number of "nervous and emotional problems" among the officers. *See Detroit News,* Nov. 9 and 12, 1967.

21. Cf. Banton, *The Policeman in the Community,* pp. 105-10.

22. I can think of only one other occupation that has the special characteristics I impute to the patrolman: that of attendant in a mental hospital. *See* Charles Perrow, "Hospitals: Technology, Structure, and Goals," in James G. March, ed., *Handbook of Organizations* (Chicago: Rand McNally & Co., 1965).

23. *See* Arthur Niederhofer, *Behind the Shield: The Police in Urban Society* (Garden City: Doubleday & Co., 1967), p. 60, and President's Commission, *The Police,* p. 179: "Typically, an officer is expected to maintain order on the street, to keep a 'clean beat,' to disperse mobs, to remove 'undesirables,' whether or not legal tools for accomplishing these results are available."

24. Selden D. Bacon, "The Early Development of American Municipal Police," unpublished Ph.D. dissertation, Yale University, (1939), esp. pp 735-87, and Roger Lane, *Policing the City: Boston, 1822-1885* (Cambridge, Mass.: Harvard University Press, 1967), pp. 58, 94, 221.

25. Egon Bittner makes the same point with respect to police handling of derelicts. *See* his "The Police in Skid-Row: A Study of Peace Keeping" and also Egon Bittner, "Police Discretion in Emergency Apprehensions of Mentally-Ill Persons," *Social Problems* 14 (Winter 1967): 278-92.

26. Banton, *The Policeman in the Community,* p. 168.

27. Bittner quotes a patrolman on skid row: "You see, there is always a risk that the man is testing you and you must let him know what is what. The best among us can usually keep the upper hand in such situations without making arrests. But when it comes down to the wire then you can't let them get away with it." Bittner, "The Police in Skid-Row," p. 711. *See also* Niederhofer, *Behind the Shield,* p. 53, and William A. Westley, "The Police: A Sociological Study of Law, Custom, and Morality" (unpublished Ph.D. dissertation, Department of Sociology, University of Chicago, 1951), p. 112.

A Sketch of the Policeman's "Working Personality"

Jerome H. Skolnick

A recurrent theme of the sociology of occupations is the effect of a man's work on his outlook on the world.[1] Doctors, janitors, lawyers, and industrial workers develop distinctive ways of perceiving and responding to their environment. Here we shall concentrate on analyzing certain outstanding elements in the police milieu, danger, authority, and efficiency, as they combine

From Jerome H. Skolnick, *Justice Without Trial: Law Enforcement in Democratic Society* (New York: John Wiley & Sons, 1967), pp. 43-59, 230-45. Reprinted by permission of the publisher.

to generate distinctive cognitive and behavioral responses in police: a "working personality." Such an analysis does not suggest that all police are alike in "working personality," but that there are distinctive cognitive tendencies in police as an occupational grouping. Some of these may be found in other occupations sharing similar problems. So far as exposure to danger is concerned, the policeman may be likened to the soldier. His problems as an authority bear a certain similarity to those of the schoolteacher, and the pressures he feels to prove himself efficient are not unlike those felt by the industrial worker. The combination of these elements, however, is unique to the policeman. Thus, the police, as a result of combined features of their social situation, tend to develop ways of looking at the world distinctive to themselves, cognitive lenses through which to see situations and events. The strength of the lenses may be weaker or stronger depending on certain conditions, but they are ground on a similar axis.

Analysis of the policeman's cognitive propensities is necessary to understand the practical dilemma faced by police required to maintain order under a democratic rule of law. We have discussed earlier how essential a conception of order is to the resolution of this dilemma. It was suggested that the paramilitary character of police organization naturally leads to a high evaluation of similarity, routine, and predictability. Our intention is to emphasize features of the policeman's environment interacting with the paramilitary police organization to generate a "working personality." Such an intervening concept should aid in explaining how the social environment of police affects their capacity to respond to the rule of law.

We also stated earlier that emphasis would be placed on the division of labor in the police department, that "operational law enforcement" could not be understood outside these special work assignments. It is therefore important to explain how the hypothesis emphasizing the generalizability of the policeman's "working personality" is compatible with the idea that police division of labor is an important analytic dimension for understanding "operational law enforcement." Compatibility is evident when one considers the different levels of analysis at which the hypotheses are being developed. Janowitz states, for example, that the military profession is more than an occupation; it is a "style of life" because the occupational claims over one's daily existence extend well beyond official duties. He is quick to point out that any profession performing a crucial "life and death" task, such as medicine, the ministry, or the police, develops such claims.[2] A conception like "working personality" of policy should be understood to suggest an analytic breadth similar to that of "style of life." That is, just as the professional behavior of military officers with similar "styles of life" may differ drastically depending upon whether they command an infantry battalion or participate in the work of an intelligence unit, so too does the professional behavior of police officers with similar "working personalities" vary with their assignments.

The policeman's "working personality" is most highly developed in his constabulary role of the man on the beat. For analytical purposes that role is sometimes regarded as an enforcement speciality, but in this general discussion of policemen as they comport themselves while working, the uniformed "cop" is seen as the foundation for the policeman's working personality. There is a sound organizational basis for making this assumption. The police, unlike the military, draw no caste distinction in socialization, even though their order of ranked titles approximates the military's. Thus, one cannot join a local police department as, for instance, a lieutenant, as a West Point graduate joins the army. Every officer of rank must serve an apprenticeship as a patrolman. This feature of police organization means that the constabulary role is the primary one for all police officers, and that whatever the special requirements of roles in enforcement specialties, they are carried out with a common background of constabulary experience.

The process by which this "personality" is developed may be summarized: the policeman's role contains two principal variables, danger and authority, which should be interpreted in the light of a "constant" pressure to appear efficient.[3] The element of danger seems to make the policeman especially attentive to signs indicating a potential for violence and lawbreaking. As a result, the policeman is generally a "suspicious" person. Furthermore, the character of the policeman's work makes him less desirable as a friend, since norms of friendship implicate others in his work. Accordingly, the element of danger isolates the policeman socially from that segment of the citizenry which he regards as symbolically dangerous and also from the conventional citizenry with whom he identifies.

The element of authority reinforces the element of danger in isolating the policeman. Typically, the policeman is required to enforce laws representing puritanical morality, such as those prohibiting drunkenness, and also laws regulating the flow of public activity, such as traffic laws. In these situations the policeman directs the citizenry, whose typical response denies recognition of his authority, and stresses his obligation to respond to danger. The kind of man who responds well to danger, however, does not normally subscribe to codes of puritanical morality. As a result, the policeman is unusually liable to the charge of hypocrisy. That the whole civilian world is an audience for the policeman further promotes police isolation and, in consequence, solidarity. Finally, danger undermines the judicious use of authority. Where danger, as in Britain, is relatively less, the judicious application of authority is facilitated. Hence, British police may appear to be somewhat more attached to the rule of law, when, in fact, they may appear so because they face less danger, and they are as a rule better skilled than American police in creating the appearance of conformity to procedural regulations.

THE SYMBOLIC ASSAILANT AND POLICE CULTURE

In attempting to understand the policeman's view of the world, it is useful to raise a more general question: What are the conditions under which police, as authorities, may be threatened?[4] To answer this, we must look to the situation of the policeman in the community. One attribute of many characterizing the policeman's role stands out: the policeman is required to respond to assaults against persons and property. When a radio call reports an armed robbery and gives a description of the man involved, every policeman, regardless of assignment, is responsible for the criminal's apprehension. The *raison d'être* of the policeman and the criminal law, the underlying collectively held moral sentiments which justify penal sanctions, arises ultimately and most clearly from the threat of violence and the possibility of danger to the community. Police who "lobby" for severe narcotics laws, for instance, justify their position on grounds that the addict is a harbinger of danger since, it is maintained, he requires one hundred dollars a day to support his habit, and he must steal to get it. Even though the addict is not typically a violent criminal, criminal penalties for addiction are supported on grounds that he may become one.

The policeman, because his work requires him to be occupied continually with potential violence, develops a perceptual shorthand to identify certain kinds of people as symbolic assailants, that is, as persons who use gesture, language, and attire that the policeman has come to recognize as a prelude to violence. This does not mean that violence by the symbolic assailant is necessarily predictable. On the contrary, the policeman responds to the vague indication of danger suggested by appearance.[5] Like the animals of the experimental psychologist, the policeman finds the threat of random damage more compelling than a predetermined and inevitable punishment.

Nor, to qualify for the status of symbolic assailant, need an individual ever have used violence. A man backing out of a jewelry store with a gun in one hand and jewelry in the other would qualify even if the gun were a toy and he had never in his life fired a real pistol. To the policeman in the situation, the man's personal history is momentarily immaterial. There is only one relevant sign: a gun signifying danger. Similarly, a young man may suggest the threat of violence to the policeman by his manner of walking or "strutting," the insolence in the demeanor being registered by the policeman as a possible preamble to later attack.[6] Signs vary from area to area, but a youth dressed in a black leather jacket and motorcycle boots is sure to draw at least a suspicious glance from a policeman.

Policemen themselves do not necessarily emphasize the peril associated with their work when questioned directly, and may even have well-developed strategies of denial. The element of danger is so integral to the policeman's work that explicit recognition might induce emotional barriers to work performance. Thus, one patrol officer observed that more police have been killed and injured in automobile accidents in the past ten years than from gunfire. Although his assertion is true, he neglected to mention that the police are the only peacetime occupational group with a systematic record of death and injury from gunfire and other weaponry. Along these lines, it is interesting that of the 224 working Westville policemen (not including the 16 juvenile policemen) responding to a question about which assignment they would like most to have in the police department,[7] 50 percent selected the job of detective, an assignment combining elements of apparent danger and initiative. The next category was adult street work, that is, patrol and traffic (37 percent). Eight percent selected the juvenile squad,[8] and only 4 percent selected administrative work. Not a single policeman chose the job of jail guard. Although these findings do not control for such factors as prestige, they suggest that confining and routine jobs are rated low on the hierarchy of police preferences, even though such jobs are least dangerous. Thus, the policeman may well, as a personality, enjoy the possibility of danger, especially its associated excitement, even though he may at the same time be fearful of it. Such "inconsistency" is easily understood. Freud has by now made it an axiom of personality theory that logical and emotional consistency are by no means the same phenomenon.

However complex the motives aroused by the element of danger, its consequences for sustaining police culture are unambiguous. This element requires him, like the combat soldier, the European Jew, the South African (white or black), to live in a world straining toward duality, and suggesting danger when "they" are perceived. Consequently, it is in the nature of the policeman's situation that his conception of order emphasize regularity and predictability. It is, therefore, a conception shaped by persistent *suspicion*. The English "copper," often portrayed as a courteous, easy-going, rather jolly sort of chap, on the one hand, or as a devil-may-care adventurer, on the other, is differently described by Colin MacInnes:

> The true copper's dominant characteristic, if the truth be known, is neither those daring nor vicious qualities that are sometimes attributed to him by friend or enemy, but an ingrained conservatism, and almost desperate love of the conventional. It is untidiness, disorder, the unusual, that a copper disapproves of most of all: far more, even than of crime which is merely a professional matter. Hence his profound dislike of people loitering in streets, dressing extravagantly, speaking with exotic accents, being strange, weak, eccentric, or simply any rare minority—of their doing, in fact, anything that cannot be safely predicted.[9]

Policemen are indeed specifically *trained* to be suspicious, to perceive events of changes in the physical surroundings that indicate the occurrence or probability of disorder. A former student who worked as a patrolman in a suburban New York police department describes this aspect of the policeman's assessment of the unusual:

> The time spent cruising one's sector or walking one's beat is not wasted time, though it can become quite routine. During this time, the most important thing for the officer to do is notice the *normal*. He must come to know the people in his area, their habits, their automobiles and their friends. He must learn what time the various shops close, how much money is kept on hand on different nights, what lights are usually left on, which houses are vacant ... only then can he decide what persons or cars under what circumstances warrant the appellation "suspicious."[10]

The individual policeman's "suspiciousness" does not hang on whether he has personally undergone an experience that could objectively be described as hazardous. Personal experience of this sort is not the key to the psychological importance of exceptionality. Each, as he routinely carries out his work, will experience situations that threaten to become dangerous. Like the American Jew who contributes to "defense" organizations such as the Anti-Defamation League in response to Nazi brutailties he has never experienced personally, the policeman identifies with his fellow cop who has been beaten, perhaps fatally, by a gang of young thugs.

SOCIAL ISOLATION

The patrolman in Westville, and probably in most communities, has come to identify the black man with danger. James Baldwin vividly expresses the isolation of the ghetto policeman:

> ... The only way to police a ghetto is to be oppressive. None of the Police Commissioner's men, even with the best will in the world, have any way of understanding the lives led by the people they swagger about in twos and threes controlling. Their very presence is an insult, and it would be, even if they spent their entire day feeding gumdrops to children. They represent the force of the white world, and that world's criminal profit and ease, to keep the black man corraled up here, in his place. The badge, the gun in the holster, and the swinging club make vivid what will happen should his rebellion become overt ...
>
> It is hard, on the other hand, to blame the policeman, blank, good-natured, thoughtless, and insuperably innocent, for being such a perfect representative of the people he serves. He, too, believes in good intentions and is astounded and offended when they are not taken for the deed. He has never, himself, done anything for which to be hated—which of us has? and yet he is facing, daily and nightly, people who would gladly see him dead, and he knows it. There is no way for him not to know it: there are few things under heaven more unnerving than the silent, accumulating contempt and hatred of a people. He moves through Harlem, therefore, like an occupying soldier in a bitterly hostile country; which is precisely what, and where he is, and is the reason he walks in twos and threes.[11]

While Baldwin's observations on police-Negro relations cannot be disputed seriously, there is greater social distance between police and "civilians" in general regardless of their color than Baldwin considers. Thus, Colin MacInnes has his English hero, Mr. Justice, explaining:

> ... The story is all coppers are just civilians like anyone else, living among them not in barracks like on the Continent, but you and I know that's just a legend for mugs. We *are* cut off: we're *not* like everyone else. Some civilians fear us and play up to us, some dislike us and keep out of our way but no one—well, very few indeed—accepts us as just ordinary like them. In one sense, dear, we're just like hostile troops occupying an enemy country. And say what you like, at times that makes us lonely.[12]

MacInnes' observation suggests that by not introducing a white control group, Baldwin has failed to see that the policeman may not get on well with anybody regardless (to use the hackneyed phrase) of race, creed, or national origin. Policemen whom one knows well often express their sense of isolation from the public as a whole, not just from those who fail to share their color. Westville police were asked, for example, to rank the most serious problems police have. The category most frequently selected was not racial problems, but some form of public relations: lack of respect for the police, lack of cooperation in enforcement of law, lack of understanding of the requirements of police work.[13] One respondent answered:

> As a policeman my most serious problem is impressing on the general public just how difficult and necessary police service is to all. There seems to be an attitude of "law is important, but it applies to my neighbor—not to me."

Of the 282 Westville policemen who rated the prestige police work receives from others, 70 percent ranked it as only fair or poor, while less than 2 percent ranked it as "excellent" and another 29 percent as "good." Similarly, in Britain, two-thirds of a sample of policemen interviewed by a Royal Commission stated difficulties in making friends outside the force; of those interviewed 58 percent thought members of the public to be reserved, suspicious, and constrained in conversation; and 12 percent attributed such difficulties to the requirement that policemen be selective in associations and behave circumspectly.[14]

A Westville policeman related the following incident:

> Several months after I joined the force, my wife and I used to be socially active with a crowd of young people, mostly married, who gave a lot of parties where there was drinking and dancing, and we enjoyed it. I've never forgotten, though, an incident that happened on one Fourth of July party. Everybody had been drinking, there was a lot of talking, people were feeling boisterous, and some kid there — he must have been twenty or twenty-two—threw a firecracker that hit my wife in the leg and burned her. I didn't know exactly what to do—punch the guy in the nose, bawl him out, just forget it. Anyway, I couldn't let it pass, so I walked over to him and told him he ought to be careful. He began to rise up at me, and when he did, somebody yelled, "Better watch out, he's a cop." I saw everybody standing there, and I could feel they were all against me and for the kid, even though he had thrown the firecracker at my wife. I went over to the host and said it was probably better if my wife and I left because a fight would put a damper on the party. Actually, I'd hoped he would ask the kid to leave, since the kid had thrown the firecracker. But he didn't so we left. After that incident, my wife and I stopped going around with that crowd, and decided that if we were going to go to parties where there was to be drinking and boisterousness, we weren't going to be the only police people there.

Another reported that he seeks to overcome his feelings by concealing his police identity:

> I try not to bring my work home with me, and that includes my social life. I like the men I work with, but I think it's better that my family doesn't become a police family. I try to put my police work into the background, and try not to let people know I'm a policeman. Once you do, you can't have normal relations with them.[15]

Although the policeman serves a people who are, as Baldwin says, the established society, the white society, these people do not make him feel accepted. As a result, he develops resources within his own world to combat social rejection.

POLICE SOLIDARITY

All occupational groups share a measure of inclusiveness and identification. People are brought together simply by doing the same work and having similar career and salary problems. As several writers have noted, however, police show an unusually high degree of occupational solidarity.[16] It is true that the police have a common employer and wear a uniform at work, but so do doctors, milkmen, and bus drivers. Yet it is doubtful that these workers have so close knit an occupation or so similar an outlook on the world as do police. Set apart from the conventional world, the policeman experiences an exceptionally strong tendency to find his social identity within his occupational milieu.

Compare the police with another skilled craft. In a study of the International Typographical Union, the authors asked printers the first names and jobs of their three closest friends. Of the 1,236 friends named by the 412 men in their sample, 35 percent were printers.[17] Similarly among the Westville police, of 700 friends listed by 250 respondents, 35 percent were policemen. The policemen, however, were far more active than printers in occupational social activities. Of the printers, more than half (54 percent) had never participated in any union clubs, benefit societies, teams, or organizations composed mostly of printers, or attended any printers' social affairs in the past 5 years. Of the Westville police, only 16 percent had failed to attend a single police banquet or dinner in the past *year* (as contrasted with the printers' 5 *years*); and of the 234 men answering this question, 54 percent had attended 3 or more such affairs *during the past year*.

These findings are striking in light of the interpretation made of the data on printers. Lipset, Trow, and Coleman do not, as a result of their findings, see printers as an unintegrated occupational group. On the contrary, they ascribe the democratic character of the union in good part to the active social and political participation of the membership. The point is not to question their interpretation, since it is doubtlessly correct when printers are held up against other manual workers. However, when seen in comparison to police, printers appear a minimally participating group; put positively, police emerge as an exceptionally socially active occupational group.

POLICE SOLIDARITY AND DANGER

There is still a question, however, as to the process through which danger and authority influence police solidarity. The effect of danger on police solidarity is revealed when we examine a chief complaint of police: lack of public support and public apathy. The complaint may have several referents including police pay, police prestige, and support from the legislature. But the repeatedly voiced broader meaning of the complaint is resentment at being taken for granted. The policeman does not believe that his status as civil servant should relieve the public of responsibility for law enforcement. He feels, however, that payment out of public coffers somehow obscures his humanity and, therefore, his need for help.[18] As one put it:

> Jerry, a cop, can get into a fight with three or four tough kids, and there will be citizens passing by, and maybe they'll look, but they'll never lend a hand. It's their country too, but you'd never know it the way some of them act. They forget that we're made of flesh and blood too. They don't care what happens to the cop so long as they don't get a little dirty.

Although the policeman sees himself as a specialist in dealing with violence, he does not want to fight alone. He does not believe that his specialization relieves the general public of citizenship duties. Indeed, if possible, he would prefer to be the foreman rather than the workingman in the battle against criminals.

The general public, of course, does withdraw from the workaday world of the policeman. The policeman's responsibility for controlling dangerous and sometimes violent persons alienates the average citizen perhaps as much as does his authority over the average citizen. If the policeman's job is to insure that public order is maintained, the citizen's inclination is to shrink from the dangers of maintaining it. The citizen prefers to see the policeman as an automaton, because once the policeman's humanity is recognized, the citizen necessarily becomes implicated in the policeman's work, which is, after all, sometimes dirty and dangerous. What the policeman typically fails to realize is the extent he becomes tainted by the character of the work he performs. The dangers of their work not only draws policemen together as a group but separates them from the rest of the population. Banton, for instance, comments:

> ... patrolmen may support their fellows over what they regard as minor infractions in order to demonstrate to them that they will be loyal in situations that make the greatest demands upon their fidelity...
> In the American departments I visited it seemed as if the supervisors shared many of the patrolmen's sentiments about solidarity. They too wanted their colleagues to back them up in an emergency, and they shared similar frustrations with the public.[19]

Thus, the element of danger contains seeds of isolation which may grow in two directions. In one, a stereotyping perceptual shorthand is formed through which the police come to see certain signs as symbols of potential violence. The police probably differ in this respect from the general middle-class white population only in degree. This difference, however, may take on enormous significance in practice. Thus, the policeman works at identifying and possibly apprehending the symbolic assailant; the ordinary citizen does not. As a result, the ordinary citizen does not assume the responsibility to implicate himself in the policeman's required response to danger. The element of danger in the policeman's role alienates him not only from populations with a potential for crime but also from the conventionally respectable (white) citizenry, in short, from that segment of the population from which friends would ordinarily be drawn. As Janowitz has noted in a paragraph suggesting similarities between the police and the military, "... any profession which is continually preoccupied with the threat of danger requires a strong sense of solidarity if it is to operate effectively. Detailed regulation of the military style of life is expected to enhance group cohesion, professional loyalty, and maintain the martial spirit."[20]

SOCIAL ISOLATION AND AUTHORITY

The element of authority also helps to account for the policeman's social isolation. Policemen themselves are aware of their isolation from the community, and are apt to weight authority heavily as a causal factor. When considering how authority influences rejection, the policeman typically singles out his responsibility for enforcement of traffic violations.[21] Resentment, even hostility, is generated in those receiving citations, in part because such contact is often the only one citizens have with police, and in part because municipal administrations and courts have been known to utilize police authority primarily to meet budgetary requirements, rather than those of public order. Thus, when a municipality engages in "speed trapping" by changing limits so quickly that drivers cannot realistically slow down to the prescribed speed or, while keeping the limits reasonable, charging high fines primarily to generate revenue, the policeman carries the brunt of public resentment.

That the policeman dislikes writing traffic tickets is suggested by the quota system police departments typically employ. In Westville, each traffic policeman has what is euphemistically described as a working "norm." A motorcyclist is supposed to write two tickets an hour for moving violations. It is doubtful that "norms" are needed because policemen are lazy. Rather, employment of quotas most likely springs from the reluctance of policemen to expose themselves to what they know to be public hostility. As a result, as one traffic policeman said:

> You learn to sniff out the places where you can catch violators when you're running behind. Of course, the department gets to know that you hang around one place, and they sometimes try to repair the situation there. But a lot of the time it would be too expensive to fix up the engineering fault, so we keep making our norm.

When meeting "production" pressures, the policeman inadvertently gives a false impression of patrolling ability to the average citizen. The traffic cyclist waits in hiding for moving violators near a tricky intersection, and is reasonably sure that such violations will occur with regularity. The violator believes he has observed a policeman displaying exceptional detection capacities and may have two thoughts, each apt to generate hostility toward the policeman: "I have been trapped," or "They can catch me; why can't they catch crooks as easily?" The answer, of course, lies in the different behavior patterns of motorists and "crooks." The latter do not act with either the frequency or predictability of motorists at poorly engineered intersections.

While traffic patrol plays a major role in separating the policemen from the respectable community, other of his tasks also have this consequence. Traffic patrol is only the most obvious illustration of the policeman's general responsibility for maintaining public order, which also includes keeping order at public accidents, sporting events, and political rallies. These activities share one feature: the policeman is called upon to *direct* ordinary citizens, and therefore to restrain their freedom of action. Resenting the restraint, the average citizen in such a situation typically thinks something along the lines of "He is supposed to catch crooks; why is he bothering me?" Thus, the citizen stresses the "dangerous" portion of the policeman's role while belittling his authority.

Closely related to the policeman's authority-based problems as *director* of the citizenry are difficulties associated with his injunction to *regulate public morality*. For instance, the policeman is obliged to investigate "lovers' lanes," and to enforce laws pertaining to gambling, prostitution, and drunkenness. His responsibility in these matters allows him much administrative discretion since he may not actually enforce the law by making an arrest, but instead merely interfere with continuation of the objectionable activity.[22] Thus, he may put the drunk in a taxi, tell the lovers to remove themselves from the back seat, and advise a man soliciting a prostitute to leave the area.

Such admonitions are in the interest of maintaining the proprieties of public order. At the same time, the policeman invites the hostility of the citizen so directed in two respects: he is likely to encourage the sort of response mentioned earlier (that is, an antagonistic reformulation of the policeman's role) and the policeman is apt to cause resentment because of the suspicion that policemen do not themselves strictly conform to the moral norms they are enforcing. Thus, the policeman, faced with enforcing a law against fornication, drunkenness, or gambling, is easily liable to a charge of hypocrisy. Even when the policeman is called on to enforce the laws relating to overt homosexuality, a form of sexual activity for which police are not especially noted, he may encounter the charge of hypocrisy on grounds that he does not adhere strictly to prescribed heterosexual codes. The policeman's difficulty in this respect is shared by all authorities responsible for maintenance of disciplined activity, including industrial foremen, political leaders, elementary schoolteachers, and college professors. All are expected to conform rigidly to the entire range of norms they espouse.[23] The policeman, however, as a result of the unique combination of the elements of danger and authority, experiences a special predicament. It is difficult to develop qualities enabling him to stand up to danger, and to conform to standards of puritanical morality. The element of danger demands that the policeman be able to carry out efforts that are in their nature overtly masculine. Police work, like soldiering, requires an exceptional caliber of physical fitness, agility, toughness, and the like. The man who ranks high on these masculine characteristics is, again like the soldier, not usually disposed to be puritanical about sex, drinking, and gambling.

On the basis of observations, policemen do not subscribe to moralistic standards for conduct. For example, the morals squad of the police department, when questioned, was unanimously against the statutory rape age limit, on grounds that as late teen-agers they themselves might not have refused an attractive offer from a

17 year-old girl.[24] Neither, from observations, are policemen by any means total abstainers from the use of alcoholic beverages. The policeman who is arresting a drunk has probably been drunk himself; he knows it and the drunk knows it.

More than that, a portion of the social isolation of the policeman can be attributed to the discrepancy between moral regulation and the norms and behavior of policemen in these areas. We have presented data indicating that police engage in a comparatively active occupational social life. One interpretation might attribute this attendance to a basic interest in such affairs; another might explain the policeman's occupational social activity as a measure of restraint in publicly violating norms he enforces. The interest in attending police affairs may grow as much out of security in "letting oneself go" in the presence of police, and a corresponding feeling of insecurity with civilians, as an authentic preference for police social affairs. Much alcohol is usually consumed at police banquets with all the melancholy and boisterousness accompanying such occasions. As Horace Cayton reports on his experience as a policeman:

> Deputy sheriffs and policemen don't know much about organized recreation; all they usually do when celebrating is get drunk and pound each other on the back, exchanging loud insults which under ordinary circumstances would result in a fight.[25]

To some degree the reason for the behavior exhibited on these occasions is the company, since the policeman would feel uncomfortable exhibiting insobriety before civilians. The policeman may be likened to other authorities who prefer to violate moralistic norms away from onlookers for whom they are routinely supposed to appear as normative models. College professors, for instance, also get drunk on occasion, but prefer to do so where students are not present. Unfortunately for the policeman, such settings are harder for him to come by than they are for the college professor. The whole civilian world watches the policeman. As a result, he tends to be limited to the company of other policemen for whom his police identity is not a stimulus to carping normative criticism.

CORRELATES OF SOCIAL ISOLATION

The element of authority, like the element of danger, is thus, seen to contribute to the solidarity of policemen. To the extent that policemen share the experience of receiving hostility from the public, they are also drawn together and become dependent upon one another. Trends in the degree to which police may exercise authority are also important considerations in understanding the dynamics of the relation between authority and solidarity. It is not simply a question of how much absolute authority police are given, but how much authority they have relative to what they had, or think they had, before. If, as Westley concludes, police violence is frequently a response to a challenge to the policeman's authority, so too may a perceived reduction in authority result in greater solidarity. Whitaker comments on the British police as follows:

> As they feel their authority decline, internal solidarity has become increasingly important to the police. Despite the individual responsibility of each police officer to pursue justice, there is sometimes a tendency to close ranks and to form a square when they themselves are concerned.[26]

These inclinations may have positive consequences for the effectiveness of police work, since notions of professional courtesy or collegueship seem unusually high among police.[27] When the nature of the policing enterprise requires much joint activity, as in robbery and narcotics enforcement, the impression is received that cooperation is high and genuine. Policemen do not appear to cooperate with one another merely because such is the policy of the chief, but because they sincerely attach a high value to teamwork. For instance, there is a norm among detectives that two who work together will protect each other when a dangerous situation arises. During one investigation, a detective stepped out of a car to question a suspect who became belligerent. The second detective, who had remained overly long in the back seat of the police car, apologized indirectly to his partner by explaining how wrong it had been of him to permit his partner to encounter a suspect alone on the street. He later repeated this explanation privately, in genuine consternation at having committed the breach (and possibly at having been culpable in the presence of an observer). Strong feelings of empathy and cooperation, indeed almost of "clannishness," a term several policemen themselves used to describe the attitude of police toward one another, may be seen in the daily activities of police. Analytically, these feelings can be traced to the elements of danger and shared experiences of hostility in the policeman's role.

Finally, to round out the sketch, policemen are notably conservative, emotionally and politically. If the element of danger in the policeman's role tends to make the policeman suspicious, and therefore emotionally attached to the status quo, a similar consequence may be attributed to the element of authority. The fact that a man is engaged in enforcing a set of rules implies that he also becomes implicated in *affirming* them. Labor disputes provide the commonest example of conditions inclining the policeman to support the status quo. In these situations, the police are necessarily pushed on the side of the defense of property. Their responsibilities thus lead them to see the striking and sometimes angry workers as their enemy and, therefore, to be cool, if not antagonistic, toward the whole conception of labor militancy.[28] If a policeman did not believe in the system of laws he was responsible for enforcing, he would have to go on living in a state of conflicting cognitions, a condition which a number of social psychologists agree is painful.[29]

* * *

NOTES

1. For previous contributions in this area, see the following: Ely Chinoy, *Automobile Workers and the American Dream* (Garden City: Doubleday & Company, Inc., 1955); Charles R. Walker and Robert H. Guest, *The Man on the Assembly Line* (Cambridge: Harvard University Press, 1952); Everett C. Hughes, "Work and the Self," in his *Men and Their Work* (Glencoe, Illinois: The Free Press, 1958), pp. 42-55; Harold L. Wilensky, *Intellectuals in Labor Unions: Organizational Pressures on Professional Roles* (Glencoe, Illinois: The Free Press, 1956); Wilensky, "Varieties of Work Experience," in Henry Borow, ed., *Man in a World at Work* (Boston: Houghton Mifflin Company, 1964), pp. 125-54; Louis Kriesberg, "The Retail Furrier: Concepts of Security and Success," *American Journal of Sociology* 57 (March 1952): 478-85; Waldo Burchard, "Role Conflicts of Military Chaplains," *American Sociological Review* 19 (October 1954): 528-35; Howard S. Becker and Blanche Geer, "The Fate of Idealism in Medical School," *American Sociological Review* 23 (1958): 50-56; and Howard S. Becker and Anselm L. Strauss, "Careers, Personality, and Adult Socialization," *American Journal of Sociology* 62 (November 1956): 253-363.

2. Morris Janowitz, *The Professional Soldier: A Social and Political Portrait* (New York: The Free Press, 1964), p. 175.

3. By no means does such an analysis suggest there are no individual or group differences among police. On the contrary, most of this study emphasizes differences, endeavoring to relate these to occupational specialities in police departments. This chapter, however, explores similarities rather than differences, attempting to account for the policeman's general disposition to perceive and to behave in certain ways.

4. William Westley was the first to raise such questions about the police, when he inquired into the conditions under which police are violent. Whatever merit this analysis has, it owes much to his prior insights, as all subsequent sociological studies of the police must. See his "Violence and the Police," *American Journal of Sociology* 59 (July 1953): 34-41; also his unpublished Ph.D. dissertation "The Police: A Sociological Study of Law, Custom, and Morality," University of Chicago, Department of Sociology, 1951.

5. Something of the flavor of the policeman's attitude toward the symbolic assailant comes across in a recent article by a police expert. In discussing the problem of selecting subjects for field interrogation, the author writes:
   A. Be suspicious. This is a healthy police attitude, but it should be controlled and not too obvious.
   B. Look for the unusual.
      1. Persons who do not "belong" where they are observed.
      2. Automobiles which do not "look right."
      3. Businesses opened at odd hours, or not according to routine or custom.
   C. Subjects who should be subjected to field interrogations.
      1. Suspicious persons known to the officer from previous arrests, field interrogations, and observations.
      2. Emaciated appearing alcoholics and narcotics users who invariably turn to crime to pay for cost of habit.
      3. Person who fits description of wanted suspect as described by radio, teletype, daily bulletins.
      4. Any person observed in the immediate vicinity of a crime very recently committed or reported as "in progress."
      5. Known trouble-makers near large gatherings.
      6. Persons who attempt to avoid or evade the officer.
      7. Exaggerated unconcern over contact with the officer.
      8. Visibly "rattled" when near the policeman.
      9. Unescorted women or young girls in public places, particularly at night in such places as cafes, bars, bus and train depots, or street corners.
      10. "Lovers" in an industrial area (make good lookouts).
      11. Persons who loiter about places where children play.
      12. Solicitors or peddlers in a residential neighborhood.
      13. Loiterers around public rest rooms.
      14. Lone male sitting in car adjacent to schoolground with newspaper or book in his lap.

15. Lone male sitting in car near shopping center who pays unusual amount of attention to women, sometimes continuously manipulating rearview mirror to avoid direct eye contact.
16. Hitchhikers.
17. Person wearing coat on hot days.
18. Car with mismatched hub caps, or dirty car with clean license plate (or vice versa).
19. Uniformed "deliverymen" with no merchandise or truck.
20. Many others. How about your own personal experiences?

From Thomas F. Adams, "Field Interrogation," *Police* (March-April 1963), p. 28.

6. See Irving Piliavin and Scott Briar, "Police Encounters with Juveniles," *American Journal of Sociology* 70 (September 1964): 206-14.

7. A questionnaire was given to all policemen in operating divisions of the police force: patrol, traffic, vice control, and all detectives. The questionnaire was administered at police line-ups over a period of three days, mainly by the author but also by some of the police personnel themselves. Before the questionnaire was administered, it was circulated to and approved by the policemen's welfare association.

8. Indeed, the journalist Paul Jacobs, who has ridden with the Westville juvenile police as part of his own work on poverty, observed in a personal communication that juvenile police appear curiously drawn to seek out dangerous situations, as if juvenile work without danger is degrading.

9. Colin McInnes, *Mr. Love and Justice* (London: New English Library, 1962), p. 74.

10. Peter J. Connell, "Handling of Complaints by Police," unpublished paper for course in Criminal Procedure, Yale Law School, Fall, 1961.

11. James Baldwin, *Nobody Knows My Name* (New York: Dell Publishing Company, 1962), pp. 65-67.

12. McInnes, op. cit., p. 20.

13. Respondents were asked "Anybody who knows anything about police work knows that police face a number of problems. Would you please state—in order—what you consider to be the two most serious problems police have." On the basis of a number of answers, the writer and J. Richard Woodworth devised a set of categories. Then Woodworth classified each response into one of the categories (*see* table below). When a response did not seem clear, he consulted with the writer. No attempt was made to independently check Woodworth's classification because the results are used impressionistically, and do not test a hypothesis. It may be, for instance, that "relations with public" is sometimes used to indicate racial problems, and vice versa. "Racial problems" include only those answers having specific reference to race. The categories and results were as follows:

WESTVILLE POLICE RANKING OF NUMBER ONE PROBLEM FACED BY POLICE

	Number	Percent
Relations with public	74	26
Racial problems and demonstrations	66	23
Juvenile delinquents and delinquency	23	8
Unpleasant police tasks	23	8
Lack of cooperation from authorities (D.A., legislature, courts)	20	7
Internal departmental problems	17	6
Irregular life of policeman	5	2
No answer or other answer	56	20
	284	100

14. Royal Commission on the Police, 1962, Appendix IV to *Minutes of Evidence,* cited in Michael Banton, *The Policeman in the Community* (London: Tavistock Publications, 1964), p. 198.

15. Similarly, Banton found Scottish police officers attempting to conceal their occupation when on holiday. He quotes one as saying: "If someone asks my wife 'What does your husband do?', I've told her to say, 'He's a clerk,' and that's the way it went because she found that being a policeman's wife—well, it wasn't quite a stigma, she didn't feel cut off, but that a sort of invisible wall was up for conversation purposes when a policeman was there" (p. 198).

16. In addition to Banton, William Westley and James Q. Wilson have noted this characteristic of police. See Westley, op. cit., p. 294; Wilson, "The Police and Their Problems: A Theory," *Public Policy* 12 (1963): 189-216.

17. S. M. Lipset, Martin H. Trow, and James S. Coleman, *Union Democracy* (New York: Anchor Books, 1962), p. 123. A complete comparison is as follows:

CLOSEST FRIENDS OF PRINTERS AND POLICE, BY OCCUPATION

	Printers N = 1236 (%)	Police N = 700 (%)
Same occupation	35	35
Professionals, business executives, and independent business owners	21	30
White-collar or sales employees	20	12
Manual workers	25	22

18. On this issue there was no variation. The statement "the policeman feels" means that there was no instance of a negative opinion expressed by the police studied.

19. Banton, op. cit., p. 114.

20. Janowitz, op. cit.

21. O. W. Wilson, for example, mentions this factor as a primary source of antagonism toward police. See his "Police Authority in a Free Society," *Journal of Criminal Law, Criminology and Police Science* 54 (June 1964): 175-77. In the current study, in addition to the police themselves, other people interviewed, such as attorneys in the system, also attribute the isolation of police to their authority. Similarly, Arthur L. Stinchcombe, in an as yet unpublished manuscript, "The Control of Citizen Resentment in Police Work," provides a stimulating analysis, to which I am indebted, of the ways police authority generates resentment.

22. See Wayne R. La Fave, "The Police and Nonenforcement of the Law," *Wisconsin Law Review* (1962), pp. 104-37, 179-239.

23. For a theoretical discussion of the problems of leadership, see George Homans, *The Human Group* (New York: Harcourt Brace Jovanovich, Inc., 1950), especially the chapter on "The Job of the Leader," pp. 415-40.

24. The work of the Westville morals squad is analyzed in detail in an unpublished master's thesis by J. Richard Woodworth, "The Administration of Statutory Rape Complaints: A Sociological Study" (Berkeley: University of California, 1964).

25. Horace R. Clayton, *Long Old Road* (New York: Trident Press, 1965), p. 154.

26. Ben Whitaker, *The Police* (Middlesex, England: Penguin Books, 1964), p. 137.

27. It would be difficult to compare this factor across occupations, since the indicators could hardly be controlled. Nevertheless, I felt that the sense of responsibility to policemen in other departments was on the whole quite strong.

28. In light of this, the most carefully drawn lesson plan in the "professionalized" Westville police department, according to the officer in charge of training, is the one dealing with the policeman's demeanor in labor disputes. A comparable concern is now being evidenced in teaching policemen appropriate demeanor in civil rights demonstrations. *See,* e.g., Judy E. Towler, *The Police Role in Racial Conflicts* (Springfield, Ill.: Charles C Thomas, 1964).

29. Indeed, one school of social psychology asserts that there is a basic "drive," a fundamental tendency of human nature, to reduce the degree of discrepancy between conflicting cognitions. For the policeman, this tenet implies that he would have to do

something to reduce the discrepancy between his beliefs and his behavior. He would have to modify his behavior, his beliefs, or introduce some outside factor to justify the discrepancy. If he were to modify his behavior, so as not to enforce the law in which he disbelieves, he would not hold his position for long. Practically, then, his alternatives are to introduce some outside factor, or to modify his beliefs. However, the outside factor would have to be compelling in order to reduce the pain resulting from the dissonance between his cognitions. For example, he would have to be able to convince himself that the only way he could possibly make a living was by being a policeman. Or he would have to modify his beliefs. *See* Leon Festinger, *A Theory of Cognitive Dissonance* (Evanston, Ill.: Row-Peterson, 1957). A brief explanation of Festinger's theory is reprinted in Edward E. Sampson ed., *Approaches, Contexts, and Problems of Social Psychology* (Englewood Cliffs, N.J.: Prentice-Hall, Inc., 1964), pp. 9-15.

SECTION TWO

Police Selection and Retention

Overview

THE ECONOMIC ASPECTS OF POLICE SELECTION: THE ORAL BOARD. Dr. James H. Rankin examines the police selection process with particular emphasis on the important function of the oral board. One of the pioneers in psychiatric evaluation of police officer candidates, Dr. Rankin has served as consulting psychiatrist for many major police departments in Southern California.

YOU CAN'T TELL BY LOOKING. Kenneth W. Sherrill, a staff member of the California Commission of Peace Officers' Standards and Training, writes of the very important process of the background investigation, the "BI." He cites some excellent case studies that illustrate his points.

LATERAL TRANSFER. Glenn A. Marin reviews the lateral transfer of qualified police professionals from one department to another on the basis of qualifications of the people and needs of the agency. This is a truly professional approach.

OPERATION: POLICE MANPOWER. James A. F. Kelley of the International Association of Chiefs of Police and Major Robert C. Barnum explain the Operation Transition training of military service men to prepare them for civilian occupations. Military services are a major supplier of manpower to the police service, and this training program is an excellent one.

KEEPING POLICEMEN ON THE JOB. Richard H. Blum and William J. Osterloh found in a study that one of the most frequently cited reasons given by resigning policemen was "public disrespect" of law enforcement. The authors studied this matter as well as other aspects of officer "turnover" and suggest that the problem may not be so factual as many officers believe. They recommend some action by the police administrators to make the facts known.

ARE YOU ORIENTED TO HOLD THEM? At the time he wrote the paper Thomas Reddin was deputy chief of police of Los Angeles under William Parker. He was promoted to chief and later retired to begin a new career as anchor man for a television news program. Chief Reddin surveys the many aspects of police management and ways in which a police department may better serve the needs of the "new breed" of professional officers. He focuses particularly on success in retaining experienced officers.

The Economic Aspects of Police Selection: The Oral Board

James H. Rankin

INTRODUCTION

Once upon a time there was a United States Senator. Through fate he became President of the United States. It has been said that he had a placard on his desk with the motto, "The Buck Stops here." The president, of course, was Harry S. Truman, a man known for being forthright and having the courage of his convictions.

It is the thesis of this paper that the "buck stops here" should more often be on the Oral Board's level of the police selection process—and to some lesser degree on the Aptitude Test. The principal reason for this proposal is a simple, straightforward one—economics. If the Oral Board can perform some of the functions of the psychiatrist, and the background investigator, it will have contributed the saving of hard cash and many man hours of time of sworn police personnel.

In order to give perspective to our examination of the economic aspects of Oral Board functions, it is in order that the earlier phases of the selection process be examined also, as they pertain to the economics of the process.

Dr. James H. Rankin is Associate Clinical Professor of Psychiatry, University of Southern California School of Medicine. A pioneer in psychiatric evaluation of police candidates in Southern California, Dr. Rankin presented this paper at the Traffic Institute of Northwestern University, Southwest Area in Palm Springs on January 19, 1967. Reprinted by permission of the author.

THE APTITUDE TEST

This initial phase of the selection process attempts to evaluate the intellectual capacity of the applicant through his education experience; to assess his ability to perform the basic mental functions of a police officer.

The aptitude test can be fairly well standardized, either higher or lower than "average" as suits the needs and convictions of individual jurisdictions. In California a number of communities utilize the facilities of the State for their aptitude tests. The results of the State test usually can be utilized by any community that so desires.

The California test examines five major areas of mental functioning—intelligence, verbal ability, numerical aptitude, spatial aptitude and form perception.

Definition of Aptitudes

1. Intelligence   This tests general learning ability. The ability to "catch on" or understand instructions and underlying principles is assessed. The ability to reason and make judgment is evaluated.

2. Verbal Ability   This measures the ability to understand the meaning of words and ideas associated with them, and to use them effectively. The ability to comprehend language, to understand relationships between words and to understand meanings of whole sentences and paragraphs is tested. The ability to present information or ideas clearly is checked.

3. Numerical Aptitude   This is the estimation of the ability to perform arithmetic problems quickly and accurately.

4. Spatial Aptitude   The ability tested here is to comprehend forms in space and understand relationships of planes and solid objects, frequently described as the ability to "visualize" objects of two or three dimensions. Thinking visually of geometric forms is assessed.

5. Form Perception   The ability to perceive pertinent details in objects or in pictorial or graphic material is included in this section. Ability to make visual comparisons and discriminations and see slight differences in shapes and shadows of figures and widths and lengths of lines is tested.

To my knowledge many communities are satisfied with the aptitude test, but some jurisdictions prefer to set up their own examination. Those who are "independent" usually demand a higher level of achievement on the aptitude test. For instance, one large jurisdiction in California, Department A, has its own, comparatively rigid, aptitude test. Another, Department B, of comparable size, uses the state test. In a recent informal spot check by me, the next to last echelon of selection, I found that approximately 20 percent of the applicants who got to me had failed Department A's aptitude test. In Department B, which uses the state test, the intelligence tests given in the Academy (the California Mental Maturity and the Wunderlich) showed a significant lowering after institution of the state test from the formerly "independent" test given by the local Civil Service Board. IQ and Intelligence tests are based fundamentally on one's exposure to, and absorption of, knowledge. I will comment later on the possible significance of this.

What is the economic significance of the aptitude test in the selection process? I'm sure there has been long and heated discussion of the merits of a high level of aptitude test versus a lowering of intellectual achievement. I might list some points in favor of both camps.

Maintenance of High Levels on the Test It is generally conceded that the greater the degree of education, the better one's chances are of advancing in life, socially and economically. Generally this is due to increased intellectual discipline engendered by the increasing standards and demands of each level of schooling. Frequently, although not absolutely, intellectual discipline and moral discipline accompany each other. The exception to this generalization can be seen frequently in the applicant who may have a bachelor's degree, yet has done little with it and is a social nonconformist, or is just not well organized in personality to cope with life. I shall comment more on moral discipline later. Departments with high level aptitude standards are less likely to get involved in teaching their recruits such things as "bone head" English. The attrition rate in the last phases of the selection process seems to be less in those applicants subjected to a more demanding aptitude test. In dollars and cents, the case for a high level test seems a good one.

Low Standard Aptitude Tests There is little need to expound on the economic and social chaos that would occur in the community with unrealistically low, or nonexistent, educational and mentally adaptive test standards.

Moderate (Perhaps Realistic) Levels of Aptitude/Intelligence Tests Those of us who are education-oriented and accustomed to educational up-striving are apt to be impatient with the person of minimal to moderate education. We tend to feel he could have done better—after all—"didn't I?" There are innumerable reasons for the under-education of our 20-year-olds—over population, for example, with pressures from below that force the student from grade to higher grade like aimless flotsam.

Many who apply for police work have a good potential of intelligence, but lack the tools to use it—spelling, grammar, reading ability, arithmetic and knowledge of his social environment. If the handicapped applicant has the Desire, the Motivation, he may overcome these handicaps through the early phases of his police career. Let me repeat! If he has Desire and Motivation. The *desire* must come from within. *Motivation* can come from his environment, either his school or his police department, or both. The written examination cannot measure Desire or Motivation. To some degree, the Oral Board can estimate these qualities. It can safely be assumed that, all things being equal, the applicant with a sounder, better basic education has had more Desire and Motivation developed in him than has the under-educated applicant. There are many exceptions to any rule, and there are, of course, many under-educated persons with Desire and Motivation. They are, however, very likely a small minority of the large army of the under-educated.

As an example of the group of under-educated who seems to have Desire and Motivation, let me comment briefly on the MDTA—Manpower Development Training Act. The Federal government subsidizes the state to train and educate certain peoples in various fields. In recent months the California State Department of Employment has embarked on an educational program to train under-educated men to pass the aptitude test for policemen. This is not a blind "do good" program, but a well-thought-out one that makes sure the applicant is physically and emotionally suited to be acceptable for training as a policeman. I have been agreeably surprised at the quality of the applicants for MDTA training. Most of them make economic sacrifice to get this further education in fundamentals. Most of them, in my opinion, have Desire, and are Motivated. It is easy to be inclined to dismiss MDTA as a "boondoggle." Several years from now we shall know. If the program salvages an appreciable number of previously nonacceptables and aims them toward successful careers as policemen, the program can be called economically sound.

Desire and Motivation are essential criteria from the first step of applying, through the probation period, and into many uncountable years of police career. It would appear that it is economically feasible to try to ascertain who, of the under-educated, *really* desire to be policemen, and assist them *outside* the police department.

On the other side of the educational coin we see young men with Desire who are going to college with the express purpose of becoming policemen. An increasing number of junior colleges are offering courses in Police Science. Without question the great majority of these students will fare better as policemen than their average or below-average educated young colleagues. Perhaps the most hopeful development in recruitment, from the aptitude/intelligence phase, is the increasing utilization of the 18- to 21-year-old student who works half time for a police department and goes to school half time. He is expected to carry a minimum of credit units and have at least a 2.0 average while working as a police cadet. I am very favorably impressed with the potential of this group. I hope the program expands.

Most departments have a large burden in carrying on an "in-service" program of career training. They should not be expected to function also in the area of general education.

It is significant that experience has shown that lower standards in the "aptitude" test has resulted in, roughly, a third higher attrition rate in the training period of one large department. In terms of economics—dollars and man hours wasted—the cost is very high. In the last four years, 1963-1966, around 300 cadets failed to meet Academy standards. When it is remembered that the attrition rate was roughly one-third higher than the preceding four years, and that the estimated total cost of training a cadet is about $3,000, the price of lowered aptitude/intelligence standards came to about $300,000 for four years.

Summary

The economics of the written portion of the process of police selection seem to point to a more demanding, relatively high-level test. The one who has applied himself in school usually is better self-disciplined and better organized, intellectually at least, to cope with the stresses of life. He usually has relatively, if diffusely, a greater desire, motivation and ambition than the under-educated and, as such, stands a better chance of performing satisfactorily as a policeman. The under-educated person who has sufficient desire will educate himself upward to the level of the demanding written test in one manner or another. It can be demonstrated that lowered standards in the written phase of police selection are costly in wasted money and man power.

THE ORAL BOARD

What the Oral Board Should Look For

In general the board should seek to determine the applicant's Morality. By this I am not talking in the ecclesiastic sense, but in the social sense. Perhaps some dictionary definitions of "moral" are in order: "pertaining to what is right or proper," "discriminating right from wrong," "conforming to, or embodying, righteous or just conduct." The word "right," from the Latin "rectus," has a number of definitions, one of which is, "obedience to lawful authority, divine or human."

The Oral Board should wish to determine, to the best of its ability, how the applicant has behaved himself through his lifetime. There are, of course, many factors that determine his behavior and his reactions to life. The probable causes of his behavior are not primarily the interest, nor the obligation, of the Oral Board. It is interested in the *results* of his behavior, and the impact of the applicant's behavior in *why* the applicant was dismissed from school, but not what causes led up to his failure.

Composition of Oral Boards

I will start with a conclusion, then try to justify it. The professionally oriented and experienced Board will do a far better job of selection of applicants than a part-time haphazardly selected Board. By analogy, a professional sports team will always beat an amateur team, especially if the amateur team is of the "pick up" variety.

The composition of Oral Boards seems to vary widely in composition. One large jurisdiction has only two members on its Oral Board, both highly professional, one being from the enforcement department itself and the other from the Personnel Department. This latter member specializes in Oral Boards of *all* nature in his quite large community, not just on police Oral Boards. This personnel member comments that a third member of other Boards, the "nonprofessional," usually turns out to be "excess baggage" who passively agrees with the "pro's." Other jurisdictions, usually smaller ones, may depend upon citizens of the community, a member of the city's Personnel Department, or a member of the Police Department concerned, and frequently, a member of a Police Department of some other jurisdiction. All of this information is, I'm sure, quite familiar to you.

It is my impression that the smaller communities do a better job of selection on the Oral Boards than the larger cities, simply because there is less volume of interviews, a clearer idea of the department expectations, and greater rapport and communication between the Police Department Board member, the Personnel member, and their superiors. If I seem to be contradicting myself about having a "pro" Board it is because I do not sufficiently emphasize that the "pro" member in the small department is a policeman who has the implicit confidence of the Chief of Police. In addition, in many departments there is direct contact with, or exposure to, the applicant by members of the department who are not directly on the Oral Board.

It should be possible to almost standardize an Oral Board's function. If a community has an at least semi-permanent quality to its Board, or Boards, its results will tend to be more consistent and of higher quality. The Police Department member should have the complete confidence and support of his Chief. His own level of achievement in the department should be such as to insure soundness of judgment and confidence in his decisions. He should know, in depth, what the department *does not want* in an applicant. This appears to be a negative approach. It is. However, we must recognize that what is left is positive personality traits. In my opinion, the Department member of the Oral Board should be, at least, a Lieutenant. It likewise would be desirable to have the visiting policeman member of the same rank. The Civil Service member should have considerable experience in assessing/hiring of employees, and like the police member, be extremely conversant with the Department's requirements. The civilian member should have had personal experience in hiring/firing and if possible have had the painful experience of "meeting the payroll."

The composition of the Oral Board is of vital importance in the proper *non*selection of applicants. If the Board is properly motivated, and in harmony with the Chief's desires, and knows what areas to explore, it will save its community considerable money.

Attitude of Board Member

After an adequate interview the Board member should be able to ask, and answer, a question of this nature: "Do I, without question, want this man to be a policeman in *my* community?" This question is essential to the theme "The Buck Stops Here." Often the reaction is, "I'm not sure." To the member: If that is your conclusion, *why* are you not sure? Of what areas are you concerned? Is to pass the applicant risky or not? Are you sorry for the applicant? The psychiatrist would phrase it: "Are you unrealistically, unwittingly, identifying yourself with the applicant?" "Have you emotionally 'put yourself' in his shoes?" Such a phenomenon is frequent in all of us. We must ever self-examine to see if we are *really* being objective.

The more familiar one is with police problems—or more broadly—problems of personnel and hiring, the easier it is to be objective and keep out of the trap of being overly sympathetic and avoiding the fatal mistake of "identifying" with the applicant. The more searching the interview, the more comprehensive the areas covered, the more likely the accuracy of his judgment. Needless to say, such a procedure generally is fundamental in most all areas of decision.

Disqualifications

Let me comment on the saving of money at the Oral Board level where, I hope, "The Buck Stops Here." In one large community, roughly 50 percent of those who passed the Oral Boards failed their physical examination. From 20 to 25 percent of those remaining failed either the psychiatric examination or the background investigation.

For some years my disqualification rate on the psychiatric examination in one Department ran consistently at about 10 percent, and the background disqualification rate was 10 to 13 percent. As I became more aware of some of the grossly anti-social aspects of the applicants' histories, the more I tended to explore these areas in my interview. More recently my disqualification rate has, at times, risen to 20 percent and levels out to about 15 or 18 percent. At the same time, interestingly enough, as my disqualification rate almost doubled, the disqualification rate of the background check reduced by half—currently about 5 percent.

The economics of the situation are readily apparent. About one out of four who passed the Oral Boards were psychiatrically failed, or failed background investigation, mostly because of unacceptable social history. The cost of the medical, the psychiatric examination, and the man hours of police time, add up to considerable amount of money. The saving in man hours' time of the investigator much more than pays for my more rigid criteria and the doubling of my rejection rate. It has been estimated in one department that, on an average, each background investigation consumes at least 30 man hours' time—a considerable expense, indeed. If the Oral Board would take a *history*—make an adequate sociological investigation, it can save its city much expense. As noted, smaller communities tend to be more thorough in their evaluation of applicants simply, in many cases, because of an opportunity for personal contacts by those in higher authority. In many of these communities my psychiatric rejection rate is less than 5 percent, likely, as noted, because the applicants are much more thoroughly screened prior to my examining them.

The almost desperate need for policemen is a lure, a seduction almost, all along the lines of the selection process, with the impulse to "take a chance," to "pass the buck." (I qualify as an expert in this, having been doing it myself for some 13 years. As the saying goes, "it takes one to catch one.") I have found that one does the Police Department no favor when an applicant is passed as a "borderline." All too frequently the doubtful one drops by the wayside after much expense, time and effort to the department. It takes courage to say "No." However, if we can base our decision to disqualify on specific reasons, we are justified in not selecting those whose history makes them, at best, doubtful risks.

Orientation

There is a good possiblity that often the Oral Board assumes too much about the applicant's interview sophistication. It can be assumed that the applicant has had some degree of experience in being interviewed for a job. Possibly the job interview is cursory, superficial and mechanical. The Oral Board should not be cursory, superficial and mechanical. The applicant must be made aware that he is not being interviewed for just another job. Police is a job requiring integrity and pride. If this approach seems, to the cynic, to be preaching, or flag waving, he is correct. It takes pride to wave the flag. The police applicant should be made aware that he is applying for a profession.

Above all, many applicants are unlikely to know how thoroughly they will be investigated. If the thoroughness of the investigation is spelled out to them in detail many unsuitable applicants will judge the situation correctly and withdraw from further effort for police work. For instance, some departments use the polygraph as part of their selection process. The applicant should know that some of his Oral Board answers will be repeated on the polygraph. He should know that discrepancies in answers will subject him to disqualification. Many departments, of course, do not use the polygraph. The applicant should be briefed on the significance of finger prints, arrest checks, credit checks, reference comments, marriage, work references and questionable associates on his chances of being accepted. He should have it spelled out to him in clear simple language that if he is evasive to the Oral Board, omits, minimizes, or lies he will ultimately be caught; if not in the selection process, probably in the probation period. He should be told bluntly that lying will not pay off for him.

What I am saying, of course, is that the applicant should be "set up" in the interview so that he is more likely to "cop out" if such is necessary. I have no illusion that all applicants will fully confess their social transgressions. However, a majority will—if probed—repeat—if probed—talk surprisingly frankly. A minority of applicants, through sheer stupidity, or resentfulness and rebelliousness to the Board authority, or even with a reckless gamble of not being caught in lie, will not "level." Others, with supreme egoism, or gall, will feel they can outsmart their inquisitors. The Jewish language has a wonderful word to describe some of these persons—"chutzpah!"[1]

Other applicants who lie can ultimately be classified as pathologic liars, or psychopaths. The official psychiatric term is "sociopath." The only way to diagnose this group is by past history, accurately and amply documented. This group of sick people, when confronted with their history, do not react with remorse or guilt. They in themselves, feel their behavior justifiable, simply because everyone else is wrong—"the end justifies the means."

Obviously neither the Oral Board, nor the psychiatrist for that matter, can pick up this small group. Usually a thorough background check will detect them. Theoretically, these should be the only cases the background investigators need to deal with. When the millennium occurs, most of the investigators will ask for a transfer due to sheer boredom. (I hope.)

Proposition

Since I am not conversant with the sequence of applicant selection in most communities, I will base this suggested variation on my experience in the Los Angeles area.

My proposal is that when an applicant is notified that he has successfully passed the aptitude/intelligence test he be instructed, in the written notification, to report to the proper area, preferably the police personnel section, to pick up his Personal History Form. When he is given the form he should be instructed, in the usual meticulous way, on how to fill out the form, and given a list of what substantiating documents are to accompany this form. It is suggested that the instructor emphasize to the applicant that the forms must be absolutely complete. Let the applicant take as much time as he desires to complete the Personal History Form—weeks, months, years! (It's his problem really.) After the applicant has completed his Personal History Form let him request from Civil Service a date to meet with the Oral Board. At that appointed time he presents his complete Personal History Form as admission to the examination.

Let me now defend my suggestion. Why do I suggest such a procedure when there has been a determined, and understandable, effort to shorten the time from filing to the Academy? Consider how many initially file for the examination and do not even bother to show up! Motivated?

I refer back to my comments on Desire and Motivation. Do the "no shows" for the Oral Board reveal a lack of Desire and Motivation? Of course! It is my premise that in this procedure variation we can test, in some degree, the Desire and Motivation to be a policeman by how the applicant rises to the challenge of the Personal History Form, in speed, promptness and completeness. As noted, some who pass the "aptitude" test will simply never show up for the Oral Board. Why? Experience has shown that some are incapable of adequately completing the form. Other applicants sense the dangers to them inherent in the questions. The questions may be too comprehensive and explicit to answer, if evasion is necessary. Other applicants are literally too lazy or mentally disorganized. Translated: They may lack Desire and Motivation to get *even to the Oral Board.*

I am aware that there likely would be technical problems raised by the proposition to put the Personal History Form ahead of the Oral examination. Frequently, objections are raised about the propriety of many aspects of police selection. Perhaps one more skirmish would not be too upsetting to the police department advocating using my "proposition."

Economics

If this suggestion is tried, and proven valid in terms of the applicant's sincerity and determination, then another step has been taken in streamlining and economizing the selection process. If this suggestion is tried it, in effect, passes the "Buck" to the applicant where it properly belongs. Should the responsibility of proper selection be exclusively the responsibility of the community? It is suggested here that more individual moral responsibility be placed on the applicant. In my opinion all too often the applicant is led to believe all he has to do is make some physical effort in passing the agility test and then the rest is up to the community that so ardently desires him. He then, in effect, presents "the body," in a passive way, to be examined. He permits himself to be informed when he may, if he desires, meet the next appointment. (Should he oversleep he will be reassigned?)

With such a passive, "please do us a favor and be a policeman!" attitude on the part of recruitment, it is a hell of a shock to those passive persons (they abound!) who have been subtly influenced to believe that once in the Academy they "have it made." I'm surprised, really, that the attrition rate is not higher. Confession: I am not without blame. I too have been influenced by the long increasing plea—"please won't you become a policeman. We need you so much!" I think the time is rapidly arriving when we should stop and, as the bridge player says, "lead from a strength," not weakness.

Referring to my ever-recurring theme, "The Buck Stops Here," perhaps the selection process machinery should, as noted, "pass the Buck" to the applicant, as suggested here. If he presents a completely satisfactory Personal History Form then they can examine him "in depth" and probe. If they use a checklist of areas to be probed, they will likely have a high efficiency of success in good applicant selection. If an airline pilot repeatedly and meticulously uses a check list, why should not an Oral Board?

Areas for Exploration

If the Oral Board adequately explores the following suggested areas it should be able to come to a fair judicious decision about the applicant's suitability for police work.

Education

Achievement in High School should be evaluated. Grades? Conduct and behavior attitudes? Group participation? An overall impression of his school environmental adjustment will help in the evaluation. College credits? Grades? Subjects? Major, if any? Specific goals and aspirations?

Military

Branch of Service? Highest rank? Assignments? Disciplinary actions? Medical, emotional problems: Ever see a military psychiatrist? How long on active duty? Type of discharge? If no military service, what classification? I-Y for instance? If so, why?

Police Record

Probe. Generally those with records will be evasive, omissive, rationalize, or just flatly lie. Remind them they can't hide their record. What is their driving license history? Suspension? Revocations? Often detailed exploration pays off in revealing adverse information. Social attitudes, and especially attitudes toward Authority, can be revealed in this area of social adjustment, or non-adjustment.

Marriage

This is an important area of evaluation in social adaptation. How many marriages? Why divorce? How much child support and/or alimony? If still married search for possible problems. Mostly the Board will have to depend on subtle indications of the marriage situation. Occasionally the applicant will be frank. The quality of inter-personal relationships can be evaluated from marriage adaptation.

Work Record

This should be explored in some depth also. This record gives an evaluation of the applicant's stability, reliability, and sense of responsibility. How many jobs has he had as an adult? What types of jobs—simple labor? Meeting the public? Degree of responsibility: Has he been fired from jobs? Why?

Debts

An applicant cannot do good work in the Academy or probationary period if he has back-breaking or impossible debts. He should not become a policeman until he can demonstrate fiscal responsibility and reasonable judgment about money management. Can he justify his debt burden? Judgment and self-control is indicated in his economic situation.

Hypothetical Questions

The "what would you do if——?" type of questions may serve some value. Sometimes I wonder if some Oral Boards may ask hypothetical questions because they don't know quite what others to ask. The not very bright applicant, or the one intellectually frozen by the stress of the interview, will likely do poorly. The average applicant should be able to give an adequate answer to hypothetical questions. The glib, plausible, confident applicant may do very well on the hypothetical question. If the Board is eager to hire him and possibly meekly offer him an immediate Sergeant's rating—disqualify him quickly! When you think an applicant is "the greatest" he often is a Psychopath. I feel the hypothetical questions should be the last area to be explored. The Academy evaluates the applicant's abilities at problem solving.

If the Board makes a reasonably comprehensive evaluation of the areas mentioned here, it will likely eliminate up to half of those formerly disqualified by the psychiatrist or the background investigator. The savings in medical examination costs, psychiatrist cost, and man hours of police personnel are evident.

It is suggested that a form checklist covering the areas listed could be made for the convenience of the Board member. In this way all pertinent areas of the applicant's social adjustment to life will be examined and evaluated. Of equal importance, each applicant will be afforded the same minimal examinations. Depending on circumstances, some Board member's impression would be desirable. This impression/conclusion should be available to the psychiatrist and background investigator to assist them in their own evaluation.

SUMMARY AND CONCLUSION

There is evidence that the aptitude/intelligence written test in police applicant selection should not be lowered from a generally accepted high level. Time and money can be saved if the applicant is adequately tested for his intellectual achievement. The Oral Board should be the level at which disqualification of most unsuitable applicants be effected. A proposal was made that the applicant complete his Personal History Form prior to examination by the Oral Board. This should facilitate information gathering and opinion formation by the Board. A checklist should be used to insure coverages of all areas of inquiry. The Board member's written impression of the applicant will help the psychiatrist and background investigator in the final decision of the applicant's worthiness to enter the Police Academy.

NOTES

1. "Chutzpah"—from Yiddish; meaning unmitigated gall. A delightful description of Chutzpah is as follows: A man kills his father and mother. When he stands before the Judge for sentence he pleads for mercy because he is an orphan.

You Can't Tell by Looking

Kenneth W. Sherrill

Armed with rifles, shotguns, tear gas, and hand guns, sheriffs' deputies and city police officers moved in toward the two-story house occupied by a family of five. Occasionally, a shot was fired from inside. The shots from inside were fired by a trained marksman. He was familiar with the tactics now being used against him. In fact, he was a veteran of the Korean War. He had suddenly and

From Kenneth W. Sherrill, "You Can't Tell by Looking," *Police* 10, no. 4 (March-April 1966): 62-65. Reprinted by permission of the author and the publisher, Charles C Thomas.

without symptomatic warning become mentally deranged. Such a confrontation can occur to you and your department at any time. Certainly you have provided some procedures for handling this situation and the thousands of variations of it. The big question is—are your men selected at an optimum level, trained in basic skills and knowledge, and disciplined to effect your procedures? In the above case, the man was taken. The hostages and the ever-present, idle, curious public were unharmed. Teamwork, intelligence, skill, and no small amount of courage are all essential parts of success. Too often the police have adhered to the philosophy exemplified by a pilot's definition of a successful landing—"It is one you walk away from." So these departments have said—"The suspect is in jail." No matter that the hostages or bystanders were injured, or worse—the end is supposed to justify the means. It has been established by numerous court cases that inadequate selection procedures and lack of training can make a jurisdiction liable in court action to anyone injured by the careless or negligent action of a police officer. While any explosive situation such as the above incident may result in injury, it is imperative that a jurisdiction provide itself with a defense. The best defense is careful selection and adequate training of officers.

In California, the first steps toward professionalization in law enforcement were taken nearly four decades ago. Capable administrators of foresight and integrity saw the impossibility of building durable organizations with inferior material. Questions were asked; meetings were arranged; experiences were exchanged. The outcome of this healthy ferment was the establishment of a consensus between the California Peace Officer's Association, The Peace Officers' Research Association of California, The League of California Cities, and many civic and service groups throughout the state. The effort to set standards of selection and training by these groups culminated in 1959 in the passage of Sections 13500 through 13523 of the Penal Code. This created the Commission on Peace Officer Standards and Training. The Commission, counseled by peace officer organizations and educators, then passed a series of regulations found in Title 11, Chapter 2, of the California Administrative Code. In addition to standards for training, these regulations set minimal requirements for inquiries that participating jurisdictions must make on candidates for employment as peace officers. Although fiscal motivation was not necessary to the more progressive administrators, the law made it possible to reimburse jurisdictions for up to 50 percent of the costs of training their new officers for those jurisdictions which, by ordinance, pledge themselves to adhere to standards. This fund is built by an assessment of $2 for every $20 fine which is imposed as a result of criminal activity.

As Field Representative of the Commission, it is my duty to inspect the screening procedures used by jurisdictions to determine compliance with the codes. Fully as important as determining compliance with minimal screening requirments is uncovering new and better methods and passing such information around the state. Our California administrators give full consideration to every innovation which comes to their attention. The moral weakling, the malingerer, the prejudiced have no place in California law enforcement. The time to screen them out is *before* they are hired.

As I go over the procedures and forms used by sheriffs and police departments, it is possible to help them shortcut the laborious and dangerous process of learning piecemeal what should be done in screeing procedures. When an administrator asks for reasons why a particular step should be performed in the background check, I am prepared with examples from all over California of what could happen if it isn't done. More and more I am able to relate instances of men with dangerous defects who were screened out because of good screening procedures. Related here are some of the examples:

John P. was an exceptionally personable, young single man. His appearance was outstanding and he expressed himself with ease and assurance. He passed all the screening tests so capably that the department—usually thoroughly professional in its approach to screening procedures—waived their own rule that *every* candidate must be interviewed in his own home. Imagine their embarrassment sometime later when they learned that the charming young man they had hired used his apartment as a studio in which he took pornographic pictures of female juveniles. It is hardly necessary to add that this department does not, under any circumstances, hire anyone prior to the home interview.

Another department that is very professional and businesslike in its selection process routinely checks the home condition of each applicant. One such applicant, James D., had passed all the tests and was considered employable. The investigator, complying with their established procedures, went to Jim's home, which was in a different county. All of the homes were neat and well-kept except Jim's. The lawn was a mass of tall weeds into which beer cans and bottles had been casually tossed. The house odors were so vile that the investigator left quickly. You can imagine the reaction of neighbors to hiring such a man as a police officer. Surely this defect would have shown up in his police work. The least we could expect would be delegations of neighbors complaining to the chief from time to time.

We sometimes have administrators tell us that they hire all or a major part of their regular force from their reserves. They sometimes believe it is not necessary to do a full-blown background investigation because they know them. It is possibly felt that undesirable characteristics will surface during his reserve duty. This is not always true. We have three variations of the following episode.

A police department liked to hire its regulars from the reserve force. Stanley B. arrived in this city, obtained a regular job as a filling station attendant, made application, and was accepted for the police reserve. About a year later, there was an opening on the regular force for which he applied and was accepted. Not long after that, while driving a police car, armed and in uniform, Stan went berserk. Fortunately, no one was injured. Only then did the department make any background inquiry. It was then discovered that Stan had spent time in two mental institutions. This department now does a careful background investigation on *every* applicant. While it is true that certain shortcuts may be made on men who are well-known, this fact should be recorded in writing and made a part of the record. This is only good administration.

We advise departments to check all hospitals and doctors listed on the Personal History Statement. Here is one that did.

Albert G. was hired in an official but auxiliary position to work with the police department of a city. His duties required him to be armed and in uniform. Fortunately, this department conducted a background investigation of Albert and found that he was classified as a homicidal maniac by two different psychiatrists. On one occasion, he had threatened to kill his mother and another time was picked up on the San Francisco bay bridge threatening to jump. When not under stress, Al was a likeable, personable individual. If he had been hired by a less professional department, it could very well have resulted in tragedy.

Departments are advised to use the acceptable military waiver form and check military records. Here is an example of the reason for this advice:

One city that does a meticulous job of background investigation routinely checks with the appropriate military records center, using the proper waiver form, when an applicant has had military service. This is done even though the man has an honorable discharge. Their standards are such that they could not accept any other type. In the instant case, Samuel R. was hired pending the outcome of the investigation. The return indicated that Sam had been a malingerer while in service. He had spent a good portion of his service in the hospital complaining of "lower back pains." After a doctor's analysis of the reports, Sam was terminated. A potential liability to the city was eliminated. Had this man been permitted to complete his probation, he might have become a useless burden to the taxpayers.

We advise departments to check the applicants' marriage license. One department hired Lester M. who turned out to be an excellent officer. He said he was married and the chief had him bring his wife in for a very casual interview. After more than a year of very capable service, Lester suddenly resigned giving vague reasons. Two weeks later, the department received a warrant alleging failure to provide for his *legal* wife and children. He had left the city and could not be located. This jurisdiction now checks marriage licenses.

Two cities had Carl T. apply from a distant state. Carl stated that he was married and his wife was with him. Both cities investigated and found that he had deserted a family in his home state and legal processes had been instigated against him by his legal wife. Embarrassment and inconvenience was avoided by the adherence of these two cities to good screening procedures.

Paul W. stated in his application for police officer that he was married and had four children. No marriage license was requested by the hiring authority. Two years after hire, there was a "family" row and it was discovered that Paul was not married. The incident was such that it caused considerable embarrassment to the city and to the department. This department now checks marriage licenses.

We suggest also that each applicant receive a thorough credit check. The following is one of many examples.

A jurisdiction hired David N. without making a credit check or adequate checks of former residence. Following the expense of training the officer, the department was deluged with demands from former places of residence for payments of judgments and overdue bills. David was immediately fired. While the chief has no knowledge of David's present location, these creditors are still writing letters, some of them indicating that the chief knows more than he is telling, even though he is completely honest in his averment.

It is important that all arrest records be obtained and that arresting and investigating officers be interviewed. (A jurisdiction that hires a man who has been convicted of a crime, the punishment for which could have been imprisonment in a federal penitentiary or state prison, is ineligible for reimbursement.)

It is required that all sheriffs and police departments located at or near the place of former residence of the applicant be checked for information. Also, those places where he worked.

Some departments are under the impression that any kind of conviction will be revealed by a CII and FBI check. Frank L. was hired by a city, and it was subsequently discovered that he had committed statutory rape. This did not show in CII or FBI fingerprint records because Frank, having learned that a warrant had been issued, got his attorney, surrendered to court and pleaded guilty. He was given a suspended sentence and a year's probation. He was never booked nor printed until he was hired as a police office. Had the department checked with the police department or the court records or the District Attorney's office in cities and counties of former residence, Frank's conviction would have been revealed. Frank has not turned out to be a police officer who would be accepted in most California jurisdictions.

Some departments hire a man from another department and fail to make an investigation, assuming that one has already been completed by the other agency.

Fortunately, the process of "unloading" a liability is on the decrease. It involves recommending a man to another department to get him to resign and take the new job. This is an avoidance of administrative responsibility and essentially unethical to the profession. One chief hired a man on the basis of one phone call to the applicant's former chief. The latter avoided mentioning the officer's defects. The man is not only worthless but had some weaknesses that made him quite unacceptable as a police officer. Even a superficial background check would have revealed this weakness. It is the responsibility of the hiring authority to do the background check or determine that a thorough background investigation has been made regardless of previous employment.

I had one "old-timer" tell me that he didn't want his officers to be pantywaists who have never been around. They wouldn't know what it's all about. Up to a point this is acceptable. The unforgivable thing is in *not knowing* what was in a man's past. Let's recruit officers of good strong character, intelligence and physique. "Hoods" have no place in the police profession and neither do "pantywaists." The only way to determine what a man is, his potential, his character, his loyalty, and his principles is by a thorough background check.

Two departments relied too strongly on a polygraph test. It was their impression that an investigation was not necessary if the men made it through the polygraph test. This instrument is of valuable assistance in recruit selection when used properly by a "Class A Examiner." We refer to people who are not recognized polygraph examiners as polygraph "operators." They are dangerous and do serious damage to the very worthwhile scientific contribution that can be made by the polygraph in the hands of an objective, intelligent, experienced examiner. Many times a polygraph "operator" will sell himself to a chief or sheriff and mislead them for months or years. His record looks good because he confidently reports the elimination of all kinds of "defective people" on the lists. The "defective" candidate could be absolutely normal. This waste of manpower is costly in the selection process.

Also, the information yielded without further checking tends to be negative. That is, it may reveal that *up to now* he had not been a thief or a wife-beater. Seldom does it reveal that he is lazy or a malingerer or overbearing or antisocial or many other things of which the subject himself seldom is aware. It does not reveal the extent of his past temptations. It does not reveal his social and moral attitudes. These can normally be determined by a thorough background investigation conducted by a competent, trained personnel investigator. There is, at this point, no substitute for it.

A very competent, progressive administrator once said:

> So long as I am forced to hire people to perform police duty, I will be confronted with latent human failings that will damage me and my profession in the eyes of the public. It is my obligation to the public to devise or accept procedures and systems to the end that these human failures are reduced to a minimum.

Sooner or later your department will be required to take action to remove a deranged and armed subject from a building, subdue a mob, or arrest a dangerous suspect in a crowd of people. This is the time that you, as an administrator, can thank your good judgment in making *sure* your men are equal to the job, or regret to the end of your days that you didn't.

NOTES

1. Publication of the Commission on Peace Officer Standards and Training, Department of Justice, State of California. Proposal for adding various regulations and specifications to Chapter 1 of Title 4 of Part 4 of the Penal Code, pursuant to the provisions of Section 13510 of the Penal Code.

2. Letter addressed to the author from the Commission of Peace Officer Standards and Training, dated 1-26-68. *See also:* President's Commission on Law Enforcement and Administration of Justice *Task Force Report: The Police,* Chapter 5.

3. "Lateral Entry and Transferability of Retirement Credits," by William H. Hewitt. Consultant's paper prepared for the President's Commission on Law Enforcement and Administration of Justice.

Lateral Transfer

Glenn A. Marin

Within the past decade there has been growing the concept, familiar to all in police-oriented fields, of *professionalization.* Within this one word lies a rather extensive and complicated range of topics. One of the small elements in the total view of the field which has received little discussion or development is the concept of the lateral transfer of police officers between police departments, i.e., the employment of an officer at any rank by a department, based upon special qualification, without following the usual selection process established by the jurisdiction for the lowest officer position.[1]

Upon the examination of this topic with the point of view of attempting to discuss it in this paper, I find two clear cut positions from which it must be approached. The first phase will be the development of the topic as an academic position with the supporting arguments. The second phase will be a discussion of the very limited attempts at implementation of the concept.

The argument for lateral transfer is based entirely within the position that advocates a professional police service.[2] The argument is that one of the mandatory steps in the achievement of a professional status is the ability of a police officer to practice his vocation wherever his services are needed. An examination of other professions discloses a general ability to move from place to place, at least within any given state, and continue to dispense professional services without fear that the move has threatened income, tenure, or professional standing. At the present time, a police officer must limit his professional growth and development to one agency or be obliged to restart his career every time he makes a change of agencies. As a result, most police agencies in this country are operated by personnel who have a relatively limited perspective and restricted awareness of various techniques, and are obliged to spend a career functioning within the local community. Officers operating under a system such as this are certainly hampered in the professional performance of duties by a lifetime of personal debts, friendships, animosities, etc., through the multitude of emotional concepts affecting a man's ability to impartially do his job. Only in select portions of the country are sufficient educational facilities available which would introduce local officers to new horizons and ideas.

Glen A. Marin is a sergeant in the Los Angeles County Sheriff's Department.
From Glenn A Marin, "Lateral Transfer," *The Police Chief* 35, no. 11 (November 1968): 26-30. Reprinted by permission of the publisher.

However, even in the best of these areas, provincialism largely prevails. To some extent, I feel, this is the reason law enforcement has had difficulty in meeting the demands of modern society. Lateral transfer could do much to eliminate this problem.

Police officers operating under this concept would increase the scope of their experience and professional maturity. A natural consequence of this would be that any given police agency would improve in terms of better ideas, new thoughts and improved public image.

While such improvement would apply for all police officers, it would seem that the greatest benefit would be to the ranking officers. The development of an administrative maturity would have its most obvious results in personnel having a voice in the operation of an agency. It would also seem that the person who has a desire to achieve would more actively attempt to improve the agency for which he works and learn better methods of operation because he would realize that it contributes to his professional knowledge and, in total, may contribute to his obtaining a higher position with another agency.

The concept of morale should not be disregarded within the context of this subject. It is common knowledge to those within the service that there are officers who for a variety of reasons desire to live in a different locality within a state or even the nation. It is presently necessary for them to give up seniority, pay, and sometimes even rank in order to accomplish the move. Since many men are not willing to do this, a frustrated, unhappy, and thereby less efficient employee is the result. It would be impossible to determine to what extent this problem has deterred men from entering the service, particularly those with substantial higher education. The police service often tends to be a dead end street in this type of situation. Another morale benefit would derive from allowing ranking personnel in smaller departments a chance to advance without waiting for the person in the next higher position to retire. This would also tend to eliminate some of the frustration of administrators in small departments who cannot move a deserving man up in rank. In other words, it would open up the field of police work at least to the state level as opposed to the previous confines of their local jurisdiction.

Lateral transfer is discussed with much favorable comment by any of the more learned organizations or reports that have considered the topic.[3] The California Peace Officers Standards and Training Commission has developed the topic possibly to a greater degree than any other organization. The California POST has taken steps to include provisions for lateral transfer into the state law controlling their commission, and, therefore, participating police agencies within the state. An officer arriving within a department by lateral transfer would be required to serve an 18-month probation. Within a requirement that all new first level supervisors complete a specified supervisory course, the commission requirements specifically state that any lateral transferee into a department at a supervisory level who has not completed the course shall be required to do so. The same rule applies to middle management positions. The commission further contends that lateral entry officers must conform to a set of minimum physical and character requirements prior to entry with the sole exception that the vision requirement is relaxed. The commission also requires an agency to so notify them of any officer hired by them via lateral transfer.

The Federal Government has developed an opinion on lateral transfer through studies of the President's Commission on Law Enforcement and Administration of Justice. In *Task Force Report: The Police,* the concept of lateral transfer is strongly supported for the reasons previously indicated in this paper. However, the position is more one of desiring advanced positions to be open to all qualified persons from both within and without the department. I take the larger view of the topic which includes officers at all levels. The *Task Force Report* feels that the police service is in need of lateral transfer immediately, but realizes the problems involved such as civil service rules, retirement systems, departmental hiring restrictions, and other administrative problems. The federal position, then, is that these restrictions should be removed and lateral entry be allowed to flourish throughout the entire police service.

An excellent analogy to the police concept of lateral transfer is found in the city manager system. This group of professionals has much in common with the police service in that it is a local government position responsible to the local citizens but governed both by the law and a set of professional ethics. Those persons associated with city management are a mobile group of men who seem to have done exceptionally well both for their profession and the cities they serve. In the opinion of the city manager of Santa Monica, Perry Scott, the ability to move about is a definite asset, without which professional progress and development would be substantially stifled. The general path of any city manager's career is one of moving from city to city in progressive steps. An individual will start out in a smaller town as an assistant city manager. As time and talent dictate, he thereupon moves to possibly a larger city as an assistant manager, or to another relatively small city as the city manager. Thus the progress of an individual's career is often marked by the moves he makes. City managers do not, as a general rule, remain in one locality for the entirety of a career. The moving about, with resultant exposure to people and ideas, produces a professional maturity that could be achieved in no other manner. As far as the mechanics of implementing such job changes goes, Mr. Scott stated that it has been his experience, and it is generally accepted within the profession, that coming into a position such as a manager spot from another location is easier and allows one to do a better job than if one was promoted from within the city administration. The lateral entry allows an approach to the position with a new and different perspective. One is not bound by personal ties, internal power struggles, or prior obligations. In other words, one is more free professionally to apply his talents. These observations most certainly bear out the theoretical arguments established for the police service lateral transfer.

The city manager concept, of course, is applicable only to the higher positions in the police service. Such views do not apply to the patrolman level, yet lateral entry would not be any less effective at this level. An officer who gains experience and training in a large city and then transfers to a smaller agency would without question be a substantial asset.

Thus far, the concept of lateral transfer has been discussed on an abstract basis with no application to any working police agency. It follows, then, that the next step is a discussion of what success has been achieved with practical application of the idea. A survey of departments within the state of California reveals a scarcity problem of concrete details. Generally, the primary manner in which any of the departments received outside personnel was for the position of police chief. It is not at all uncommon to encounter cities with open examinations for chief of police. Among them, Union City, Glendora, Whittier, El Segundo, and Downey have attempted to obtain talent from outside the confines of their agency.

The Covina Police Department has, in the past, had open exams for the position of captain. For this reason I had an interview with Chief Fred Ferguson. He stated that the reason an open examination was held was because of the size and newness of their department. There simply were not enough qualified men in the department from which to choose. Thus they were forced to look elsewhere for the candidates. The department found that the idea worked quite well and the persons filling the position performed quite adequately. As a result of this experience, Chief Ferguson feels that the idea of lateral transfer is practical with no unusual or unpredictable problems developing. Surprisingly, with only one possible exception, personnel problems did not arise as a result of promoting a man from the outside. However, since this would be an obvious problem, the reasons for the outside promotion were thoroughly explained to the personnel of the department prior to its implementation. Chief Ferguson was completely in favor of the lateral entry concept—in theory. He felt it would be a benefit for himself, other police officers, and the police service as a whole, particularly smaller agencies. However, he also realizes that he has a responsibility to his men to assist them in their professional development as they become ready. Thus, when he has adequate numbers of men within his own department capable of handling an advanced position within the department he has an obligation to them to allow one of them to ascend to it rather than recruit someone from outside the agency. The simple matter of the morale of his men would demand at least this from the Chief. However, due to his belief in the value to be derived from lateral transfers, he attempted to balance this concern for his personnel by requesting the Covina city manager to confer with other city managers within the San Gabriel Valley on setting up a mutual lateral transfer pact. This pact was to be limited to promotional exams only, allowing officers from all of the other pact departments to apply and compete. However, the idea never got off the ground; the other managers simply were not interested in such an idea.

Chief Ferguson was not in favor of unlimited or uncontrolled lateral transfers among the lowest level personnel. He believes that rules should be enforced not allowing a transfer within the same county or geographical area to inhibit those persons who are perpetually unhappy wherever they are from abusing the program. In other words, there would have to be a good reason for the move, not just an impulsive desire to change.

I contacted Police Chief Kenneth H. Huck of Union City, California, who was one of the Captains in Covina when the open door policy was made effective. He was strongly in favor of the concept with realistic reservations. He did not think that law enforcement was really ready for such a radical concept since current thinking is still too much bound by tradition. He also strongly emphasized his objection to the possibility of any state licensing and control of police officers in the manner in which teachers are licensed. He stated local autonomy must be maintained in the hiring, firing, and discipline of all employees without the intervention of the state.

In discussing the present state of lateral transfer, it is impossible to ignore the position the POST certificate plays. While the holding of a POST certificate is still completely voluntary on the part of individual police officers, it is the only common standard of measuring a police officer's education and experience in this state today. As such, it is being accepted by some agencies as a *prima facie* level of achievement when presented by applicants. The County of Lake and the cities of Sierra Madre and Palm Springs will employ an applicant laterally without a competitive examination if he holds a basic POST certificate. The city of Glendora, which just recently held an open examination for Chief of Police, listed as one requirement among others, that an applicant must hold an advanced POST certificate. The Peace Officers Standards and Training Commission is desirous that the certificate become a mark of professional competence that would allow the holder to practice anywhere in the state.

The cities of Alameda and Torrance recently conducted an exchange of personnel that is not what would be considered a lateral transfer, but would seem to bear mentioning within the framework of this topic. The situation was that the two cities exchanged two officers each, complete with equipment. Then, for a period of time, they worked in each other's city, observing how the other department carried out the daily chores of policing a medium-sized city. This certainly is a progressive move, and may be one manner of bringing about enlightening ideas and exposing policemen to new horizons.

OBSTACLES TO LATERAL TRANSFER

As previously stated, the *Task Force Report* felt that the major obstacles to the implementation of lateral transfer are such technical problems as civil service rules, retirement credits, and general employment restrictions. I completely disagree that these are major obstacles. These are factors to be considered and solved. However, it is my opinion that these are relatively minor factors that need only some study and resultant administrative decisions to eliminate. I feel the real problem is a much more intangible and harder to define problem that has to do with the feelings and attitudes of power elements within this society toward the purpose and use to which police power should be used.

In order to lay the groundwork for understanding what I feel to be the obstacle to lateral transfer, I would ask the reader to recall the prior situation described by Chief Ferguson of Covina when the city manager of that city attempted and failed to gain support from other managers for a limited application of the lateral transfer concept. I would then elaborate upon this one situation with an interview I had with City Manager Perry Scott of Santa Monica. Mr. Scott felt that the concept in question was not feasible or even particularly applicable to police agencies. My impression from his statements was that lateral transfer as the city manager system uses the concept is not applicable to police agencies as a group. The reason for this would be the nature of the work performed, its relationship to the people of the community, and its relationship within the structure of local government. In regard to the command level positions within a police agency, I quite frankly do not see how it differed in any significant manner from the city manager lateral transfer situation. I pointed this out to Mr. Scott, but his response was that he felt the police service could not be compared to the city manager service because the police service was a horse of a different color. This sets the scene for the true roadblock to the implementation of lateral transfer to the police service. Professionalization, and all of the progressive ideals that are included in that word, are basically only in the minds of police administrators, *and not in the minds of other persons of power in our form of government.* In fact, I am sure that many police leaders have some difficulty in grasping such a concept. The attitude of the general power structure does not seem to hold the police service in very high esteem nor do they grant it, at least, mentally, a professional status. Visions of a professional law enforcement agency do not readily come to the minds of local mayors, city councils, city managers, county supervisors, and the like because they desire that the police be kept within their power to control. In a word, subservience of the police service to local power is desired. If a local agency were to be operated by men dedicated to professional principles and ethics, and who, in addition, were attempting to establish a professional reputation, there would be some substantial problems with the local power groups in having a voice in when, where, and how the law is to be enforced in their community. A department consisting of professional administrators would be substantially more difficult to control, and while the system is not nearly as overt as the old political patronage system, to a greater or lesser extent, this attitude still prevails. This is a basically traditional attitude of the power structure toward police agencies which has considerable traditional support. Thus it seems that the greatest problem in gaining acceptance of the lateral transfer concept is not in solving the technical problems of employment practices, but in overcoming these traditional practices and attitudes.

With the analysis of the problem as I see it, there seems to be only one means of bringing about the implementation that is so necessary for the advancement of the police service. In California, the necessary organization exists and the first steps have already been taken in the right direction. The California Peace Officers Standards and Training Commission is the organization that has the authority to override local resistance and to require police agencies to comply with progressive standards. This agency has both the political power of the state behind it and the equally powerful ability to control funds to local police departments. Many states have their own equivalent of this professional agency. As the state spokesman for professional law enforcement, these organizations must necessarily accept the burden of battling local indifference or opposition to improvement of the police service. Within this context, I would also like to see the International Association of Chiefs of Police take an active and aggressive role in this regard.

The above discussion is not intended to discount those progressive agencies which already have or will on their own initiative inaugurate lateral transfer programs. The problem is that they are too few and too far between—and the need for professional action is too great for the police service to wait decades for the idea to gain acceptance within the multitude of more mundane agencies and self-serving local power groups.

In summary, my view of the concept of lateral transfer is that in the course of professional development of the American police service, it must come to pass. There is substantial academic and professional support for the idea at levels removed from local municipalities. However, at the working level, the idea has met with very little success except in the most progressive of agencies. Law enforcement is still too bound by traditionalism to accept the idea very readily. Within the framework of traditionalism, one also finds local politics opposed to the loss of control that would come with any professional administration of the police agency. Thus it seems that a concerted effort would be required by agencies removed from the local level and that local agencies would have to be pushed into accepting the concept.

In substance, then, the basic responsibility for the statewide implementation of the lateral transfer concept lies in the hands of the professional state agency set up for the purpose of furthering professional law enforcement within the state. If this can be accomplished, a nationwide lateral transfer policy for the police service would be but a complicated administrative decision away.

Operation: Police Manpower

James A. F. Kelly and Robert C. Barnum

In response to the president's request the Department of Defense established its TRANSITION Program in January, 1968. This program offers the more than 800,000 enlisted men who depart the military service each year "a path to more productive civilian careers." Under the TRANSITION program, personnel with from one to six months of service time remaining, who have not had an opportunity to develop a saleable civilian skill, are offered an opportunity to develop or upgrade the skills they will require when they return to civilian life. The program provides counseling, training and job placement assistance to those who volunteer for this service. These services are currently provided at more than 250 military installations throughout the United States and overseas. To date, these installations have provided consulting services to approximately 200,000 servicemen and more than 60,000 have received training under the program.

LAW ENFORCEMENT TRAINING

Since the inception of TRANSITION several military installations with the cooperation of local police departments have implemented training programs in the criminal justice field. To date, this has allowed more than 1200 individuals to receive introductory training in this vital area of public service. Pilot programs were conducted at Fort Irwin and Camp Pendleton, California, in cooperation with the Los Angeles Police Department. The success of these initial efforts has led ten other installations to adopt similar programs. OPERATION: POLICE MANPOWER is an extension on a national scale of these previous individual efforts.

Recognizing that the department serviceman, with his relative maturity and disciplined background, represent a prime manpower source for the law enforcement profession, the military services have been cooperating for some

---

James A. F. Kelly is a consultant, IACP Professional Standards Division, IACP Headquarters, Washington. Robert C. Barnum is a major, U.S. Army Military Police Corps, Department of Defense Transition Program, Government Relations Section.

From James A. F. Kelly and Robert C. Barnum, "Operation Police Manpower," *The Police Chief* 36, no. 7 (July 1969): 45-52. Reprinted by permission of the publisher.

time in the Police Recruiting Program. Under this program the individual is discharged up to 90 days early if he has been accepted for police service. This recruiting program conducted by major cities on military installations has proven highly successful in meeting some of the critical manpower shortages in the police field.

The training offered prior to separation under OPERATION: POLICE MANPOWER and similar programs is an additional effort designed to motivate and train the individual prior to his release from service. As such, the program not only helps some of the larger cities, but provides real thrust toward assisting the small-to-medium departments with limited recruitment and training capabilities.

RECRUITMENT AND SCREENING

Under this program the Department of Defense personnel will recruit, screen, test and place prerelease servicemen into the training program. The Transition Program is not limited to law enforcement. A vast number of other careers are available through these offices. Because of this, the Transition offices are already manned, geared and experienced in carrying out these responsibilities.

Announcements concerning career opportunities are widely and predominately placed throughout the military installations and these evince considerable interest. The bulletins direct those who are interested to the Transition office.

The screening and placement phases of this program are very significant. Some applicants are unable to meet the basic requirements set by state minimum standards and therefore must be eliminated. Others who lack educational qualifications are guided into programs to fit their specific needs, such as completion of high school under the GED program. Upon completion of that work, the placement services of the program will still be available. **(See** Chart 1.)

The Transition officer has access to individual military personnel and medical files which are useful in screening the applicant's basic qualifications. In each of the five centers where a Police Manpower program is offered there is a copy of IACP's *Model Police Standards Council Program.* A summary of selection requirements for the course follows:

1. U.S. citizenship.
2. Background information:
    a. Individuals must be free of convictions in felony charges, serious military offenses and cases involving moral turpitude.
    b. Individuals with a chronic record of misdemeanors or minor offenses are also disqualified.
    c. It is explained to *each* individual that acceptance by any police organization will require a further investigation.
3. Vision: (determined by medical records):
    a. At least 20/40 correctable to 20/20 in better eye and 20/25 in the weaker eye.
    b. Normal color vision.

4. Hearing: normal (determined by medical records).
5. Height: 5'7" minimum to 6'4" maximum.
6. Weight proportionate to height.
7. Age: minimum 21 years, maximum 29 years upon completion of course.
8. High school diploma or the equivalent.
9. General intelligence quotient of 100 or higher.
10. Good health, emotional stability and passing score in the annual combat physical proficiency test.

CHART 1

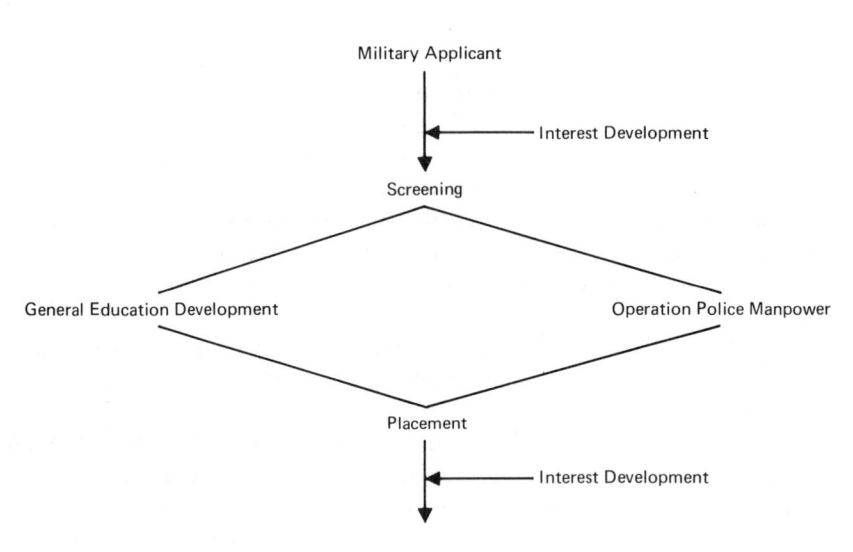

```
                        Military Applicant
                              |
                              |◄─────── Interest Development
                              ▼
                           Screening
                          /         \
                         /           \
General Education Development     Operation Police Manpower
                         \           /
                          \         /
                           Placement
                              |
                              |◄─────── Interest Development
                              ▼
                   Local Law Enforcement Career
```

POLICE MANPOWER TRAINING PROGRAMS

Under OPERATION: POLICE MANPOWER, the International Association of Chiefs of Police will be the national contractor for the preparation of approximately 400 servicemen entering the field of local law enforcement. All trainees are active members of the military with six months of service or less to complete. They continue to be subject to the Uniform Code of Military Justice and are housed, clothed and fed by their respective armed forces unit.

IACP negotiated with local academic institutions to establish training and education programs to meet the requirements of surrounding boards and councils of police training and state minimum standards. Minimum standards for police training vary within the United States. The Police Manpower program consists of 240 hours of police training which currently meets the highest mandatory state standards required in the United States. It also complies with IACP's Model Minimum Standards Program. (*See* Chart 2.) As a result, the individual with minimum local indoctrination will be job-ready for immediate entry into the law enforcement field. Of course, it will be necessary for him to be indoctrinated in local law, ordinances and procedures. This offers considerable saving for the employing departments by greatly decreasing training costs and salaries paid to individuals during the training phase.

CHART 2 SUMMARY
BASIC RECRUIT SCHOOL CURRICULUM
RECOMMENDED BY THE IACP

	Contact Hours
Introduction to Law Enforcement	3
Criminal Law	16
Criminal Evidence	8
Administration of Criminal Law	2
Criminal Investigation	54
Patrol Procedures	38
Traffic Control	20
Juvenile Procedures	6
Defensive Tactics	14
Firearms	26
First Aid	10
Examinations	3
Sub-Total	200

Part of the 240 contact hours may be awarded college credit. The additional motivation of college credit for a portion of the course is designed to encourage continued professional growth upon entry into the field. An effort was made to utilize institutions with recognized qualifications in law enforcement education and training.

In order to reach and maintain a high level of quality, programs are held on college campuses whenever possible. This reinforces an academic approach to the program and permits the use of the college faculties and facilities. This point is considered to be a major factor in controlling the quality variance. In addition, all the instructors must meet qualifications as established by the nearest state standards commissions. Some subjects, of course, require the use of instructors who are veterans of the police service. The added advantage of having local coordination is to keep the program within the framework of an organized police training structure. The following institutions were contracted because they have the qualities necessary and are near appropriate military installations:

Mira Costa College and Camp Pendleton, California
Pensacola Junior College and Pensacola Naval Air Station, Florida
Central Texas College and Fort Hood, Texas
El Paso Community College, Colorado Springs, Colorado
Trenton Technical Institute and Fort Dix, New Jersey

Outstanding assistance in the development of viable curricula and the procurement of qualified instructor personnel has been received from state and local authorities where the programs were planned. Police training commissions have been invited to visit and assess these programs and where possible certify successful graduates. The Police Training Commission of the State of New Jersey and the Municipal Police Training Council of New York State cooperated in the development of a curriculum that was mutually agreeable for certification by both states for the Fort Dix project. This is a noteworthy step forward in the police training field.

The program takes cognizance of the differences in education and training. The purpose of education is to develop judgment ability and this is accomplished through classroom discussion, outside study and research. Training is intended to impart skills through classroom explanation, demonstration through the use of audio visual aids and actual practice of the skill. The use of firearms and driving an automobile are good examples. This program is intended to wed the two methods of learning and thus award college credit for the academic work. A course awarding 3 hours of college credit would require approximately 50 contact hours in a 12 week period. An example is the course, *Introduction to Law Enforcement and Criminal Justice,* being offered by Central Texas College. (*See* Chart 3.)

CHART 3 CENTRAL TEXAS COLLEGE
ADMINISTRATION OF CRIMINAL JUSTICE
3 CREDIT HOURS

Course	*Contact Hours*
History and Philosophy of Law Enforcement	3
An Overview of the Criminal Justice System	3
A Career in Law Enforcement	1
Professionalization of the Police Service	1
Law Enforcement Ethics	1
Government Organization at the Local, State and Federal Levels	4
Organization & Jurisdictions of Law Enforcement Agencies: Federal, State and Local Levels	3
Crime and Delinquency Causation: Theories	6
Court Systems	5
Probation and Parole	4
Correctional Institutions' Programs for Rehabilitation	4
Community Sociology	3
Contemporary Urban Problems	4
Crime Prevention and Education	4
Supporting Public Resources	2
Exams and Critique	2
Total Contact Hours	50

There is no universally recognized curriculum for a police recruit school. There are some common core subjects but the balance and emphasis vary in different localities. IACP has offered a model basic program that has received some acceptance but the differing number of training hours in each community disrupts the design.

CHART 4 BASIC RECRUIT SCHOOL CURRICULUM
RECOMMENDED BY THE IACP

Introduction to Law Enforcement		3
Criminal Law		16
Law	12	
Law of Arrest	4	
Criminal Evidence		8
Evidence	4	
Search and Seizure	4	
Administration of Criminal Law		2
Criminal Investigation		54
Report Writing	10	
Assaults	2	
Auto Theft	2	
Burglary	2	
Collection of Evidence	6	
Injury & Death Investigations	6	
Interviews and Interrogations	6	
Robbery	2	
Sex Crimes	2	
Larceny and Stolen Property	4	
Scientific Aids	2	
Fingerprint Evidence	2	
Vice Investigations	6	
Miscellaneous Investigations	2	
Patrol Procedures		38
Courtroom Demeanor	2	
Disorderly Conduct Cases	2	
Domestic Complaints	2	
Drunk and Drunk Driving Cases	2	
Field Notetaking and Crime Scene Recording	6	
Mental Illness	2	
Patrol Techniques	8	
Prowler and Disturbance Calls	2	
Public Relations	6	
Human Relations	2	
Crime Scene Procedure	4	
Traffic Control		20
Traffic Direction Techniques	2	
Citations	2	
Traffic Law Enforcement	2	
Accident Reporting	4	
Accident Investigation	10	
Juvenile Procedures		6
Defensive Tactics		14
Arrest Techniques	6	
Defensive Tactics	8	
Firearms		26
First Aid		10
Examinations		3

CHART 5 PENSACOLA JUNIOR COLLEGE
HUMAN RELATIONS
3 CREDIT HOURS

	Contact Hours
Police Philosophy	2
Political, Economic and Social Factors in the Community	3
Ethnic Groups and Subcultures	3
Community Organization and Government	2
History of Civil Rights and Review of Civil Rights Legislation	2
Civil Rights and Anti-Civil Rights Activists	2
Contemporary Social Problems	3
History and Analysis of Civil Disorders	2
Psychology of Human Development	2
The Mechanisms of Prejudice	3
Interpersonal Relations	2
Basic Principles of Conflict	2
Communications	2
Implications for Police Work: Its Social Role and Status	2
Elements of Social Disorganization	2
Groups: Their Structures and Processes	2
The Psychology of Crowds and Mobs	2
Adolescence and Youth	2
The Impact of Performance of the Individual Officer on the Police Image	2
Public Opinion, the Press and the Police	2
Practical Police Programs for the Prevention of Crime and Disorder	2
The Individual Officer's Part in Police Community Relations	2
Examination and Critique	2
Total Contact Hours	50

Local institutions of higher learning frequently work at cross purposes to the training effort. Some colleges tend to offer only those credit courses now appearing in their catalogue and show little initiative in offering special programs or schedules.

Therefore under OPERATION: POLICE MANPOWER it became necessary to match the capability of the local institutions, to an acceptable and transferable academic subject curriculum while at the same time meeting the requirements of the neighboring state minimum standards. This was no menial task. The IACP's basic recruit school curriculum recommended in the Model Police Standards Council Program was the basic instrument used to lace together the subjects so as to come to some universal acceptance. (*See* Chart 4.) The 40 additional contact hours in the Police Manpower program permitted enough flexibility to meet these varying needs. For example, the Florida Police Standards Council requires a 200-hour curriculum, several hours of which concern Human and Public Relations. Pensacola Junior College offers an academic course entitled *Human Relations* for 3 hours of college credit requiring 50 contact hours. (*See* Chart 5—*Human Relations course outline designed by the IACP Research and Development Division.*) This course was incorporated into the police program for the Naval Air Station in Pensacola.

A requirement for periodic testing is included in each curriculum. If the student falls below the acceptable grade point of the institution, he will be referred for guidance. The Transition guidance service again comes into effect at this time. This is important, not only in evaluating the program, but also in insuring that the participant has maximum placement potential. Each school is required to submit a syllabus for each subject and a copy of each examination. The students will be given a final grade and rank in their class. This is intended to motivate the student and assist in maintaining a high quality program. Hopefully, a graduate of OPERATION: POLICE MANPOWER will recognize his future potential based on the training offered him. He can then continue toward a higher level of education under the G.I. Bill and/or LEAA Academic Assistance while working as a local police officer.

This vast base of young personnel could have a marked affect upon local law enforcement. Local police administrators will be interested in taking advantage of OPERATION: POLICE MANPOWER. In the future, with success, this program could handle a greater share of the 800,000 men released from the military service each year. Cooperation, understanding, and support can assist professional law enforcement through the United States. Personnel officers, civil service commissions and state standards councils working together can develop more uniform selection procedure and standards. To benefit from this broadened recruiting base, local municipalities may wish to consider the advisability of retaining outmoded residence requirements and other restrictive entrance procedures. This can be accomplished without reducing standards.

Cooperation is needed to place successful graduates of the proposed program. The training and education phase of the program will be regionalized at various military installations in keeping with the assignment of the individual. However, the placement of recruits will be made on a national basis according to personal desires of the individual.

THE FUTURE POTENTIAL

There is a need to press forward to perfect this initial program effort. Previous pilot programs and this experimental national effort financed by federal funds prove the potential value and practicability of such a program. The current training effort is intended to graduate 400 recruits within a 12-month period at a cost of $100,000. This figure is exclusive of the military's cost for testing and maintaining the man in the service. The return from this program is quite small in relation to the manpower needs of police departments in the United States. However, future efforts might attain even greater results. Law enforcement recruiting might be conducted throughout all of the military service units, both in the United States and abroad. Testing and counseling could be conducted at an earlier date within the six-month pre-release period. This effort would indicate the acceptability of the applicant for a career in law enforcement as well as which phase of criminal justice the applicant desires and for which he is best suited. An effort could be made to specify the department or region where the applicant will work.

The current system admittedly leaves a great void in the sea of available manpower. The training program is open only to personnel who are stationed at the training site or other military installations in close proximity. This is an accidental relationship which limits the number of potential applicants. To overcome this problem there is a clear need to increase the efficiency of this program without unnecessarily burdening the military services. The Transition Program is one of many tasks which confronts the local military commander. The scheduling and utilization of the manpower involved is sometimes difficult in light of other priorities. Therefore, a serviceman assigned to Transition training normally works with his unit for half a day and attends school the other half. In working positions a relief must be found for him. In training situations, the man may have to be released from field exercises or other training tasks. If the student worked a full day with his unit and went to school at night, he could doubtfully do justice to the program. Therefore, adjustments and a commitment must be made both by the individual and his military organization.

An optional solution might be to test an applicant at his duty post and then transfer the acceptable enrollees to one of five police manpower training centers regionally located throughout the United States. This could be done at a time coincident with the beginning of the course best allied with his estimated time of discharge. He would be attached to a center during the training period of approximately three months. Upon successful completion of the program, he would be discharged from the service to begin his law enforcement career. The centers would be located at a military installation in close proximity to civilian education and training resources. The enrollee's responsibility would be that of a student plus the duties necessary to support his environment. He would remain under the jurisdiction of the Code of Military Justice and under the command of the officer in charge of the center. Instructor and material resources could be better utilized, course quality maintained and placement efforts better directed.

Regardless of future improvements, OPERATION: POLICE MANPOWER and similar programs of this nature are positive efforts to assist state and local authorities in overcoming personnel shortages and improving police professional standards. The spirit with which the military services and state and local authorities involved have undertaken this task is a commendable step in the right direction. With increased support and cooperation from professional law enforcement officials throughout the United States even greater accomplishments will be attained.

Keeping Policemen on the Job: Some Recommendations Arising from a Study of Men and Morale

Richard H. Blum and William J. Osterloh

For many years we have been studying problems of selection, work adjustment, and job termination among policemen. As preparation for participating in a peace officers' symposium on the subject, two questionnaires were designed by the authors, a psychologist-criminologist and a police lieutenant who was to serve as the institute's moderator. One was directed to men who had entered the police vocation within a preceding year, and the other to persons who had left the police field during a three-year period. Distribution was made through a sample of urban California police and sheriffs' offices. The object of our inquiry has been to learn something more about the special characteristics of men who become policemen, to learn about their job satisfactions and dissatisfactions, and to identify some of the major problems which modern urban peace officers experience. The purpose of this article is to share some of our findings and our conclusions with you, the police reader, who we are sure share our interest and concerns.

Let us look first at the reasons young men give for joining a metropolitan police force. Foremost among career motivations is a strong sense of morality: these young men want to protect society, reduce danger and corruption, and to act as moral agents by punishing wrongdoers. A second set of motives are simply economic: they want to earn good salaries in a job setting which provides secure income and later pension-retirement opportunities. The third set of motives are personal but consistent: young men joining the force look forward to action, excitement, and adventure. They appear to be career-dedicated young men almost to a man; only a few would consider any career shifts at this stage (on the force less than six months) in their lives. Most intend to remain policemen until they retire.

Assuming now that other men joining other California police departments felt the same when they were new recruits, we must ask what goes wrong to cause so

From Richard H. Blum and William J. Osterloh, "Keeping Policemen on the Job: Some Recommendations Arising from a Study of Men and Morale," *Police* 10, no. 5 (May-June 1966): 28-32. Reprinted by permission of the authors and the publisher, Charles C Thomas.

many of them to leave police work voluntarily in spite of their earlier career plans? For at least a partial answer to this question we turn to the comments of the men who have quit. First, however, let us attend, not to what these men disliked, but to what they liked about police work even though they were leaving it.

First of all, they like their fellow officers. We presume that a fundamental satisfaction in police work is that spirit or sense of brotherhood which is so clearly evident to any observer in a good police department; the group itself, the police fraternity, is a source of work and personal pleasure. Secondly, the men do enjoy their role in society; they want to be of service, to protect the community, and to serve those moral ends which are part of their role in society, and part of their character and career motivation. They also enjoy the work; it does hold for many of them the sense of action and excitement, the sense of worth too, which brought them into the career. Finally they are, nearly all of them, satisfied with the salary and security which their jobs have offered.

The reader will see a paradox here. Men join the force for reasons moral, economic, and personal and, at the time they leave police work, they report these same reasons as their basic satisfactions in police work. How can it be that men—or at least some men—(those in our sample of 72) who have chosen a career which in fact satisfies their major expectations nevertheless quit that career?

We asked our terminating men what had gone wrong, "What was the biggest difference between what you expected police work to be like and what you found it to be like?" The most frequent answer? "Public disrespect." Here then is something that was implicit in career expectations—that the public would appreciate what a peace officer is and does—which is not fulfilled. Is, however, this public disrespect the major reason given for quitting police work? No, it is not. The reasons our sample of terminating policemen gave were more immediate and personal: Poor opportunity for promotion, night work, politics and unfairness in advancement—these were the immediate factors that rankled most. These and one other crucial sentiment summarized by the phrase, "recent court decisions." It would appear that however surprising and disappointing "public disrespect" is, it may be a very particular segment of the public which "bugs" the officer most, that segment being the high court judges whose recent rulings many police officers view as votes of "no confidence" in the police as well as a set of obstacles imposed upon the police in their work to apprehend criminals. While immediate factors of promotion, politics, hours, and also lack of supervisorial "backing" loom large in stated reasons for quitting, the importance to morale of the police view of recent court decisions affecting search and seizure, arrest and interrogation, is emphasized by the reply our terminating sample gave to yet another question. We asked, "As you stayed in police work, what were the biggest changes over time which affected your own job satisfaction?" The most frequent answer? "Court decisions" (recent and adverse to the policeman's view of things). Again, in another section of the questionnaire offering a long list of possible reasons for quitting, "recent court decisions" is checked more often than any other statement. Consistent with earlier spontaneous statements, we find politics in advancement and limitations in promotion ranking second as reasons for quitting. Here on the checklist we find "poor supervision" and "public disrespect" ranking about third as reasons for quitting.

Given the sentiments expressed about sources of dissatisfaction, it will be well to attend to dissatisfactions which were not mentioned. Again the findings are consistent. Although given an opportunity both in reply to "open ended" questions and a check list, very few of the terminating men said they had quit because of any dissatisfaction with salary or security, because of any dislike for danger, conflict, or being in a uniformed and command or authoritarian setting, or because of any souring of their moral convictions which necessarily require them to be exposed to corruption, crime, and the seamy side of things, and to act the role of a moral authority *vis à vis* the criminal.

These statements, which express the sentiments of recruits about why they join a police force and which express the joys and sorrows of terminating men saying why they quit and why they'd like to stay on in police work, lead us to two further sets of observations. One set of observations links our findings here to the research of others who have described the personal characteristics of police officers. While those descriptions are not entirely consistent with one another, the findings in general[1] suggest that the average officer enjoys adventure and conflict, can be comfortable with routine tasks, accepts orders easily, is conventional in a moral and social sense, and enjoys directing others. Superior policemen are consistently intelligent, ambitious, personally effective, and have superior emotional adjustments. The statements that our recruits and terminating men make about their goals and satisfactions in a police career are consistent with these findings by others. Combining them all, one gets a picture of men who are strongly moral in conventional ways and who are willing to risk their own safety and ease to safeguard traditional morality in their communities. In doing so, they are directly involved in conflict, do experience danger and adventure, and do impose their moral views on others; each of these experiences and actions being a source of personal and moral satisfaction as well as part of the job which the community demands of the police. In terms of economics, the officer reasonably seeks a good salary, security, and retirement protection in his job, and in return for that is quite willing to accept life-long work routines and to adjust to a uniformed hierarchical and authoritarian structure. *However,* personally and economically, the superior officer also demands an opportunity to achieve, to be promoted, to receive adequate and honest supervision, and to rise in the service free from the taint of unfairness which occurs when "city hall" or "department politics," or an archaic and invalid promotional system interferes with equitable and adequate advancement opportunities. Those interferences the officer will not tolerate, and however much he enjoys his colleagues and career, the superior officer will quit if he is denied the chance for achievement and the honest working conditions which he deserves. Some may also quit if their hours and shifts are consistently undersirable. This issue seems unrelated to fairness or opportunity, although it may be necessarily a matter of departmental policies and supervisorial goodness as well as being part of the nature of police work.

Let us put our findings so far into a set of conclusions and recommendations for police administrators and supervisors. It is clear that most of the men (in our samples at least) who have gone into police work enjoy their colleagues and the work and would stay in police careers if they had the choice. That means that the odds in personnel management are on the side of the administrator. It seems clear that good men who quit police work could have been kept in police work, if politics and influence were kept out of advancement, if promotion was dependent on valid tests of ability and suitability, if department tables of organization allowed for men at higher echelons, or if there were some other means of awarding men with a sense of achievement and satisfaction of ambition even if the higher ranks cannot be expanded. Good men can also be kept in police work if supervisors themselves get better training in how to do their jobs, if they back their men up when right, and if they are sensitive to the needs of their men. It is on this latter count that we see the only hope for keeping the men who quit because of dislike of night shift. We presume that to the extent that undesirable duty hours are fairly rotated among men, then envious comparisons and complaints of unfairness will be reduced. We also presume that night shifts can be made attractive, and perhaps staffed by more volunteers, if extra pay can be awarded those volunteering. Beyond that the matter is, as it always has been, a matter of the supervisor showing his sympathy and proving his fairness should reasonable complaints be aired.

Earlier we tried to link the personal characteristics of police officers to working conditions to show how satisfactions are obtained and to warn supervisors about conditions which are so dissatisfying they will lead to the loss of personnel. Now we turn to a much more difficult and pervasive issue, the problem of low police morale which arises from "public disrespect" and "recent court decisions."

We shall begin by emphasizing our findings that the terminating policemen in our sample report their greatest surprise and disappointment between what is expected from police work and what is found, and between what police work is said once to have been as opposed to its present form, in regard to the actions of judges and public toward the police. Officers feel betrayed or criticized, frustrated and disrespected, interfered with and criticized by people whose opinions matter to them. Although officers' dismay is important, indeed crucial since we believe the terminating officer speaks for large numbers of his still working fellows, it is important to bear in mind that public disrespect and court decisions are not—to our way of thinking—sufficient reasons for quitting police work; to quit, a man must have personal reasons: dissatisfaction over advance, politics, hours, or supervision. Nevertheless, the felt position of the policeman as an embattled minority member unappreciated by the public or distrusted or flayed by judges looms large as a morale problem and as a set of sentiments which either make it easier to quit or automatically insure sympathy from colleagues when offered as a reason for resigning from the force.

Examining the problem of police dismay over public disrespect and recent court decisions, both of which we take to be "real" social phenomena not just distorted police perceptions of the world, we would propose two separate considerations, one of which is related to the personal characteristics of the average policeman as earlier described, and one related to a larger social circumstance. The first consideration is moral. The average policeman is a moral man. He is also a man of action and one who has fewer qualms than the ordinary citizen about imposing his morality on those around him, especially those who are violators of the socially established moral order. Thus he acts as a moral authority with the conviction that what he does is right, if not righteous, and represents the will of the community, i.e., the shared moral sentiments of the larger society he represents.

The problem that this moral man faces is that the community is not of one mind about what morality is. Many important and generally law-abiding segments of the community disagree with the conventional morality of the police officer. We see this in the "civil disobedience" demonstrations by equally moral—but differing—public segments such as students, professors, ministers, etc. We also see it in drug use by respectable citizens[2] in the move to legalize marijuana, in recent suggested steps to treat homosexuals as ordinary law-abiding citizens, and in similar "liberal" or "humane" social action movements. When the peace officer acts out of his own convictions—as well as the law—to represent and maintain traditional morality, he now finds himself in conflict with decent citizens with a different set of values. Those citizens do not take kindly to his "old fashioned" morality, and the policeman, to his surprise, finds respectable people accusing him of "brutality," forcing him to arrest them, and otherwise giving him a very hard time indeed. We think this is the essence of one aspect of "public disrespect" which is so unsettling to the officer. It challenges his equanimity about the absolute rightness of his own morality, it makes him insecure about community backing, it subjects him to insult and ridicule, and since the people who disrespect him are not otherwise criminal or immoral, the peace officer cannot easily resort to his usual view of the moral deviant as a "criminal." Indeed the reverse may be true; the forces of the new or merely reaffirmed morality in the community teach the officer that his conventional views are the "criminal" ones; as has happened in recent years with the introduction in the South of civil rights to previously repressed Negro populations, where the Southern peace officer finds the old order turned topsy-turvy.

The action morality of the policeman has also led him into conflict with the courts. Since the policeman acts out of conviction as well as duty, he feels personally that he is an agent of society's morality and that he acts properly when he is an instrument seeking the punishment of wrongdoers. The community, however, is of several minds as to whether "punishment" is the treatment of choice for wrongdoers, just as the community is of several minds about who in fact the "wrongdoers" are. Furthermore, the community, represented by the statutes enacted and the judges who interpret and apply them, is not of one mind about the nature of the menace posed by wrongdoers. Some are convinced that the community is best protected by apprehending wrongdoers at all costs. Others are equally convinced that the community is best protected by safeguarding individuals from any risk that their rights may be violated by any form of arbitrary authority. The first group, among whom many policemen and prosecutors are found, call for strenuous action to punish individual wrongdoers. The second group, among whom many civil-liberties people are to be found, call for strong controls on the exercise—in administering criminal justice—of governmental power.

Because they do act as legitimate moral authorities, police officers cannot help but be judges. Each decision to arrest or not to arrest is a juridical one, regardless of what the statutes may say about police powers being separated from judicial powers. Similarly, in the act of arrest and interrogation the policeman is already "punishing" the suspect by depriving him of liberty. It is possible that on occasion an arresting officer has handed out other "punishment" to a suspect whose crime or person is emotionally distasteful to the officer. While certainly infrequent, it is probable that there have been cases where arresting officers have harassed or abused those moral wrongdoers who are potentially offensive to the conventional morality of society, or those who stand for what is to law enforcement too extraordinary a change in society's conventional order. We suggest that it is this socially standardized morality of the policeman, acting in good faith as a representative social agent, which expresses itself in moral and effective conduct *vis à vis* the criminal, but nevertheless conduct which may not be in strict conformity with law or recognized niceties and this has contributed to the reaction of the courts in "putting down" the police and their "bad cases." The more broad the body of law which the judge must interpret, and the more complex the social and legal community in which judge and jury reside, the more likely they are to differ from the clear-and-simple, traditional moral position of at least some police officers.

We do not propose that the current conflicts and antagonisms between the police and other sectors of the public are simply a matter of the individual predispositions of policeman versus a differing morality or different concept of menace among other citizens and higher court judges. Obviously, the problems are very complex and, as yet, hardly understood. Other sources of trouble certainly exist, for example, as Director Edward Comber has pointed out, the enactment of new law lags far behind social change and evolving public sentiments, but the police must enforce the old law, and consequently are perennially found in untenable public but legally correct positions. Certainly much careful thinking and research will be necessary before we fully understand the present dilemma and distress of the police.

In the meantime it would seem unwise—for the sake of police morale and the prevention of further loss of effective police personnel—for police administrators to sit back and let police personnel suffer the loss of esteem and security, which is associated with their perception of public and judicial criticism, without attempting some interim assistance. It appears to us that three immediate steps can be taken, each a matter of education. First, and with reference to court decisions affecting search and seizure, arrest and interrogation, etc., each department can examine its record of arrests and prosecutions to see if there is not, in fact, a higher record of convictions based on "better cases" in the last few years (since *Cahan* for example) than before. Our expectation is based on the experience of departments known to us. If that is the case, officers in the department need to be told about it, for it will restore their confidence not only in the effectiveness of their own moral role as effective punishers of crime, but can lead them to reevaluate at least some of the court decisions, so that these are not seen to be as hostile and impeding to police work as some officers have been convinced they are.

A second step would be to ask local newspapers or public opinion survey groups to conduct surveys of public opinion to see just how many citizens are in fact disrespectful of the police. We predict that very few decent citizens are disrespectful, but that many may be critical. Those criticisms need not be reasonable or rational ones, but some will be. When criticisms are valid, the department can reduce public antagonism by putting its own house in order. We predict officers will be at least somewhat reassured to find the general sentiment of the public to be one in which the need for law enforcement is very strongly stated and deep respect for peace officers, however clouded by emotional ambivalence, is quite clearly present. That knowledge, presented as part of regular training programs or in daily bulletins, should help reduce—although it cannot eliminate—some of the feeling that "the rug has been pulled out from under the police."

A third step requires no searching for outside facts to be compared against departmental worries or fears. It does require that there be open but firmly guided discussions, as for example, in in-service training, which allow officers to vent their dismay over changing public and judicial standards, but which provide reasoned and understanding instruction to the rank-and-file, aimed to help the officer understand that social changes are inevitable in a great modern society. Basic morality if, of course, also changing.[3] Disagreements between police and public groups, or between police and higher courts, need not be taken as calamaties but rather as inevitable aspects of life in an industrial society. Dealing with them is just another part of the difficult police job, a part requiring broad understanding and a commitment to self-examination and open communication of differences, rather than an occasion for despair or unyielding rigid hostility of any one group toward another. What is proposed here is that the current problems of police morale *vis à vis* the public and courts be treated as another challenge to be met by administrators through the usual procedures of problem identification, fact-finding, solution testing, and personnel training. These will not be complete solutions, nor will they touch the larger social issues which generate the differing social conceptions of menace, morality, and the proper administration of justice in our society. They are, however, steps which can be taken now within departments themselves to help build morale and to keep effective officers at work.

NOTES

1. *See* Richard H. Blum, ed., *Police Section* (Springfield, Ill.: Charles C Thomas, 1964) for a summary of the findings.
2. Richard H. Blum, et al., *Utopiates: A Study of the Use and Users of LSD-15,* (New York: Atherton Press, 1964).
3. S. Rettig and B. Pasamanick, "Changes in Moral Values over Three Decades, 1929-1958," *Social Problems* 6 (1959): 320-28.

Are You Oriented to Hold Them?

Thomas Reddin

Historically, law enforcement has gone through several administrative eras. Some 25 years ago there was great involvement in organizational planning. We started developing organization charts with related activities placed in neat little boxes and grouped together under precise headings. Then we joined them all together with solid and broken lines which, hopefully, showed their interrelationships and provided means of getting the job done with least organizational friction.

Time passed and we entered the semantics period. We had to tell people what all of our terms meant so that they could best understand existing charts and procedures. All sorts of manuals were written telling how things should be done. About this time it appeared that despite organization charts, well defined terms and lots of manuals, more still was needed. Emphasis was then placed on supervision, the first line supervisor became the culprit, it was his responsibility to get the job done. So, emphasis was put on the supervisor. After the supervisor was brought into line, the workers weren't going along with the gag and the

At the time the article was written, Thomas Reddin was deputy chief of police for Los Angeles.

From Thomas Reddin, "Are You Oriented to Hold Them?: A Searching Look at Police Management," *The Police Chief* 33, no. 3 (March 1966): 12-20. Reprinted by permission of the publisher.

psychological era embracing human dynamics, human relations and human affairs came into being.

Now we had gone the full circle, organization planning plus semantics plus supervisory development plus internal human relations all added up to an infallible combination. But we weren't quite ready for what followed; we still had problems. So we spent several years ruminating about communications. Messages must get up and down the hierarchical structure. Lines of communications must be kept open.

Then something new happened—automation, mechanical gimmicks, computers became the problem of the day. So systems and analysis, long range planning, and procedural analysis began to gake great amounts of our time.

This brings us to today and suddenly we find ourselves in a transitional period. We are beset from all sides by all sorts of political, economic, and social pressures. We are utilizing the best lessons learned from history. We are searching for answers for the present. We conclude, inescapably, that our great present internal problem is people. One major question keeps arising, how can we best keep our individual officers happy, working and on the job?

INDIVIDUAL NEEDS

Psychologists tell us that there are many different ways in which the basic psychological needs of an individual can be satisfied. After eliminating the needs which primarily concern physical matters and confining our thinking to the management-employee relationship, we find it possible to reduce an employee's psychological needs to a very elemental level.

In his relationship to his organization, an employee wants basically three things: to do, to belong, to be recognized—to do something, something worthwhile, and to do it well; to belong to a group, an organization, a group with a mission, an efficient well-recognized organization; to be recognized as a worthwhile employee, as a member of an outstanding group, to be accepted as either a master craftsman in his work or as one who has the potential to achieve such status. If management is to keep its employees, to keep them happy and working, these basic psychological needs must be fulfilled. Today we hear much talk of great turnover, resignations and early retirements. This gives rise to the question *"Are we oriented to hold them?"*

One word of warning, an organization cannot hold employees, keeping them happy and morale high, simply by giving them things. Fringe benefits do not automatically produce happy, well-adjusted workers. Employees must be made to feel that they belong, that they are participating.

LEADERSHIP

Any discussion concerning how to hold or achieve the best performance from employees immediately focuses attention upon leadership. Leadership generally follows dictates set down by management. Management, unfortunately, does not always operate in such a way that proper direction is given to its leaders.

Too often one observes management by crisis, management by detail, management by fear, and management by organization chart. If we examine the underlying implication of these terms, we discover many things we should not do and very few things that we should do. Any type of management or leadership involves people. We cannot escape the fact that the efficiency of an organization depends virtually entirely upon the efficiency of those individuals performing the first level job. Providing proper leadership is a tremendous challenge to management.

Obviously, we do not wish to manage our organization by crisis, detail, fear, or organization chart; nor, should we delude ourselves into the belief that we can achieve desired results through the type of "nice guy" leadership. However, the fact is inescapable that we are working with people and the manner in which we provide leadership must contain the ability to satisy our employees' needs if we are to keep them happy and working.

If you don't have proper leadership you can appoint committees, draw organization charts and make speeches until you're blue in the face, but nothing will happen.

NEW OFFICERS

Hiring a new policeman is a great deal different than hiring a new employee in most other forms of endeavor. Law enforcement hires, or hopes to be hiring, career officers. It is up to management to make career officers of them. There are many routine ways of so doing. The police probationer is in a strange, new environment and needs expert help and guidance. This especially is true in his earliest assignments.

A long time ago an erudite, early pioneer in the field of police administration announced that new men should work the graveyard shift. There was less to do there; ergo, there was more time to learn. The new man could be brought along slowly and (if he lived long enough) through seniority advance to the night shift. The premise advanced overlooks several important points. With less to do, the man does less and in the process learns less. Most of the newer men are on the same shift, so who is going to teach whom? The little activity of the graveyard shift can easily lead to boredom and the development of bad habits.

Employees should be assigned in such a way that they will be exposed to all watches and the greatest varieties of assignments possible within the administrative limitations of the department.

A supervisor has little if any time to teach the young officer how to become a skilled policeman. With increased rates of hiring we have seen a rise in the use of senior officers as training officers in on-the-job training. Use of training officers serves two purposes. In addition to providing step-by-step training in the field, the training officer himself benefits from the experience. He is doing something extra and he is getting recognition.

SHIFT ASSIGNMENTS

Many discussions have been held concerning shift assignments. Arguments have been advanced in favor of the seniority plan, the rotation plan and the watch preference plan. In our discussion of assignment of new officers we covered, and indicated a disapproval of, the seniority plan.

The rotation plan calls for watch changes based on prearranged schedules. Proponents argue that through rotation an officer receives wider experience and becomes acquainted with the overall problem. They claim that rotation minimizes the development of cliques and that morale for the whole force is better since the majority of assignments are not reserved to the preferred few with lots of seniority.

The watch preference plan can provide most of the benefits claimed for the other two methods, but it is by far the most difficult to administer. Under the watch preference plan each officer who so desires submits, in order, his preference for watches. Insofar as possible, the man is assigned the watch he requests. It might prove surprising that many men might prefer other than day work. If requests involving changes balance out (which is highly unlikely) your problem is solved. If not, certain ground rules should be followed. For examples: A man cannot routinely request a change until he has been on a watch for a specified period of time (three months-six months). If a change is requested and no one wants off of the watch requested, then the one with the longest service (if over the specified period of time) is moved. Unless, of course, there is some administrative reason why one or the other should not be moved.

Despite the difficulty in administering the watch preference plan, it often pays off well in production, morale and efficiency. Certainly problems exist when an employee does not get a watch he requests or when an employee is bounced from a watch he does not wish to leave. When this occurs an explanation should be given the employee so he will have a complete understanding. In the long haul, a well-administered, consistently operated watch preference plan will pay dividends.

SPECIALIZATION

Organization as a process depends primarily upon specialization. The larger the department, the greater degree of specialization occurs. A good general rule to follow is to specialize if you must, generalize if you can.

Even where specialization is deemed necessary it is often wise to provide for time limits in given assignments and to leave spots open for training purposes in other assignments.

One might liken police work to furniture building. In the old days, one craftsman might have made an entire dining room set. Today he probably makes left front legs only and thus finds it difficult to identify with the end product. A certain feeling of doing, of accomplishment, is necessarily missing. Recognition is hard to attain simply because he makes better and more left front legs than any other worker. Much more satisfaction obviously would exist if he were a trained practitioner in the complete art.

Specialization does have certain benefits but for an organization experiencing increasing specialization, the trend has serious implications. Most important of all, it tends to separate the worker from the end product. Additionally, specialization tends to narrow the probability of a potential supervisor. People who advance in a department should have broad experience and background.

Specialization early in a man's career is a particularly bad practice. He may never get a chance to become a generalist. He may get spoiled for other assignments or he may quit or become disgruntled from working an assignment he does not particularly care for.

Broad, general knowledge is not an end in itself but it does give an appreciation of the part he plays in the whole picture and tells him what his efforts contribute to the total purpose of the organization.

Developments through direct experience should be handled by job rotation, the planned interchange of selected personnel. This is a basic necessity if we are to raise a man's sights above his specialty.

DECISION MAKING

Almost any employee wants to know how he is doing and where he is going. In addition, each likes to have authority delegated to him that allows him, in turn, to make decisions on his own and to provide some substance of leadership—even if it is only self-leadership.

The decision-making process should be pushed down to the lowest possible level in an organization. The best situation exists where the individual performing the task feels that he can and should make decisions on the spot. He should not have his decision making powers diminished by fear of criticism or second guessing. His decisions should not be based on a slavishness to rules, regulations and procedures. Books and files should not become a substitute for thinking. The man on the spot should decide and act, he should not report, request and wait. In many organizations, the decision gets so far away from the fact that seemingly nobody is responsible for it. In this process purposes are lost sight of, initiative decreases and the responsibility for decision making moves ever upward.

We have said before that the vitality of any organization will be found in its people, not in its organization charts, rules or manuals. People should be encouraged to act and make decisions on their own. Sure they might make mistakes—we all do. But they will learn from their mistakes and develop that indeterminate thing called judgment. Judgment, we have been told, is nothing more than the ability to profit by our mistakes. But, one often hears that there is no room for mistakes in law enforcement. If we address our comments to careless decisions, where life and liberty are concerned, this may be true. But, we are not talking about careless decisions; we are discussing carefully considered decisions. Most people have a liberal measure of intelligence, imagination and reasoning ability. This should equip them to make decisions on what makes sense at the moment to accomplish the goal.

Once you make a decision for a man when that man should have made the decision himself, you are assisting in destroying his initiative and in so doing lessening his value to your organization. When you are asked a question under circumstances where the man should provide his own answer, use the "rebound technique." Ask him what he thinks, assist him in reasoning his way through to the decision. Let him know the cake of ice is in his lap; he's the one who has to get rid of it.

It has been said that once you start making decisions for a person, you are taking unto yourself the responsibility for even more of his decisions in the future. When a person makes a decision he is doing something, he is contributing to his organization, he is developing himself, he feels important, he is preparing for leadership.

Push that decision-making process downward in your organization. Encourage men to act on their own. Be tolerant of mistakes. The important thing is that the man makes a decision and that he profits from the results of that decision, right or wrong. Certainly we must have rules, regulations and procedures and they should be followed. But they are no substitute for initiative and intelligence. The more a man is given an opportunity to make decisions, and in the process to learn, the more rules and regulations will be followed.

IDEAS

Management should provide attitudes and procedures that welcome ideas. Among the most successful managers will be found those who can stimulate thinking, tap experience and encourage imagination. Among the happiest employees will be found those who have been afforded the opportunity to make suggestions and who have been provided with a good listener. When an employee is given the opportunity to make a suggestion, there results a feeling of belonging, of importance. He has contributed something to the workings of his organization, he is participating, he is doing something extra.

Many daily problems can use the help of idea people. Obviously, no one knows a job better than the one who works at it eight hours a day. Chances are that you may not even hear most of the good ideas of the people who work for you. Channels of communication must be kept open. People should be urged to be alert for improvements and should be encouraged to talk about their ideas. Any idea advanced should be given a fair hearing.

There are several admonitions about your reactions to ideas. Don't kill an idea because it does not solve all of the problems in a situation. Solve the easy portions of the problem first. In killing an idea, you might kill the source of future ideas. Don't let personal antagonism against an idea interfere with an objective analysis. Don't be a credit-grabber, even if you did think of it first. You gain nothing and lose a great deal. Don't eliminate a suggestion because it has been tried before. Times change, and we should change with them; it might work today. Yesterday's impractical idea might be practical today.

Don't just hang up a suggestion box. You cannot create an atmosphere conducive to the formation of ideas by this simple rule. Suggestion boxes, unfortunately, are too often a convenient receptacle for gum wrappers, cigarette butts and locker room humor. Further, there is a certain anonymity connected with suggestion boxes. They seem to imply that the source of suggestions should be kept secret.

Ask questions. Invite suggestions. Encourage participation. Provide time for listening. Be a positive listener. Give recognition. Give it openly and warmly, in a penciled note or verbally, or in a letter or in a magazine. Give it any way you wish, but give it.

When an organization has the active participation of people down the line, rather than their passive compliance to established procedures, it simulates interest and loyalties.

CREATIVITY

A deep-thinking idea man is generally a creative person. The art of creating an air favorable to creativity needs much study. Creation of such an atmosphere is sometimes difficult. Creativity necessarily involves the suggestion of change and among the many problems of modern management, there arises the question of how to accept continued change as inevitable, just and desirable.

A very real problem in human relations is how to foster a healthy attitude toward change and at the same time a healthy attitude toward authority. Too often the tendency is to attempt to obtain good morale by avoiding change and thus almost eliminating authority. Emphasis is placed on so-called participation and the development of the organization man. As a result we often see the continuance of cozy, unchanged units. There is plenty of "participation," not much action and very little change. Creativity within an organization is a healthy sign. Many organizations have a tendency to stifle creativity since creativity invariably means conflict, either because the old ways are challenged or because it represents something wholly new.

As technological and social problems increase, the need for creative thinking multiplies. Most people are born with more creativity than they ever use. The manager's problem is to get more ideas out of the few creative people he might have and additionally to improve the creativity of the people he does have.

Actually law enforcement does a pretty good job of stifling creativity and encouraging conformity. A strong body of opinion exists that the conformist is the one who gets ahead. And let's not kid ourselves, many men make their way to upper levels by pursuing conventional standard approaches. But a word of warning—where conformity is being accepted, or even encouraged, a lot of good talent goes into hiding and is being wasted.

Too often conformity to established thinking and procedure is considered the keystone of a smooth running organization. And, when you think of it, why not? Under such conditions, decision making is routine. There will be no serious problems. Work performances will be adequate, though conventional. Leaders look good because all seems to be going smoothly. It appears that one would almost be a fool to experiment, encourage creativity, suggest changes and in so doing perhaps risk his reputation. But, as the doctrine of an organization, conformity can spell stagnation and a descent into mediocrity.

An organization is not represented in an organization chart but in its people. There is a need to recognize organization charts for what they are—history; sometimes ancient, sometimes contemporary, but virtually always a reflection of a static condition—a reflection to be tested and evaluated against ideas and suggestions.

Encourage your people to have ideas, make suggestions, be creative and they will truly be participating in and belonging to an organization.

PROBLEM EMPLOYEES

Even in the unlikely event that every supervisor practiced the top leadership methods and even if each supervisor could acquire a sincere and understanding attitude toward each of their subordinates, boredom and inefficiency would still remain. We would still have the problem employee and we would still have to strive to bring out the best in him. We are not speaking of the employee who should be fired outright, but the one who is, for various reasons, inadequate. It is extremely difficult to motivate a meatball, but as they say in the restaurants, they can't be all bad.

First, and most important, if an employee is lacking in any quality, he should be told. We are dealing with men in a competitive world. Even though you may think he is inadequate, he may think he is doing fine. Tell him why he is considered inadequate, discuss his shortcomings with him, listen to his point of view, offer your aid in improving him, work with him on a program of development. Down deep he has the same psychological needs as the outstanding officer. Help him meet those needs. After determining the cause for substandard performance, you may choose one of several methods to rehabilitate him; load him with work assignments, set deadlines, make spotchecks on his progress in such a manner as to appear that you are interested in the project and not his lack of interest. Don't penalize, don't carp. If he fails, *you* have failed. Use "we" in assignments. What can we do about the parking problem for the officers' cars? What can we do about this burglar? Talk to him frequently, establish rapport. Be willing to spend the time to rehabilitate.

One phase of supervisorial activities that provides great satisfaction is to plan a rehabilitative program for a problem employee, discuss it with the employee and watch it through to a successful end. But, it cannot be done without planning and it cannot be done if you do not have the courage to openly discuss problems with the employee.

When all else fails, then and only then, feed him to the sharks. Institute disciplinary proceedings.

CONCLUSION

The work situation should be one of the most gratifying aspects of a man's life. Management can help keep employees "gratified" but it takes effort and understanding. Understanding sometimes comes from a review of past successes and failures. From our review we reach several conclusions. Social pressures are not entirely to blame for all of the internal problems facing us.

We give too little thought to the work itself. Work must be more than congenial; it must be absorbing, meaningful and challenging. There just isn't any "work" as inherently rich in these qualities as police work. Yet, in many cases we have done such a successful job of strangling and stifling the juices out of the "work" that we now find ourselves searching for ways to "make" it interesting.

As organizations have developed, there has been a tendency to take for granted that people would accept a highly controlled environment. It was just so logical that employees would be happy when an organization was well organized, well regulated and well run that the human factor was given insufficient consideration. Employees are not automatically pleased with such an organization. Their psychological needs still must be met.

Recent developments indicate that we sometimes *over-manage* our organizations to the extent that initiative and ingenuity are driven to seek outlets away from the job. Over-managing leaves too little leeway for the exercise of judgment.

Management can be automated and tightly regulated but people cannot. In the end, management must accommodate itself to people and not vice versa. It has always been thus. It is not easy and it takes work. But if we give our people the opportunity to do, to belong, to be recognized, our organizations will grow more flexible, viable and productive.

SECTION THREE

Professionalization

Overview

THE ELUSIVE PROFESSIONALIZATION THAT POLICE OFFICERS SEEK. Walter E. Kreutzer discusses the characteristics of a profession and compares the police service to his own criteria. He outlines a workable plan that would assure its ultimate professionalization. He calls for changes in educational requirements and a system of certification based on education, skill training, and experience levels. Professional mobility, or "lateral transfer," is also a must for professionalization. Ethical standards and codes of conduct also must be universally established and enforced, according to the authors.

THE WORKING POLICEMAN, POLICE "PROFESSIONALIZATION," AND THE RULE OF LAW. Jerome H. Skolnick's *Justice Without Trial is an* incisive study of the police and their operational characteristics. In this chapter of his book, Skolnick studies the concept of police professionalization from an objective viewpoint. He points out the dilemma of the police in democratic society; The fulfillment of their personal goals, initiative, and ambitions versus restraints upon their individuality demanded by the "rule of law." Skolnick then points out the limitations of police professionalization when considered in terms of "managerial efficiency" and the officers' own self-concept of professionalization.

THE POLICE: A MISSION AND ROLE. Dr. A. C. Germann, a long-time advocate for dramatic change in theory and practice of law enforcement, presents his views on professionalization. He discusses the police today and as he hopes to see them in the future. Although his writing appears to reflect the views of a cynic, Germann states that he looks forward with optimism to changes as the "old guard" of law enforcement administrators is replaced by a different type of professional leadership.

IMPLICATIONS OF PROFESSIONALISM IN LAW ENFORCEMENT FOR POLICE-COMMUNITY RELATIONS. Professor Louis Radelet discusses the concept of "professionalism" as it applies to community relations. He points out that there is more to professionalization of the police service than mere proclamation and "image changing." There is a great deal of work to be done from the inside, starting with the self-image, and then concentrating on police attitudes, at the same time building public recognition of the "profession."

The Elusive Professionalization that Police Officers Seek

Walter E. Kreutzer

The police of the United States have long sought professional status and recognition as professionals. Yet this recognition has not been forthcoming. Why have the police failed to achieve this status? How can professional status be achieved? And lastly, probably the most difficult question, will the body of police want professional status that will require them to conform to a strict code of ethical standards which will yield sanctions for nonconformity? Nonconformity to criminal law is expected to produce punishment by probation, jail or prison. Nonconformity of police officers to professional or ethical standards should also yield sanctions such as loss of professional status, which in turn would mean permanent or temporary loss of employment as a police officer.

Professionalization implies an obligation, willingly taken, but an obligation to what? It is an obligation, "rooted in religious or ethical philosophy."[1] A professional is one who has an obligation toward mankind and this obligation is "rooted in religious or ethical philosophy." The following quote aptly describes the basic criteria for professionalization.

> A profession is that occupational group which practices its skills with the following basic obligations:
> 1. A duty to serve mankind generally rather than self, individuals, or groups.

From Walter E. Kreutzer, "The Elusive Professionalization that Police Officers Seek," *The Police Chief* 35, no. 8 (August 1968): 26-31. Reprinted by permission of the publisher.

2. A duty to prepare as fully as practicable for service before entering active practice.
3. A duty to work continually to improve skills by all means available and to freely communicate professional information gained.
4. A duty to employ full skill at all times regardless of considerations of personal gain, comfort, or safety, and at all times to assist fellow professionals upon demand.
5. A duty to regulate practice by the franchising of practitioners, setting the highest practicable intellectual and technical minimums; to accept and upgrade fellow professionals solely upon considerations of merit; and to be constantly alert to protect society from fraudulent, substandard, or unethical practice through ready and swift disfranchisement.
6. A duty to zealously guard the honor of the profession by living exemplary lives publicly, and privately, recognizing that injury to a group serving society injures society.
7. A duty to give constant attention to the improvement of self-discipline, recognizing that the individual must be the master of himself to be the servant of others.

By these standards it is clear that police work is not a profession.[2]

There is a significant difference between technology and professionalism that must be realized. The time has come to combine the tremendous technological advances law enforcement has made in the last 20 years with a strong pragmatic ethical code that has resolution and fortitude. There must also be a melting of municipal or civil service police requirements and the professional requirements of the body of police which may be enumerated through such organizations as the International Association of Chiefs of Police or, as in medicine, the American Medical Association.

This paper will explore the combining of technical requirements of law enforcement with the ethical standards of the body of police that might evolve into the professional status so sought by police officers throughout the United States.

TECHNICAL REQUIREMENTS FOR PROFESSIONALIZATION

A professional group has a bond of common knowledge. That is information that is not generally known to the public. This is quickly seen in law, medicine and, to a degree, in education. These people have trained for their professional status for a period of from four years to as many as ten or twelve years, or more in the case of psychiatry. They then have a body of knowledge that is peculiar to their particular group.

Law enforcement has begun the serious training of its working members and those individuals now entering law enforcement. The California Peace Officers Standards and Training (POST) is a leading example of a state effort to set minimum recruitment and training standards for the police. The 372 hours of basic instruction, which the POST training averages, does give the entrance level police officer a fund of basic knowledge on which to build a profession. But how much of a fund is it when compared to other professional groups? Educators might be considered a comparable group. Like the police, many educators are employed by a government body and deal with a large segment of the population. A beginning teacher, at a minimum, must have a baccalaureate degree for a permanent teaching position. In many states, however, the B.A. degree is not sufficient and five years or more of training are required to complete all courses in the particular teacher training program. Assume that four years will, at the minimum, at least open the door to the profession of education, how does this compare to the police requirements? A baccalaureate degree of 120 semester units or hours is equivalent to approximately 1,920 hours of training—or 120 units times 16 weeks equals 1,920 hours. The concentrated 640-hour police program equals 40 units or one-third of the minimum requirements of a teacher. This, then, is one of the technical facets that must be faced. The basic fund of knowledge common to the police is somewhat shallow. The colleges and universities are, especially in California, trying to overcome this situation. But college or university training *per se* will not necessarily make a competent police officer. Accademic training must be mixed or compounded with practical experience acquired in the field to create the truly professional police officer. Often some experience can be obtained through on-the-job training, or cadet training. Table 1 compares the number of hours of training requirements for various academic degrees and police academy training courses.

From this, it would appear that the academic approach to law enforcement must be strengthened. This is now being done in some areas; however, we must not look at training as having been completed once the first course has ended. On the contrary, the first course is just an introduction or the opening of one of many doors ahead for the new police officer. Fortunately, the police are making steady progress to deepen the fund of knowledge so necessary for a group on the path toward professionalization.

CERTIFICATION PROGRAM

For a doctor or lawyer to practice his profession, he must first receive certification through the state. For a California police officer to be employed, or practice his trade, he must be 21, a United States citizen, have good moral character, have a 12th grade education and be able to pass a written examination and an oral interview.[3] For the most part he is not required to bring into the police service anything more than a healthy body that is able to learn and that has not been convicted of a felony. This is, of course, far different from the lawyer, doctor, or educator, each of whom must have the basic, in-depth knowledge of his skill prior to practicing it.

The potential of certification for the police is unlimited. In the past, civil service has been concerned primarily with keeping the rascals out and not necessarily with attracting and obtaining the most competent people in the shortest possible period of time.

TABLE 1 COMPARABLE STATISTICS OF POLICE TRAINING PROGRAMS AND ACADEMIC DEGREES

Police Training Courses		Academic Programs		
Hours	Units	Units	Hours*	Degrees
200	12.5	63	1,008	A.A.
372	23.2	120	1,920	B.A.
640	40.0	30	480	M.S.
		45*	720	Ph.D.

*Estimated

The police certificate program can offer a new dynamic approach to the field of law enforcement. The following four tables are based upon two primary assumptions:

1. There is a POST or similar program available with at least five training courses offered: basic, intermediate, advanced, command and administrative which may be coupled to a college program.
2. No permanent police rank will be attainable without the appropriate police certificate.

The California POST program has utilized a combination of experience and education to produce the requirements for receipt of the various POST certificates. The concept enumerated in this article will also use a ratio of experience and education for certification. The difference between the concepts is in the application, the meaning, need, and desirability of certification. All examinations in this program would be of the open type. That is, anyone who meets the requirements may compete for the positions. A person holding the appropriate credential would have the written portion of the particular entrance or promotional examination waived and would only be given the oral portion of the examination. The persons holding the required credential and successfully passing the oral portion of the examination would then head the particular list for entrance or for promotion. This concept of certification would place a premium on a combination of academic attainment and experience.

A revalidation program might also be utilized that would require four semester credits every second year to revalidate the highest credential held.

Examine Table 2. Note that each respective police rank would have a certain credential requirement for permanent rank; this, of course, being in addition to the probationary period.

Credentials would be issued based on a combination of experience, police academy courses and formal academic training. The term "experience" is defined as the sum total of experience as a fulltime (paid) police officer regardless of rank. Thus, a person seeking promotion to the permanent rank of sergeant would be required to hold an intermediate credential.

The intermediate credential would require a combination of training and experience of six credential points with a minimum of two points from the academic/academy segment and a minimum of two points from the experience segment. The other two points would then come from either experience or

TABLE 2 CREDENTIAL REQUIREMENTS

Ranks	Credentials				
	Basic	Intermediate	Advanced	Command	Administrative
Chief					Required
Deputy Chief					Required
Captain				Required	
Lieutenant			Required		
Sergeant		Required			
Patrolman	Required				

academic attainment. *See* Tables 3 and 4. In the case of the sergeant, it would mean that at a minimum he might have attended an intermediate police academy course and have taken 30 college units and have been a police officer not less than one year. This combination would account for four points of the required six for permanent appointment to the rank of Sergeant. The other two points would be acquired through two more years of experience, additional college units or a combination of these. Through the system described, highly motivated people will be attracted and retained in the active field of law enforcement. The credentials awarded would have meaning because they are a license to practice the law enforcement skills acquired, just as the lawyer may practice his skills once he has been admitted to the bar. But we still find ourselves a long way from the goal —professionalization.

TABLE 3 MINIMUM CREDENTIAL POINT REQUIREMENTS

Requirements	Credentials				
	Basic	Intermediate	Advanced	Command	Administrative
College or Police Academy	1	2	3	4	5
Experience	1	2	3	4	5
Minimum Points Required for Credentials	4	6	8	10	14

TABLE 4 CREDENTIAL POINTS

Educational Points Towards Certificate		Experience Points		Academy Course Points	
	Points		Points		Points
30 Units	1	9 months less than one year	1	Basic	1
60 Units	2	1 yr. less than 2 yrs.	2	Intermediate	1
A.A.	3	2 yrs. less than 3 yrs.	3	Advanced	1
90 Units	4	3 yrs. less than 4 yrs.	4	Command	1
B.A./B.S.	5	4 yrs. less than 5 yrs.	5	Administrative	1
M.S.	7	5 yrs. less than 6 yrs.	6		
Ph.D.	10	6 yrs. less than 7 yrs.	7		
		7 yrs. less than 8 yrs.	8		
		8 yrs. less than 9 yrs.	9		
		9 yrs. less than 10 yrs.	10		
		10 yrs. (and over)	11		

PROFESSIONAL MOBILITY

A professional can move, if not from state to state, at the minimum intrastate. If a position becomes available in another city he can compete for it without necessarily being forced to start at the bottom or entrance level again. Mobility also infers a certain amount of security acquired through practice in the profession. Educators, for example, who are members in a state teachers' pension system may move from school to school or from school system to school system within the state and retain their retirement program. This provides both mobility and security. City managers are another example of mobility in employment. A city manager may become a participant in the International Association of City Managers retirement program. This too allows mobility yet maintains a program for eventual retirement.

Most states have some type of employee retirement program for their state employees. It would be a relatively simple matter for the police employee and the city to contribute to this retirement program instead of a local program if the employee so elected. By being a member of a state retirement program, the individual police officer might then, if he desired, have mobility throughout the state and not lose his retirement program.

"Lateral entry has been suggested as another means of obtaining professional personnel."[4] Mobility, or the ability to move from one police department to another, while disliked by many police administrators, would bring new ideas and concepts into each police department and reduce the tendency toward ingrown practices that can mean stagnation.

Mobility is based upon technical competence and not upon political "know who." The benefits to be derived are potentially unlimited. This is, of course, based upon the dynamics of the individual police department. The liabilities are few in comparison. The concept of mobility would mean that each police department would have an opportunity of increasing its fund of knowledge and compete for personnel. This would be true for the large, as well as the small police department. In some respects, the smaller police departments may offer greater appeal than the large police department. This is especially true of the person who is seeking to broaden his experience in law enforcement. The larger departments tend to turn personnel into specialists. While specialization is highly desirable at the working level or supervisory level, administrative personnel need an expanded view of the police operation, not the limited perspective of one who is highly specialized. An officer qualified for greater responsibility would not necessarily be stymied if promotion were not possible in the department he now serves. Old methodology that has withstood the test of time simply because "we have always done it that way" would be challenged and new ideas, even if not adopted, would at least surface in the police administration.

Open competition increases the opportunity for both the employee and the employer. The police certificate would be the key to this employment opportunity. The certificate holders would in fact be competing among themselves and those within the police department who do not possess the certificate would compete among themselves. But the certificate holders would have the greater probability of employment since they would be placed at the top of the final employment list. Many will say this is unfair to the non-certificate personnel. This, in one sense, is true until one examines the fact that those who do not possess the certificate have the same opportunity to acquire certification as those who are so motivated. The benefits to be derived by the particular police department and to the individual police officer through improved quality of performance are untold. Time, competition, and performance would tend to improve both the police department and the individual police officer.

The certified employee through mobility now comes closer to the status of a professional than ever before, but at least one more obstacle must be traversed before professional status is a reality.

PROFESSIONAL ETHICS AND SANCTIONS

The dishonest lawyer who is tried and convicted is disbarred. A malpracticing doctor, found guilty, loses his license to practice and so should an errant police officer. An officer who uses a credential as part of the requirements for appointment should be deprived of this credential and employment if found to be performing in an unethical or illegal manner. What is an unethical manner for a police officer? Most police departments have operational manuals that clearly outline the ethical conduct for each police officer. Violation of these rules would mean either temporary or permanent loss of the credential under which the officer was employed. Permanent loss of an advanced certificate, for example, would mean demotion if the person were in the rank which required that certificate.

Harsh treatment, yes, but the treatment must be exacting if the patient is to survive and grow into maturity. "Many law enforcement administrators lament the fact that we are not a recognized profession. Yet, they tolerate and sanction the acceptance of gifts and gratuities by police personnel."[5]

Police Chief James F. Bale of Whittier, California, explores professionalization with such questions as, "It would be interesting to note whether the doctors and lawyers receive free coffee or a discount on their meals at the local restaurant. Or would they feel insulted at the offer of a handout?"[6] How many times has a police officer commented on how he went to a particular store in uniform and purchased an item, only to find the merchant wants to give him a discount. This is perfectly all right, if the merchant gives *every* customer a discount, but if not, this is extortion by uniform. Extortion is a harsh word, but let the same man go into the same store, unknown and out of uniform, and the merchant would undoubtedly never think of giving a discount. First of all, the police officer had no legitimate reason for being in the store in uniform if he were not there on police business. Many police officers have a prosaic attitude toward the power the police uniform implies. The morality required of the police is far different from that of a "good" businessman. The businessman courts favor as part of doing business. This is a violation of the ethical practices of law enforcement. The police officer must be impartial—above temptation and able to weigh each situation on its merits. The law enforcement code of ethics should serve as the guide for police conduct.[7]

But why do police officers fail to obey this code? They fail to obey because there is little or no punishment for noncompliance. The police officer who fails to conform to the standards of police ethics must be brought to trial before his peers—the police. But why not a civil review board or a citizens committee? Why the police? Because the ethics of the nonpolice world are different from the police world. What is sound "business practice" in the nonpolice world may be an unethical practice in the police world. But what type of court should hear charges against an errant police officer? The police trial board has certain advantages if conducted properly. First, formal charges must be made against the accused. For example, that he did violate rule 5 of the police operating orders, to wit, accepted passes to the Esquire Theater, 101 Main Street, from John Jones, Manager, and so used the passes to go to the theater on (date). The trial board would be convened upon formal receipt of charges made to the Chief of Police. The Chief of Police would convene a five-man board chaired by a division commander, having at least three officers of the rank of lieutenant or above and two sergeants. The defendant may request that one patrolman be assigned to the board in place of one sergeant. There would be a prosecutor assigned by the Chief of Police with the defense selected by the defendant from within the active field of law enforcement. The trial board would be conducted in a formal manner, with a transcript taken. The trial board would find the defendant guilty, not guilty or the charges constitute a false report. If guilty, a punishment recommendation would be made by the board. If not guilty, the recommendation would be to return the officer to duty with appropriate remuneration. If a false report, a recommendation would be made that formal charges be brought against the person making the false report. All recommendations would then be forwarded to the Chief of Police for final determination.

"In effect, the Trial Board in the police department is an administrative court set up by city ordinance, by statute, or by charter amendment voted on by the people, in lieu of utilizing the civil service or personnel hearing board procedure."[8]

However, the average Civil Service Commission could also be heard during the proceedings. All penalties of suspension of more than 30 days, fines in excess of $100 or dismissal could be affirmed by the Civil Service Commission. The role of the Civil Service Commission should be only to assure that the trial board was fair, impartial, and the charges if the person was found guilty, were proved beyond a reasonable doubt and a moral certainty. The findings of the trial board would also be forwarded to the agency issuing the certificate, if the defendant held a certificate. This body would then revoke the certificate based upon the findings of the trial board.

A great deal of trouble for accepting two passes to the show? Certainly, but there is a price to pay for professionalization. The body of law enforcement has verbalized the desire and need of professional status. It is now mandatory that the individual police officer squarely address himself to the realism of just what professionalization means.

The question that policemen must now ask is: Are they really willing to pay the price for professional status?

SUMMARY

The requirements of professionalization are exacting and demand, in part, a true in-depth fund of knowledge, standardization (certification), mobility, ethics and sanctions if the obligations and ethics of the service are violated. This article has been one approach to the difficult and complex subject of police professionalization. Standards through certification, mobility and pension provisions are all aspects of professionalization. But the paramount question that remains unanswered is, as stated before, are the police truly willing to accept and use these requirements to gain the status of professionals?

NOTES

1. *Municipal Police Administration* (Chicago, Ill.: The International City Managers' Association, 1961), p. 458.
2. Ibid.
3. George H. Shepard, "Are We Aiming Too Low in Recruitment? *The Police Chief* (January 1967), p. 25.
4. James F. Bale, "Brother, Can You Spare a Dime?" *FBI Law Enforcement Bulletin* (September 1967), p. 7.
6. Ibid.
7. *Task Force Report: The Police* (Washington, D.C.: The President's Commission on Law Enforcement and Administration of Justice), p. 213.
8. John P. Kennedy, *Police Management Planning* (Springfield, Ill.: Charles C Thomas, Publisher, 1959), p. 73.

The Working Policeman, Police "Professionalism," and the Rule of Law

Jerome H. Skolnick

The traditional concern of criminology and of writers on "social control" is the maintenance of order in society. This study suggests that such a view is limited both philosophically and sociologically. "Social control" must deal not

From Jerome H. Skolnick, *Justice Without Trial: Law Enforcement in Democratic Society* (New York: John Wiley & Sons, 1967), pp. 230-45. Reprinted by permission of the publisher.

merely with the maintenance of order, but with the quality of the order that a given system is capable of sustaining and the procedures appropriate to the achievement of such order. Thus, a given set of social and legal conditions may lead to order in a stable democracy but not in a stable totalitarianism. Meaningful sociological analysis of order cannot, therefore, be value-free, because such a posture falsely assumes the equivalence of all types of order.

This research rejects the "value-free" approach, and concentrates instead upon the social foundations of legal procedures designed to protect democratic order. In the workings of democratic society, where the highest stated commitment is to the ideal of legality, a focal point of tension exists between the substance of order and the procedures for its accomplishment. "The basic and anguishing dilemma of form and substance in law can be alleviated, but never resolved, for the structure of legal domination retains its distinguishing features only as long as this dilemma is perpetuated."[1] This dilemma is most clearly manifested in law enforcement organizations, where both sets of demands make forceful normative claims upon police conduct.

In addition to this fundamental dilemma, there are further complications. Neither form nor substance, law nor order, is an entirely clear conception; and what it means for police to use law to enforce order is also somewhat problematic. The empirical portion of this study looked into the question of how the police themselves conceive the meaning of "law" and "order" to find out how these conceptions develop and are implemented in police practices. Social conditions in the varying assignments of police heightened or diminished the conflict between the obligations of maintaining order and observing the rule of law.

This chapter considers the implications of the research. First we summarize findings about these issues and suggest that the dilemma of the police in democratic society arises out of the conflict between the extent of initiative contemplated by nontotalitarian norms of work and restraints upon police demanded by the rule of law. Second, we consider the meaning of police professionalization, pointing out its limitations according to the idea of managerial efficiency. Finally, we discuss how the policeman's conception of himself as a craftsman is rooted in community expectations, and how the ideology of police professionalization is linked to these expectations. Thus, this chapter focuses upon the relation between the policeman's conception of his work and his capacity to contribute to the development of a society based upon the rule of law as its master ideal.

OCCUPATIONAL ENVIRONMENT
AND THE RULE OF LAW

Five features of the policeman's occupational environment weaken the conception of the rule of law as a primary objective of police conduct. One is the social psychology of police work, that is, the relation between occupational environment, working personality, and the rule of law. Second is the policeman's stake in maintaining his position of authority, especially his interest in bolstering accepted patterns of enforcement. Third is police socialization, especially as it influences the policeman's administrative bias. A related factor is the pressure put upon individual policemen to "produce"—to be efficient rather than legal when the two norms are in conflict. Finally, there is the policeman's opportunity to behave inconsistently with the rule of law as a result of the low visibility of much of his conduct.

Although it is difficult to weigh the relative import of these factors, they all seem analytically to be joined to the conception of policeman as *craftsman* rather than as *legal actor*, as a skilled worker rather than as a civil servant obliged to subscribe to the rule of law. The significance of the conception of the policeman as a craftsman derives from the differences in ideology of work and authority in totalitarian and nontotalitarian societies. Reinhard Bendix has contended that the most important difference between totalitarian and nontotalitarian forms of subordination is to be found in the managerial handling of problems of authority and subordination.[2]

Subordinates in totalitarian society are offered little opportunity to introduce new means of achieving the goals of the organization, since subordination implies obedience rather than initiative. As Bendix says, ". . . managerial refusal to accept the tacit evasion of rules and norms or the uncontrolled exercise of judgment is related to a specific type of bureaucratization which constitutes the fundamental principle of totalitarian government."[3] By contrast, in nontotalitarian society, subordinates are encouraged to introduce their own strategies and ideas into the working situation. Bendix does not look upon rule violation or evasion as necessarily subverting the foundations of bureaucratic organization, but rather sees these innovations as "strategies of independence" by which the employees "seek to modify the implementation of the rules as their personal interests and their commitment (or lack of commitment) to the goals of the organization dictate."[4] In brief, the managerial ideology of nontotalitarian society maximizes the exercise of discretion by subordinates, while totalitarian society minimizes innovation by working officials.[5]

This dilemma of democratic theory manifests itself in every aspect of the policeman's work, as evidenced by the findings of this study. In explaining the development of the policeman's "working personality," the dangerous and authoritative elements of police work were emphasized. The combination of these elements undermines attachment to the rule of law in the context of a "constant" pressure to produce. Under such pressure, the variables of danger and authority tend to alienate the policeman from the general public, and at the same time to heighten his perception of symbols portending danger to him and to the community. Under the same pressure to produce, the policeman not only perceives possible criminality according to the symbolic status of the suspect; he also develops a stake in organized patterns of enforcement. To the extent that a suspect is seen as interfering with such arrangements, the policeman will respond negatively to him. On the other hand, the "cooperative" suspect, that is, one who contributes to the smooth operation of the enforcement pattern, will be rewarded. Accordingly, a detailed investigation was made of exchange relations between police and informers, in part to ascertain how informers are differentially treated according to the extent to which they support enforcement patterns, and partly to analyze how the policeman creates and uses the resources given to him.

In attempting to enrich his exchange position, the policeman necessarily involves the prosecutor in supporting his enforcement needs. The prosecutor, of course, also has a stake in the policeman's work performance, since the policeman provides him with the raw materials of prosecutorial achievement. Our observations suggested, however, that although he is ultimately the policeman's spokesman, the prosecutor performs a quasi-magisterial function by conveying a conception of legality to the policeman.

Most interesting, of course, is the basis on which the prosecutor's greater attachment to legality rests. We may point here to pertinent differences between policeman and prosecutor. One, of course, has to do with socialization. The prosecutor is a product of a law school, with larger understanding and appreciation of the judiciary and its restraints, especially constitutional ones. The policeman, on the other hand, generally has less formal education, less legal training, and a sense of belonging to a different sort of organization. Such differences in background go far to explain the development of the policeman's conception of self as a craftsman, coupled with a guildlike affirmation of worker autonomy. The policeman views himself as a specialist in criminological investigation, and does not react indifferently either to having his conclusions challenged by a distant judiciary or to having "obstacles" placed in his administrative path. He therefore views the judiciary, especially the appellate courts, as saboteurs of his capacity to satisfy what he sees as the requirements of social order. Each appellate decision limiting police initiative comes to be defined as a "handcuffing" of law enforcement, and may unintentionally sever further the policeman's attachment to the rule of law as an overriding value. In addition, the policeman is offended by judicial assumptions running contrary to probabilistic fact—the notion of due process of law staunchly maintains a rebuttable presumption of innocence in the face of the policeman's everyday experience of an administrative presumption of regularity.

Although the prosecutor is legally accorded a wider area of discretion than the policeman, the setting of the policeman's role offers greater opportunity to behave inconsistently with the rule of law. Police discretion is "hidden" insofar as the policeman often makes decisions in direct interaction with the suspect. The prosecutor typically serves at most as advisor to these dealings. Whether it is a question of writing out a traffic citation, of arresting a spouse on a charge of "assault with a deadly weapon," or of apprehending an addict informer, the policeman has enormous power; he may halt the legal process right there. Such discretionary activity is difficult to observe. By contrast, prosecutorial discretion frequently takes place at a later stage in the system, after the initial charge has been made public. The public character of the charge may restrict the prosecutor's discretion in practice more than the policeman's, even though the scope of the prosecutor's discretion is far wider in theory.

Internal controls over policeman reinforce the importance of administrative and craft values over civil libertarian values. These controls are more likely to emphasize efficiency as a goal rather than legality, or, more precisely, legality as a means to the end of efficiency. Two analyses were made along these lines. One was of the clearance rate as an internal control process. Here it was suggested that the policeman operates according to his most concrete and specific understanding of the control system, and that the clearance rate control system emphasizes measures stressing the detective's ability to "solve" crimes. It was further shown how it is possible for this control system to reverse the penalty structure associated with substantive criminal law by rewarding those evidencing a high degree of criminality. Thus, persons with greater criminal experience are frequently better "equipped" to contribute to the "solution" of crimes, thereby enhancing the policeman's appearance as a competent craftsman. The introduction of this control system into police work was analyzed to illustrate a response to the difficulties experienced by organizations that produce a fundamentally intangible service, or at least where "output" is subject to a variety of interpretations. Such an organization requires internal measures of the competence of employees, plus a set of measures (which may be the same) for assessment by outside evaluators.

The dilemma of democratic society requiring the police to maintain order and at the same time to be accountable to the rule of law is thus further complicated. Not only is the rule of law often incompatible with the maintenance of order but the principles by which police are governed by the rule of law in a democratic society may be antagonistic to the ideology of worker initiative associated with a nontotalitarian philosophy of work. In the same society, the ideal of legality rejects discretionary innovation by police, while the ideal of worker freedom and autonomy encourages such initiative. Bureaucratic rules are seen in a democracy as "enabling" regulations, while the regulations deriving from the rule of law are intended to constrain the conduct of officials.

The conflict between the democratic ideology of work and the legal philosophy of a democracy brings into focus the essential problem of the role of the police. The police are not simply "bad guys" or "good guys," authoritarians or heroes. Nor are they merely "men doing their jobs." They are legal officials whose tendencies to be arbitrary have roots in a conception of the freedom of the worker inhering in the nontotalitarian ideology of the relation between work and authority, a conception carried out in the context of police work. Seeing themselves as craftsmen, the police tend to conduct themselves according to the norms pertaining to a working bureaucracy in democratic society. Therefore, the more police tend to regard themselves as "workers" or "craftsmen," the more they demand a lack of constraint upon initiative. By contrast, *legal actors* are sympathetic toward the necessity for constraint and review.

PROFESSIONALISM AND POLICE CONDUCT

The idea of professionalism is often invoked as the solution to the conflict between the policeman's task of maintaining order and his accountability to the rule of law. The meaning of this idea, however, is by no means clear. In sociology, there have been two main traditions, one emphasizing professional ideals and values, the other stressing technical competence. In Durkheim's view, what is distinctive about the idea of "professional" groups is not merely that such groups have high status, or high skill, or a politically supported monopoly over certain kinds of work, or a distinctive structure of control over work—most important is an infusion of work and collective organization with moral values, plus the use of sanctions to insure that these moral values are upheld. Arguing against the laissez-faire doctrines of the classical economists, for example, Durkheim pleaded for the introduction of morality into economic life:

> When we wish to see guilds reorganized on a pattern we will presently try to define, it is not simply to have new codes superimposed on those existing; it is mainly so that economic activity should be permeated by ideas and needs other than individual ideas and needs . . .with the aim that the professions should become so many moral *milieu* and that these (comprising always the various organs of industrial and commercial life) should constantly foster the morality of the professions. As to the rules, although necessary and inevitable, they are but the outward expression of these fundamental principles. It is not a matter of coordinating any changes outwardly and mechanically, but of bringing men's minds into mutual understanding.[6]

An alternative concept of "professionalism" is associated with a managerial view emphasizing rationality, efficiency, and universalism. This view envisages the professional as a bureaucrat, almost as a machine calculating alternative courses of action by a stated program of rules, and possessing the technical ability to carry out decisions irrespective of personal feelings. As Weber says:

> Above all, bureaucratization offers the optimal possibility for the realization of the principle of division of labor in administration according to purely technical considerations, allocating individual tasks to functionaries who are trained as specialists and who continuously add to their experience by constant practice. "Professional" execution in this case means primarily execution "without regard to person" in accordance with calculable rules.[7]

In the effort to introduce fairness, calculability, and impersonality into an American administration of criminal justice that was often riddled with corruption and political favoritism, most writers who have seriously examined police have also tended to subscribe to reforms based upon the managerial conception of "professional." Reviewing the works of such police reformers as O. W. Wilson or William Parker, we find that the conception of "professional" emphasizes managerial efficiency based upon a body of "expert" knowledge. A recently completed volume by law professor Wayne LaFave contains a similar point of view. In his concluding chapter, LaFave advocates a conception of the police as an administrative agency, with, presumably, the presumptions of regulation associated with such "expertise." He writes:

> The development of police expertness should be encouraged, and its existence should be recognized when appropriate .... There is need, and ample precedent in other fields, for the development of methods of communicating the existence of police expertness to trial or appellate courts which are called upon to decide arrest issues. The relationship between the court and the economic regulatory agency might serve as a model in the absence of a more highly developed proposal.[8]

There are, however, costs in developing a professional code based upon the model of administrative efficiency. Such a conception of professionalism not only fails to bridge the gap between the maintenance of order and the rule of law; in addition it comes to serve as an ideology undermining the capacity of police to be accountable to the rule of law. The idea of organization based on principles of administrative efficiency is often misunderstood by officials who are themselves responsible for administering such organizations. In practice, standardized rules and procedures are frequently molded to facilitate the tasks of acting officials. The materials of this study have clearly demonstrated that the policeman is an especially "nonmechanical" offical. As Bruce Smith says:

> The policeman's art ... consists in applying and enforcing a multitude of laws and ordinances in such degree or proportion and in such manner that the greatest degree of protection will be secured. The degree of enforcement and the method of application will vary with each neighborhood and community. There are no set rules, nor even general principles, to the policy to be applied. Each policeman must, in a sense, determine the standard to be set in the area for which he is responsible. Immediate superiors may be able to impress upon him some of the lessons of experience, but for the most part such experience must be his own. ... Thus he is a policy-forming police administrator in miniature, who operates beyond the scope of the usual devices for control. ... [9]

Smith may be making his point too strongly. Nevertheless, as a system or organization, bureaucracy can hope to achieve efficiency only by allowing officials to initiate their own means for solving specific problems that interfere with their capacity to achieve productive results. Some of these procedures may arise out of personal feelings—for example, relations between police and traffic violators—while others may become a routine part of the organizational structure. Examination of a procedural code, for example, would disclose no reference to the systematic use of informants. Given the task of enforcing crimes without citizen complainants, however, it becomes necessary for police to develop alternative methods to those used to apprehend violators in "standard" or "victimizing" crimes. These techniques of apprehension may demand considerable organization and skill on the part of the individual official, skill not so much in a formal administrative sense as in the sense of knowledge and ability to work within the effective limits of formal organization. As described, for example, the informer system requires so much ability that an aesthetic of execution has come to be associated with its use; it has become such an intrinsic component of police work that the abilities of the "professional" detective have come to be defined in terms of capacity to utilize this system.

As a bureaucratic organization, however, the police and governmental institutions, increasingly and generally, have a distinctive relationship to the development of the rule of law. The rule of law develops in response to the innovations introduced by officials to achieve organizational goals. It is certainly true, as Bendix asserts, that "A belief in legality means first and foremost that certain formal procedures must be obeyed if the enactment or execution of a law is to be considered legal."[10] At the same time, while legality may be seen as comprising a set of unchanging ideals, it may also be seen as a working normative system which develops in response to official conduct. The structure of authoritative regulations is such that legal superiors are not part of the same organization as officials and are expected to be "insensitive" to "productive capacity" as contrasted with legality. Thus, for example, a body of case law has been emerging that attempts to define the conditions and limits of the use of informants. Legality, therefore, develops as the other side of the coin of official innovation. As such, it is both a variable and an achievement. To the extent that police organizations operate mainly on grounds of administrative efficiency, the development of the rule of law is frustrated. Therefore, a conception of professionalism based mainly on satisfying the demands of administrative efficiency also hampers the capacity of the rule of law to develop.

The police are increasingly articulating a conception of professionalism based on narrow view of managerial efficiency and organizational interest. A sociologist is not surprised at such a development. Under the rule of law it is not up to the agency of enforcement to generate the limitations governing its actions, and bureaucrats typically and understandably try to conceal the knowledge of their operations so that they may regulate themselves unless they are forced to make disclosures. But the police in a democracy are not merely bureaucrats. They are also, or can be conceived of as, legal officials, that is, men belonging to an institution charged with strengthening the rule of law in society. If professionalism is ever to resolve some of the strains between order and legality, it must be a professionalism based upon a deeper set of values than currently prevails in police literature and the "professional" police department studied, whose operations are ordered on this literature.

The needed philosophy of professionalism must rest on a set of values conveying the idea that the police are as much an institution dedicated to the achievement of legality in society as they are an official social organization designed to control misconduct through the invocation of punitive sanctions. The problem of police in a democratic society is not merely a matter of obtaining newer police cars, a higher order technical equipment or of recruiting men who have to their credit more years of education. What must occur is a significant alteration in the ideology of police, so that police "professionalization" rests on the values of a democratic legal order, rather than on technological proficiency.

No thoughtful person can believe that such a transformation is easily achieved. In an article estimating the prospects for the rule of law in the Soviet Union, Leonard Schapiro has written, "It is perhaps difficult for dictators to get accustomed to the idea that the main purpose of law is, in fact, to make their task more difficult."[11] It is also hard for police officials in a democracy to accept this idea. In the same article, Schapiro reports the case of two professors who were criticized for urging the desirability of adopting certain principles of bourgeois law and criminal procedure, arguing that observance of legal norms must prevail over expediency in government legislation and administration. They were officially criticized for incorrectly understanding "the role of legal science in the solution of the practical tasks of government,"[12] a criticism not too different from the sort often leveled by "professional" police administrators in the United States against those who, for example, insist that the police must act legally for their evidence against the accused to be admitted. The argument is always essentially the same: that the efficient administration of criminal law will be hampered by the adoption of procedures designed to protect individual liberties. The police administrators on the whole are correct. They have been given wide and direct responsibility for the existence of crime in the community, and it is intrinsically difficult for them to accustom themselves to the basic idea of the rule of law: "that the main purpose of law is, in fact, to make their task more difficult."

THE COMMUNITY AND POLICE CONDUCT

If the police are ever to develop a conception of *legal* as opposed to *managerial* professionalism, they will do so only if the surrounding community demands compliance with the rule of law by rewarding police for such compliance, instead of looking to the police as an institution solely responsible for controlling criminality. In practice, however, the reverse has been true. The police function in a milieu tending to support, normatively and substantively, the idea of administrative efficiency that has become the hallmark of police professionalism. Legality, as expressed by both the criminal courts community with which the police have direct contact, and the political community responsible for the working conditions and prerogatives of police, is a weak ideal. This concluding section will attempt to locate the main sources of support for the managerial concept of police professionalism.

A posthumously published article by Professor Edmond Cahn distinguishes between "the imperial or official perspective" on law and "the consumer perspective."[13] The official perspective, according to the author, is so called "because it has been largely determined by the dominant interests of rulers, governors, and other officials.[14] In contrast, the "consumer" perspective reflects the interest and opinion of those on the receiving end of law. In the "consumer" view, therefore, constraints on the decision-making powers of officials are given more importance than the requirements of the processing system and those who carry out its administration. Cahn adds, in addition, that "A free and open society calls on its official processors to perform their functions according to the perspective of consumers."[15] At the same time that he argues against it, however, Cahn demonstrates in his own article the empirical strength of the presumption of correctness in official conduct. So in large part do the materials in this study.

The "official perspective" is most persuasive because it operates as the "established" mode of law enforcement, in the broadest sense of that term. The administration of criminal justice has become a major industry in modern urban society. FBI data show that during 1963 there were 4,437,786 arrests reported by 3,988 police agencies covering areas totaling 127 million in population. In California alone during 1963 there were 98,535 adult felony arrests and 595,992 adult misdemeanor arrests. There were in addition 244,312 arrests of juveniles.[16] During 1962 to 1963, the District Attorney of Los Angeles County had a staff of 546 (with 180 lawyers) and a budget of just over $4,800,000.[17]

Under these circumstances of mass administration of criminal justice, presumptions necessarily run to regularity and administrative efficiency. The negation of the presumption of innocence permeates the entire system of justice without trial. All involved in the system, the defense attorneys and judges, as well as the prosecutors and policemen, operate according to a working presumption of the guilt of persons accused of crime. As accused after accused is processed through the system, participants are prone to develop a routinized callousness, akin to the absence of emotional involvement characterizing the physician's attitude toward illness and disease. That the accused is entitled to counsel is an accepted part of the system, but this guarantee implies no specific affirmation of "adversariness" in an interactional sense. Indeed, the most respected attorneys, prosecuting and defense alike, are those who can "reasonably" see eye-to-eye in a system where most defendants are guilty of some crime.

The overwhelming presence of the "official" system of justice without trial provides normative support for the policeman's own attachment to principles of administrative regularity in opposition to due process of law. Under such circumstances, it should not be surprising to find the policeman adopting the "official" perspective too, since his role is to make the initial decision as to whether a charge has been warranted. Having made the charge, he of all people can hardly be expected to presume the innocence of the defendant. He has, in practice, listened to the defendant's story and assured himself of the latter's culpability. In his own mind, there are numerous guilty parties whom he has not arrested because he does not feel their cases will hold up in court, even though he is personally convinced of their guilt to a moral certainty. Police may feel most strongly about the "irrationality" of due process, but in fact other role players in the system of criminal justice may also be observed to be more concerned with efficiency than legality. If the policeman is the strongest advocate of a "rational bureaucratic" system emphasizing factual over legal guilt, he may well be simply because it is the definition of his ability as a worker that is most affected by the application of the rule of law.

An "order" perspective based upon managerial efficiency also tends to be supported by the civic community. The so-called power structure of the community, for example, often stresses to the police the importance of "keeping the streets clear of crime." The La Loma County Grand Jury, composed of "prominent" citizens—mainly businessmen and bankers—typically expresses concern not over violations of due process of law, but over a seemingly ever-rising crime rate and the inability of police to cope with it. Similarly, the Westville Courier, the city's only newspaper, makes much of crime news, exaggerating criminality and deploring its existence. The police, quite sensitive to press criticism, find little support for the rule of law from that quarter. Indeed, when a newspaper runs an editorial, or a political figure emphasizes the importance of "making the streets safe for decent people," the statements are rarely qualified to warn law enforcement officials that they should proceed according to the rule of law. On the contrary, such injunctions are typically phrased as calls for zealous law enforcement or strict law enforcement. James Q. Wilson has described this as the "problem of the crusade." As he says:

> Even if the force has but one set of consistent ends specified for it by the commissioner or superintendent, and even if adherence to those ends is enforced as far as possible, it is almost inevitable that there will come a time when the commissioner will decide that something must be done "at all costs"—that some civic goal justifies any police means. This might be the case when a commissioner is hard pressed by the newspapers to solve some particularly heinous crime (say, the rape and murder of a little girl). A "crusade" is launched. Policemen who have been trained to act in accord with one set of rules ("Use no violence," "Respect civil liberties," "Avoid becoming involved with criminal informants.") are suddenly told to act in accord with another rule—"catch the murderer"—no matter what it costs in terms of the normal rules.[18]

The emphasis on the maintenance of order is also typically expressed by the political community controlling the significant rewards for the police—money, promotions, vacations. Mayors, city councilmen, city managers draw up police budgets, hire and fire chiefs of police, and call for "shake-ups" within the department. Even the so-called "liberal" politician is inclined to urge police to disregard the rule of law when he perceives circumstances as exceedingly threatening. Thus, Wilson adds:

> When Fiorello La Guardia became mayor of New York City he is said to have instructed his police force to adopt a "muss 'em up" policy toward racketeers, to the considerable consternation of groups interested in protecting civil liberties. The effort to instill one set of procedural rules in

the force was at cross-purposes with the effort to attain a certain substantive end.[19]

In contrast to that of political authority, the power of appellate courts over the police is limited. In practice, the greatest authority of judges is to deny the merit of the prosecution. Thus, by comparison to the direct sanctions held by political authority, the judiciary has highly restricted *power* to modify police behavior. Not only do appellate courts lack direct sanctions over the police but there are also powerful political forces that, by their open opposition to the judiciary, suggest an alternative frame of reference to the police. By this time, however, the police have themselves become so much a part of this same frame of reference that it is often difficult to determine whether it is the political figure who urges "stricter law enforcement" on the policeman, or the law enforcement spokesman who urges the press and the politician to support his demands against laws "coddling criminals," by which he typically means rulings of appellate courts upholding constitutional guarantees, usually under the Fourth, Fifth, Sixth, and Fourteenth Amendments. Whether the policeman is the "man in the middle," as Wilson portrays him, and as police prefer to present themselves, or whether police have by this time come to be the tail wagging the press and the politician, is the subject for another study. Beyond doubt, however, there are enough forces within the community, perhaps by now including the police themselves, to provide the working policeman with a normative framework praising managerial efficiency and opposing due process of law.

CONCLUSION

This chapter has indicated, how the police respond to the pressures of the dilemma of having two sets of ideals thrust upon them. As workers in a democratic society, the police seek the opportunity to introduce the means necessary to carry out "production demands." The means used to achieve these ends, however, may frequently conflict with the conduct required of them as legal actors. In response to this dilemma, police "experts" have increasingly adopted a philosophy of professionalism based upon managerial efficiency, with the implied hope that advancing technology will somehow resolve their dilemma. As indicated, it has not, and by its very assumptions cannot. First of all, in those areas where violations of the rule of law occur, advanced technology often results in greater violation. Technological advances in the form of wiretaps, polygraphs, stronger binoculars, and so forth only make the police more competent to interfere with individual liberty. Secondly, the model of efficiency based on bureaucracy simply does not work out in practice. Warren Bennis has catalogued the limitations of bureaucracy in general, and such limits are certainly applicable to large urban police forces. The following is a sample:

1. Bureaucracy does not adequately allow for personal growth and development of mature personalities.

2. It develops conformity and "group-think."
3. It does not take into account the "informal organization" and the emergent and unanticipated problems.
4. Its systems of control and authority are hopelessly outdated.
5. It has no adequate juridical process.
6. It does not possess adequate means for resolving differences and conflicts between ranks, and most particularly, between functional groups.
7. Communication (and innovative ideas) are thwarted or distorted due to hierarchical division.[20]

The working policeman is well aware of the limitations of "scientific" advances in police work and organization. He realizes that this work consists mostly of dealing with human beings, and that these skills are his main achievement. The strictures of the rule of law often clash with the policeman's ability to carry out this sort of work, but he is satisfied to have the argument presented in terms of technological achievement rather than human interaction, since he rightly fears that the public "will not understand" the human devices he uses, such as paying off informers, allowing "fences" to operate, and reducing charges, to achieve the enforcement ends demanded of him.

Police are generally under no illusions about the capacity of elected officials and the general public to make contradictory demands upon them. A certain amount of lip-service may be paid to the need for lawful enforcement of substantive criminal law, but the police are rarely, if ever, rewarded for complying with or expanding the area of due process of law. On the contrary, they are rewarded primarily for apprehension of so-called "notorious" criminals, for breaking "dope-rings," and the like. As a matter of fact, police are often much more sophisticated about their practices than the politicians who reward them. Police, for example, generally recognize the complexities of the meaning of such a term as "hardened criminal" and of the difficulties involved in carrying out a system of enforcement in line with the strictures of due process of law. The working detective who has used an informant for years, who has developed a relationship with the man in which each can depend on the word of the other, is not taken in by newspaper exaggerations of the man's "criminal" character.

Finally, the dilemma can never be resolved since it contains a built-in dialectic. Appellate decisions upholding the integrity procedural requirements may well move large segments of the community to a greater concern for the security of the substantive ends of criminal law. Especially when the police are burdened with the responsibility of enforcing unenforceable laws, thereby raising the spectre of a "crime-ridden" community,[21] decisions that specifically protect individual liberty may increase the pressure from an anxious community to soften these, and thus contain the seeds of a more "order-oriented" redefinition of procedural requirements. Over the past twenty years, courts have been increasingly indulgent of the rights of the accused. Whether this trend will continue, or whether the courts will redefine "due process of law" to offer legitimacy to what is presently considered unlawful official behavior may well be contingent upon the disposition of the civic community.

If this analysis is correct in placing ultimate responsibility for the quality of "law and order" in American society upon the citizenry, then the prospects for the infusion of the rule of law into the police institution may be bleak indeed. As an institution dependent on rewards from the civic community, police can hardly be expected to be much better or worse than the political context in which they operate. When the political community is itself corrupt, the police will also be corrupt. If the popular notion of justice reaches no greater sophistication than that "the guilty should not go free," then the police will respond to this conception of justice. When prominent members of the community become far more aroused over an apparent rise in criminality than over the fact that Negroes are frequently subjected to unwarranted police interrogation, detention, and invasions of privacy, the police will continue to engage in such practices. Without widespread support for the rule of law, it is hardly to be expected that the courts will be able to continue advancing individual rights, or that the police will themselves develop a professional orientation as *legal* actors, rather than as efficient administrators of criminal law.

NOTES

1. Reinhard Bendix, *Nation-Building and Citizenship* (New York: John Wiley & Sons, 1964), p. 112.

2. *See* his *Work and Authority in Industry* (New York: Harper Torchbook, 1963); and *Nation-Building and Citizenship* (New York: John Wiley & Sons, 1964).

3. *Work and Authority*, p. 446.

4. Ibid., p. 445.

5. There is, perhaps, some ambiguity in this posing of the situation of the worker in totalitarian society. Police in a totalitarian society may have the opportunity to exercise a great deal of "initiative." *See* Simon Wolin and Robert M. Slusser eds., *The Soviet Secret Police* (New York: Frederick A. Praeger, Inc., 1957), *passim;* and Jacques Delarue, *The Gestapo,* trans. Mervyn Sevill (New York: William Morrow Co., Inc., 1964), *passim.*

6. Emile Durkheim, *Professional Ethics and Civic Morals* trans. Cornelia Brookfield (Glencoe: The Free Press, 1958), p. 29.

7. *Max Weber on Law in Economy and Society* ed. Max Rheinstein, trans. Max Rheinstein and Edward Shils (Cambridge: Harvard University Press, 1954), p. 350.

8. Wayne R. LaFave, *Arrest: The Decision to Take a Suspect into Custody* (Boston: Little, Brown and Company, 1965), pp. 512-13.

9. Bruce Smith, *Police Systems in the United States* (New York: Harper & Row, Publishers, 1960), p. 19.

10. Bendix, op. cit., p. 112.

11. Leonard Schapiro, "Prospects for the Rule of Law," *Problems of Communism* 14 (March-April 1965): 2.

12. Ibid., p. 7.

13. "Law in the Consumer Perspective," *University of Pennsylvania Law Review* 112 (November 1963): 1-21.

14. Ibid., p. 4.

15. Ibid., p. 9.

16. Edward L. Barrett, "Criminal Justice and the Problem of Mass Production," in Harry W. Jones (ed.), *The Courts and the Public, and the Law Explosion* (Englewood Cliffs, N.J.: Prentice-Hall, Inc., 1965), p. 95.

17. Ibid., p. 98.

18. James Q. Wilson, "The Police and Their Problems: A Theory," *Public Policy* 12 (1963): 199.

19. Ibid.

20. Warren Bennis, "Beyond Bureaucracy." *Trans-action* 2 (July-August 1965): 32.
21. Police statistics also contribute to this perception. *See* Gilbert Geis, "Statistics Concerning Race and Crime," *Crime and Delinquency* (April 1965), p. 142-50.

The Police: A Mission and Role

A. C. Germann

The word "police" is currently used to identify that institution of social control which, for the community, attempts to prevent crime and disorder and preserve the peace, and which, for the individual, attempts to protect life, property, and personal liberty. The police mission is thus simply stated.

Historically, policing as we know it today has relatively recent origins. Prior to the nineteenth century, protection and service was largely random and unorganized, operating through the watch and ward, the merchant police, the parish police, and the intermittent efforts of private citizens and community organizations. Some parallels can be seen today in terms of diversity and lack of coordination. The criminal law was highly punitive and greatly disregarded due to the conditions of the day. (Much like the current scene.) With the advent of the Peelian reforms, the criminal law was simplified and clarified, and the responsibility for policing was assumed by the state which consolidated, centralized, and coordinated the police function. These reforms, occurring in England, around 1829, set the mold for modern policing as we know it today.

The "role" of the police has never been clearly delineated and accepted by vocation, and has varied from time to time and from place to place. Many persons have a narrow view of the police role and identify it with the limited function of crime repression and suppression—the mechanical treadmill of investigation, identification, apprehension, and prosecution. Other persons, through the years, have insisted that more is involved, such as crime prevention activities, and the provision of social services.

Crime prevention, a function that involves all attempts to keep crime from happening, is not a new idea in the police field. A general order issued to the new police of London, England, in 1829, by Commissioner Charles Rowan, stated:

Dr. A. C. Germann is Professor of Criminology at California State College, Long Beach.
From Dr. A. C. Germann, "The Police: A Mission and Role," *The Police Chief* 37, no. 1 (August 1968): 16-19. Reprinted by permission of the author and the publisher.

It should be understood, at the outset, that the principal object to be obtained is the prevention of crime. To this great end, every effort of the police is to be directed. The security of person and property, the preservation of the public tranquility and all other objects of a police establishment would thus be better effected than by the detention and punishment of the offender after he has succeeded in committing the crime.

Some people, even today, see the police with a limited perspective, that of "catching crooks," and are unable to identify with any police activities of an educational, counseling, communications, and service nature. David Bordua states that "police have come to be identified almost entirely with the coercive function of the state."[1] (A study of the fashion in which we measure the accomplishments of an officer or a department would find majority stress on arrests and coercive activities as measurement criteria.)

Social services, by the police, are, likewise, not new ideas in the police field. In 1928, we read:

> ....most of the work of a patrolman should be done quietly, with the social service point of view always in mind, under circumstances which make mere size and brawn count for little .... Both personnel and police administrators have made little attempt to secure as members of the police force men and women with a social attitude and training in social service work; in fact, they have all too often opposed the appointment of the police officers with such an attitude and background.[2]

In 1931, August Vollmer, revered mentor of American policing, said that "The policeman is no longer merely the suppressor of crime, but the social worker of the community as well."[3]

THE CURRENT SCENE

As we look about us, we see a variety of repressive and coercive police activities, all over the nation, but only an unrepresentative smattering of crime prevention and social services—and these only to a very limited degree. Common observation indicates that not only are we not stressing crime prevention and social services, but we seem to be moving in the direction of paramilitary and political police, expanding the repressive and coercive role of police.

From coast to coast, police and sheriff departments have initiated radical changes in programs and equipment as they prepare themselves for riots or guerrilla warfare. This has been done with very little questioning of the property of American police to assume duties and functions which traditionally have been the responsibility of the National Guard or Regular Military Forces of the nation. As a matter of fact, it would seem that the American policeman welcomes the role of "soldier" and some police leaders have used that exact word in describing current police role.

The Newark, New Jersey, Ledger, of August 9, 1967, reported some $331,000 budgeted by the city for riot equipment including AR-15 rifles, barbed wire, armored cars, and high intensity lights to blind snipers. The *Los*

Angeles Times, February 15, 1968, reported a secret police program to put down riots which included riflemen with telescopic sights, a "general staff" plan similar to the military commands, black cloth covers for "their glistening white helmets," fibre shields "similar in appearance to those carried by Crusaders," and the budgeting of two armored cars.

Dean Richard A. Myren, School of Criminal Justice, State University of New York at Albany, submitted a paper on "The Role of the Police" to the president's Commission on Law Enforcement and Administration of Justice. In that paper, speaking of functions that are regularly assigned to police agencies, he said:

> Although they do have an important role to play in civil defense in case of invasion, police do not have authority nor responsibility for maintaining tank, paratroop, and similar military units as do the para-military police organizations of other countries. Police in the United States are also not lawfully assigned the role of controlling and suppressing political opposition to the party in power, although there have been instances, at particular times and places, when they have seemingly assumed or been assigned this role illicitly.

W. H. Ferry, long associated with the Center for the Study of Democratic Institutions, Santa Barbara, this month drew analogies with Hitler's Germany and suggested that a police state now exists in the United States with respect to our black ghettoes, and exists with the backing of white America. He spoke of "sati-pression"—the repression of the dissatisfied by the satisfied—and said:

> Whitetown easily tolerates practices in blacktown that it would not stand for in its own neighborhoods. The good Germans, when they were willing to pay any attention, easily tolerated the frightful tactics of their police in dealing with Communists and Jews. They did not—most of them, anyway—think that they were living in a police state. They thought they were sanctioning only those laws and practices needed to preserve order and keep the nation secure against its enemies. Since these laws and practices took effect only in distant ghettoes and against strange, despicable people, how could Germans consider them anything but the most reasonable preservations of law and order?[4]

Whether or not we stress the roles of repression and coercion, or crime prevention, or social service, or paramilitary operations, or political police, depends, not only on the education, motivation, and perspectives of the police vocation, but on the voice and heart of the American Community.

Changes in our society have become imperative—but vitally necessary changes—available low cost housing, increased employment opportunity, crash programs in education, humanization of the criminal justice system—have received but token attention. Many people who will not support open housing, curbs on job discrimination, money for schools, or reform in criminal justice, react very predictably when ill-advised action programs seek to achieve change by use of violence—they immediately excoriate communists, criminals, and outside agitators and call for strong repression and heavy sanctions. If the majority community is more interested in order than liberty, more interested in property than human beings, more interested in community security than personal freedom, more interested in entertainment than in injustices, that community surely is inviting the police state. Its police may form an accurate barometer of community values; its police may precisely mirror the attitudes of the majority. And any police agency that accepts the task of "community bully," even if tacitly agreed to by community silence, and regularly bugs the living hell out of its minority groups, peace groups, hippie groups, youth groups—unpopular groups—will sooner or later have "a lot of chickens coming home to roost," and be forced to increase repression and coercion. Anyone who would seek to blame the American police service for current orientation and attitudes would be well advised to study the majority community in terms of orientations and attitudes.

Some communities seem to desire their police "to make people good," a very commendable goal, but not the proper function of police. Some communities seem to want their police to protect the community from the nonconformist, from the questioner of the status quo—and such a desire, in these days of social protest, may be most unreasonable.

It would seem dangerous to our national future if the American police function can be perverted into a political tool to coerce virtue or suppress dissent. I, for one, hope that such will not be the developing role of our police—but I am very frightened by what I observe these days.

THE FUTURE SCENE

The police services of America exist largely as they have always been. Change is dilatory, minimal, and grudging. Recommendations for change have come from private, academic, and governmental sources—and have been repeated and reiterated and recalled and restated and presented in a variey of forms for many years but always with the same predictable outcome: negligible change. Whether we recommend higher educational qualifications, new position classifications, lateral entrance, more rapid promotion of the qualified, revision of training emphases, changes of field practices, modification of civil service rigidities, complaint review procedures, community relations programs, public participation in decision making—or whatever—we find interest only in those projects which make the current ineffective police operation more efficient. Thus, our police continually become more efficient in doing the same old ineffective operations. Nowhere is there indication of radical, revolutionary, massive change of attitude, role, and methods. Slavishness to custom and tradition and precedent make one police agency, in essence, indistinguishable form any other. And this environment has produced a police officer who is so locked in the system, so brain-washed, so determined in his mental sets, so predictable in his attitudes and behavior, that, with but few exceptions, one police officer is indistinguishable from any other.

I have observed the police scene for 20 years and I am not as totally cynical and pessimistic as I may sound to you. I have many friends in the police service, from coast to coast—and many enemies. (The friends, you might well assume, are those progressive and enlightened people whose biases agree with my biases; the enemies, naturally, are those neanderthal and rigid people whose biases differ from my biases). Let me tell you what I see—in the future.

As I look ahead, and see the current tunnel-visioned, myopic, narrow police leadership retired (or replaced) and imaginative, creative, innovative people taking the helm (and this may mean going outside of the vocation if police leadership continues to be a mirror-image perpetuation of prior leadership)—I see the police establishment changing dramatically:

I see police headquarters operated much like a large County hospital (and its peripheral clinics) with many different types of personnel—professional, subprofessional, technical, mechanical, clerical, maintenance, volunteer, student, resident, intern, specialist, and the like, and an end to the silly "sworn/civilian" dichotomy we now live with. I see the agency engaging in services to the public, in research, in education and training, and working closely with the social scientist and the university and college. In other words, I see it "opening up."

I see a change in name for the policeman as he becomes to assume a broader role than that of "crook catcher," and as he changes from a "law and arrest" oriented person to a "people and service" oriented person. Perhaps "human affairs officer," or "public welfare specialist," or "public serviceman," or "human relations officer," or "social psychiatric field worker," will replace the current "patrolman" designation.

I see a change in uniformed appearance of the men in the field. Instead of a frightening, glittering, helmeted, goggled, armed-to-the-teeth apparition, I see a neatly dressed (blazer jacket and slacks?), friendly and accessible partner with the public. Although I do not think it wise to disarm our police, I do think that certain control services—such as sap, sap gloves, iron claw—could be eliminated, and perhaps not all officers need be armed with .357 magnum and hollow point bullets—or the riot gun. If we don't "deescalate," we will soon come to see hand grenades and flame-throwers in the police armamentarium.

I see a change in the Criminal Law with many current "crimes" redesignated as administrative infractions, or as mandatory counseling matters, for non-punitive supervision by psychiatric social worker, psychologist, or psychiatrist. In that light, many traffic functions might move to a separate agency—for certainly we can regard an overtime parking violation as other than a criminal act—a crime to be investigated and handled by the police. Thus may many juvenile functions move to a separate agency—for certainly we can regard a curfew violation as other than a criminal act—a crime to be investigated and handled by the police. Thus may many vice functions move to a separate agency—for certainly we can regard consenting adult homosexuality as other than a criminal act—a crime to be investigated and handled by the police. At any rate, a thoroughgoing reform in Criminal Law will certainly radically alter the role of the police in many areas.

I see change in police education and training. The educational programs will increasingly insist on a board liberal education for criminal justice careers, with accent on the humanities and behavioral sciences, and with lesser accent on the technical, skills oriented subject matters. The colleges and universities, I think, will be less interested in justifying the anachronistic and making it more efficient, and more interested in the kind of research and analysis that will lead to wide-scale innovation and experimentation—much of which will literally wipe out many currently revered police customs and practices.

I see a change in police academy programs so that they will produce a self-directed and autonomous officer, rather than an indoctrinated automation. The police officer spends the great majority of his time in public service activities, and a very small part of his time in "crook catching"; the academies, I hope, will restructure their programs so that the bulk of training is in the community services-human relations area. I see more civilian involvement in academy training, with sociologists, psychologists, anthropologists, social workers, public administrators, and other community oriented people used as instructors and as advisors.

I see many changes in police field practices as objective research critically evaluates what is now done and its overall impact on the total community. There may well be a change of policy for tactical squads, aggressive preventive patrol, intelligence units, use of informers, mass arrests, and the like, if such objective research takes place. I see, ultimately, acceptance of the National Crime Commission firearms use policy—prohibition of any lethal force except in self-defense or the defense of a citizen after all other means have failed—for I think we will come to see that lethal force should not only be legally justified, but socially warranted as well, and in keeping with the ideals of rational and humane social control.

I see, as the educational qualifications for policing increase, some of our brightest and most highly motivated students taking an interest in criminal justice careers. But, unless changes are made in the current authoritarian, anti-intellectual, bureaucratic environments of the police service, I see them becoming frustrated and angry, either leaving for other career opportunities, or staying on at the cost of cynicism, bitterness, disillusionment, and with the feeling that they have sold their souls for security.

I see in the future, high compensation for professional work. I see a change in organizational structure, with far less rigid military overtones, such as "rank," and much more development of professional competence as a measure of merit and worth. I see a change in rigid civil service rules that will permit lateral entrance of a wide variety of personnel, and that will permit very rapid advancement of the qualified.

I see better relationships with the public. I see internal investigations units that are not "the world's best washing machine—everything that goes in dirty comes out clean!"—but truly dedicated to serving the people. I see increased citizen participation in decision making and policy making as the police service decentralizes its operations in order to involve the people in the police function. I see community relations programs that are not public relations programs, not crime prevention programs, not youth programs, but programs designed to involve the total community. I see less efforts to deal only with the responsive and acceptive elements of the community, and more efforts to deal with individuals and groups who are critical of the police, who do not cooperate with the police, and who are unpopular in the community, for that is at the heart of any viable and productive and realistic community relations program.

I see, as time goes by, the possibility of having a wide variety of political, social, religious, economic, and philosophical views represented within the police establishment. The late Chief William H. Parker, Los Angeles, noted that most of the police of America are "conservative, ultra-conservative and very right-wing."[5] I think there is evidence to indicate that the policeman has been, traditionally, authoritarian in attitude, and holding a conservative social philosophy, which has made for automatic conflict in contracts with behavioral scientists, civil libertarians, nonconformists, and humanists.

I see increased commitments to those who lack social position, economic advantage, or political power—the police becoming the "ombudsman" for the weak and exploited. For example, I see new units formed to deal with white collar crime, consumer frauds, and any economic skullduggery. I see new units formed to deal with political graft and corruption. And I see new units formed to assist all social groups and enclaves receive just and fair treatment from private and government institutions.

I see the mission and role of American police developing in spite of the current police leadership—and in spite of the current dedication to the status quo by police unions, associations, fraternal organizations; and so-called professional groups. Either massive change will come from internal generation (I have no great hopes here), or from external pressures (In the next 10-20 years we will have a different public and public representative, or a total police state, I do believe). I wish I could tell you that I think that massive change will be initiated from within the police establishment, but I cannot, for there are far too few people able and willing to take risks, make mistakes, venture into unknown areas, and do battle with the centers of power—which are often the centers of fossilization. I have observed the work and progress of the most praised police institutions—the Los Angeles Police Department, the Federal Bureau of Investigation, the International Association of Chiefs of Police—and I see some very dedicated and professional people, I see marvelous use of science and technology, I see wonderous developments in communications and mechanized records, I see facilities and equipment that are unparalleled in all the world, but no real change of objectives or methods or attitudes, no meaningful responses to the people-centered needs of our cities, no genuine willingness to consider renewal and reform and radically "root out" the ongoing outrages of illegal, irrational, and noncompassionate policing that almost daily blight the American civil landscape.

All that I see will come only over the battered or removed bodies of the current police leadership, for they (understandably) feel very threatened, and are hostile to the idea of change. (I must say that there are some notable exceptions here, and some of the most heartening changes are coming from the leadership in medium and small police agencies.)

I do not expect much development of police mission and role unless or until our police become or are made aware of the social dynamics of the contemporary scene and react sensitively by making massive changes in administration, supervision, and operations. I do not expect much development of police mission and role unless or until policing becomes as committed to social service and due process as it is to crime control and repression, unless or until policing becomes totally respectable, humanized, relevant, and alert to the needs of the day.

I see Command Officers of Police, as potentially obstructive and constructive. For me, the most constructive role you can play in the obviously emerging battle between the neanderthals and the professionals is to take sides—to speak out—to risk your current status and reputation and comfort for the reward of being counted among those brave souls who are so sensitively dedicated to the ideals of a professional service that they will not settle for anything less—today or tomorrow.

Implications of Professionalism in Law Enforcement for Police-Community Relations

Louis A. Radelet

Everybody talks about professionalism in law enforcement, and everybody assumes that everybody means exactly the same thing by it. One of the most important things to know about another person is what he takes for granted—what he assumes—e.g., in a matter like the definition of "professionalism." It strikes me that there is an abundance of talk about professionalism in law enforcement, but a scarcity of talk at the level of defining terms and reaching some measure of consensus regarding what might be called "professional specifications." Indeed, I heard Jim Slavin speak, a few years ago, to the National Institute on Police and Community Relations at Michigan State,

Louis A. Radelet is director of the National Center on Police and Community Relations at Michigan State University.

From Louis A. Radelet, "Implications of Professionalism in Law Enforcement for Police-Community Relations," *Police* 10, no. 6 (July-August 1966): 82-86. Reprinted by permission of the author and the publisher, Charles C Thomas.

and his topic was, *Six Reasons Why American Police Will Never Be Professional.* It was, as I recall, partly a typical Slavin leg pulling job, but he wouldn't admit it if you asked him! I can remember two of the reasons he cited: one was the lack of consensus among police leaders as to the "police product" in a free society; another was the present rigid patterns of structural and functional organization in American law enforcement agencies. It led me to ask myself the question. what is the difference between a *profession* and a *professional*? If medicine is a profession, and a hospital is a place where medicine is practiced, are all the people who work in the hospital professionals? Is it necessary that they be professionals? If not, then who are we talking about?

I think I need not belabor the possible analogy to law enforcement. The point is that these are, it seems to me, examples of good questions to raise—and to discuss—in this matter of professionalism.

As long as this reference to medicine is at hand, we might fiddle with it a bit more. It seems to me that I sense some rather common concern among medical doctors about their "collective image" today, if you will please forgive the Madison Avenue jargon. Evidently, many physicians have been persuaded to woo their client's favor, and there are some references to "your friendly family doctor," and similar nonsense. Now I would maintain that a profession serves needs, not wants. I don't particularly care about being a pal with my doctor, but I do want to respect him for his competence, his skill, and his attitude as a professional. I don't think he should go out of his way to be a pal to me either. When I need his help, I want something more from him than soothing assertions that he'll never let me down.

Returning, then, to the analogy to law enforcement, may I suggest what I regard as the first implication of the professional concept for police-community relations: to woo the client's respect, not his favor—in short, to reassert authority as a necessary corollary to responsibility. I would submit that this principle is at once one of the vital trademarks of a true profession, and a significant implication of it for police-community relations. I am suggesting that so-called "imagery," as applied to the police relationship with the community in a professional sense, can be carried to ridiculous extremes. A police agency can become so preoccupied with the gimmicks of creating a positive image—in effect, of trying to be "pals" with all citizens and groups—that it hasn't time to do "police work." Even though given the most imaginative and effective total program of police-public relations, there can be no rescue from the difficult, the dangerous, and the dirty business of policing in enforcing the law and the protection of rights and property. There is, in short, a provocative distinction between looking good and being good! Surely, therefore, the goal in police-community relations, professionaly defined, is not simply a matter of improved imagery.

Let us return to medicine again. The president of the American Society of Internal Medicine, Doctor Robert E. Westlake, writing recently in the magazine *The Internist,* said this:

In those areas of community life dealing with health, the physician, as an individual, must not take a back seat to anyone. We must excel in the organization of medical care at all levels, as well as in medical care itself ... This means leadership in many aspects of hospital affairs, recently left to administrators; special attention to welfare medical programs, usually left to politicians; and involvement in voluntary health organizations and community health planning, so often left to business leaders ... Finally, only review by practicing physicians of the quality of (medical) care and the use of facilities is effective and acceptable. Professional review committees of physicians are here to stay.

I can sense the undercurrent surge from police executives, almost literally itching to apply to the field of law enforcement what Doctor Westlake has said so well about the medical profession. Of course, my intention in quoting him was to suggest again the possible analogy. But let's not snap too quickly at the bait! Doctor Westlake is talking about a field universally acknowledged to be "a profession." He is talking about the obligations and responsibilities of professionalism. In a field not as yet, by any means, widely recognized as a profession, i.e., law enforcement or policing, there is—I think—a strong tendency to stress the privileges and prerogatives of professionalism, and to speak only very softly about the obligations and responsibilities. I fear that too many police officers today plead emotionally for community support and recognition of their professional aspirations, while yet failing to perceive what this means in the way of responsibility to the community. In effect, what they apparently desire is public support and acclaim, to go on doing the same old police job in the same old way. These are the police officers who resist the idea of training and college education, but want better pay; they do not see why the courts should insist upon *legal* means for conducting interrogations or searches, but they want to be loved by all groups; they resent discussion of licensing or certification for police officers, but they like the pension system; they fly into a rage when the notion of the review board for processing citizen complaints is mentioned, but they stubbornly refuse to study and to evaluate existing machinery for this purpose to determine whether it meets reasonable requirements of justice for all parties; they become exasperated if someone hints that today's society requires that a truly professional police officer be a community leader and social practitioner, but they think the PAL is a perfectly splendid organization; finally, they may become violent if it is recommended that traditional descriptions of proper police function urgently need reassessment, and probable recasting, in the light of today's community conditions, but they will at the same time orate publicly that the real problem in Watts was "people who resist arrest."

I could extend this recitation of fairly obvious inconsistency and ambivalence to much greater length. So could any of you. The fundamental point I am advancing is, of course, that authentic professionalism in policing, as it bears upon community relations, must not be a pattern—as it seems to me it is now, in too many respects—of all "gimme" and no give.

It may be useful to review, briefly, the criteria by which a profession may be recognized. These criteria are pretty well established, and it is not difficult to find them listed in relevant texts. You are familiar with them:

1. A systematic body of knowledge and skills, oriented to intellectual pursuit.
2. More or less well-established principles, methods, theory, etc.
3. A clearly defined purpose (product) of service.
4. An esoteric terminology.
5. Pecuniary profit is not a primary objective.
6. Associations within the field are concerned with standards, accrediation, ethics, a certain self-monitoring element, etc.

The best definition of a professional, in any field, that I have heard is one that takes these various criteria for granted. It *assumes* all these things, but it adds a factor that may well be the most telling characteristic of a professional. The definition was coined by the late Alexander Woolcott, as follows: "A professional is a person who does his best job when he feels worst." In effect, Woolcott is saying that it is *attitude* that makes a professional. Perhaps there is no field of public service where attitude is more important than it is in law enforcement. Insofar as police-community relations are concerned, there is surely no more important implication of the professional concept. Perhaps this point should be further elaborated.

It is hardly news that child psychologists are deeply interested in the development in children of what they call "a positive self-image." Among other personality attributes with which this matter of self-image is related, there is the psychological phenomenon called "prejudice"—and this is a phenomenon that is quite well known in the field of police-community relations. To an important degree, prejudice is a way of trying to deal with a negative picture of one's self. Prejudiced persons are often characterized by what the psychiatrists call a "weak ego." They are fearful of their own impulses: their picture of themselves, which has been reflected back to them by the behavior of others toward them, is an uncomplimentary one, and they are afraid of it. Because they are insecure, they become rigid-minded in an attempt to get some stability and predictability in life. It is difficult for them to adapt and adjust to the forces of change.

But what, you ask, has this to do with professionalism and its implications for police-community relations? A simple way to answer this question is to say that respect for others begins with respect for self. To put it another way, community recognition of the police as professionals begins with the attitude of the individual police officer toward himself. From this point on, the professional concept becomes a means as well as an end. Take a simple example in the matter of police equipment and tools. The first step is for police administrators to convince themselves that a given new or better tool is needed (for professional advancement, the first step is that the police must *want* it—a question of *motivation,* as the psychologists put it). When, and as, the new or better tool is secured (because the police administrator has persuaded the appropriate public representatives that the tool is needed, and they agree to support it), the theory then is that this tool will produce, in some sense, better police work. This "product" is, therefore, communicated and interpreted to the public (community), and on this basis the public is persuaded to support more and better tools, for better police work. Translate this theory into more and better personnel, professionally speaking—elevation in recruitment standards, increased education and training for police, emphatic attention to the *attitudes* of police personnel toward themselves and others with whom they come into contact—add to it a *professional* quality in related police administrative matters such as policy, supervision, line service, planning and research, and indeed in complaint procedure—and we have the essential ingredients of a truly sophisticated, imaginative, effective, productive program in police-community relations. All of it begins with commitment to the professional concept in law enforcement—in large part, a professional *attitude,* a professional way of thinking and acting. Obviously, this implies—for instance in questions of race relations and civil rights that a police officer, as an individual, will have his personal views, opinions, and indeed, prejudices, as all of us do—and to which he is, in a sense, "entitled." But as a police officer, he will be expected to sublimate his personal views, in favor of his responsibilities as a *professional.* As a policeman, it is his *professional* attitude that is important, as he relates to various persons and groups in the community. The acid test will be the extent he is able to keep distinct his personal views and his professional attitude. He will often do his best job when, perchance, he feels worst!

There is, of course, nothing new or revolutionary about these considerations, for seasoned police officials. In our efforts through the years in the National Institute on Police and Community Relations, and now in the National Center, we have incorporated these notions in our basic assumptions with consistency and cardinal emphasis. We have had no monopoly in this, bearing in mind the numerous concrete and tangible evidences of the professional advancement of American law enforcement in recent years, signs with which we are all familiar and they need not be recited here. Indeed, the very encouraging development of police leadership in the field of community relations during the past ten to fifteen years is one of the significant "signs" to which I refer. For example, take a recent statement by San Francisco Police Chief Thomas J. Cahill—and I cite him only as illustrative of the current thinking of many police executives:

> The police administrator must, of necessity today, concern himself more than ever with the factors that bring about bitter cultural conflicts, the results of which must inevitably wind up on his doorstep. Because of this period of rapid sociological change, he must become more concerned with the development of proper human relationships between the police agency and the public. It is not easy being a police officer in a large urban community criss-crossed by cultural conflict, but it is a job that must be done, and done well. The police administrator today must understand that the desired relationship between the police and the public can be obtained only by a deliberate and calculated effort. It cannot be expected to develop by chance or at random, as in the past.

An interesting sidelight on this statement by Chief Cahill is that he admits candidly that he would not have made such a statement five years ago. This in itself is suggestive of a highly desirable quality in the professional police administrator, i.e., a capacity to adjust and to move with flexibility and wisdom *with*, rather than *against*, the tide of social change.

Incidentally, Chief Cahill's position is also in pleasing contrast to the position of the police official (*not* Bill Parker!) who defined the problem in Watts as "people who resist arrest." It might be argued that this is to define the problem "in police terms," and I would agree—the police terms of 25 years ago! It simply will not do for the community that today's police are endeavoring to serve. The relief of problems of slum housing, chronic unemployment, the relocation of urban renewal-affected families, etc., may not, it is true, be "police problems" in a direct and explicit sense, but I see no reason to excuse *professionally* motivated police officials from dedicated service as deeply concerned members of a community team bending to the task of doing something constructive about such problems. Call it *social work*, if you must, but "methinks thou dost protest too much!" Who knows—such work might improve police-community relationships in a profound and meaningful sense: it might help the police acquire the stature of genuine *community leaders*, and even in a negative sense, it might be argued that the police should be involved in efforts to deal with the *causes* of personal and social disorganization, since they must always deal with the tragic *effects*. In our big cities, such police leadership might even engender a sense of *community*, where none now exists. It seems to me that this is exactly what the better programs in police-community relations are currently doing in some of our metropolitan centers. It is the best that we know today in police professionalism, as I see it.

I refered earlier to what I call "imagery" in police-community relations, and I may have left the impression of referring to it disparagingly. What I intended to suggest was, of course, that a program built with "gimmicks," and gimmicks only, will fall flat on its face. One cannot build a successful business simply on the basis of the merchandise on display in the show window. Now permit me to say a good word about imagery. In a sense, the police are a kind of "community parent" for a lot of people. Many citizens turn to the police for help in precisely the way they once turned to parents. Regardless of the problem, they believe the police are well-nigh omnipotent, and hopefully seek help for anything from clogged sink drains to wayward daughters. Actually, the incredible resourcefulness and *Job*-like patience of some officers has made their role as "omnipotent parents" almost believable!

But this is to refer to a general public attitude. *Specific* public attitudes toward the police are more difficult to diagnose. Yet we do know that children learn a little from what they are taught, and a lot from the examples they see. Consequently, as psychologist Claudine Gibson Wirths has well indicated, the actions and attitudes of law enforcement people themselves probably constitute the greatest single cultural influence on public attitudes toward law enforcement. It is law enforcement *officers* who mold public attitudes, for when people think of "the law," they tend to think of the officers they know in their own town, county and state—or the stereotype of police officers which is so profitably cultivated by such media as *Dick Tracy, True Detective, Earle Stanley Gardner, Car 54—Where Are You,* and even *Agent 007.* It gets to the point where real police officers are forced to take up the jargon of their fictional prototypes, or people complain that they don't know their job!

There are some fascinating monographs in recent literature, of the scholarly variety, which deal with certain aspects of the subject we are exploring. For instance, there is Michael Banton of the Department of Social Anthropology at the University of Edinburgh in Scotland. In an article appearing in the April, 1963 issue of *The Police Chief* (and in a book published in 1964, *The Policeman in the Community*), Doctor Banton brilliantly develops his thesis of the policeman as what he terms a "professional citizen," and the idea that professionalism in law enforcement creates a morality of its own. I heartily recommend Banton's work to you. Likewise do I recommend a monograph entitled, *The Police and Their Problems: A Theory,* by James Q. Wilson of the faculty of the Harvard University Graduate School of Public Administration, appearing in the 1963 *Yearbook* of that distinguished school.

I have just recently read an excellent paper on the function of the police in today's democratic society, by Professor John Pfiffner of the University of Southern California, not as yet published. He will forgive me, I am sure, if I reveal that a central question in his study is this: Will the welfare-therapeutic-bureaucratic (his term!) society demand a team approach in which the police role will be but one phase of society's cooperative effort to deal with defective humanity? He tactfully ventures the view that the police subculture of our society still possesses a set of values, standards, and job goals more appropriate to the days of public hangings than to a society which is making some progress toward ameliorating the lot of those who, for one reason or another, have not adjusted to the demands of society. In short, Doctor Pfiffner wonders whether the sacred cows are compatible with the demands of an age in which it may be easier to jump over the moon than we once imagined. Which reminds me, and by way of conclusion, of the following poem, author not known:

>One day through the primeval wood
>A calf walked home as good calves
>   should,
>But made a trail all bent askew
>A crooked trail as all calves do.
>
>Since then three hundred years have
>   fled,
>And I infer the calf is dead
>But still he left behind his trail,
>And thereby hangs my moral tale.

The trail was taken up next day
By a lone dog that passed that way;
And then a wise bellwether sheep
Pursued the trail o'er vale and steep.

And drew the flock behind him too
As good bellwethers always do.
And from that day, o'er hill and glade
Through these old woods a path was
    made.

And many men wound in and out
and dodged and turned and bent
    about.
And uttered words of righteous wrath
Because 'twas such a crooked path.

But still they followed . . . do not
    laugh.
The first migrations of that calf.
This forest path became a lane
That bent and turned and turned
    again.

This crooked lane became a road,
Where many a poor horse with his
    load,
Toiled on beneath the burning sun
And traveled some three miles in one.

And thus a century and a half
They trod the footsteps of that calf.
The years passed on in swiftness fleet,
The road became a village street:

And this, before men were aware,
A City's crowded thoroughfare.
And soon the central street was this
Of a renowned metropolis.

And men two centuries and a half
Trod in the footsteps of that calf—
A hundred thousand men were led
By one calf near three centuries dead.

For men are prone to go it blind
Along the calf-paths of the mind
And work away from sun to sun
To do what other men have done.

They follow in the beaten track
And out and in, and forth and back,
And still their devious course pursue,
To keep the path that others do.

They keep the path a sacred groove
Along which all their lives they move,
But how the wise old wood gods laugh
Who saw the first primeval calf.

SECTION FOUR

Academic Progress In Law Enforcement

Overview

UPGRADING THE SERVICE. Larry D. Soderquist discusses the demands of law enforcement with respect to education. Because of the intricacies of the occupation it is becoming imperative that policemen have considerable educational experience. The article discusses the various tasks that a police officer must perform, and argues for specific types of education necessary to fulfill the policeman position adequately. In addition to educational standards, the author addresses the need for change in entrance requirements, specifically, touching on the existing physical requirements and the rule requiring local residence for a specified period of time prior to employment. He also discusses other topics, such as increased salary, lateral entry, realistic promotional policies, and job security provisions.

LAW ENFORCEMENT TRAINING AND THE COMMUNITY COLLEGE: ALTERNATIVES FOR AFFILIATION. Denny F. Pace, James D. Stinchcomb, and Jimmie C. Styles discuss the police training programs—specifically basic training academies—that are operated jointly with local police agencies and a community college. In California the trend is going in this direction. One exception is an academic affiliation between the Los Angeles Police Department and California State College at Los Angeles, where the Academy recruit has the option concurrently to enroll in a correlated set of courses. The community colleges that offer such programs also grant college credit to officers who have successfully completed out-of-college courses to stimulate the new officers to continue their college education.

LEEP—ITS DEVELOPMENT AND POTENTIAL. William E. Caldwell discusses the historical development of the Office of Law Enforcement Assistance and its successor, the Law Enforcement Assistance Administration, beginning in 1966. Caldwell outlines the many loan grant options available to the student of criminal justice.

FEDERAL AID TO LOCAL POLICE—TRICK OR TREAT? W. Cleon Skousen traces the historical development of federal aid programs, the role of the federal government in education, and gives his views of the problems attendant to such programs. The serious student should explore all sides of this important issue, beginning with Caldwell's and Skousen's articles in this section.

Upgrading the Service

Larry D. Soderquist

Thesis: The police service needs to be upgraded. This upgrading can and should be effectuated by increasing the educational requirements for appointment to the police service.

PRESENT LEVELS

What is the average educational level attained by police officers in the United States? This question must be answered before one can meaningfully discuss the need to raise the minimum educational requirements for appointment to the police service. Unfortunately, there is not a wealth of information on this subject. The only extensive, recent study was done by George W. O'Connor and Nelson A. Watson of the International Association of Chiefs of Police. In connection with this study, they sent 9,884 questionnaires to a fairly representative sample of sworn police personnel in the United States. "Of the 6,200 officers who responded to the educational question on the questionnaire, 76.7 percent indicated they had completed high school, and another 11.4 percent said they had earned an equivalency certificate, while 11.9 percent indicated they had done neither.[1] Only 7.3 percent said they had one or more college degrees (including the two-year Associate degrees), but 30.3 percent

---

Larry D. Soderquist worked as a police officer while earning his bachelor's degree.
From Larry D. Soderquist, "Upgrading the Service," *The Police Chief* 36 no. 8 (August 1969): 53-76. Reprinted by permission of the publisher.

indicated they were attending college.[2] Of those holding college degrees 414 had one degree, 42 had two, one had three, one had four."[3] The educational levels varied greatly by region. The Pacific region had the highest percentage of high school graduates (89.9 percent), and the highest percentage of college degree holders (18.6 percent). New England had the lowest percentage of high school graduates (64.5 percent), and the Middle Atlantic states had the lowest percentage of college degree holders (4.1 percent). Though there was some difference between the percentage of administrators who had one or more college degrees (9.2 percent) and the number of patrolmen who possessed degrees (4.4 percent), there was no significant difference between the percentage of administrators who had graduated from high school (76.5 percent) and the percentage of patrolmen who had done so (74.4 percent).[4]

It is also important to note the almost uniformly low educational requirements that prevail in police departments. Another O'Connor survey, conducted in 1961 showed that 24 percent of the 300 departments surveyed had no minimum educational requirements for appointment, and less than 1 percent required any college education. Over 72 percent of the New England departments surveyed had either no educational requirements, or one which required less than high school.[5] Admittedly, this 24 percent figure has become somewhat out-of-date. We know that some departments which did not previously require a high school diploma for appointment now do so, but one doubts the 1961 figures have changed significantly. It seems only one non-federal law enforcement agency requires a four-year college degree as a prerequisite to appointment. This is the Multnomah County Sheriff's Department in Oregon. As of 1966, only 21 other police departments required some college training before appointment, and 20 of these departments were in California.[6]

NATURE OF THE POLICE TASK

What kind of job are we asking these minimally educated policemen to perform? Unfortunately, a large portion of society views the police function as ministerial. As noted by the President's Commission on Law Enforcement and the Administration of Justice, the public generally assumes "that the police enforce the criminal laws and preserve peace mechanically, by simply arresting anyone who has deviated from legislative norms of acceptable behavior."[7] This is simply not correct. Except for the work of those few police officers who specialize in relatively simple, largely repetitive tasks such as writing parking tickets or directing traffic, the work we expect our police to do is highly discretionary. "First, the police do not have the resources to enforce all criminal provisions equally. Second, the other parts of the criminal justice system simply cannot cope with all law violators."[8] And, third, at least given the way laws are presently written, justice would not be done by the mechanical enforcement of all laws. Many laws, the gambling laws being the most obvious, were not meant to apply to all situations in which they could technically be applied. Finally, justice requires that the police consider the foreseeable consequences of an arrest (for instance, might it precipitate a riot), the degree to which the law was broken (did the violator, for instance, utter one profane word in contravention of a statute, or did he repeatedly shout obscenities in a crowd), whether an arrest is necessary to protect an individual or society from some harm (such as arresting one man on a drunkenness charge if he has no place to go and setting another equally intoxicated man free if he does), whether more harm will come to the victim of a crime if the perpetrator is arrested (for instance, where a husband has slapped his wife and the arrest may cause further domestic problems).

On this point, the President's Commission on Law Enforcement and the Administration of Justice aptly noted:

> In light of these inherent limitations, individual police officers must, of necessity, be given considerable latitude in exercising their arrest power. As a result, no task committed to individual judgment is more complex or delicate. A mistake in judgment can precipitate a riot or culminate in subsequent criminal activity by a person who is erroneously released by an officer. An unjustified arrest can seriously, and perhaps permanently, effect the future course of a man's life. The importance of the arrest power and the need for rational exercise of this power cannot be overstated. [9]

Many Americans also view the police task as one requiring little knowledge or skill. Some even go so far as to say that college educated people should not be accepted for the police service because the task involved is so mundane that the boredom necessarily associated with it would prevent such a person from competently handling the job.[10] Some of the advocates of that policy can hardly be blamed for their misconception as many of them have never seen the police function properly carried out. And, without exposure to a proper functioning department, it is easy for them to assume that the way things are being done is not only the proper way, but perhaps even the only way.

Also, much of America sees its police officers only from a distance or only through the medium of television or the movies. At a distance, one sees only the badge, the gun, and police cars with flashing lights; in the movies and on television, one sees only the "action cops" fighting criminals, shooting criminals, and chasing criminals. As a result, a large portion of American society never sees the "thinking cops" as they try to solve domestic problems, attempt to turn juvenile offenders from delinquency, or decide how best to prevent a small disturbance from becoming a major one.

Some individuals have difficulty understanding that a man can be both a "man of action" and a "man of thought." Applying this idea specifically to the police, Jean-Baptiste Colbert said, in a memorandum to Louis XIV: "Our Lieutenant of Police must be a man of the gown and of the sword; while the doctor's learned ermine floats about his shoulders, the knight's spur must ring upon his heel."[11] Amplifying this same idea, Doctor Ruth Levy said much more recently:

Reviewing the tasks we expect of our law enforcement officers, it is my impression that their complexity is perhaps greater than that of any other profession. On the one hand we expect our law enforcement officer to possess the nurturing, caretaking, sympathetic, empathizing, gentle characteristics of a physician, nurse, teacher, and social worker as he deals with school traffic, acute illness and injury, juvenile delinquency, suicidal threats and gestures, and missing persons. On the other hand we expect him to command respect, demonstrate courage, control hostile impulses, and meet great physical hazards.... He is to control crowds, prevent riots, apprehend criminals, and chase after speeding vehicles. I can think of no other profession which constantly demands such seemingly opposite characteristics.[12]

The above discussion deals only with the reasons for the misconception, without refuting it. The man who most succinctly stated the refuting argument is Quinn Tamm, Executive Director of the International Association of Chiefs of Police, who said:

It is nonsense to state or to assume that the enforcement of the law is so simple that it can be done best by those unencumbered by a study of the liberal arts. A man who goes into our streets in hopes of regulating, directing or controlling human behavior must be armed with more than a gun and the ability to perform mechanical movements in response to a situation. Such men as these engage in the difficult, complex and important business of human behavior. Their intellectual armament—so long restricted to the minimum—must be no less than their physical prowess....[13]

KNOWLEDGE AND SKILL REQUIRED

What specifically is required of the policeman in the way of knowledge and skill? First, he must have a knowledge of the laws he is expected to enforce. Here it must be remembered that "the local officer is ... a law enforcement generalist; he must know federal law, state law, county and municipal law, traffic law, criminal procedures and their applications in his community."[14] A further complication is that the framework of procedural rules within which the police must function is often unclear and difficult to apply. Only years of litigation may resolve ambiguities in procedural rules, but a police officer must make his own resolution instantly, under stress, and often without advice.[15] As any lawyer knows, the substantive criminal law is as complicated and ambiguous as the procedural criminal law. Without above-average intelligence and experience in reading complicated prose the police officer has little hope of understanding the law he is supposed to enforce.

The skeleton which a law is has very little meaning unless considered in light of the legislative policy behind the law. For instance, an officer who does not understand that the gambling laws were meant to discourage or stop "commercialized" gambling and not a "friendly" dollar bet on a baseball game simply cannot do an effective job of law enforcement. An even larger problem is created by the officer who does not understand that it is the policy of the "Law" that particular laws should not be enforced in those circumstances where such enforcement would likely lead to breaches of more important laws. Many officers who lack a knowledge of this legislative policy have touched off riots because they could not see the wisdom in foregoing the making of a minor traffic arrest.

The effective officer must have thorough knowledge of what is now generally called police science or nonsociological criminology. True, the officer does not have to be a fingerprint expert, a photographer, a pathologist or an expert on paint, blood, or poison. In a way, however, his task is more difficult than the fingerprint expert's or the forensic chemist's. He must have enough knowledge about each of these and other scientific or quasi-scientific fields to know when to call on an expert to aid in a criminal investigation. Without this knowledge valuable clues are not recognized, thus leading to the escape of the guilty or the conviction of the innocent.

Anyone who doubts the intellectual difficulty of mastering even limited amounts of knowledge about police science should peruse such books as Gonzales et. al., *Legal Medicine, Pathology and Toxicology* or Svensson and Wendel's *Techniques of Crime Scene Investigation.*

The effective police officer must also be knowledgeable in the field I will call, for want of a better name, practical psychology. Most police functions involve dealings with human beings, and frequently these dealings are in stress situations. The officer does not necessarily have to know Adlerian or Freudian psychology, but he does have to understand what causes thought and behavior in individuals. With such knowledge he is better able to investigate and solve crimes, convince an individual he should or should not follow a particular pattern of behavior, and handle almost any situation with a minimum of conflict with the individuals involved. It is partly because so many police officers presently lack any knowledge of psychology or human relations techniques that so many police-citizen interactions are characterized by physical or verbal conflicts and long lasting animosity.

Especially in heterogeneous urban areas, the officer must understand sociology. As Stanley R. Schrotel, Chief of Police of Cincinnati, Ohio, has said:

> The gregarious nature of man has produced in our country an urban community that has become increasingly more congested, and the social interrelations more complex. These concentrations of humanity are characterized by political and socioeconomic problems of a dimension heretofore unknown. These mixtures of culture, education, skills and status offer unprecedented opportunities for conflict. In this morass, those charged with supervising human behavior and maintaining the peace, must enjoy a competence equal to the task.[16]

There can be little doubt that much of the unrest and many of the disturbances and riots in our ghetto areas are caused to a large extent by the actions of officers who have an almost total lack of knowledge of the particular modes of living, ways of thinking, and institutions characteristic of the racial or ethnic groups with which they deal. For instance:

> Many officers simply fail to understand the effects of their actions because of their limited knowledge of the Negro community. Calling a Negro teenager by his first name may arouse resentment because whites still refuse to extend to adult Negroes the courtesy of a title, "Mister." A patrolman may take the arm of a person he is leading to the patrol car. Negroes are more likely to resent this than whites because the action implies that they are on the verge of flight and may degrade them in the eyes of friends or onlookers.[17]

This particular police inadequacy also almost uniformly manifests itself generally in the way the ghetto is patrolled. For instance, ghetto dwellers often complain that:

> When calls for help are registered, it is all too frequent that police respond too slowly or not at all. ... When they do come, [they] arrive with many more men and cars than are necessary ... brandishing guns and adding to the confusion.[18]

Admittedly, some of this type of behavior is purely spiteful or done purposefully to harass. Most such behavior, however, results from a lack of understanding of the people with whom the police are dealing. As must be expected, a lack of understanding leads to fear, and fear leads to the technique of leaving situations alone as long as possible and then using too much force when action is taken.

Police supervisors and command officers have an even more difficult job, and, as stated above, the level of education among police administrators is universally low, with high school clearly being the norm. Since almost all police administrators are promoted from the ranks, it is logically impossible for them to have much more than the high school level of education which is the norm among lower-level officers. In no other field are persons with such little education asked to perform such a complicated function.

> The job of the chief administrator is a complex task in a world made more complex by the growth of our society. He is required to administrate in the areas of traffic enforcement; radio patrol; investigations; records; communications; personnel; business management; and many other specific functions dependent upon the particular geographic areas, the population and the industry involved. More than ever this requires not only good sound business practices but, more importantly, good administrators to fulfill the objectives of the police organization, no matter how big or how small it may be. Today's chief administrator must be aware of enforcement indexes; crime rates; statistical interpretation; use of storage and retrieval process, where applicable; manpower use; and budgetary analysis if he is to get the job done properly. And he must make his junior executives equally aware of these management tools and their proper use.[19]

It is probably desirable that top police administrators be professional policemen, but their work is much more analogous to that of a business executive than it is to that of a patrolman or detective. In a real sense police departments are "big business," and to function efficiently and effectively the "executives" of this "business" must have the knowledge, skills, and intellectual attributes of their counterparts in private industry. One needs only to look at the size of police budgets—over $360,000,000 in New York and $90,000,000 in Chicago—or at the complex organizational chart of a large police department to get an idea of the magnitude and complexity of the job.[20]

NECESSITY FOR COLLEGE TRAINING

Many individuals and many organizations, such as the International Association of Chiefs of Police and the President's Commission on Law Enforcement and the Administration of Justice, who understand the complexity and difficulty of the police task have come to the conclusion that police personnel must have college training if they are to perform effectively their function. In evaluating this idea one must realize that most young men who have the basic personal characteristics which are necessary for the effective handling of the police task now go to college. "In 1966, 55 percent of all high school graduates enrolled in college and this percentage will continue to increase."[21] And it is predicted that within the next three or four years "some 40 percent of the adult population will have obtained the equivalent of a junior college education."[22] Considering these statistics, and considering the fact that the police task requires men of the intelligence, ambition, and seriousness characteristic of the individual going to college, it seems clear that the police service must either compete with colleges for these desirable individuals or else recruit them after they have gone to college. Even if the first possibility were considered desirable it would be almost impossible since the average college freshman is only 18 years old and most police departments do not now, and perhaps should not in the future, hire men who are under 21 years old. On this point, the experience of the Berkeley, California, Police Department, which in 1960 established a two-year college requirement for appointment, is important to consider. Their Director of Personnel has said: "A significant factor in adopting the two-year college requirement was that persons who had qualified for employment in preceding years, in almost every case, could meet the two-year college minimum requirement."[23]

This, of course, only means that college-trained people should be recruited, but does not prove that college training should be required. There are reasons why there should be such a requirement. Foregoing for the present a discussion of why the college experience itself is valuable and should be made a prerequisite for appointment, there is another reason why the requirement should be established: The college trained man will want to go to a department where his education is taken note of and appreciated, and where he will be working with men with a like background. Also, it seems clear that one of the factors which makes recruitment of college men difficult is the fact that the police service is now regarded as a "low status" position. Simply establishing higher educational minimums for appointment will raise the status of the job and thus aid in recruiting. Here again, the Berkeley experience is relevant. The Personnel Director has said: "I am certain that the establishment of a two-year college requirement has given us a recruiting advantage in continuing to attract highly qualified young men to apply for the Berkeley Police Department."[24]

Amplifying this idea, the Chief of the El Monte, California Police Department has said:

> We have had no problem in recruiting well-qualified personnel. In fact, it has been our experience that our college requirement has aided us in competing with the metropolitan departments of this area such as the Los Angeles Department and the Los Angeles County Sheriff's Office for manpower. Since both of these Departments pay over $50 per month more than we do we decided to seek why applicants who were on our list and at the same time on one or both of the other departments' lists decided to accept employment with us. Almost to a man they stated the reason they chose El Monte was that they felt a department that required college work presented a more professional type police organization and afforded them the opportunity in the long run to be recognized for their individual efforts. [25]

Why is the college experience a necessary prerequisite for effective police work? Since the above-quoted statistics indicate that within a very few years some college training will be the educational norm of the population of the United States, it is necessary that the officers who deal so intimately with the citizenry have comparable background and experience. One often hears the criticism that the police are an insular society. If this is true—and there is good evidence that it is—then the educational level of police officers must rise with the educational level of the general population or this insularity will increase. And, as one commentator has said:

> The police officer who must work with, and for, members of his community will not command respect or perform his task satisfactorily unless his educational achievements are at least equal to the average citizen whom he contacts. [26]

As stated above, police officers must have broad knowledge in a number of academic or quasi-academic areas, such as psychology and sociology, English, and such social sciences as political science and history. Only in college can the officer gain this training.

Even with the best of aptitude, intelligence, and achievement tests, it is very difficult for police departments to evaluate the personal qualities of applicants. Departments can, however, rely upon colleges to have tested the intelligence, drive, ambition, creativity, and adaptability of applicants. To succeed in almost any college the student must demonstrate an above average ability in all of these areas. Affirming this proposition R. E. Neth, Chief of the Costa Mesa, California, Police Department, has said:

> We have found that officers recruited under this plan [a two-year college requirement] are easier to train, have generally better ability to reason through a problem to a successful solution, and are less inclined to lose sight of the responsibility they bear by the nature of their work. [27]

Finally, the college experience forces an individual to meet and associate with many different kinds of people from many different kinds of backgrounds. On the importance of this experience, O. W Wilson has said:

> He [the college trained officer] has had broader experience with people and new situations; his adaptability has been tested; he has had the opportunity to meet students of many different nationalities, cultural backgrounds, and racial characteristics, and, consequently should have lost much of any previous bias or prejudice he may have held. His studies will have given him a new perspective on the problems and aspirations common to all men, and he will have learned to some degree to withhold judgment and to restrain his actions and impulses in favor of calm consideration and analysis.[28]

We can expect, then, that college trained officers will in general do a substantially better job of policing than non-college trained officers. Will more intelligence, creativity, sensitivity, and the insights and knowledge gained from the college experience make a white man capable of effectively patrolling a Negro or other minority group ghetto? Some think not. Some "Black Power" advocates say the Negro is simply not going to allow white men to come into black neighborhoods to enforce the "White Man's" law. Others, including many whites, believe it necessary for the police officer to be a member of the minority group he is working with in order for him to understand their problems and their ways of thinking and behaving.

If one looks at the specific complaints of ghetto dwellers, however, it seems clear that what they are really complaining about is simply poor law enforcement—and not the color of the law enforcement officer. The National Advisory Commission on Civil Disorders noted that "Negroes firmly believe that police brutality and harassment occur repeatedly in Negro neighborhoods. This belief is unquestionably one of the major reasons for intense Negro resentment aginst the police." [29] This Commission also reported that:

> Physical abuse is only one source of aggravation in the ghetto. In nearly every city surveyed, the Commission heard complaints of harassment of interracial couples, dispersal of social street gatherings, and the stopping of Negroes on foot or in cars without obvious basis. These, together with contemptuous and degrading verbal abuse, have great impact in the ghetto. As one Commission witness said, these strip the Negro of the one thing that he may have left—his dignity, "the question of being a man." [30]

The Commission also found that ghetto dwellers complain strongly and frequently about the inadequacy of the police protection they are given. It reported:

> This belief is founded on two basic types of complaints. The first is that the police maintain a much less rigorous standard of law enforcement in the ghetto, tolerating their illegal activities, like drug addiction, prostitution and street violence that they would not tolerate elsewhere. The second is that the police treat complaints and calls for help from Negro areas much less urgently than from white areas. [31]

There is no reason to believe that a police force made up of intelligent, highly motivated, and educated white police officers could not thoroughly and quickly put down the bad reputation which police have acquired in the ghetto because of the above-discussed behavior. This type of police officer could be expected to function in such a way that the above-mentioned complaint would not be registered in the future. This would not, of course, solve the problem of the new Negro individuals who do not want any white men having authority over them. It does not seem, however, that society should support this type of "reverse prejudice" by adopting it as a policy. Also, since the holders of this view are in the minority in the ghetto, their desires should not be fulfilled at the expense of the majority who demand the type of police protection that can only be achieved through the selection of officers who possess the above-discussed qualification.

This is not to say great effort should not be made to recruit Negroes and members of other minority groups into the police service. Those members of minority groups who possess the above-discussed qualifications would be highly valuable. As the National Advisory Commission on Civil Disorders found;

> Negro officers can help to avoid stereotypes and prejudices in the minds of white officers. Negro officers can also increase departmental insight into ghetto problems, and provide information necessary for early anticipation of tensions and grievances that can lead to disorders. [32]

What the problem comes down to is this:

> Recruiting more Negro officers, alone, will not solve the problems of lack of communication and hostility toward police. A Negro's understanding of the ghetto is not enough to make him a good officer. He must also meet the same high standards as white officers and pass the same screening process. [33]

PROPOSALS FOR INCREASING EDUCATIONAL REQUIREMENTS

There are two basic types of proposals which have been made for increasing the minimum educational requirements. The first, which is characterized by the IACP Model Police Standards Council Act, is that the educational requirements should be raised to a certain uniform level for all sworn police who are hired in the future. In its relevant parts, the Model Act reads, "[no] person shall be appointed as a police officer ... unless such person ... is the holder of a Bachelor's degree from an accredited institution."[34]

The second type proposal involves the reclassification of police functions by their degree of difficulty and according to the amount of skill required to perform them, and the establishment of minimum educational requirements for each new classification. The best known such proposal is that made by the President's Commission on Law Enforcement and the Administration of Justice:

> The Commission recommends that police departments give up single entry and establish three levels at which candidates may begin their police careers. The Commission calls these three levels the "Community Service Officer," the "Police Officer," and the "Police Agent."
>
> * * *
>
> [The Commission's proposal concerning the "Community Service Officer" is excluded here and will not be discussed since this type officer would not be sworn, and would not be charged with general law enforcement responsibilities. This part of the proposal seems important and worthwhile, but simply outside the thesis of this paper.]
>
> The Police Officer would respond to calls for service, perform routine patrol, render emergency services, make preliminary investigations, and enforce traffic regulations. In order to qualify as a police officer at the present time, a candidate should possess a high school diploma and should demonstrate a capacity for college work.
>
> The Police Agent would do whatever police jobs were most complicated, most sensitive, and most demanding. He might be a specialist in police community-relations or juvenile delinquency. He might have staff duties. He might be in uniform patrolling a high-crime neighborhood. To become a police agent would require at least two years of college work and preferably a baccalaureate degree in the liberal arts or social sciences.
>
> As an ultimate goal, the Commission recommends that all police personnel with general enforcement powers have baccalaureate degrees. [35]

In the end, then, these two proposals call for the same educational requirements—a baccalaureate degree for all personnel charged with general enforcement responsibilities. Also, the educational requirements which both proposals call for in the short run may be very much alike since the IACP Model Act education proposal is prefaced by the words "At the earliest practicable time," thus leaving the way open for the same type of gradual increases contained in the Commission's proposal. Where they differ is in the matter of the reclassification of police functions. Would such reclassifications be desirable? Before answering this question, one must consider present policies for use of police personnel.

Presently, almost all police departments have patrolmen and detectives as operational level personnel. The patrolmen answer every call which comes into the police switchboard and initially investigate any matter for which the police have responsibility, whether brought to their attention by some person on their beat or which they themselves observe. As is obvious, this melange includes crimes from the most serious and complex to the mundane, and all manner of noncriminal human problems—from rescuing cats from trees to attempting to solve complicated and emotionally charged domestic problems. Only in a very few cities do departments go so far as to have special squads which do nothing but investigate traffic accidents or answer obvious felony calls—such as armed robberies in progress or assaults in which a weapon is used. In almost no case are patrolmen expected or allowed to do any investigation even in the case of very minor crimes. Investigation is a job of the detectives and, theoretically, they are supposed to investigate every crime the patrolman reports. Since, however, "there are relatively few detectives in a police department—normally about 10 percent of all sworn personnel—they ... are overwhelmed by their caseloads."[36] As a result, only serious crime is investigated—and even then not to the extent society might desire—and minor crime cannot be investigated at all. What this means is that in the case of the minor crime there is little chance for a solution of the crime or the apprehension of the perpetrator unless the patrolman catches the culprit in the act; or unless some witness identifies the perpetrator and is either present when the patrolman investigates the crime, and thus can be asked about it then; or unless the witness comes into the police station and volunteers the information.

For many reasons the present organization makes little sense. First, "The existing wide range of patrol responsibility hampers efforts to attract more highly qualified personnel into the police service."[37] Presently, virtually all persons entering the police service, no matter how highly qualified, must enter as patrolmen. Further,

> personnel must remain in this category from 1 to 5 years before being eligible for promotion or transfer. ... Police work, therefore, tends to attract persons who are willing to perform its mechanical aspects and to accept its status and compensation.[38]

It is obvious that very few highly qualified or highly educated persons are going to be willing to enter the police service under such conditions even at salaries substantially higher than they are now. This fact was noted by the British Commission in its 1960 Interim Report on Police:

> The reason for this failure [to recruit a proper share of able and well-educated young men] is not in our view, that the police service is inherently unattractive as a career. ... It lies in the neglect of those responsible to adjust the opening stages of a police career, in the way that other professions have found it necessary to do, so as to attract able candidates. It cannot be doubted that it is the early prospects that influence young people to choose one career rather than another.
>
> Nor does it call for any great insight or a deep knowledge of psychology to understand how the police service must appear at a disadvantage in this respect compared with almost any other profession today.[39]

The present system also results in a very inefficient use of manpower. First, even if the detectives had time to investigate minor crime it makes no sense to have them do so. A great many of these investigations could be done by the individual who answers the initial call. In this way extra reports would not have to be filed—reports which are now necessary simply to fill in the detective on what happened—and there would be no repetition of effort such as occurs when the detective must necessarily go over the same ground covered by the patrolmen. Second, it results in a situation in which the least qualified men are assigned to answer the most important calls whenever such calls happen to occur on their beat, and in which the most highly qualified men either spend a large portion of their time handling the least important police tasks, as patrolmen, or else are used to perform only one specialized function—as detectives. This latter situation is particularly unfortunate since by definition the detective is almost always the most highly qualified operational level person in the department (one becomes a detective through promotion from the patrolman ranks), and yet as a detective he cannot be used where he is often most needed: answering serious calls, making difficult arrests, and patroling high crime areas.[40]

In the system proposed by the President's Commission on Law Enforcement and the Administration of Justice these problems would be solved. Many tasks currently performed by detectives, such as routine follow-up investigations on certain types of cases, could be assigned to police officers, leaving the agent to perform the traditional functions of the detective and also:

1. Serve as a uniformed patrol officer in high tension areas;
2. Investigate major crimes in a plainclothes capacity;
3. Acquire an understanding of and develop solutions for police-community problems;
4. Make difficult arrests;
5. Investigate crimes in which juveniles are involved;
6. Enforce gambling, vice, and narcotic statutes;
7. Maintain contact with citizens in the community to ascertain potential signs of strife. [41]

As a result of this reclassification the position of the agent would emerge as a high-status, challenging, professional position for which highly qualified, educated individuals could be recruited.

The Commission's proposal is very good—as far as it goes. However, at the very outset of the program two years of college should be required as a prerequisite for appointment as officer and four years of college should be required as a prerequisite for appointment as agent. The latter requirement should be left flexible enough, as discussed below, to allow present officers or detectives to be appointed to the agent position without fulfilling the educational requirement. This stricter requirement is important for two reasons: First, it would force departments to try to recruit more highly educated persons, whereas the Commission's proposal would allow them to forego doing so on the unproved assumption that such persons were not available. Second, in light of the recruitment experience of departments who now have college educational requirements (discussed above), it seems probable that most or perhaps all departments, at least in medium or large size cities, could recruit sufficient numbers of these more highly qualified individuals. As the Commission noted, as soon as possible the minimum educational requirements for officer should also be raised to equal those for agent.

The Commission did not discuss how its proposal could best be put into effect. It seems the only way to do this would be to reclassify all patrolmen and detectives as either officers or agents, depending on their past performance, intelligence, education, and willingness to obtain further education. Since at the same time it may be necessary to expand the number of operational level personnel, and since in many cities many authorized patrolman positions are unfilled, there will probably be an immediate need for recruitment. In order to introduce the largest number of the most educated persons possible into the departments at the earliest possible time, most of the present patrolmen and a number of the present detectives should be reclassed as officers, leaving a large percentage of the agent positions to be filled by recruitment of college graduates. Only those persons who have attained the goal-education should be hired or promoted unless it is impossible to fill open positions otherwise, or unless a "nonqualifying" candidate proved to be so otherwise outstanding that it would be unfair and unwise not to promote or hire him. This is much the same system used in industry, and it should be used much as it is there; that is, very infrequently and only when a person's special qualifications make him clearly the best choice. In order to insure that all reasonable efforts have been made to hire or promote those persons who had met the educational minimums, the permission of a special board—perhaps appointed by a mayor or governor—should be necessary before any nonqualifying person could be hired or promoted. Also, any nonqualifying person who is hired or promoted should be required to earn a certain number of college credits (perhaps 3 to 6) each year until he can meet the education minimums for the position he holds.

On the question of educational requirements for police administrators the President's Commission on Law Enforcement and the Administration of Justice stated:

> With few exceptions, the completion of 4 years at a college or university is a minimum requirement for top administrative and staff positions in other branches of government. No less should be demanded of administrative and supervisory personnel in our police departments.
>
> Therefore police departments, and particularly larger departments, should take immediate steps to establish the minimum educational requirement of a baccalaureate degree at an accredited institution for all major administrative and supervisory positions. [42]

Again, the Commission has aimed too low. Considering the complexity and importance of the task performed by police administrators (as discussed above) at least a master's degree or equivalent should be required. [43] This requirement seems high only when considered in light of the present circumstances. In considering the fact that public school principals in a great many states are required to possess the master's degree, [44] and that most business executives who have as much responsibility or power as police administrators almost necessarily must have the master's degree to be hired, this requirement does not seem high at all. As in the case of operational level personnel, departments should be able to hire or promote to administrative positions men who do not meet the minimum educational requirements, but here also their appointment or promotion should be cleared through the above discussed special board, and they should, unless their duties are so unusually pressing that they do not have time, be required to earn a certain number of college credits each year until they have earned a master's or equivalent degree.

TYPE OF COLLEGE PROGRAM DESIRED

Charles Tenney, Dean of the College of Criminal Justice at Northeastern University, has said:

> There is agreement that education for law enforcement is an important feature of improving police performance and relations with and within the community.
> However, there is no real consensus on what "education" *means* for law enforcement.... [45]

This theme was amplified by the President's Commission on Law Enforcement and the Administration of Justice when it stated:

> While there has been some progress made in determining the training needs of police personnel, there has been far too little analysis either by the police or by colleges and universities of their educational needs. [46]

This fact must be kept in mind when attempting to decide what type of college program should be recommended for or required of police personnel. Some recommendations, however, can be made with certainty. One concerns the inclusion of vocational or technical courses in the college program. One need only peruse the list of course offerings in many of the "police science" programs offered by colleges to see that in many cases large percentages of their course offerings can only be characterized as vocational. [47] The President's Commission on Law Enforcement and the Administration of Justice noted this, saying:

> College credit is given for example, for such courses as traffic control, defense tactics and patrol procedures. Although there is a need for vocational training, it is not and cannot be a substitute for a liberal arts education.... [48]

Those advocating that such courses make up any substantial portion of a college program must be reminded of the difference between training and education:

The trained man has developed skills and attitudes needed to perform a complex task. The educated man has developed his capacity to judge the worth, the performance, and the excellence of human action.[49]

The inclusion of a substantial number of such courses would be "as inappropriate in a collegiate law enforcement program as would a course in auto repair in a school of engineering."[50]

This does not mean, however, that such courses could not be included in a college program. There are very few colleges or universities in the United States that do not give a limited amount of credit for physical education courses, technical ROTC courses, or any number of vocational courses given in schools of business administration, nursing, and journalism. The point is, very few such courses should be included in the curriculum. Certainly no great question should be raised if such vocational courses are taken to meet the almost universally present physical education requirements.[51] And, there is a benefit to be derived from giving credit for a very limited number of such courses. These would very likely be chosen as the first college courses taken by a police officer. If these courses serve no other function than that of introducing police personnel to college they are valuable and should be offered for credit.

There seems to be little disagreement on the proposition that police personnel should be trained in the liberal arts and social sciences. The nature of the police task, as outlined above, points directly to this conclusion; that field personnel need to have a background in psychology, sociology, English, history, and political science, seems logically determined by the nature of the task.

> The complex responsibilities and duties of police work require that field personnel understand their community and conditions which breed criminal and delinquent conduct. This understanding can best be gained through a liberal education.[52]

This does not, however, mean a student should not major in police science. Many of the police science programs presently offered by 234 colleges and universities seem not to be academically sound,[53] and though there is genuine doubt about the relevancy of such programs to the career needs of today's law enforcement students,[54] such need not be the case. The properly formulated police science program offers an interdisciplinary liberal arts curriculum which blends and applies to law enforcement problems such disciplines as psychology, sociology, political science, history and philosophy. The School of Criminology at the University of California at Berkeley offers such a model program. Even a cursory look at a fairly representative sample of their course offerings shows the interdisciplinary nature of the curriculum: The Etiology of Crime, Sociological, Psychological, Psychiatric; Ethnic Tensions and Conflict in Relation to Law Enforcement; Social Policy and Penal Practice; Law Enforcement Policies and Social Structure; Social and Historical Origins of Major Theories of Criminal Behavior; and the History of Crime and Its Treatment.[55]

Much can be said for such a program in that it gives fairly good assurance of relating the liberal arts disciplines to police problems, and assures that, over a four-year period, the student will have given considerable thought to the intelligent solution of these police problems. Even if it is at some time proven that such a program does not better prepare the student for a career in law enforcement considering the academic quality of such instruction, it is doubtful that a program including a major in another liberal arts field would prove better preparation. Even it if proved to be only of equal value in the long run, it would enhance his initial effectiveness vis-à-vis that of a nonpolice science graduate. This would certainly be of interest to the hiring police departments and could help to make the proposal for raising the minimum educational requirements more acceptable to police departments. At least until much more is known about the educational needs of the police service, however, a major in police science should not be required, and since there are so few programs (and especially programs that equal Berkeley's) this would be impossible anyway.

ENTRY LEVELS FOR NEW GRADUATES

Once it has been decided that police personnel should be reclassified as officers, agents, and supervisors, and that various levels of college education should be required for appointment at each level, it is necessary to decide at what level or levels recent graduates will be allowed to enter the police service. It seems only two policies are possible: require each person to enter at the officer level regardless of his education, or allow some persons to enter at higher levels. In determining which policy to follow, it must be understood that:

> It is doubtful whether suitable graduates will be attracted to police service if they are required in all cases to initiate their career at the lowest level of a department.... [56]

Especially if a department is interested in hiring the very best people, this point cannot be overstated. Considering the other opportunities which confront a college graduate, and especially one holding a graduate degree, it is highly unlikely that any such persons could be enticed to begin at the bottom.

Equally important is the fact that such a "start at the bottom" policy would not be an appropriate method of utilizing highly educated and talented personnel.[57] Even if the holder of a master's degree in public administration or criminology, for example, could be induced to begin as an officer it seems a great waste of talent to have him do so. Considering the dearth of supervisors and administrators with graduate training, very little can be said for a policy which kept persons with such training from exercising their skill. One hears very little disagreement with these ideas, but critics of such a plan attack it on the grounds that it will not work, the usual reason given being that on-the-job experience is needed to handle any job above that of officer. While such an argument sounds as if it has some validity, the experience of European police departments, the military, and industry with lateral entry programs has proven they do work.

> Most police systems on the continent make at least some provision for lateral entry. Since World War II this feature has become highly developed in France. Half of the candidates for the French equivalent of a lieutenancy are chosen from among nonpolice candidates who hold a baccalaureate degree, while half the candidates for the *commissaire* or inspector grade, are chosen from nonpolice applicants who hold a law degree. German police forces recruit ten percent of their detective forces directly from the legal profession, while the Swedish police recruit lawyers to fill some 300 of their top positions. [58]

Although the literature on these European police programs is very sparse, particularly in the English language, that which is available is highly laudatory and gives no hint that the lateral entrance programs are not working.

Our military has used the lateral entry system since the country was founded. All but a very few military officers begin their careers as lieutenants or ensigns, with only a few officers "coming up through the ranks." Also, many individuals begin their military careers at levels above ensign or lieutenant. Appointments to the rank of captain are very common, especially for persons with medical, dental, or law degrees. In attempting to analogize the military system to the police system, one might be misled by assuming that military officers are given a large amount of special preparatory training. While this is so in the case of service academy graduates, it must be remembered that such graduates make up a very small percentage of the officer corps and that most officers are appointed after minimal ROTC or OCS training, and many are appointed who have no military training at all. It seems interesting to note, also, that even in this age when the military establishment comes under diverse and frequent criticism one never hears the military criticized for its officer appointment policies.

Industry also makes extensive use of the lateral entry concept. Only a very small number of supervisory or administrative personnel in industry above the foreman level ever worked at the operational level. Also, not only do almost all supervisors begin in some executive or administrative position, but many persons enter at quite high levels directly from college or graduate school. On the workability of this procedure as it concerns police departments R. W. Walters, Director of College Employment, American Telephone and Telegraph Company, has said:

> Men can learn details of low-level experiences, never having actually gone through the "musical chairs" routine. It means, in our business, that a man can be a management foreman even if he has never installed a telephone. It means that he must know the details and be held responsible for his people doing the technical job, but it doesn't mean that he has had to experience the job. In your work, it means that men can be good administrative officers even if they have never been a patrolman. [59]

Concerning lateral entry, the President's Commission on Law Enforcement and the Administration of Justice has proposed:

College graduates should, after an adequate internship, be eligible to serve as police agents. Persons who have adequate education and experience should be allowed to enter directly into staff and administrative positions.[60]

It would seem that the only sensible way to implement this program would be to appoint persons at the level for which their education qualifies them if they are nearly equal on other grounds with competing candidates who lack the goal education. Experience should not be treated as another ground per se, but should be considered insofar as it bears on such qualities as judgment and knowledge. This approach is necessary if present personnel are to be encouraged to obtain more education and if highly educated persons are to be attracted to the police service. The idea would be that education is not absolutely necessary, but that only in extraordinary cases would one be promoted or hired without meeting the goal educational requirements.

NECESSITY FOR CHANGING PHYSICAL REQUIREMENTS

If police departments are to be able to hire highly educate and highly qualified persons there are a number of changes which must be made. First, the present physical and residence requirements which are in effect in most departments must be changed. "Minimum height requirements are often set at five feet eight inches or five feet nine inches"[61] and "minimum and maximum weights, when set, usually range from 150 pounds to 250 pounds."[62] The visual requirements are even more stringent, often being "set at 20/20 both eyes, or slightly less for one eye, correctable to 20/20."[63] Very rarely, it seems, are requirements set at less than 20/50, correctable to 20/20.[64] Such rigid requirements not only result in the summary rejection of otherwise exceptionally qualified canidates, but with the raising of educational requirements the physical requirements must be lowered if the recruitment base is to be large enough to supply the needed number of candidates. Office or supervisory personnel should be required to be free of physical defects which would unduly impede their mobility or ability to communicate. Field personnel should not be appointed or retained if they do not possess the physical capacity to handle thier job. Since police jobs vary, and therefore the physical requirements vary, it seems wise to do away with all rigid physical requirements, and assess each situation on an individual basis.[65] In making these evaluations a department should remember that the FBI has a minimum height requirement of only five feet seven inches,[66] and "the Federal Aviation Agency will license commercial pilots whose vision is 20/100, as long as the vision is correctable to 20/20."[67]

NECESSITY FOR CHANGING RESIDENCE REQUIREMENTS

The widely prevailing residence requirements must also be changed if highly qualified persons are to be available for appointment. "A 1961 survey by the

International Association of Chiefs of police revealed that nearly 75 percent of the responding departments had preservice residency requirements varying from 6 months to 5 years."[68] The major arguments for hiring only "local" people seem to be:

1. They should have job priority by right.
2. They are more familiar with the topography, governmental organization, local mores and philosophies than "outsiders."
3. They are voters and taxpayers, and thus more loyal to the community.
4. They are more easily and economically recruited.
5. The background investigation is more easily completed.[69]

Why local residents should have job priotity by right is not clear. It seems that this idea grew out of the depression when there was some justification for the idea that the government had a responsibility to provide employment for its members. During times of full employment, however, this argument seems to have no validity. That local residents are more familiar with the local topography, governmental organization, and local mores is true, but unimportant. Some of these things might not be important to learn at all, and an educated and intelligent person should have no trouble obtaining the necessary information in a very short time. That they are voters and taxpayers is also true, but this may be to their detriment as police officers since what is desired is objectivity and neutrality rather than "loyalty." That they are more easily and economically recruited, and that the background investigation can be more easily completed, should certainly be of little import when one considers the advantages to be gained by hiring the best people available rather than hiring those most easily available.[70]

As to residence requirements, the President's Commission on Law Enforcement and the Administration of Justice has recommended:

> Each department should attempt to obtain the best policemen that can be recruited anywhere in the country. Police and city administrators should immediately take steps, therefore, to remove local residency requirements and should also encourage the removal of state residency requirements, if they exist.[71]

NECESSITY FOR INCREASING COMPENSATION

Salary levels must also be changed if departments are to recruit highly educated and highly qualified persons. "If the police service is to be an attractive career opportunity, it must offer compensation that is competitive with other occupations or professions that seek men of education or ability."[72] A quick review of present police salaries shows that very few departments offer competitive salaries to the college graduate. "In 1966, the median starting salaries for Patrolmen ranged from $4,920 in small communities to $5,834 in cities of over 500,000 population."[73] This level is not only below that offered by other employers seeking college graduates, but is even below the level offered to most skilled tradesmen.[74] The median salary for police chiefs is also low, with a range of "from $7,504 in population."[75]

The President's Commission on Law Enforcement and the Administration of Justice recommends a starting salary of from $7,000 to $10,000 (based on 1967 wage levels) for college graduates recruited for police agent jobs, and a maximum salary for this job exceeding $15,000.[76] There seems to be no reason to doubt the need for such salaries, and it is obvious that most cities will have to initiate substantial raises in order to meet these requirements. Undoubtedly, there will be much argument against such raises on the grounds that cities cannot afford them. What must be understood, however, is that "too often our least expensive help has turned out to be our most expensive help... We cannot afford not to pay ample wages."[77]

Along with making substantial raises in the base salary, cities should look carefully into the possibility of establishing incentive pay plans whereby persons would receive extra salary for each course taken or each degree held. As of May 1967, 15 municipal police departments—eight of which are in California—offered incentives ranging from $1.00 per month for each semester credit earned to 10 percent additional salary for four years of college.[78] Especially in the years immediately succeeding the time when increased educational requirements are instituted, an incentive plan would have the effect of encouraging the "hold over" employees who do not meet the educational requirements to work toward meeting these requirements. After such time as all employees meet the minimum requirement the plan would still be valuable in that it would encourage members of the department to obtain further education.

In considering the level at which salaries should be set it is very important to understand that "pay...has rarely enjoyed first place among the employment conditions the better employee-applicant is seeking. More likely such aspects as 'interesting and important work' and 'opportunity for advancement' are sought."[79] This must be remembered for two reasons: First, competitive salaries alone will not bring in highly motivated and highly qualified applicants. Even salaries which are much higher than that offered by the competition will not do so either unless the work is interesting and challenging. Second, salaries higher than those offered by the competition are not necessary for attracting the highly qualified if the work is interesting and challenging. In fact, if highly educated persons are given positions of great responsibility and challenge many or even most would be willing to work for salaries somewhat less than those offered by the competition.

NECESSITY FOR CHANGING PROMOTIONAL SYSTEMS

The promotional systems in effect in most departments must be changed. Presently, promotions are usually made in one of three ways: arbitrary selection by the administrator, promotion by strict seniority, or by the competivite processes.[80] The first of these methods seems to have little merit. Even if it were true that the administrator could make the very best decisions in a somewhat arbitrary way, the system is bad because such arbitrariness would not be good for morale, and if the administrator were able to pick the best qualified person this same person should also be promoted as a result of a more structured, formalized system. Obviously, little can be said for a system which promotes only by seniority. To the extent that it is true that a more experienced officer is more qualified for promotion this higher competency should make itself evident in some overt way. On this point, O. W. Wilson has said: "Seniority by itself should be given no consideration; if experience has developed leadership ability, promotion should be based on it—not on the number of years of service."[81] The use of competitive proccesses offers the most rational method of deciding who should be promoted. Care must be taken, however, to insure that the candidates compete upon relevant grounds. Clearly, it is unwise to rely too heavily upon high achievement in written examinations:

> Written promotional examinations ... do not test those qualities of leadership or administrative capacity which are presumably a major consideration in promotion to high ranks. Such qualities are, therefore, largely ignored before the more familiar techniques of personnel management which do not attempt any such evaluation of human personality.[82]

Upon this point, the President's Commission on Law Enforcement and the Administration of Justice noted:

> While there may be merit in requiring all candidates to take a competitive written examination, the results of such an examination should be only one of the many factors to be considered. Other factors should include: (1) an officer's prior performance and reputation in previous jobs as well as within the department and in the community, (2) an officer's educational achievement, and (3) an officer's demonstrated leadership potential and ability to assume greater responsibility.[83]

In addition to changing the promotional process it will also be necessary to modify or eliminate time-in-rank requirements, and also to allow for open competition for vacancies. Presently, in most jurisdictions, officers must serve five or six years before being considered for the next higher rank.[84]

> Time-on-job, as a rigid qualification, seems somewhat inane, for some officers, of great background and capacity, assimilate experience and knowledge very quickly, whereas others may merely repeat one week's or one month's experience for ten or more years without appreciable development.[85]

Not only does such a requirement lead to inefficient use of manpower, but it erects a formidable barrier to the recruitment of highly motivated and qualified individuals. To those who think experience is absolutely necessary to handle all but the lowest police jobs, it can only be said that if that is true the lack of a time-in-rank requirement should do no harm, as low time-in-rank candidates should show themselves to be less qualified than their more experienced competitors through their performance in some competitive process.

NECESSITY FOR HAVING OPEN COMPETITION

Open competition for vacancies is also necessary if police agencies are to attract the highly motivated. Very few highly educated and highly talented individuals are going to enter a field in which their whole future depends upon advancement within one department. Obviously within one department one's promotion depends upon the existence of a limited number of vacancies in higher positions, and, to a great extent, upon one's ability to impress one particular group of superiors. Since college graduates do not face this barrier in industry it would be impossible for the police service to attract the very best people without offering them the same chances for advancement as they find in industry. Also, open competition—and its handmaiden, lateral entry—are to be favored because of the chance they offer for the infusion of "new blood" and fresh ideas. "The symptoms of a closed system are mediocrity, sterility, isolation, and insulation or self-protection. On the other hand, migration and mobility can be an effective mechanism for matching people and jobs over space and time . . ."[86] Indeed, some of our best police administrators have entered departments through lateral entry. In attempting to decide what candidates should be eligible for promotion, or for lateral entry, one commentator has said:

> In most police promotional processes, only the next lower rank is eligible to compete for promotion. Assuming that a promotional probationary period is effectively utilized, there would seem to be a certain logic in allowing eligibility to the two next lower ranks in order to increase competition within the department. This would tend to promote greater attention to work and performance, and stimulate study. Further, such a provision would provide an excellent recruiting aid, for men of great capacity would be more inclined to consider the police service if the opportunities for advancement were opened somewhat wider than they are under current civil service rules.[87]

If this is true why put any limits on the competition? Nothing could be lost by such a policy, and much could be gained both because such a policy would aid in recruitment and would allow departments to look for the best candidates wherever they can find them.

NECESSITY FOR CHANGING PENSION SYSTEMS

If open competition and lateral entry are to be practically possible the present pension systems of police departments must be changed. What is wholly lacking, and absolutely necessary, is a nationwide portable pension system which would allow one's pension to "move" with him without any financial loss. Since the war, multi-employer pension plans have been founded in a large number of industries.[88] Some of the better known and larger plans include United Mine Workers of America Welfare and Retirement Fund, The International Brotherhood of Electrical Workers Pension and Benefit Trust Fund, and the Amalgamated Insurance Fund-Pension Fund.[89] While some of these funds have over 250,000 members, some have as few as 26 members.[90] Characteristically, these plans allow for the easy transfer of pensions within the industry and insure each worker that he will incur no financial loss from a job change within the industry.[91] There seems to be no reason to believe there would be any problem in establishing such a pension plan within the police service. The easiest and best way to do this would be simply to consolidate "all local, city and county, local and state, state and federal pension programs into one nationwide portable pension, retirement plan."[92]

NECESSITY FOR PROVIDING JOB SECURITY FOR PRESENT PERSONNEL

Present members of police departments must be assured a reasonable amount of job security, chance for advancement and chance to further their education. One clause of the International Association of Chiefs of Police Model Standards Council Act, states:

> Police officers already serving under permanent appointment on the effective date of this Act shall not be required to meet any requirement of subsection (B) and (C) [pertaining to education, training, and other such requirements] of this Section as a condition of tenure or continued employment; nor shall failure of any such police officer to fulfill such requirements make him ineligible for any promotional examination for which he is otherwise eligible."[93]

Such consideration for present personnel seems absolutely necessary. So as to aid morale and keep qualified present employees, each department should make it clear that any new requirements will not affect the jobs of present members if they can do a minimally effective job at their present position, and if they are willing to undertake a realistic amount of additional training. The standard used to determine if present employees are doing a minimally effective job should be *whether they could do a minimally effective job in the department as it was constituted prior to the enactment of new requirements and procedures.* In many cases, additional training would be deemed necessary if these present men are to work effectively under the new system. The type and extent of such training must almost necessarily be determined individually—certainly in many cases this would include college courses. As discussed above, competition for any open position would be absolutely open. Under this system each employee, whether he met educational or other requirements or not, would be eligible to compete for any position. Lastly, the chance to take college courses must be provided for present employees. The rapidly expanding number of community colleges should be used to provide this education, and departments should explore the possibility of granting leaves of absence with full or part pay to any employee who wants to attend college. Also, departments should explore the possibility of establishing a half-and-half program which would entail a shortened work week and a less than full load at college. Clearly, departments should be willing to pay for any college courses they require their members to take.

POLICE ATTITUDES ON PERSONNEL CHANGES

Will the above proposals be accepted by the persons who must institute the suggested changes? To obtain a partial answer to this question, George W. O'Connor, of the International Association of Chiefs of Police, and the writer sent questionnaires (Fig. 1) to 424 police chiefs in the United States—to every chief in a city of over 50,000 population and to chiefs in one in every four cities of 25,000 to 50,000 population. We asked these chiefs what educational requirements were presently in effect in their departments, what requirements they would favor for the future, and their opinion on 11 of the recommendations for changes in personnel policy which were made by the President's Commission on Law Enforcement and the Administration of Justice. We sent the complete explanatory text of each of the 11 recommendations along with the questionnaires.

A total of 239 completed questionnaires were received, representing a 56.4 percent return rate. Tabulation was both by geographical location and population group of the city. The reader may wish to study this more detailed data for divergences of opinion between chiefs in different regions or in cities of varying sizes.[94] Comparison of actual and desired educational requirements for selected ranks and position are shown in Fig. 2, and responses to the recommendations are shown in Fig. 3.

Of the 11 recommendations submitted (See Fig. 1) number two, which is also a major recommendation of this paper, met with the least acceptance, with only 33.9 percent either agreeing or strongly agreeing. (Agree and strongly agree will be referred to here as *agree,* while disagree and strongly disagree will be referred to as *disagree* and the percentages will be calculated on this basis.) The fact that there was such a large number of "no opinion" (22.2 percent) seems significant, however, and if they are not considered, only 10.0 percent more chiefs disagreed with the recommendation than agreed with it. It seems likely from occasional comments written on the returned questionnaires that a large proportion of chiefs either had no opinion or disagreed because they did not understand the proposal or its desired effects. Perhaps, if adequate explanation of the proposal were given a large proportion of the chiefs who registered no opinion and at least some of the chiefs who disagreed would have agreed.

Recommendations three and four, which were also proposed in the body of the paper, received substantial acceptance (85.8 percent and 64.8 percent, respectively). However, it must be noted that in Section B only 15.0 percent of the chiefs thought four years of college was a desirable level of education for patrolmen. The difference between 15.0 percent and 64.8 percent can probably be explained by the fact that recommendation four contains the clause "ultimate aim of all police departments" and the question in Section B implies a more immediate desirability. It seems, then, that while chiefs are not disagreeable to the ultimate raising of educational levels in police departments in general, the majority of those questioned are at the moment reluctant to call a college degree desirable for patrolmen in their own departments.

Recommendation five, which in earlier reference was said to be aiming too low—a graduate degree should be required—was agreed to by the majority of chiefs (57.3 percent). This seems encouraging since the recommendation must seem threatening to any chief who does not understand the Commission's position (not apparent from the recommendation itself or from the explanatory text which accompanied the questionnaires) that present supervisory and executive personnel would not lose their jobs because they could not meet the educational requirement. Also, 72.6 percent set four years or more of college as the desired educational level for chiefs in response to the first question in Section B. From the comments several chiefs made on the "immediate" in recommendation five, it appears this qualification caused at least some chiefs to disagree with the recommendation who otherwise find higher educational levels for police supervisory and executive positions desirable. It should be noted here that 5.6 percent of the chiefs did agree with the proposal made in this paper that a graduate or law degree be required of chiefs.

There is little that can be said about the opinions concerning recommendations seven, eight, ten and eleven (the other recommendations most relevant to the proposals made in this paper), except that recommendations seven, eight and ten were overwhelmingly agreed with, and that 63.9 percent of the chiefs agreed with recommendation eleven, though more than one of them noted that this recommendation was fairly complicated and involved more than one question.

Recommendation	Strongly Disagree	Disagree	No Opinion	Agree	Strongly Agree
1. Each municipality, and other jurisdiction responsible for law enforcement, should carefully assess the manpower needs of its police agency on the basis of efficient use of all its personnel and should provide the resources required to meet the need for increased personnel if such a need is found to exist.					
2. Basic police functions, especially in large and medium sized urban departments, should be divided among three kinds of officers, here termed the "community service officer," the "police officer," and the "police agent."					
3. Police departments should recruit far more actively than they now do, with special attention to college campuses and innercity neighborhoods.					
4. The ultimate aim of all police departments should be that all personnel with general enforcement powers have baccalaureate degrees.					
5. Police departments should take immediate steps to establish a minimum requirement of a baccalaureate degree for all supervisory and executive positions.					
6. Until reliable tests are devised for identifying and measuring the personal characteristics that contribute to good police work, intelligence tests, thorough background investigations and personal interviews should be used by all departments as absolute minimum techniques to determine the moral character and the intellectual and emotional fitness of police candidates.					
7. Police departments and civil service commissions should reexamine and, if necessary, modify present recruitment standards on age, height, weight, visual acuity, and prior residence. The appointing authority should place primary emphasis on the education, background, character and personality of a candidate for police service.					
8. Police salaries must be raised, particularly by increasing maximums. In order to attract college graduates to police service, starting and maximum salaries must be competitive with other professions and occupations that seek the same graduates.					
9. Salary proposals for each department within local government should be considered on their own merits and should not be joined with the demands of other departments within a city.					
10. Promotion eligibility requirements should stress ability above seniority. Promotion "lists" should be compiled on the basis not only of scores on technical examinations but on prior performance, character, educational achievement and leadership potential.					
11. Personnel to perform all specialized police functions not involving a need for general enforcement powers should be selected for their talents and abilities without regard to prior police service. Professional policemen should have the same opportunities as other professionals to seek employment where they are most needed. The inhibitions that civil service regulations, retirement plans and hiring policies place on lateral entry should be removed. To encourage lateral movement of police personnel, a nationwide retirement system should be devised that permits the transferring of retirement credits.					

FIGURE 1

The Eleven Recommendations Submitted to a Group of Chiefs of Police in Opinion Survey of Personnel Policy Changes Recommended by the President's Commission on Law Enforcement and the Administration of Justice

Rank/Position		None	Less than High School	High School Diploma	College Totals	2 Years of College	4 Years of College	Some College	1 Year of College	3 Years of College	Graduate Degree	Law Degree
Chief	Actual	6.8	.9	75.2	17.1	8.1	9.0					
	Desired	.9		15.0	84.1	9.4	67.0	1.7	.4		4.7	.9
Command Level (Captain, Lieutenant)	Actual	3.9	2.2	84.9	9.0	7.3	1.7					
	Desired	.4		15.8	83.7	29.5	53.0	.4	.4		.4	
Supervisors (Sergeants)	Actual	3.8	2.1	89.8	4.2	3.4		.4	.4			
	Desired	.4		24.0	75.5	51.5	22.3	.9	.4	.4		
Investigators (Detective, Juvenile)	Actual	3.9	1.7	90.9	3.4	3.4		.4				
	Desired	.4		27.8	71.7	50.8	19.7	.4	.8			
Patrolmen	Actual	2.1	3.4	92.3	2.1	1.3	.4	.4				
	Desired	.4		34.3	65.2	48.9	15.0	.4	.9			

FIGURE 2

Comparison of Actual and Desired Educational Requirements for Selected Ranks and Positions by Percent of 239 Responses

Recommendation	Strongly Disagree	Disagree	No Opinion	Agree	Strongly Agree
	-478 4 3	2 1	0	1 2	3 4 +478
1. Each municipality, and other jurisdiction responsible for law enforcement, should carefully assess the manpower needs of its police agency on the basis of efficient use of all its personnel and should provide the resources required to meet the need for increased personnel if such a need is found to exist. (SD = 0, D = 0, NO = 3, A = 77, SA = 159)					+395
2. Basic police functions, especially in large and medium sized urban departments, should be divided among three kinds of officers, here termed the "community service officer," the "police officer," and the "police agent." (SD = 25, D = 80, NO = 53, A = 74, SA = 7)			−42		
3. Police departments should recruit far more actively than they now do, with special attention to college campuses and innercity neighborhoods. (SD = 3, D = 15, NO = 16, A = 146, SA = 59)				+243	
4. The ultimate aim of all police departments should be that all personnel with general enforcement powers have baccalaureate degrees. (SD = 5, D = 53, NO = 26, A = 116, SA = 39)				+131	
5. Police departments should take immediate steps to establish a minimum requirement of a baccalaureate degree for all supervisory and executive positions. (SD = 6, D = 78, NO = 18, A = 105, SA = 32)				+79	

FIGURE 3

Graphic display achieved on a scale of minus 478 to plus 478 by weighting responses as follows: Strongly Disagree (SD) = −2, Disagree (D) = −1, No Opinion (No) = 0, Agree (A) = +1, and Strongly Agree (SA) = +2. The number of responses in each category is indicated below the recommendation.

6. Until reliable tests are devised for identifying and measuring the personal characteristics that contribute to good police work, intelligence tests, thorough background investigations and personal interviews should be used by all departments as absolute minimum techniques to determine the moral character and the intellectual and emotional fitness of police candidates.
(SD = 1, D = 0, NO = 6, A = 73, SA = 159) **+316**

7. Police departments and civil service commissions should reexamine and, if necessary, modify present recruitment standards on age, height, weight, visual acuity, and prior residence. The appointing authority should place primary emphasis on the education, background, character and personality of a candidate for police service.
(SD = 2, D = 22, NO = 4, A = 118, SA = 93) **+278**

8. Police salaries must be raised, particularly by increasing maximums. In order to attract college graduates to police service, starting and maximum salaries must be competitive with other professions and occupations that seek the same graduates.
(SD = 0, D = 1, NO = 2, A = 88, SA = 148) **+383**

9. Salary proposals for each department within local government should be considered on their own merits and should not be joined with the demands of other departments within a city.
(SD = 0, D = 0, NO = 2, A = 53, SA = 184) **+421**

10. Promotion eligibility requirements should stress ability above seniority. Promotion "lists" should be compiled on the basis not only of scores on technical examinations but on prior performance, character, educational achievement and leadership potential.
(SD = 0, D = 3, NO = 4, A = 88, SA = 144) **+373**

11. Personnel to perform all specialized police functions not involving a need for general enforcement powers should be selected for their talents and abilities without regard to prior police service. Professional policemen should have the same opportunities as other professionals to seek employment where they are most needed. The inhibitions that civil service regulations, retirement plans and hiring policies place on lateral entry should be removed. To encourage lateral movement of police personnel, a nationwide retirement system should be devised that permits the transferring of retirement credits.
(SD = 8, D = 53, NO = 26, A = 97, SA = 55) **+138**

FIGURE 3 (Continued)

NOTES

1. George W. O'Connor and Nelson A. Watson, *Juvenile Delinquency and Youth Crimes: The Police Role* (Washington: International Association of Chiefs of Police, 1964), p. 77.
2. Ibid., p. 79.
3. Ibid., p. 78.
4. Ibid., pp. 78-79.
5. *Survey of Selection Methods,* cited in the President's Commission on Law Enforcement and the Administration of Justice, *Task Force Report: The Police* (Washington: U.S. Government Printing Office, 1967), p. 126.
6. *A Forward Step: Educational Backgrounds for Policemen,* pp. 3, 21, cited by the President's Commission on Law Enforcement and the Administration of Justice, op. cit., p. 126.
7. Ibid., p. 120.
8. Ibid., p. 120.
9. Ibid., p. 120.
10. Raymond E. Clift, *Guide to Modern Police Thinking* (Cincinnati: W. H. Anderson, 1965), p. 48.
11. From the personal files of George Berkley, Tufts University, listing the quotation as coming from Stead's, *The Police of Paris.*
12. Statement Presented at Conference for Police Professions, Michigan State University, April 6-8, 1966, quoted in the President's Commission on Law Enforcement and the Administration of Justice, op. cit., p. 121.
13. "A Change For The Better" in *The Police Chief,* 1962, p. 5, quoted in the President's Commission on Law Enforcement and the Administration of Justice, op. cit., p. 126.
14. A. C. Germann, *Police Personnel Management* (Springfield, Ill.: Charles C Thomas, 1958), p. 24.
15. The President's Commission on Law Enforcement and the Administration of Justice, op. cit., p. 120.
16. Stanley R. Schrotel, "Attracting and Keeping College Trained Personnel in Law Enforcement," *The Police Yearbook, 1966* (Washington: International Association of Chiefs of Police, 1966), p. 109.
17. The National Advisory Commission on Civil Disorders, *Report* (New York: Bantam Books, 1968), p. 303.
18. "In Search of Fair and Adequate Law Enforcement," pp. 12-13, quoted in the National Advisory Commission on Civil Disorders, op. cit., p. 308.
19. Norman C. Kassoff, "Selecting Recruits," *The Police Chief,* (August 1965), p. 38.
20. *Municipal Yearbook, 1966,* p. 444 cited by the President's Commission on Law Enforcement and the Administration of Justice, op. cit., p. 121.
21. The President's Commission on Law Enforcement and the Administration of Justice, op. cit., p. 127.
22. Norman C. Kassoff, "A Model Police Standards Council Act," *The Police Chief* (August 1967), p. 12.
23. A. C. Germann, *Recruitment, Selection, Promotion and Civil Service* (unpublished paper submitted to the President's Commission on Law Enforcement and the Administration of Justice, 1967), p. 25.
24. Ibid.
25. Ibid., p. 27.
26. Schrotel, op. cit., p. 110.
27. Germann, *Recruitment,* p. 27.

28. O. W. Wilson, *Police Administration* (2nd ed.; New York: McGraw-Hill, 1963), p. 139.

29. The National Advisory Commission on Civil Disorders, *op. cit.,* p. 302.

30. Ibid., p. 303.

31. Ibid., p. 307.

32.,Ibid., p. 315.

33. Ibid., p. 317.

34. Kassoff, "Model Standards," p. 14.

35. The President's Commission on Law Enforcement and the Administration of Justice, *The Challenge of Crime in a Free Society* (Washington: U.S. Government Printing Office, 1967), p. ix.

36. The President's Commission on Law Enforcement and the Administration of Justice, *The Police,* p. 121.

37. Ibid.

38. Ibid.

39. "Interim Report of the Royal Commission on Police, 1960," p. 19, quoted in the President's Commission on Law Enforcement and the Administration of Justice, *The Police,* pp. 121-122.

40. The President's Commission on Law Enforcement and the Administration of Justice, *The Police,* p. 122.

41. Ibid.

42. Ibid., p. 127.

43. See Germann, Recruitment, p. 21.

44. Kassoff, "Model Standards," p. 16.

45. Charles W. Tenney, Jr., "Education of Law Enforcement," *Trial* (October-November 1969), p. 19.

46. The President's Commission on Law Enforcement and the Administration of Justice, *The Police,* p. 128.

47. Thomas S. Crockett, *Law Enforcement Education, 1968* (Washington: International Association of Chiefs of Police, 1968).

48. The President's Commission on Law Enforcement and the Administration of Justice, *The Police,* p. 127.

49. "The Role of Colleges and Universities in Police, Management," p. 39, quoted in the President's Commission on Law Enforcement and the Administration of Justice, *The Police,* p. 127.

50. Tenney, op. cit., p. 20.

51. Crockett, op. cit., p. 1.12.

52. The President's Commission on Law Enforcement and the Administration of Justice, *The Police,* p. 128.

53. Crockett, op. cit., p. 1.2.

54. Ibid., p. 1.11.

55. Ibid., p. 2.22.

56. The President's Commission on Law Enforcement and the Administration of Justice, *The Police,* p. 142.

57. Ibid.

58. George Berkley, "The European Police: Challenge and Change," *Public Administration Review,* (September-October 1968), p. 425.

59. R. W. Walters, Jr., "Management Development," *The Police Chief* (September 1965), p. 20.

60. The President's Commission on Law Enforcement and the Administration,*The Police,* p. 142.

61. Germann, REcruitment, p. 6.

62. Ibid., p. 7.
63. Ibid., p. 8.
64. International Association of Chiefs of Police, "Police Personnel Selection Survey" (Washington: International Association of Chiefs of Police, 1968).
65. The President's Commission on Law Enforcement and the Administration of Justice, *The Police*, p. 130.
66. Germann, Recruitment, p. 6.
67. "Regulations: Part 57, Medical Standards and Certification," cited by the President's Commission on Law Enforcement and the Administration of Justice, *The Police*, p. 130.
68. *Survey of Selection Methods*, cited in the President's Commission on Law Enforcement and the Administration of Justice, *The Police*, p. 130.
69. Germann, *Police Personnel Management*, p. 21.
70. Ibid., pp. 21-22.
71. The President's Commission on Law Enforcement and the Administration of Justice, *The Police*, p. 131.
72. Ibid., p. 134.
73. *Municipal Yearbook, 1966*, p. 435, cited in the President's Commission on Law Enforcement and the Administration of Justice, *The Police*, p. 134.
74. The President's Commission on Law Enforcement and the Administration of Justice, *The Police*, p. 135.
75. *Municipal Yearbook, 1966*, p. 436, cited in the President's Commission on Law Enforcement and the Administration of Justice. *The Police*, p. 135.
76. The President's Commission on Law Enforcement and the Administration of Justice, *The Police*, p. 135.
77. William H. Hewitt, *Lateral Entry and Transferability of Retirement Credits* (unpublished paper submitted to the President's Commission on Law Enforcement and the Administration of Justice, 1967), p. 23.
78. James D. Stinchcomb, inter-office memorandum to staff of the International Association of Chiefs of Police, May 2, 1967.
79. Hewitt, op. cit., p. 23.
80. Richard H. Blum, *Police Selection* (Springfield: Charles C Thomas, 1964), p. 70.
81. O. W. Wilson, "Toward a Better Merit System," *The Annals of the American Academy of Political and Social Science*, (January 1954), p. 92.
82. *Police Systems in the United States*, p. 134, quoted by the President's Commission on Law Enforcement and the Administration of Justice, *The Police*, p. 142.
83. The President's Commission on Law Enforcement and the Administration of Justice, *The Police*, p. 142.
84. Germann, *Police Personnel Management*, p. 73.
85. Ibid.
86. Hewitt, op. cit. p. 34.
87. Germann, Police Personnel Management, p. 73.
88. Hewitt, op. cit., p. 94.
89. Ibid., p. 95.
90. Ibid., p. 94.
91. Ibid., p. 100.
92. Ibid., p. 103.
93. Kassoff, "Model Standards," p. 14.
94. Tabulations by geographical regions and population groups are available from the Professional Standards Division, IACP, 1319 18th St., N.W., Washington, D.C. 20036.

Law Enforcement Training and the Community College: Alternatives for Affiliation

Denny F. Pace, James D. Stinchcomb and Jimmie C. Styles

TRAINING FOR LAW ENFORCEMENT: THE COMMUNITY COLLEGE ROLE

Law enforcement agencies are increasingly concerned about their ability to deliver the variety of training demanded of them. And there is increasing national concern about better job qualifications for all public employees, due to the complexity of society which demands greater understanding and better performance from all citizens.

An accelerated training and education program has been recommended by the President's Crime Commission Reports. If society is to survive in its acknowledged democratic form, these programs must be put into effect.

Law enforcement agencies are struggling to meet a minimum standard of training, and some 250 community and junior colleges are engaged in law enforcement, police science or police administration education. Because of limited tax dollars available for law enforcement training and education, the community college should be studied as a resource for training criminal justice personnel.

The law enforcement system employing one-half million persons plus those employed in corrections, probation, parole, and the court system, admits that adequate training programs using existing personnel and facilities, would take years to develop. Moreover, there is considerable doubt as to whether this could be achieved with existing agency facilities.

Crime Commission Recommendations

The recommendations of the President's Crime Commission form the foundation for community college affiliated training programs. After viewing their recommendations it becomes apparent that present training personnel and facilities of local agencies are incapable of meeting a minimum training need for

From Denny F. Pace, James D. Stinchcomb, and Jimmie C. Styles, *Law Enforcement Training and the Community College: Alternatives for Affiliation* (Washington, D.C.: American Association of Junior Colleges, 1970), pp. 1-11. Reprinted by permission of the authors and the publisher.

long range programs. Some of the recommendations dealing with education and training are:

1. All training programs should provide instruction on subjects that prepare recruits to exercise discretion properly, and to understand the community, the role of the police, and what the criminal justice system can and cannot do. Professional educators and civilian experts should be used to each specialized courses—law and psychology for example.... [1]
2. Formal police training programs for recruits in all departments, large and small, should consist of an absolute minimum of 400 hours of classroom work spread over a 4 to 6 months period so that it can be combined with carefully selected and supervised field training.[2]
3. Every general enforcement officer should have at least 1 week of intensive in-service training a year. Every officer should be given incentives to continue his general education or acquire skills outside his department.[3]
4. Deficiencies in current police training are not limited to recruit programs. The enforcement needs of a community change, and new concepts of police technology and department policy emerge. These facts dictate that training be a continuing process.[4]
5. Additional skills needed by prospective administrators and supervisors must be acquired through advanced education and specialized training. It is essential that departments undertake massive programs to provide the opportunity for interested personnel to continue their education.[5]
6. Colleges and universities should cooperate with individual departments in order to provide model career development programs....[6]

Other publications have supplemented these suggestions with such program areas as work experience and education for corrections. In the work experience programs developed for cooperation between the agency and the college these observations are drawn:[7]

1. If the student, the agency and the educational institution are to receive maximum benefits, they need to recognize the urgency for practical as well as academic experience.
2. ...Departments should progressively increase educational standards for supervisors and administrators at the earliest opportunity.... Only an educational institution can perform that task.

In the field of corrections, Vernon Fox makes this observation:

The Community and Junior college can provide basic education to the field of corrections. Education of personnel is the most effective way of improving correctional services. When 75 to 85 percent of the budget of a correctional institution or agency goes into its personnel, then improvement of the personnel must be the most appropriate approach to improvement of the program.

These publications have pointed out vividly that agencies and departments involved in the criminal justice process are not going to meet these needs with either local or regional training academies. Agencies have been strongly urged to utilize the already-established educational system. The benefits to be derived from agency involvement with established educational programs are clearly established in the publications of the American Association of Junior Colleges.

The one institution throughout the country that is locally oriented, locally supported, and most adaptable to insuring change in its own physical environment is the two-year institution—referred to as the junior college, the comprehensive community college, the county college, or the technical institute. This logical source of assistance, then, which in many instances already possesses a physical plant and a substantial staff, should assist in providing an effective training and education program. The utilization of all institutions of higher learning, but more specifically the comprehensive community colleges, with their growing national network of modern facilities and their mandates for local involvement, offer an obvious resource for both training and education. If agency administrators make their needs known, colleges will respond.

Several strengths characterize training programs affiliated with community colleges. The programs, by retaining local autonomy, are readily adaptable to local agency requirements. Community colleges can prepare a man to upgrade his technical expertise horizontally in the agency, and educational by-products of college relationships will provide for his vertical growth. This growth will result from the strong relationship between what is done in the training program and what follows in the educational program. The maintenance of a relationship with the entire educational spectrum allows the community college program to make a greater contribution to the individual. An additional advantage of college affiliation for criminal justice agencies is that education is becoming more and more recognized as a part of the basic requirement for the law enforcement officer and other agents of the criminal justice system.

The strength of an academic program lies in the foresight of criminal justice administrators. If educational increments and an across the board-upgrading of personnel are not major goals of the law enforcement administrator, then a college-based program will not be used effectively. College affiliation expands existing law enforcement training into a more meaningful and comprehensive instructional program.

Alternatives for Agency and College Affiliation

There are a number of possible combinations of training and education that may develop within the agency and the college. A few alternatives include:

1. A law enforcement agency provides training exclusively, with the possibility of some formal ties to a community college. This allows for agency control, but gradually may infuse some content from educational sources.
2. A community college provides services at an agency, with control of the academy retained by the agency. Several programs are developing in this manner. This plan assures a high degree of program quality, both academic and technical.
3. Shared control and responsibility for the academy through a

coordinating council, with defined responsibilities for the agency and the community college respectively. Over the next few years, this could be the most promising.
4. Law enforcement agencies provide services at a community college with direction of the academy resting with the educational institution. This has been used successfully in a number of programs, notably in California.
5. A community college provides law enforcement training on its campus with exclusive control, but with the possibility of an informal tie existing between the law enforcement agency and the college. There is less chance of this alternative developing, and logically so, since the agency has such a strong vested interest in the personnel the institution provides. This alternative does, of course, offer a possible solution to the training needs of dozens of small agencies that might exist in a community college district. However, in these cases, the third of the above alternatives would appear to be more sound.

Combinations of elements from the above alternatives can be expected to develop. Local needs and concerns along with varying leadership views will continue to influence the precise form these events may take in a particular situation. When we view training programs emanating from the college campus, it may be a single course of instruction, or it may be an entire training curriculum. The curriculum may be vocational, technical, or general education or any combination thereof and still be a training program. What the student should receive in a training program must depend upon local decisions.

Academically oriented training programs have the following desirable features:

1. The officer receives a more diverse view of the role and function of law enforcement in society.
2. The officer is exposed to college courses, thus breaking the barrier to higher education.
3. The officer receives the benefit of the professional expert in the field of social sciences in how to understand and deal with the prime commodity of law enforcement, which is people.
4. The image of the law enforcement officer to the public is enhanced because of his college education and exposure.
5. The law enforcement officer gains a new perspective when he finds he is capable of meeting the social challenge offered in education.

To illustrate the potential for training programs on the college campus, the American Association of Junior Colleges' guidelines on law enforcement education cited specific types of training with emphasis upon in-service short courses. The rationale is summarized as follows:[10]

1. The college-based program is responsive to the police administrator (and others) who furnish personnel and guidance for the program.
2. Law enforcement courses can be scheduled to meet job demands, yet on-going programs of suitable length to have lasting knowledge for the participant can be presented.
3. Short courses can do a great deal to enhance the operations of a law

enforcement organization when they can be related to actual performance in the field.
4. The community college can set the academic levels and areas of knowledge.
5. There is the availability of a staff which is highly specialized in areas peripherally related to law enforcement.
6. Supplemental instructional materials not normally found in training academies are available at the college level.

Training in colleges is as old as academia. Since the beginning of learning the proper balance between training and education has been debated. Educational theorists have categorized and strongly supported the merits of education versus those of training. Each school of thought has offered substantial support for its views. What has become apparent is that complete and comprehensive educational programs have included training activities. Conversely, a sound training program will include much education. If either education or training is being presented properly, each will have a substantial amount of the other included in its curriculum. Affiliation between law enforcement agencies and community colleges opens the way for a sound balance of training and education in developing competent personnel.

THE COMMUNITY COLLEGE SYSTEM: ITS SIGNIFICANCE TO LAW ENFORCEMENT TRAINING

As we move into the 1970s it is important to consider the impact community college systems may have upon law enforcement training and education. The direct influences will depend upon how colleges relate to community needs in the following areas:

1. Local option, a basic ideal for law enforcement training.
2. Stimulating the cooperative processes between law enforcement agencies and the colleges.
3. The capabilities of the community college to deliver quality programs.

Local Option

The term *local option* is dear to the hearts of most Americans. The connotation of this term at times seems to override economic and operational efficiency when it is evident there is a need to initiate or expedite public services. Whether there is some logical reason for retaining local option is open to debate.

A strong argument for retaining law enforcement education in community colleges is that its control will be local. Community colleges have moved to consolidate services, yet they retain the image of being locally sponsored institutions because they are dedicated to meeting community needs in their service areas. A community college district will serve several law enforcement jurisdictions and still retain the flexibility to service local training needs.

Pressure builds in a community to retain small police departments so that local control may be assured. Studies have indicated trends are now to integrate functions of the criminal justice system. One such study by Norrgard makes the following observations concerning the direction of police agencies in sponsored services.

> Regardless of size, financial resources, or proximity to other units of general government, the vast majority of local governments in governments in metropolitan areas deem themselves capable of administering a complete law enforcement program within their respective jurisdictions. This is one significant illustration of the failure to seek alternative means of problem solving.[11]

With particular reference to police service (*and this would apply equally to other agencies of the criminal justice system*), he says, "... the supportive activities can be consolidated and coordinated while reserving the important responsibility of providing necessary patrol service to each local government."[12] Training is specifically enumerated as being one of the staff services which lends well to some form of cooperative venture.

It is possible to retain local option and still have services of a cooperative nature by working together. A major advantage of this type of operation would be realized through better planning for the allocation of financial and other resources.

The Cooperative Processes Between Law Enforcement Agencies and the College

The opportunities being offered law enforcement education and training in the United States are being drastically weakened by the establishment of unrealistic goals with inadequate financial resources, shortages of qualified personnel, and a lack of efficient coordination at all levels. These weaknesses can be attacked only if there are concisely developed plans for a comprehensive training and educational system. Such a system, if it is to best serve the community, must bring the resources of law enforcement technology and educational expertise into focus. For a number of reasons community colleges offer the most logical locations to bring these coordinated concepts of education and training into being.

For the past two decades law enforcement education and training have experienced such rapid growth that there has been little time to pause and analyze the quality of these rapidly evolving programs. These programs have developed primarily as a stop-gap liaison between college programs and functional field operations. This has brought about a situation in which educational quality of some programs has been compromised. The education offered has, by necessity, been either training-oriented or outside the disciplines directly related to law enforcement.

Many educational programs developed in these two decades have, however, adapted to the changing needs of law enforcement in society. It is these quality programs that should be involved in the training processes. Because community colleges have been flexible in their approach to social issues confronting society, where law enforcement agencies and colleges work together to provide linkages between training and education, criminal justice personnel with broader professional preparation are produced.

Cooperation between law enforcement agencies and colleges will tend to build a stronger program for these reasons:

1. It places the recruit trainee in a viable educational environment and builds his interest and confidence in continuing off-duty educational programs.
2. It exposes the trainee to other local agency personnel and other department procedures. With consolidated curricula in the system there will tend to be cross-fertilization of procedures and policies.
3. It permits a pooling of the best available instructor talent. Colleges, in most instances, can and will utilize all agency personnel who are qualified to teach.
4. It is a highly visible demonstration of the college's interests in local needs. This also extends to the regional need for consolidation which is becoming more acceptable.
5. It allows greater innovation and experimentation in teaching techniques and curriculum planning than is presently being accomplished through unilateral training efforts.
6. It will develop a sounder relationship between the professional law enforcement administrator and the academic community and between the different agencies of the criminal justice system.
7. It can serve as a catalyst for developing and improving degree producing programs in the criminal justice field.
8. It will help improve the public image of agency personnel along with improvement in technical expertise.
9. It will tend to unveil the "mystique" which surrounds law enforcement training to the unknowing public insofar as what is taught or if it is taught at all.
10. It offers the agency administrator who is hampered by local, political, or budget considerations an opportunity to demonstrate what training can accomplish.

The Capabilities of the Community College to Deliver Quality Programs

The capability of the comprehensive community college is created by its general philosophy in responding to local needs. There is great variety in terms of communities being served and, of course, the needs of the suburban community are common to a degree, yet different from those of densely populated areas. For this reason, it cannot be said "this is the way to do it everywhere." The fact that community colleges are different and are *where the action is* makes them a good resource.

How effective colleges can be in assisting the training effort is going to depend upon:

1. Relating the training to a total systems concept.
2. The cost of training.
3. Staffing.

Training: The Total Systems Concept. The criminal justice system has become fragmented to the extent that each agency looks to its unique function as the final solution for the complex problems of law enforcement and administration. There are many common areas of training and education for police, probation, parole and corrections. For example, the understanding of human behavior is just as important for the police as it is for any of the criminal justice agencies. There is a grouping of common knowledge or core courses that should be common to agents of each service in the criminal justice system.

The total systems concept as proposed in this publication offers some unique advantages. There is need for concern when all agencies within the system insist upon a role of "going it alone." In a sense this gives each agency the opportunity to reinvent the wheel. This duplication is a waste of financial resources.

The Cost of Training: The Academy and the College. In the area of cost analysis, either agency can present arguments to support and justify a training program. The purpose of this publication is to maximize the total effort of a training program, not to justify or support one over the other. All monies are coming from the same taxpayer and the responsibility of those in training and education is to see that maximum use is made of the money available. The criteria should not be dollars, but the human resources that emerge to function in the democratic system. Since finances are going to have strong political impact on community leaders, some comments on the different criteria for evaluation of program cost are presented.

1. The administrative cost of the program will probably be less if the testing, records, or grading are included with other students in a college setting.
2. The amount of money available for training is limited, just as is manpower. Through flexible campus-based training, it is possible for a person to obtain some advanced training on his own time. This is especially true if educational inducements are a part of the total program.
3. Training for a local agency may not be less expensive than it has been in the past, simply because there has been no scheduled training. In any event training is not low in cost, but it has been found to be a solid investment.
4. The pooling of resources and facilities is going to constitute a major saving for taxpayers. In an organization that has the facilities already available, monies can then go to improved staffing rather than to building construction and facility maintenance.
5. The intangibles of college-based programs should be considered. Community colleges have supporting services, expertise in resource materials, training in instructional techniques and the administrative structure for enforcing standards of performance.
6. Community colleges have residual services for securing grants or special endowments that may not be otherwise available to operating agencies.

Staffing. Community colleges have done a rather remarkable job of attracting to their faculties individuals with not only appropriate academic credentials, but also with varieties of law enforcement backgrounds and experience. These individuals have been largely responsible for law enforcement program growth, since they have exerted leadership not only among in-service personnel, but also as career counselors in giving guidance to recent high school graduates.

Since many of them had been associated with law enforcement training during their careers, there was a personal adjustment necessary when they moved into the higher education environment and became responsible for theoretical material and less concerned with day-to-day practical procedural skills. It should not be surprising then that these newly emerging professors are in reality far better qualified to plan, coordinate, and evaluate short term delivery of knowledge. Having taught in the college classroom and having associated with the community college faculty, the former law enforcement officer has achieved a better concept of such essential reinforcements to learning as outside readings, research papers, and the value of essay-style responses to questions.

There is every reason to believe that both recruit and in-service learning can be increased substantially when it includes visual reinforcement, individualized study, and retention-demonstrated answers that evoke self-expression. Most authorities agree that serious deficiencies in the makeup of law enforcement personnel result from their unfamiliarity with their own literature as well as that from allied bodies of knowledge. An obvious ingredient in any professional is the desire to continually keep informed in areas of concern to him.

The community college library with its many inter-related resources can be readily available to assist the training function in the same way that it supports educational programs. An isolated law enforcement library in and of itself would certainly have usefulness, but the bodies of knowledge within which the police function operates are not isolated, but interwoven, and so must be all learning experiences.

Relying upon the community college law enforcement staff for coordination of training programs should insure a more unified approach to the presentation of lectures, particularly those given by guest instructors brought in to cover materials in their special field of competence. A program planned, coordinated, and supervised by an institution whose main purpose is delivering knowledge should have a considerable advantage over even the most worthy efforts that originate from organizations whose primary mission is not directed toward identifying, reassessing, and effectively presenting the world of knowledge.

NOTES

1. Report of the President's Commission on Law Enforcement and the Administration of Justice (Washington, D.C.: U.S. Government Printing Office, 1967).
2. Ibid.
3. Task Force Report, op. cit., p. 113.
4. Task Force Report: *The Police,* (Washington, D.C.: U.S. Government Printing Office, 1967), p. 139.
5. Ibid., p. 140.

6. Ibid., p. 141.

7. Jimmie C. Styles and Denny F. Pace, *Guidelines for Work Experience Programs in the Criminal Justice System,* (Washington, D.C.: American Association of Junior Colleges, 1969).

8. Vernon B. Fox, *Guidelines for Corrections Programs in Community and Junior Colleges* (Washington, D.C.: American Association of Junior Colleges, 1969), p. 9.

9. James D. Stinchcomb and Thompson S. Crockett, *Guidelines for Law Enforcement Education Programs in Community and Junior Colleges* (Washington, D.C.: American Association of Junior Colleges, 1968).

10. Stinchcomb and Crockett, *Guidelines for Law Enforcement,* pp. 20-21.

11. David L. Norrgard, *Regional Law Enforcement,* Public Administration Service, 1969, p. 1.

12. Ibid., p. 2.

LEEP — Its Development and Potential

William E. Caldwell

Prior to the twentieth century formalized police training as we know it today did not exist. The most prevalent method of preparation for police work was "on-the-job training." [1] Available records disclose that some of the earliest training programs in this country for basic police recruit training were Pennsylvania State Police, 1906; and Detroit and New York cities, 1911; and New York, New Jersey and Michigan State Police organizations had recruit programs by 1921.

However, it was not until 1916 that the first recorded involvement of an institution of higher education occurred. This was at the University of California in Berkeley when August Vollmer, then Chief of the Berkeley, California, Police Department, in conjunction with a Berkeley law faculty member, devised a summer program in criminology. Summer courses were offered almost every year from 1916 to 1931 at which time the School of Criminology was founded. [2]

In the summer of 1918, the University of California at Los Angeles offered a program in the Department of Criminology for policewomen. This school offered the added dimensions of field trips and outside lecturers (psychologists, judges, attorneys, probations officers, etc.).

William E. Caldwell is director of the office of Law Enforcement Assistance Administration in Washington, D.C.

From William E. Caldwell, "LEEP: Its Development and Potential,' *The Police Chief* 37, no. 8 (August 1970): 24-30. Reprinted by permission of the publisher.

By 1920, three trends in formalized preparation for police work were discernible:
1. Police programs were sponsored by institutions of higher education.
2. Formal training was provided for policemen and policewomen.
3. Law enforcement and the academic world were cooperating to a limited degree. [3]

In 1923, a "first" was recorded when the University of California, Berkeley, awarded an A.B. degree to a police officer with a minor in criminology. In 1925, the Graduate School of Harvard University established the Bureau of Street Traffic Research. While this was not a degree program, it was the initial entry of a prestigious eastern university into the area of specialized law enforcement programs.

While through the twenties cooperation between law enforcement agencies and institutions of higher education increased it was not until 1930 that the first two-year college police program in the United States was established at San Jose Junior College. [4] In rapid succession, other institutions followed suit: Los Angeles City College, 1932; the University of Southern California, 1933; Michigan State University, 1935. Also in 1935, after necessary curriculum adjustments, San Jose State Teachers College was authorized to grant the A.B. degree. [5]

Although new programs continued to be developed, it was not until after World War II, with the increasing number of junior colleges, that a significant expansion of police programs occurred. By 1957, there were 27 junior colleges offering A.A. degree programs. In 1961, there were 49. By 1962, the number of four-year institutions offering degree programs in law enforcement fields was 40. [6] According to a survey conducted by the International Association of Chiefs of Police, there were 261 programs in law enforcement available in 234 separate institutions by the fall of 1968. [7]

OLEA

Most of these programs developed on their own initiative without outside financial support. It was in 1966 that the next significant event in law enforcement education took place. The Office of Law Enforcement Assistance (OLEA), the predecessor of the Law Enforcement Assistance Administration (LEAA), started a small grant program to stimulate the development of police science degree programs. These were two-stage grants which provided up to $15,000 for first-year development funds and up to $25,000 for second-year implementation funds. Both stages required something in the way of a contribution on the part of the school. The purpose of these grants was consistent with developments in the President's Commission on Law Enforcement and Administration of Justice. (The final report of the Commission had not as yet been submitted but it was clear that some type of assistance should be started to provide educational opportunities to law enforcement personnel.)

It is noteworthy that the guidelines for this OLEA grant program did not attempt to dictate a model curriculum but rather laid down the following broad principles and conditions:

1. The school had to be accredited by the recognized state accrediting unit and by a regional accrediting association. Exceptions were permitted where the school did not have enough time for full accreditation.
2. The curriculum designed during the development phase must have been approved by the appropriate state higher education authority.
3. In addition to courses directly relating to police science the curriculum should include whatever other basic courses are considered a prerequisite for the Associate (or baccalaureate) degree.

It was anticipated that the required degree offerings would include public administration, law and government, behavioral sciences, and liberal arts subjects in addition to the specialized courses for the law enforcement officer. However, this was further qualified by the requirement that the curriculum balance for associate degrees would be approximately half the courses in general academic subjects and the other half in police science. In programs leading to the Bachelor's degree, the anticipated curriculum balance as between technical and general academic courses was expected to be comparable to that prevailing for other degree program areas of study within the institution.

With these very broad guidelines 28 colleges and universities received 48 grants totalling nearly one million dollars. Of the 28 schools; 14 developed two-year programs; 8 developed four-year programs; and 6 developed both two- and four-year programs. The only two priorities for the distribution of grants were first to schools in states which had no higher education programs in criminal justice and second to schools in metropolitan areas without such programs.

OTHER EFFORTS

Concurrent with the OLEA program, the American Association of Junior Colleges developed "Guidelines for Law Enforcement Education Programs in Community and Junior Colleges." It proposed a balanced curriculum for a two-year program which leaned toward instruction in general and liberal arts subjects but still retained a heavy load of professional subjects. To the best of my knowledge this was the first concerted attempt at bringing a standard curriculum to educational institutions in the area of police science.

The other major moving force in law enforcement education during this period was The President's Commission on Law Enforcement and Administration of Justice. It recommended that police departments take immediate steps to establish a minimum requirement of a baccalaureate degree for all supervisory and executive positions. It further stated that the ultimate aim of all police departments should be that all personnel with general enforcement powers have baccalaureate degrees.[8] While setting such a high ultimate goal for police agencies, the Commission attempted to distinguish between education and training and questioned the wisdom of giving degree credit for technical courses.[9] Regardless of the validity of the Commission recommendations it nevertheless set the tone for emphasizing the need for education in law enforcement.

While the main concern had been about the police, the Commission did not neglect corrections. It stressed the need for solidifying the correctional discipline by encouraging the funding of faculty recruitment and retention, research programs, fellowships and stipends, and sustained support for internships and field placement programs.[10]

As the Commission was developing substantive background information to persuade a program of law enforcement education, Congress too was developing plans in this area. Most notable were bills introduced in the respective houses by Representative William R. Anderson of Tennessee and Senator Abraham A. Ribicoff of Connecticut. These laid the foundation for the ultimate language of subsequent legislation.

SAFE STREETS ACT

The sum of all of these efforts is reflected in the next significant happening in law enforcement education—the Omnibus Crime Control and Safe Streets Act of 1968, P.L. 90-351. Section 406 of this law authorized the LEAA to carry out programs of academic educational assistance to improve and strengthen law enforcement. Basically, it provided for a program of financial assistance to make loans and grants available to students enrolled in courses leading to degrees in programs of higher education relevant to law enforcement. Although the Act defines law enforcement as all activities pertaining to crime prevention or reduction and enforcement of the criminal law, including police, courts, and corrections. I will only discuss the effects upon the police community in this article.

Section 406 being a relatively noncontroversial section, there was very little legislative history in either of the committees. Although this required a narrow interpretation of the Section, the absence of administrative provisions allowed LEAA to develop a broad and viable program of implementation. As head of the task force to implement this section, after consultation with the Office of Education, Department of Health, Education and Welfare (OE, DHEW), I recommended to the Administration that the provisions of Section 406 be administered through the Law Enforcement Education Program (LEEP). This was in June, 1968. For the first time in history, the federal government was committed to furnishing massive aid for the educational upgrading of personnel in the criminal justice system. Because the first year's appropriation of $6.5 million was available for only one semester, the spring session of the 1968-69 academic year, one could project the effective use of $13 million for a complete academic year.

WHAT IS LEEP?

LEEP is an aid program which provides funds in the form of loans and grants for study in areas related to law enforcement. The LEAA enters into an agreement with a college or university to make grants and loans under the terms prescribed by the Administration. At the schools, the LEEP is usually administered by the Student Financial Aid Officer (SFAO). In order for a school to be eligible to participate it must be accredited by one of the six regional accrediting associations. No funds are awarded by LEAA directly to student—only through the SFAO.

LOAN PROGRAM

The loan program is geared mainly toward bringing new young people into the field with a background of higher education. It provides for loans up to $1,800 per academic year for *anyone* desiring a career in criminal justice who is enrolled *full-time* in a degree program *related directly* to law enforcement. It is significant to note that Congress used the term *directly related* in establishing program eligibility. This required the LEAA in effect to approve curriculum and to determine what is actually relevant to performance within the criminal justice system. It would have been presumptuous on the part of LEAA to have come out with a model curriculum so early in the program because general agreement to disagree on the best approach to law enforcement education then existed, and still does, within the field. However, if a narrow position with respect to directly related programs had been taken only about 325 schools in the country would have been eligible to make loans. There would have been no geographic dispersion, most of the schools being located in nine states.

To satisfy the requirements of the statute and to broaden the coverage of the loan program, LEEP defined a directly related program as a course of study which included semester credit hours of directly related subjects—and a broad definition was given to directly related subjects. Preliminary studies and discussions with the Advisory Committee and with practitioners indicated that perhaps a broad liberal education was the best way to prepare students for work in the criminal justice system.

Further, to use the loan program as a recruiting device, the SFAO's were told that no needs analysis was necessary when computing the direct education expenses of the student. It was felt that, regardless of need, the loan could serve as a lure to bring new people into the system if the student were guaranteed at least the cost of his education; i.e., tuition fees, books, supplies, and transportation. The difference between this figure and the statutory limit of $1,800 per academic year was left to the discretion of the SFAO.

Because the loan program required the student to carry a full-time academic load and because so few officers are able to do this, we felt that priority in awards should go to in-service officers and to those officers on academic leave from their agencies to attend school. Second priority was to go to any student who expressed an intent to pursue a career in criminal justice. The SFAO's were asked to screen applicants as closely as possible with respect to intent and most of them require the prospective student to furnish a letter in this regard.

USE OF THE LOAN PROGRAM

Agencies having a unique opportunity to formalize recruiting efforts and to guarantee a steady source of educated personnel by establishing close working ties with local colleges and universities. Because most criminal justice agencies do not hire people under 21 years of age, they have a limited source of manpower from which to recruit. Most talented high school graduates have already committed themsleves to definite career objectives by the time they are 21 and therefore criminal justice agencies must generally select from a small supply of possibly less capable people or to happenstance. A program which is properly coordinated among the agency, the college representative, and high school counselors can attract talented high school students to criminal justice careers. This would have the effect of upgrading the quality of recruits, thereby raising entrance standards and possibly establishing a personnel force which would be enhanced in the public's image. Although the agency could not guarantee the student a position upon completion of his studies, it nevertheless could assure him of possible candidacy for positions within the system.

Because LEEP loans are forgiven at a rate of 25 percent for each year of service in the criminal justice system, many prospective students would be attracted to the system. Further, in-service law enforcement officers have the advantage of working and earning concurrent forgiveness. However, anyone failing to enter the criminal justice system after completion of his education must repay the loan to the LEAA on the basis of minimum payments of $50.00 per month and at a rate of 7 percent interest per year on the unpaid balance of the loan.

GRANT PROGRAM

The main emphasis of the grant program is to upgrade the educational level of personnel within the criminal justice system. It provides grants of up to $200 per quarter or $300 per semester for officers of publicly funded law enforcement agencies enrolled on a full-time or part-time basis in courses in graduate and undergraduate programs which are either related to law enforcement or are in an area suitable for persons employed in law enforcement. The two major differences between the grant program and the loan program is that only in-service officers are eligible for participation in the grant program and the grant program course of study does not have to be in an area *directly* related to law enforcement.

By omitting the word *directly* Congress recognized that law enforcement is a multi-disciplined profession, and LEEP reflects that in its guidelines. Full discretion for program eligibility is placed in the hands of the employing executive who certifies that the student's course of study is relevant to law enforcement. In the early stages, and still today, many chiefs feel that because the man or woman is working for a police agency, police science is the only subject area that the person should be or could be studying under LEEP. A better use of manpower might be to try to relate the program of education more closely to functional needs of the agency. For example, if a man is involved in recruitment or personnel processing then he might properly be studying Personnel Management. Where he is working in a large communications section, particularly in a major metropolitan departments, then he should perhaps be enrolled in a Computer Science program. The same applies to Business Administration, Accounting, and other disciplines. If he is in a community relations unit he ought to be enrolled in a Behavioral Science program. The point is that as long as the agency has a need for a particular type of expertise, it is fundable under the grant program. If the chief is imaginative he can enhance the efficiency of his agency by taking a close look at what his men are studying.

This is especially true when examining the quality of local offerings. The agency should demand quality in education. It should insist on qualified faculty and not be satisfied merely with the years of practical experience the teacher has but also determine what academic credentials to teach he possesses. Quality should not be compromised just because local funds are not involved. The role of the school is to serve the community. Give them that opportunity by expressing your needs.

Although it is referred to as a grant program the student incurs an obligation to remain with his employing agency for two years following the completion of his education; otherwise, the grant must be repaid on the same terms as a loan except that there is no forgiveness attached. While this may seem restrictive to the students, in most cases agencies must revise schedules to accommodate the students and it is not unreasonable to expect some return from the student in the way of service for this accommodation.

OTHER ASPECTS

There are other aspects to LEEP beyond the mere conditions of the grant and loan provisions. With respect to administration, because the Act did not provide for administrative expenses to the schools for handling the program and because this program was meant to make it as easy as possible to allow criminal justice personnel to raise its educational level, it was decided during the task force days to make this program as free from bureaucratic snarls as possible. It is generally accepted in student financial aid circles that this has been accomplished. Funds are moved easily to the schools and then to the students. Transfers of unused funds from one school to another school with needs is accomplished in minimum time.

At first it may appear that LEEP is an uncomplicated and an insignificant phase of the total LEAA program because of its budget size in relationship to the Planning and Block Program, but this is far from true. LEEP has implications which affect not only the criminal justice system but the academic community as well.

The police world must be prepared to accept the flow of educated students who will be coming to it as a result of LEEP. Take, for example, the graduates of criminal justice education programs. In order to have their loans forgiven they must secure employment in the law enforcement community. Regardless of what the entrance requirements are they will be competing with applicants who at best have high school diplomas. It is to be expected that the college graduate will prevail in the selection process. And even though no salary incentives are offered he will accept the job in order to earn his forgiveness. Thus the police agency, even through its present method of screening, will be beset by college trained individuals.

The educated officer, if this educational experience has been worthwhile and if he has any initiative, will be dissatisfied with performing some of the mundane, monotonous police tasks that presently exist. He will want a mental challenge to correspond with the physical challenge of police work. He will want to apply his education to his job. Hopefully, this will stimulate agencies to perform job analyses which will result in better manpower utilization.

POLICE IMAGE

Regardless of what impact educated individuals will have upon the police system, it is equally important to assess the impact this will have on society as a whole. One noted sociologist has cited three problems which appear to be an integral part of the police profession. He mentions specifically *social isolation* from the community at large; *solidarity* of law enforcement personnel among themselves; and *alienation* of minority and underprivileged groups. [11] Hopefully, an education which involves an understanding of the environment in which he functions will be a part of any program of higher education for criminal justice personnel and will assist in resolving the aforementioned problems.

In addition to the above, the educational process must create an understanding of the total system in which the police officer functions. He must understand not only the police subsystem, but the subsystems of courts and corrections as well. As he rises through the executive echelon of the police agency he must be educated in management techniques. Education must be complemented by in-service training to acquaint the man with the new responsibilities he will encounter in his next step up the ladder. LEEP can help in all of this.

From its modest beginning of $6.5 million, LEEP grew to $18 million in fiscal year 1970. The House of Representatives has, at this writing, approved a budget of $21 million for fiscal 1971. Over 19,000 in-service law enforcement officers took advantage of LEEP during its first six months of operation. Preliminary reports indicate that as many as 50,000 may have been enrolled during the 1969-70 academic year. Already schools have requested funds to support over 105,000 students for the 1970-71 academic year. These figures echo a resounding acceptance on the part of law enforcement. Those agencies which are lagging behind in encouraging and in making possible education for their men will find it more difficult to compete in the manpower market. The competition for capable personnel is keen. Educational incentives and modern management techniques will help retain these people. LEEP will help.

WHAT IS NEEDED

Educational institutions must assess their offerings. Are they providing for the needs of the real world? The men presently going through school are the potential chiefs of police later in this century. Are we only providing the skills for day-to-day operations and ignoring the future? Do all police officers really need a baccalaureate education? Should we perhaps be concentrating on the A.A. degree for the rank and file and using the four-year program for areas of specialty and for education of the potential hierarchy of law enforcement? These are all questions with which we are wrestling. As the answers unfold, LEEP will be the vehicle for moving forward with improvements in the system.

As the education of society as a whole increases, police officers must at least strive for the norm. From the response to date, I believe that there is no other group in this country more anxious to take advantage of educational opportunities than policemen. As long as we make these opportunities available to them I believe that they will use them and that they will raise themselves as a profession above the educational norm of society as a whole. We can provide all of the sophisticated equipment we want but if the man is ill-prepared to use it, it is money poorly spent. Manpower development is what we are talking about and that is what LEEP is.

NOTES

1. *The Police, The President's Commission on Law Enforcement and Administration of Justice*, p. 10.

2. *University of California, Berkeley,* Bulletin of the School of Criminology (1966-67), p. 7.

3. Allen E. Gammage, *Police Training in the United States* (Springfield, Ill.: Charles C Thomas, 1963), p. 62.

4. T. W. MacQuarrie, San Jose State College Police School, *Journal of Criminal Law, Criminology and Police Science,* vol. 26, no. 2 (July-August 1935): 255.

5. Gammage: *Op. cit.,* p. 65.

6. A. C. Germann, Frank D. Day and Robert R. J. Gallatti, *Introduction to Law Enforcement,* (Springfield, Illinois: Charles C Thomas, p. 243.

7. Crockett, *Law Enforcement Education: 1968* (IACP, 1968).

8. *The President's Commission on Law Enforcement and Administration of Justice,* p. 109, 110.

9. *The Police:* op. cit., p. 128.
10. *Corrections, The President's Commission on Law Enforcement and Administration of Justice,* p. 100.
11. Marvin E. Wolfgang, Address at Michigan State University, May, 1965. "The Police and Their Problems," *Papers Presented at the Eleventh Annual National Institute on Police and Community Relations, P. G.*

Federal Aid to Local Police — Trick or Treat?

W. Cleon Skousen

This was the startling proposal made by the White House in a Presidential message to Congress during February of this year. It was the first hint that plans were afoot for a massive Federal Aid program for local police. Of course, the police were not to be the only recipients—correctional and judicial agencies were included—but it was obvious that the police were intended to receive the bulk of the benefit.

At first the announcement was received with loud huzzas from local political leaders. Unfortunately, it has become commonplace for many home-town officials who have been guilty of neglecting their local responsibility to look to Washington as the giver of all blessings and ask that the general funds of the U.S. Treasury be employed to remedy the ravages of their own derelictions. Surveys have shown that the biggest single factor retarding the rapid development of a first-class police service throughout the United States has been the careless indifference of many local politicians to the manifest needs of their respective police agencies. But the prospect of massive finances from Washington—now there was something to cheer a politician's heart, and surely this must be the logical cure for the current crime crisis.

But is it?

A LESSON FROM FEDERAL FINANCING OF LOCAL EDUCATION

Cautious police administrators have been recently noting the Federal Government's use of naked coercive authority over local educational affairs as a result of power acquired through Washington's multi-billion dollar program of financial aid to education. They have wondered if the same devious pattern

From W. Cleon Skousen, "Federal Aid to Local Police—Trick or Treat?" *Law and Order* 15, no. 6 (June 1967): 10-12, 42-45. Reprinted by permission of the publisher.

might not be contemplated for the purpose of gradually nationalizing the police.

The Chicago superintendent of schools found himself being ordered to take steps which were specifically forbidden under the law authorizing Federal aid to education. Yet 30 million dollars in U.S. funds were being withheld by the Federal administrator unless the Chicago schools knuckled under. What bothered the Chicago superintendent the most was the fact that the Federal official was demanding a procedure which was bad for the Chicago schools and bad for the students. Widespread publicity was required to make the Federal administrator back down.

Just recently the University of Michigan found itself being threatened with a loss of all Government grants and contracts unless the administration began recruiting students and faculty on a basis which was blatantly ethnical discrimination. University officals were told that instead of recruiting on the basis of "equal opportunity" and "intellectual competence" as in the past, they must now give preferential treatment to a designated ethnic group. This was to be the price for future Federal financing on which the University had become extremely dependent.

There has been a rapid escalation of scandalous incidents such as these where school administrators have protested the improper meddling of Federal officials in the procedures and policies of local school system. Ironically, some of the educators currently making the loudest protests were among the most vocal advocates of Federal aid to education when it was first proposed. They assured their colleagues the "Federal aid most assuredly did not mean Federal control." But intervening events led the Chicago Tribune to declare, "We are learning the truth of the Supreme Court dictum of 25 years ago, 'It is hardly lack of due process for the government to regulate that which it subsidizes.' The fiat to the University of Michigan verifies a self-evident fact." (Editorial Page, March 14, 1967)

LAUNCHING OF THE ORIGINAL
LAW ENFORCEMENT ASSISTANCE ACT

It was in 1965 that the Federal Government made its first modest entry into the area of financial aid to local police. Sponsors of the bill were perfectly aware of the existing suspicion that Washington might be trying to inject itself into local police matters. The bill was therefore signed into law with the absolute assurance that "nothing will be done to indicate federal direction, supervision, or control over the organization, administration, or personnel of any state or local police force or other law enforcement agency." But this was exactly the same kind of disclaimer that came out of Washington with the launching of the first program of Federal aid to education!

The Law Enforcement Assistance Act of 1965 was very modest. It started out with a mere $7,249,000. The President said it was simply to provide "support for research, for experiments, and for new programs." The administration of the Act was assigned to the Department of Justice and several outstanding professional police administrators were employed to supervise the dispersal of funds. These administrators conscientiously interpreted the Act in its strictest sense and set up a number of criteria which had to be satisfied before any grant would be made. They provided safeguards so that the Federal Government would not become involved in administering local police power. No money could be spent for regular police equipment or to subsidize established salary schedules. Funds were only available in quantities of $15,000 to $150,000 and these were restricted to the actual costs of new experiments in crime prevention, police techniques, police training or establishing uniform programs of minimum standards for police personnel.

Anyone who is familiar with the reasonable costs of such limited projects will immediately recognize that these are relatively modest plans. There was nothing at that point which would raise any issue of Federal interference in local police affairs. Nevertheless, the annual convention of the IACP passed a resolution in 1965 declaring that the International Association of Chiefs of Police was definitely opposed to "any attempted encroachment by the federal government into state or local government in the law enforcement field."

It was right after the report of the President's Commission on Law Enforcement and Administration of Justice that there began to be widespread proposals for massive Federal aid to local police. This resulted in the President's request for $50,000,000 in 1968 and $300,000,000 in 1969. It was obvious that the Washington planners had a lot more in mind than the modest dimensions provided in the Law Enforcement Assistance Act of 1965.

Senate Bill 824 was introduced calling for a comprehensive subsidy of education for policemen and potential recruits, also the outright purchase of certain types of equipment for police departments and the construction of certain of facilities. The payments for salaries of police cadets and subsidies for technical equipment were brought up for consideration. Proposed Federal participation was indicated as being between 50 and 90 percent, the balance being provided by the States. All of this would lead the professional police administrator to only one conclusion: here the Law Enforcement Assistance Program was less than two years old and already the original guidelines were collapsing and the Federal Government had begun talking about massive spending in areas which would inevitably lead to policy-making and supervisory control.

THE LEGITIMATE ROLE OF THE FEDERAL GOVERNMENT

Back in the Gangster Era of the 'Thirties' when a frantic Congress was considering the possibility of creating a national police force, J. Edgar Hoover testified against it. He stated that the creation of a national police force would mark the beginning of the end for American democracy. He recognized that under the Tenth Amendment the states had never delegated authority to the Federal Government to intervene in local or intra-state police problems. He therefore suggested that the Federal Government restrict itself to the areas where it could legitimately "promote the general welfare" without violating Constitutional barriers.

At that time these areas were considered to be:

1. The creation of a National Police Academy to train local officers.
2. The creation of a scientific crime laboratory to service departments which could not afford laboratories of their own.
3. Development of a uniform system for the reporting of crimes and monthly collection of them on a nationwide basis.
4. Granting of Federal jurisdiction over major crimes involving certain inter-state offenses.

Funds to provide for these four areas of activity were enacted into law. Within a very short time they paid tremendous dividends. Not only were the gangster elements forced out of many areas of inter-state crime, but the services provided by the FBI soon became a most significant factor in the upgrading and professionalizing of American law enforcement. During the first ten years after World War II the American police were making tremendous strides.

Then something happened.

THE FEDERAL GOVERNMENT CREATES A CRISIS

Beginning in the latter 1950s the U.S. Supreme Court began overturning decisions of the lower Federal courts and of the State Supreme Courts with reference to police procedures in gathering evidence against criminals. These rulings were first applied only to the police in the District of Columbia but eventually the Court employed the Fourteenth Amendment to force their decisions upon the police procedures of all the States. The impact was immediate. Crime, which had been significantly reduced in the District of Columbia, immediately shot up after the Mallory decision. As procedural restrictions spread to the police of the states, crime increased substantially all over the country.

While this was going on, the Executive branch of the Federal Government commenced playing havoc with law and order in many cities by openly promoting and encouraging as a matter of official policy certain private groups who claimed to be representing the under-privileged minorities. These private groups were operating under self-appointed leadership which steadily moved from pious pretentions of non-violence to flagrant provocations leading to widespread rioting, burning, looting, shooting and other forms of illegal and irresponsible mob action. A number of top government officials publicly praised the actions of these groups in violating state laws or local ordinances with which they disagreed. Local law enforcement found itself caught in the Washington-supported cross-fire of this completely un-American approach to bring about social change by violence and lawlessness.

Law enforcement was further harassed by other private groups professing strong anti-police sentiments which decided it was a good time to take advantage of the confusion and crime by blaming it on the police. They recklessly charged these disastrous developments on "police brutality" and urged that the police be shackled under the disciplinary authority of civilian review boards.

All this had its influence in creating overt public hostility toward the police. With growing frequency officers found themselves being attacked by boisterous crowds as the officers tried to make arrests or prevent crimes from being perpetrated. The police image which had gained so much stature during the years after World War II sudenly began to lose its luster under the smudge and smear tactics of all these inimical influences. But the police were not the only casualties.

It soon became obvious that the whole nation was suffering from the impact of these corrosive influences. Narcotics, pornography, assaults, vandalism, murder, robbery, rape and theft have been gradually becoming a way of life in many sectors of the nation. And no place can boast of being much worse than the headquarters city of the Federal Government, Washington, D.C.

Exasperated Congressmen tried a number of times to remedy the situation but were astonished to find their efforts being opposed by high-level central planners in the Executive branch of government. The foggy bottom intellects used their influence on the President so that when a bill was passed to tighten up on pornography it was vetoed. Last year a crime bill drafted to rectify the damage resulting from a host of Supreme Court decisions also was vetoed. The White House as much as told the Congressmen that they didn't know what the police really needed and therefore the Executive branch would come up with its own plan. It turned out to be $50,000,000 for 1968 and $300,000,000 for 1969.

But millions from the Federal Government with all the Federal controls which are inherent in such subsidies is not what is going to win the war on crime. And police administrators know it. When veteran Police Chief Thomas J. Cahill of San Francisco saw what the President's Commission on Law Enforcement was going to recommend, he joined the six other members of the Commission to write a strong dissent. Over one third of the members of the Commission including three past-presidents of the American Bar Association, the California Attorney General, the President of the National Association of District Attorneys and Chief Cahill all signed this minority report. They suggested that in lieu of all the impractical cornstarch being strewn about to confuse the issues, that the nation return to some very elementary brass-tack facts which have demonstrated their reliability in fighting crime in the past. They then went ahead and recommended almost the same identical program which Congress had previously passed and which the President had vetoed!

CONCLUSION

The traditional separation of powers provided by the Constitution has been seriously impaired by Federal authorities in recent years. A powerful clique of central planners have used multi-billion subsidy programs to invade numerous areas originally intended to be excluded from Federal control. The local police appear to be the next target. Police administrators have seen what is happening in Federally subsidized public education, and it is perfectly obvious what will happen if the central planners abandon the legitimate Federal areas identified by J. Edgar Hoover and start moving in the direction of massive Federal aid which portends the nationalizing of all American police.

It is true that in many cases community leaders have not given their local departments sufficient funds to function efficiently but this is no excuse for following the dangerous practice of getting them from million dollar grants-in-aid out of Washington. A more wholesome alternative is provided in House Bill 4479 introduced by Congressman Edward J. Gurney. His proposal would return a certain percentage of all Federal income taxes to the states to be used exclusively for law enforcement and be administered under the exclusive control of the states.

But equally important is the need for a proper functioning of government on all levels. Congress has the responsibility under the Constitution of compelling the Supreme Court to stay within its designated limits. It also has the task of following the suggestion of the minority report of the President's Commission and redefining authorized police procedures. The Executive branch of the government has the responsibility of restoring the dignity of government by law and not by private whims and capriciousness of individual men. We want to see a return to a policy of orderly change by due process instead of legislative intimidation by mobs and violence.

As for the police, they deserve to have the local financial support which is absolutely essential if they are to continue the improvement of their professional service. This should be accomplished without their being made to feel beholden to a Washington bureaucracy for their salaries and equipment. They want a legitimate relationship with the Federal government based on cooperation, not consolidation.

All of these are important facets of the overall strategy if we are to win the nation's war against crime.

SECTION FIVE

Police Discretion

Overview

"ALICE" WOULD HAVE QUESTIONS TRAVELING IN A POLICE PATROL CAR. FBI Inspector Dwight J. Dalbey takes an imaginary "Alice in Wonderland" tour through the land of criminal justice with a police officer on patrol. The tour is through an imaginary major city in the United States. The time is now. The police officer has so many important decisions to make under stress and under conditions calling for immediate action, most of the time alone. The officer's guidelines are vague and ill-defined in many cases, in view of conflicting jurisdictions and court philosophies. He points out that the policeman serves two masters: the community and the law—sometimes a nearly impossible task.

POLICE DISCRETION. Professor James Q. Wilson critically examines the professional behavior of police officers and points out some variety in their behavior. The book from which this chapter was excerpted is *Varieties of Police Behavior*. The reading is an objective appraisal of the broad discretionary powers of the working police officer, and an assessment of how he uses that power.

POLICE DISCRETION. A few months ago Thomas F. Adams and several graduate students set about to study the police officer's concept of the discretionary power that he has as an individual professional within the criminal justice system. Not a comprehensive study by far, but more of a survey to determine the scope and depth of future studies, this paper does point out that the officer is both aware of his discretionary powers and that he uses them. The hypothesis "that the personal value systems of individual police officers determine the parameters of law enforcement practices by the police" was tested and tentatively affirmed.

"Alice" Would Have Questions Traveling in a Police Patrol Car

Dwight J. Dalbey

One hundred years ago an Englishman whose pen name was Lewis Carroll wrote one of the great classics of literature, which came to be called "Alice in Wonderland." It is a fanciful tale of a small child in a summer meadow who followed a talking rabbit into his burrow and discovered deep underground a topsy-turvy world. Birds and animals talked to her like human beings, and although she always said and did what seemed to her judgment to be quite right on earth, it was always the wrong thing down there. She was forever in trouble. Of course, it was only a dream, as she happily discovered on waking to find herself beside an older sister who had been reading a book.

If Lewis Carroll were writing his classic story in America today, he would have no need for the fictional device of sending Alice down a rabbit hole in a cow pasture. He could arrange for her to discover a topsy-turvy world much more simply by putting her into a police patrol car making the rounds in one of our major cities. Suppose we put Alice in the patrol car and see through her eyes what she finds.

But first we must set the stage with some common police incident which combines the two factors typical of so many situations with which the police officer is confronted—first, a high degree of ambiguity of fact, and second, an equally high degree of compulsion to act. The facts of the case often are obscure and difficult of ascertainment, but the law requires, and the public expects, that the officer will act quickly, decisively, and accurately in sorting them out. This is the world of the police officer on patrol.

Setting the stage, it is 3 a.m, on a soft summer night in a modest residential section of the city. A householder awakens from his sleep with a vague premonition of danger and walks to the window looking out on his backyard. There in the half light of night he sees the figure of a man staring intently at his house. The man holds some dimly outlined object. It may be a weapon, but the householder cannot know for sure.

From Dwight J. Dalbey, *"Alice* Would Have Questions Traveling in a Police Patrol Car," *FBI Law Enforcement Bulletin* (July 1966), pp. 9-13, 22-27. Reprinted by permission of the author. Footnotes have been deleted by the editor.

Moving quietly to an adjoining room, the householder calls the police. Two officers in a radio car answer the call. Alice is with them. Now they are rounding the back corner of the house and coming through the gate to confront the situation. Many an officer has answered a call of this same general nature in the past and many will do so in the future. Change the scene, if you wish, to any one of a thousand different common police situations and the result is the same. The officer still is confronted with his constant problem—a high degree of ambiguity of fact and a high degree of compulsion to act.

"Who is this man," Alice wonders. "Is he a murderer, a burglar, an escaped convict, or only a diabetic wandering aimlessly in shock for lack of insulin?" Perhaps he is none of these—nothing more than an irate neighbor intending to wreak vengeance upon a tomcat that has been keeping him awake half the night.

And whoever he is, what will he do? Will he shoot? Will he slash at the officers with a knife? Will he run? Or will he merely beg their pardon for having done something foolish?

Alice does not know it, but these same questions are running through the minds of the officers. They have met these types and these reactions before, and some of them bear the scars of knives, bullets, and broken bottles to prove it. And the officers know something else—a fact that Alice in her childlike innocence may not quite grasp. They know that they are alone and must find all the immediate answers for themselves. They know that if Alice might rub Aladdin's lamp and direct that mythical character to instantly summon into emergency session the Supreme Court of the United States, surrounded by the most eminent scholars of the law, the prosecutors, and the defense lawyers—all those who may speak learnedly of this case after months or years of deliberation—none of them, either singly or collectively, could possibly shed the slightest ray of light on who this man is, why he is here, or what he will do next; no one knows. They would limit themselves to one single opinion—that the police must do something. But this the officers already know. They are charged by the law with a duty to act. So they must act alone, without legal counsel until morning. This is a police officer's world.

Moving closer now, the officers identify themselves. They see that the man holds in his hand a short, stout stick. It is not a weapon, really, yet a burglar or a murderer could put it to his uses. He drops the stick to the ground. Now the danger of physical attack is past, unless he carries a gun, or a knife, or prefers to use his fists.

The officers do what they can. One asks the man who he is and what he is doing here. Now we can stage the scene in two different ways, either of which conforms to reality. Perhaps the man stands mute; some do. Or he gives an answer which only deepens the ambiguity of the circumstances. Police officers often receive answers that are ambiguous and unresponsive to their questions.

Alice is puzzled by the failure of the officers to arrest immediately, and so is the family watching from the window upstairs. Anyone who has read a detective story or seen crimes solved on television knows what to do—arrest him on the spot and take him to the station. But Alice has forgotten something and so have the sheltered observers upstairs. This is 1966, not 1960.

In 1960 the officers, on receiving an ambiguous reply, or no response at all, would have placed the man under arrest. Then, searching him immediately, they would have taken the gun or knife with which he might have attacked them, and any instrumentality, fruit, or contraband of crime found in his possession. Had they found in the neighborhood an automobile with a warm radiator, they would have searched that, too, and taken the things of crime found therein. At the station house they would have interrogated this man. If they found that he had committed a crime, the man would most likely have confessed and pleaded guilty. If he elected to stand trial, the question of the legality of the arrest may not have been raised at all since it was not then a Federal constitutional issue, or would have been resolved against him, and the courts in approximately half the states would have allowed into evidence against him the things of crime found in his automobile without questioning and legality of the search. And, of course, if the officers found the man to be sick, they would have taken him to a doctor or a hospital. If he had done no more than chase a lovesick tomcat, they would have chided him for his indiscretion and sent him home—in the patrol car. But, as I said, this is 1966. The rules have changed, but Alice and many others do not know it.

How have the rules changed? In 1964 the Supreme Court of the United States said that from this time forward no officer in the land lawfully may arrest anyone, at any time or place, unless there is at the moment of arrest a sufficient quantity and quality of information to show probable cause for belief of guilt as defined under the Fourth Amendment to the Constitution of the United States.

Of course, the officer still makes the arrest according to the law of his state, as he used to do, but if the arrested man thinks the state law is out of kilter with the Federal Constitution, he now can take his case all the way to the Supreme Court. If that High Court finds that the arrest did not meet the standards of the Fourth Amendment because there was not enough information to make an arrest, then the arrest simply was illegal, regardless of what the state law and state court said.

In 1961 the Supreme Court said that from now on every officer in the land who makes a search and seizure must do it in a manner that is reasonable under its interpretation of the Fourth Amendment of the Federal Constitution. If the officer fails to make his search in a manner approved by the Federal court, none of the things of crime which he finds can be used as evidence against this man in any court, either state or Federal. In 1961 the Supreme Court held that if an officer violates a Federal constitutional right, such as the right to be free from unreasonable searches, or arrest without probable cause, the person whose right has been violated may bring the officer into Federal Court and sue him personally for damages. In 1963 the Supreme Court said that if any person is brought into court charged with a felony, he automatically has a Federal constitutional right to a lawyer for his defense. A lawyer, studying the case at his leisure, has a good chance of finding some fatal flaw in the legality of the action taken by the officers here tonight under the pressure of danger and their duty to act swiftly and decisively. The lawyer, like the judges, has been trained in the constitutional law of arrest and search, but the officers have not. And he has the luxury of time to think and study before acting.

The officers know the law has changed. They are now more cautious. That is why they do not yet arrest, here in 1966.

The officers tell Alice why they are cautious. They explain that for the law, as well as for their own safety, this is the most critical moment of the case. As to the law, still another decision of the Supreme Court in 1963 held that if the arrest is illegal because there is not sufficient probable cause for belief of guilt, all evidence obtained directly from the illegal arrest is equally unlawful. The search of the man made incidental to the illegal arrest is unreasonable and the evidence of crime found on his person cannot be used in court. Moreover, any confession or admission of guilt which he makes as a direct result of the illegal arrest must also be excluded from evidence. The result is that these officers must arrest on probable cause or not arrest at all. And for the sake of their safety, this decision must be made quickly. The longer they delay in arresting the man and searching him, if they have the power to take this action, the greater his opportunity to attack them with a gun, or knife, or any other weapon in his possession.

Alice ponders over this explanation for just a moment and then exclaims, "What a topsy-turvy world! They tell you that you must make decisions on the constitutional law of arrest and search, and make them fast, and make them right, and make them when maybe everyone is a little bit scared, and the lawyers and the judges will study them and argue over them, maybe for years and years, and then if they disagree with what you did, they will tell you that you made a mistake here in the backyard facing a stranger in the dead of night. Your job looks as hard to me as theirs. You must make decisions of constitutional law, as they do, but under conditions much more difficult and dangerous. Why doesn't someone at least teach you the law like they do the lawyers and the judges?"

"That," the officer replied, "is a hard question to answer. I suspect that the reason is that those who control such things are still six years behind the Supreme Court. They have not caught up to the fact that as a result of judicial decisions handed down during recent years, every law enforcement officer has become, in effect, a constitutional lawyer on the Fourth Amendment, the Fifth Amendment, and the Sixth Amendment—on those parts of the Federal Constitution which cover the legality of arrests, searches, and confessions. I say he is a constitutional lawyer because he is forced to make decisions on questions of constitutional law which may go as high as the Supreme Court of the United States for ultimate decision. In my view, that makes him a constitutional lawyer whether he wants the job or not. No matter whether he is trained in the law or untrained, the law holds him responsible for a knowledge of constitutional law in certain areas and that is the controlling and undeniable fact."

But the family upstairs is impatient, even after the officer has explained these things. "Hang the law," they shout, "arrest him and get him out of here. Don't we have a constitutional right to be protected?"

"You know," Alice said, "I think they have a point. From reading the papers, I get the impression that plain people like these bear too great a share of an always unequal burden of crime. They seem more likely to be murdered, robbed at gunpoint, and all that than—well, than anyone else. The reason, perhaps, is that economic circumstances force so many of them to live and work in the high-crime areas. I wonder if they aren't the principal victims of the increase in crime that Director Hoover of the FBI has pointed out in figures so clear that anyone can see except for those who are blind because they do not wish to see. And since there are so many of them, surely there must be, as Abe Lincoln suggested, somebody who loves them. Doesn't that Constitution of ours say anything about the rights of these people?"

"Of course it does," the officer replied. "Don't be foolish. Constitutional rights apply equally to everyone. If one of those people upstairs ever is charged with murder, he will have a right to a lawyer and a right to say nothing to the police and a right . . ."

"Just one minute, please," Alice interrupted rather sharply. "Do you really need the glare of a morning sun to see the terror in that woman's eyes as she holds her child in her arms? Don't you see her husband's arm around her to quiet her fears? Perhaps I am being foolish, but if you will pardon a personal view, I think those rights which you just rattled off the tip of your tongue are not precisely what these people mean when they ask whether they have any rights. Can't you find just one single constitutional right that you can use to protect them right here and now?"

"I suppose I can," the officer replied, "but you see I have been so busy lately with the defendant's rights under the Fourth Amendment, and the Fifth, and the Sixth, and . . ."

"Yes," Alice said "yes, I know."

Then Alice remembers something else—something she read in the newspapers recently. It was about two officers who arrested two men in an alley in a large city, after a citizen had complained of those two men, and the officers were viciously attacked with a broken bottle which one of the men held in his hand. One of the officers spent a long time in a hospital and came out with many disfiguring scars. And the judge, hearing the case later on, studied the matter and reached the conclusion that the men who attacked the officers were right, and the officers were wrong, because the officers did not have enough information of guilt to make a lawful arrest. So Alice wondered aloud, "Is that why these officers are hesitating? Is that why they are not quite sure of what to do next? Does the law really give this man a right to physically attack these officers?"

Now one officer tells Alice the rest of the story. The scholars went back to their lawbooks and read them slowly and carefully, and some of them said the judge was right on the letter of the law. In all but a handful of the states of this Nation, a person illegally arrested has a right to physically resist the arrest, even when the officer's decision to arrest must be made swiftly, under circumstances of danger to life and limb, and under facts so close that no one may know that the arrest was illegal until years later when the Supreme Court of the United

States so holds by a narrow majority of 5 to 4.

"Why does the law say that?" Alice asks. So one of the officers explains. The right to resist illegal arrest came into the law centuries ago in England when most arrests were made by private citizens and both participants were armed with no more than barrel staves or swords, much less dangerous than six-shooters and automatics. It was a time when bail for a felony usually could not be had, when there was not right to speedy trial—years might pass before the royal judges heard the case. The jails were dungeons, torture chambers, in which the prisoner might die before trial. It was a time totally unlike today when jails are relatively clean and humanely operated, when bail is a constitutional right in most cases and is now being widely and quickly allowed under a broadening concept of that right, and when the accused has a constitutional right to a speedy trial (to say nothing of instant habeas corpus), a right to make no confession to the officers, and a right to demand a lawyer, relative or friend before the officers interrogate him for evidence of his own guilt.

"What a topsy-turvy world," Alice said again, half to herself. "You would think that with all these constitutional rights available to a person under arrest, civilized people in this day and age would make it the law that this man must go peacefully with the officers and decide the legality of the arrest in the courts instead of starting a fist fight over it in the street. And wouldn't that be better for everyone? If we let someone kick an officer's teeth in because he made a mistake of constitutional law, won't the officer—like anyone else—perhaps be afraid to arrest the next time, and not arrest someone who should be arrested and who will hurt some innocent person if he isn't? Do we let a man kick a lawyer's or a judge's teeth out if he makes an honest mistake on the constitutional law of arrest?"

"No," the officer said, "we do not—the law says that's not right, and I agree. And you have some good company when you say it should not be right in the case of a police officer either. A few states have abolished the right to resist illegal arrest. The Superior Court of New Jersey recently did so in that state. They said that resistance to arrest is 'antisocial in an urbanized society. It is potentially dangerous to all involved. It is no longer necessary because of the legal remedies available.'

"And newspaper editors in big cities have said the same thing. One said, 'Strange as it may seem, it is now lawful to kick, bite, or punch an arresting officer in uniform, if the arrest is one that a court lawyer finds is technically defective and hence unlawful. In these days of increasing hoodlumism and street crime, the community rightly expects the police to assume risks in the course of their duty, but in return it owes them reasonable protection. Policemen forced to make instantaneous decisions under trying circumstances should not become fair game for a mob.'

"Another said that if the law does condone a vicious assault upon a policeman with a broken bottle, then the law ought to be changed because 'Otherwise the police will predictably find it far harder than it already is to control the hoodlums who prey upon the public in every large city in this era of growing lawlessness and whose particular pleasure seems to be to maim or kill policemen. A police officer's job is perilous and thankless enough without leaving this kind of legal weapon in the hands of thugs.'"

"But look," Alice said, "there's another way out. Even if you don't have enough facts indicating crime to make a legal arrest, why don't you search him for a gun or a knife now and take it if he has it—then, at least, he can't hurt you while you are asking questions of him. All that you would be doing is protecting your own lives and mine, and maybe even his. Surely there is no law against that."

"No," the officer said, "you are wrong again. A search like that might be unreasonable under the Fourth Amendment to the Constitution. We don't have a search warrant, or his consent to search, and we haven't arrested him, so we still don't have a right to search him. A few states have laws saying we could search him before arrest for our own protection, but we aren't in any of those states now. Anyway, some lawyers say the Supreme Court will make those states change their minds as soon as it gets a good chance."

"You mean to tell me," Alice said, "that while you stand here making up your mind on probable cause for arrest, a difficult decision of constitutional law, the law will not let you search that man first, just to prevent him from pulling out a gun and killing you, or those people up there in the window, or me?"

"Yes," the officer said. "That is the way it is."

"Would the law let him shoot a judge in court while the judge was making up his mind on a question of constitutional law?" Alice asked.

"No," the officers said. "It would not."

Again Alice was heard to say, half to herself, "What a topsy-turvy world!"

"But there is a way, there is a way," Alice shouted excitedly, "even if he does have a gun. There are two of you and only one of him and you can just arrest him, even if the arrest isn't legal, and grab him by both arms and handcuff him and then he can't hurt you. Do it that way."

"No," the officer said. "That's not so good either—it might hurt in my pocketbook."

"You mean he would kick you?" Alice asked.

"Well, sort of. You see, Alice, the Supreme Court said in 1961 that if an officer violates a man's constitutional rights—such as the right of this man right here not to be arrested without probable cause for belief of guilt—the man can haul the officer into Federal Court and sue him personally for damages. This possibility of being sued frightens us, because in many of the states, or perhaps most, the officer has to pay the judgment out of his own pocket. The state either will not pay it for him or it pays only a part.

"Now some of the scholars in the law say this is bad because if an officer allows his pocketbook to influence his decision to arrest, the public interest in good law enforcement is sure to suffer. You know what they mean—the officer often will be afraid to arrest when he should arrest, and his fear will leave a dangerous criminal on the street to kill, rob, or steal. And the scholars say it isn't right on principle because this same man is not allowed to sue anyone else. He cannot sue the state's attorney for prosecuting him on evidence which is just not quite enough to convict, and he cannot sue the judge who erroneously makes a ruling against him on the law. So why should he have the right to make the officer pay a judgment out of his own pocketbook for the same kind of mistake? The scholars may be right. The newspapers that I read say that some policemen are now beginning to be afraid to arrest for fear they will be sued for all they've got. If that is true, we have created a condition dangerous to society.

"A few years before you were born, Alice, a wise old man on the Supreme Court of the United States said something I think more people should remember. He was talking about the difficult problem that officers have in deciding whether to arrest or not, and he said that because officers must face many situations which are more or less ambiguous, some room must be allowed for this mistakes, so long as their mistakes are those of reasonable men. But I guess most everyone has forgotten what he said.

"The law seems to tell me now that if I make any mistake of judgment at all on this constitutional law question of probably cause for arrest, then 'bingo,' no matter how honest I am, I can be sued for every penny I have. So I am very careful, and sometimes, perhaps, I fail to arrest when I should, and I wonder if that really is proper for the public good. Would it not be much better if I used my own judgment and, when I made an honest mistake, the government would say to the man arrested illegally, that the officer made a mistake in your case, but he did it not for his own profit but in performance of a public duty, so here is the money paid by the state to compensate you for this mistake? When the law won't let a judge or a prosecutor be sued for a mistake of constitutional law, it says the reason is that he must be allowed to do his duty as he sees it without fear and without having to risk being used for making a wrong guess on the law. Shouldn't that apply equally to a police officer, here in this backyard in the dead of night?"

"Very odd," Alice said, "very odd."

"Then there's nothing to do," Alice suggested, "but to hope that the man will not run away while we call the state's attorney to see if he will approve a warrant of arrest. That will settle the issue of probable cause and you won't have to stick your neck out."

"Basically a good idea," the officer said. "Arrest by warrant is the American system, and the fairest of all. The magistrate who decides whether the warrant shall be issued is neutral and unbiased and he doesn't care, at least theoretically, whether the arrest is made or not. Being neutral makes him a good judge of probable cause, fair to both sides. The Supreme Court likes it that way. Sometimes they criticize us for not getting warrants. Not long ago they warned us, as they have done several times before, that 'The point of the Fourth Amendment, which often is not grasped by zealous officers, is not that it denies law enforcement the support of the usual inferences which reasonable men draw from evidence. Its protection consists in requiring that those inferences be drawn by a neutral and detached magistrate instead of being judged by the officer engaged in the often competitive enterprise of ferreting out crime. Any assumption that evidence sufficient to support a magistrate's disinterested determination to issue a search warrant will justify the officers in making a search without a warrant would reduce the Amendment to a nullity and leave the people's homes secure only in the discretion of police officers.'

"But the fact which I think the courts sometimes fail to grasp, Alice, is that the officer whom they criticize for not getting a warrant is not *allowed* to decide whether he will ask for a warrant or not. Someone made a scholarly study of this matter and found that the prosecutor dominates the warrant decision. By that I mean that the prosecutor—not the officer—decides whether the officer can have a warrant or not, and he usually tells the officer to go ahead and arrest without a warrant. You see, Alice, this is exactly the opposite of what the Supreme Court says we should do. The Court tells us to get a warrant and the prosecutor tells us to arrest without a warrant. And that's not all. If the state's attorney did approve a warrant, who would issue it to us at this time of night? Most magistrates keep office hours, which crime and the criminal do not. At this time of night the magistrates are deep in the arms of Morpheus" (the mythical Greek God of sleep).

"That doesn't make sense!" Alice exclaimed. "The Supreme Court telling you to make arrests on warrants as much as you can, and being really quite right at that, but no one will permit you to have the warrant and no one to give it to you even should it be approved. If this man's constitutional right not to be arrested without probable cause for belief of guilt is as important as the Supreme Court says it is, and the function of the magistrate in making a fair decision on probable cause is as critical as the Supreme Court says it is, why can't one of those—one of those magistrate people—be appointed to work nights like you do?"

"You think too much," the officer replied. "Kids like you are dangerous."

The conversation between Alice and the officers continued. Alice and the people upstairs grew increasingly impatient with both the officers and the law. As to the officers, it seemed so elementary that something must be done here, and what could be more simple and direct than for two big and burly policemen to take the man down to the station and learn what he was up to. As to the technical requirements of the law, which had now been explained to Alice and the people upstairs for the first time in their lives, they echoed the view of Dickens' famous character, Mr. Bumble, who said, "If the law supposes that, ... the law is an ass, an idiot." Yet, when the officers asked them to specify which crime this man had committed, Alice and the people upstairs fell silent. They did not know, either.

Then Alice had still another idea. If the officers doubted that they had sufficient information of crime to make probable cause for arrest, why not simply keep the man here while they investigate. One officer could hold him and the other could check through the neighborhood for breakins, a suspicious car, or anything else. "Not a bad idea," one officer said, "at first glance. The law of a few states has allowed this action for many years, mostly under the Uniform Arrest Act. Some call it detention for investigation. If the officer has a reasonable basis for simply *suspecting* that the man in front of him might have committed a crime, he can hold that man for two hours or so, whatever the law of that state specifies, while he investigates. If the officer then finds enough facts to make probable cause for arrest, he can arrest the man. And if he doesn't he must turn the man loose, but the act of the officers in detaining the man during investigation is not an arrest and the man cannot sue the officer for false arrest."

"Now that," said Alice, "sounds like the answer."

"Not so fast," the officer replied, "We are not in one of those states. Outside of a few states an officer does not really know whether he has the power to detain or not. A Federal judge said not long ago that American law has 'inadequately articulated' the power of an officer to detain for investigation, which I take to be a judge's scholarly way of saying that the law simply does not say for sure whether we can detain to investigate or not. Because the law hems and haws on this point, some other scholars who call themselves the American Law Institute recently proposed that the law clearly and unequivocally gives us this power. But do you know what happened? It was no sooner suggested than some other scholars on the other side of the fence hit the ceiling, if you don't mind me mixing my metaphors. So where does that leave the officer like me? Everybody hollers for him to obey the law so he hollers back, 'what is it?' And then they start fighting among themselves while he stands there facing an unknown quantity in the dead of night."

"Okay," said Alice, "we're licked, let's get out of here."

"No," the officer said, "we can't. We wouldn't get three blocks before the night chief would come bawling over the radio for us to come in to explain why a citizen had complained that two cowards in blue uniforms had run out on him. I have a wife and kids to feed. We will arrest this man for vagrancy. It isn't a very good answer. Arrest for vagrancy have been bitterly criticized in recent years. If the critics get hold of this case, they will shout that it is just another example of illegal arrest on suspicion only—another example of tyrannical abuse by the police. If we walk away from here and this man attacks the people upstairs, or someone else, the law and the critics will condemn us—and perhaps worse—for dereliction of duty. If we walk away and nothing happens, the people upstairs will register a complaint against us anyway. We are squeezed between the law which restricts our action and often fails to tell us what we can do, and the demand of the citizen that we do something. Do you see the problem?"

"I see the problem," Alice replied, "but I don't see why the critics who are so certain on what you should not have done after you did it are so uncertain on what you should do before you do it. I should think that they have some responsibility for coming up with the other half of the answer. They ought to tell you what you *can* do. If they think this arrest is illegal, they should tell you to not make an arrest in a case like this, and then defend you all the way to the Supreme Court when the mayor tries to fire you for not doing your job."

Alice was relieved, nevertheless, as were the people upstairs, that an arrest would be made. But one officer cut their relief short with a reminder that his troubles with the law were by no means ended. "The requirements of the law on confessions," he said, "interacting with the community demand that the case be solved will baffle us again before the night ends. The high courts of some states, interpreting a 1964 decision of the Supreme Court, have told the officers that a confession of guilt given under arrest and in the interrogation room of the police station is not admissible in evidence against that man unless the officer first tells the man that he has a right to remain silent and a right to counsel. The high courts of some other states disagree. They say it is enough if the man is told only that he has a right to remain silent. The high courts of still other states have disagreed with both these positions. They say the officer doesn't need to tell the man anything so long as the man's request for counsel, if he makes it, is not denied. So the officer is left standing at the crossroads with at least three signposts, each pointing in a different direction and each saying that it alone shows the true path. Some say that the officer needs to know more law. I agree, but he also needs the patience of Job and a sense of humor.

"Of course," the officer continued, "it would be easy enough for us to tell this man that he has a right to silence and a right to counsel. But commonsense tells you that the more we warn him against confessing, the less likely he is to tell us the truth. That isn't so true, I'm sure, of cases where a long investigation before arrest gives the interrogating officer a file of facts 10 inches thick on the man and his crime. If the officer recites a few of the facts from that file and shows the man that he is caught cold, the man can see that the game is lost and that perhaps the intelligent thing for him to do is confess and throw himself on the mercy of the court. But that isn't our case, Alice, and it isn't the case with which police officers so often are confronted. Our case contains, through no fault of our own, a minimum of fact and a maximum of ambiguity. If we solve this case—and that is what the people upstairs and the people of this community expect—we will do it only from what this man tells us. In circumstances like these you can understand our reluctance to say anything which might encourage him to say nothing.

"The heart of the problem, Alice, is that we serve two masters, and we have it on high authority from long ago that no man can accomplish that feat. He will cleave to the one and reject the other, or reject the one and cleave to the other. One master is the community which we serve. This master is powerful. It can hire us and fire us, raise our pay, or refuse a raise, according to how well we satisfy its demands. This master wants an honest confession, because from a confession it learns the facts important to its health and well-being. The other master, also very powerful, is the law, which instructs us that we can obtain the confession only under legal restrictions which the first master neither knows nor understands. A confession pleases one master but often displeases the other. In fact, our master in the law seems sometimes to doubt that we ever need a confession to solve a criminal case. This master seems occasionally to suggest that we can solve any case by talking with witnesses and by finding the gun, the tire track in the mud, the vial of poison, and all those other things with which Mr. Hoover's FBI Laboratory can do so much. That is not true. As a wise old man who sat on the Supreme Court not so long ago—two of them, in fact—said so well, there are crimes, often of the worse kind, in which there simply are no witnesses, no guns, no tire tracks, and no vials of poison to be found. And moreover, these two learned men of the law asked how the police can possibly solve such cases except by getting information from the man who committed the crime. Those two wise men of the law asked that question on two different occasions, Alice, during the last two decades. We are still waiting to hear the final answer. If the law thinks we should not try to solve a murder or any other crime by asking questions of the man whom we have arrested, then let it say so, straight out, loud and clear, and we will obey. The crime may go unsolved, of course, and a criminal may be set free in the street once more, but that will not be our fault."

"But haven't you forgotten something?" Alice asked, "Suppose this man had kidnapped my baby brother and you arrested him for that crime. Now my father and mother and I want to know where he has hidden the baby, who might die if we don't find him. If you ask the man, but tell him first that he has a right to refuse to answer, do you not perhaps sign a death warrant for that child? Isn't this a corruption of values? They teach us, you know, in school and at home and in your office and in church that we have a moral and religious obligation to tell the truth. And then they turn right around and say that you must tell this man that *he* has no such obligation, even when the likely result will be to deprive an innocent child of life itself. What do you suppose the experts on the law would say if it were their baby instead of ours?"

"You are all mixed up," the officer replied. "I don't know how to explain it, but you seem to think religion and the law live in the same house, so to speak. They did once, way back in the days of Moses, but it is my impression that they are now divorced. Anyway, that's no subject to discuss with a kid like you—let's get on with this case."

"No," said Alice, glancing at her watch, "I can't. You have been saying nothing but 'No' to me all night whenever I mentioned the law. You sound like you have picked up a bad habit from one of your masters. Now it is my turn to say 'No.' My parents knew that I would be with you, but they must be wondering about me. I live just down the block. You can watch me until I go in the door. And it was awfully nice to meet you. I will see you again and if I ever need you, I will call you."

"Thank you." the officer replied, "but don't be disappointed if we don't show up."

"But surely you don't mean . . . !" Alice exclaimed.

"No, again," the officer said, "that is not what I mean. I just mean that there are not enough of us to everything. Our department, like so many others all over this nation, is understaffed. We have a budget for a certain number of officers, but we can't get that many. We are trying to recruit new officers in areas hundreds of miles beyond the city, reaching into other states, and still we can't find enough officers to fill the jobs. More and more of the young men who would become fine policemen are taking a long look at the pay and the working conditions offered. They see the law taking away some of the tools which law enforcement officers always have used in all civilized countries since time began, including this one until a very few years ago, and the apparent assumption on the part of the public that the officers still have all the power necessary to do the job demanded of them. They see the odd hours and dangerous conditions under which we must work. They see the increasingly frequent physical assaults upon policemen by persons being arrested. They see that mobs form and start riots, that blind and unreasoning mobs can be controlled only by physical force, that if we fail to attempt to stop the mob, we can be discharged or prosecuted for dereliction of duty. That if we do stop the mob, the tumult of battle has scarcely died down before we are charged with police brutality, for which we can be discharged or prosecuted. They see the facts, and more and more of them appear to be making the same decision that the critics of the police made long ago—that they do not want the job for themselves."

"Well, no offense intended to a good friend," Alice said as she started away, "but that is the only smart decision that I have heard all night."

EPILOGUE

This was "Alice in a Patrol Car." The comparison with the original is not perfect of course. The Alice of "Alice in Wonderland" was only dreaming, but our Alice is now. What our Alice says here is the raw stuff of Life itself, the material out of which the law should be shaped and reshaped as necessary in a Nation whose criminal environment is now newly dominated by the sprawling metropolis where dense concentrations of millions of human beings make possible a rate of criminal activity greater than ever before in our history. With few exceptions, however, this raw stuff of Life is known only to a few—to police officers and to the victims of crime, to those who by occupation or unfortunate circumstance bear in their bodies and in their fortunes the unequal burden of crime. It has been said that these are predominately the poor and those of modest income. Most others turn a blind eye and a deaf ear to the facts. Some call it apathy.

Federal Circuit Judge Edward Lumbard said a few years ago that "Police officers need to know their powers to question, detain and arrest, but federal laws and the laws of all the states on these questions are in great confusion ... no one can say with any certainty what powers the police officer has until the particular case is decided by the courts." Federal Circuit Judge Horner Thornberry said that "There is a crying need for reform in criminal law and procedure, but little has been accomplished ..." Past President Lewis F. Powell, Jr., of the American Bar Association said that "There is a growing consensus that outmoded criminal codes and the dramatic reinterpretation of constitutional safeguards have rendered the process of law enforcement far more difficult."

Director Hoover of the FBI has repeatedly warned us of the rising volume of crime. Mr. Katzenbach, Attorney General of the United States, is concerned. The President of the United States is calling for action against crime. If these acknowledged authorities are correct in their views on crime and the criminal law, then "Alice in a Patrol Car" is the wrong title. The title should be, "You in a Patrol Car"—you who belong to a profession whose members are charged with the continuing duty of acting as the architects of the law, you whose function it is to enact and to interpret the law so that justice may be done, as Mr. Justice Cardozo once said, to the accuser as well as to the accused, and you, the responsible citizen who depends upon the police for protection of person and property. Take a ride with the police officer and see this "topsy-turvy" world for yourselves.

Police Discretion

James Q. Wilson

Though the legal and organizational constraints under which the police work are everywhere the same or nearly so, police behavior differs from community to community. First, the conduct with which the police must cope varies from place to place. Both crime and disorder are more common in low-income areas than in high-income ones. How frequently the police intervene in a situation, and whether they intervene by making an arrest, will depend in part on the number and seriousness of the demands the city places on them. Second, some police behavior will be affected by the tastes, interests, and style of the police administrator. Finally, the administrator's views of both particular problems and the general level and vigor of enforcement may be influenced, intentionally or unintentionally, by local politics.

In this chapter, the extent to which police behavior varies among eight American communities will be considered, especially the degree to which that variation is in accord with the intentions of the administrator. In the next three chapters, these differences will be grouped into three archetypal police strategies or styles, and the departmental policies and organizational codes, implicit and explicit, that seem to animate and sustain those strategies will be discussed, along with the consequences of such strategies for various groups in the

From James Q. Wilson, *Varieties of Police Behavior: The Management of Law and Order in Eight Communities* (Cambridge, Mass.: Harvard University Press), pp. 83-88. Copyright ©1968 by the President and Fellows of Harvard College. Reprinted by permission of the author and the publisher.

community, especially, but not exclusively, for Negroes and community notables. Succeeding chapters will deal with the extent to which these strategies are, or can be, influenced by specific political decisions or by the general distribution of power within the community.

THE DETERMINANTS OF DISCRETION

The patrolman's decision whether and how to intervene in a situation depends on his evaluation of the costs and benefits of various kinds of action. Though the substantive criminal law seems to imply a mandate, based on duty or morality, that the law be applied wherever and whenever its injunctions have been violated, in fact for most officers there are considerations of utility that equal or exceed in importance those of duty or morality, especially for the more common and less serious laws. Though the officer may tell a person he is arresting that he is "only doing his duty," such a statement is intended mostly to reduce any personal antagonism (that is, psychic costs to the officer incurred by being thought a bad fellow). Whatever he may say, however, his actual decision whether and how to intervene involves such questions as these: Has anyone been hurt or deprived? Will anyone be hurt or deprived if I do nothing? Will an arrest improve the situation or only make matters worse? Is a complaint more likely if there is *no* arrest, or if there *is* an arrest? What does the sergeant expect of me? Am I getting near the end of my tour of duty? Will I have to go to court on my day off? If I do appear in court, will the charge stand up or will it be withdrawn or dismissed by the prosecutor? Will my partner think that an arrest shows I can handle things or that I can't handle things? What will the guy do if I let him go?

The decision to arrest, or to intervene in any other way, results from a comparison, different perhaps for each officer, of the net gain and loss to the suspect, the neighborhood, and the officer himself of various courses of action. Under certain circumstances, the policy of his department may set the terms of trade among these various considerations or alter the scales on which these values are measured. Such policies may in some cases make arrest (or no arrest) so desirable that, for all practical purposes, the patrolman has no discretion: he is doing what the department wants done. In other cases departmental policies may have little or no effect, and thus such discretion as is exercised is almost entirely the officer's and not the department's.

To explain fully the uses of discretion many factors would have to be considered. For simplicity, two major determinants (major in the sense that they explain "enough" of the variation) suffice: whether the situation is primarily one of *law enforcement* or one of *order maintenance* and whether the police response is *police-invoked* or *citizen-invoked*. To repeat the difference between law enforcement and order maintenance, the former involves a violation of a law in which only guilt need be assessed; the latter, though it often entails a legal infraction, involves in addition a dispute in which the law must be interpreted, standards of right conduct determined, and blame assigned. A police-invoked response is one in which the officer acts on his own authority, rather than as the agent of a citizen who has made a specific verbal or sworn complaint (though citizens "in general" may have complained about "the situation"); a citizen-invoked response is one in which the officer acts on the particular complaint or warrant of the citizen. Although some situations cannot be nearly placed in any category, enough can, I hope, so that we can imagine four kinds of situations in which discretion is exercised, as illustrated by the following figure.

Basis of police response

	Police-invoked action	Citizen-invoked action
Law enforcement (Nature of situation)	I	II
Order maintenance	III	IV

FIGURE 1 FOUR KINDS OF DISCRETIONARY SITUATIONS

Each case offers a different degree of discretion for the patrolman, the department, or both.

Case I: Police-Invoked Law Enforcement

In this situation the police themselves initiate the action in the specific instance, though sometimes in response to a general public concern over the problem, and whatever action they take is on their own authority. If there is an arrest, the officer is the complaining witness. Many crimes handled in this way are "crimes without victims"—that is, no citizen has been deprived and thus no citizen has called the police. Such calls as the police may get are from "busybodies"—persons who dislike "what is going on" but who themselves are not participants. Enforcement of laws dealing with vice, gambling, and traffic offenses are of this character. The rate and form of police interventions in these situations can be strongly influenced by the policy of the administrator. He can apply a performance measure to his subordinates, though (to introduce a further distinction) that measure differs with the particular offense. With respect to certain forms of vice and gambling, his measure will be whether a brothel or a bookie operates; if they do, his men are "not performing" and the administrator, if he is so inclined, will urge them to greater efforts. His performance measure is *goal-oriented*—that is, it is based on his observation of whether the substantive law enforcement goal has been attained. Accordingly, not only does the administrator have substantial control over his officers, but the community (the mayor, the city council, the newspapers), being able to make the same observations, has substantial opportunity to control the administrator. With regard to traffic enforcement, however, the administrator's measure will be how many traffic tickets the officers have written, not how safe the streets are or how smoothly traffic flows. He cannot judge his men, except perhaps in the extreme case, on these substantive grounds because he knows that writing traffic tickets has only a small effect on actual traffic conditions. Accordingly, his performance measure will be *means-oriented* and as a result, the community will be less able to hold him responsible for traffic conditions. Should they accuse him, which is unlikely, of letting the accident rate rise, he can reply reasonably that, unlike police attitudes toward brothels, police attitudes toward traffic law enforcement are not the sole or even the major determinant of whether there will be accidents.

Case II: Citizen-Invoked Law Enforcement

Here a citizen is the victim of a crime and he or she complains to the police. The vast majority of crimes with victims are those against property—larceny, auto theft, and burglary—and the vast majority of these are crimes of stealth for which the suspect is unknown. As a result, only a small percentage are solved by an arrest. The patrolman in these circumstances functions primarily as a report taker and information gatherer except when the suspect is still on the scene or has been caught by the victim or an onlooker. This is often the case, for example, with shoplifting. Here the patrolman must decide whether to make an arrest, to tell the citizen that it is up to him to handle the matter by getting a complaint and taking the suspect to court himself, or to encourage him to effect a citizen's arrest on the spot. The police department in turn may insist that prosecutions once started, either by an officer or a citizen, may not be dropped; conversely, it may make it easy for the arresting party to change his mind and forget the whole thing. The patrolman's attitude and departmental policy are amenable to some control by the administrator, especially since a majority of the suspects are likely to be juveniles.[1] The police are formally and legally vested with considerable discretion over juveniles (any person in New York under the age of 16 and in California and Illinois under the age of 18). They can decide, if not *whether* to intervene (that is decided for them by the citizen who invokes the law), at least *how* to intervene (to arrest, take into temporary custody, warn and release, and so forth). The police administrator can influence the use of that discretion significantly, not, as with Case I, by observing substantive outcomes or by measuring the output of individual officers, but by setting guidelines on how such cases will be handled and by devoting, or failing to devote, specialized resources (in the form of juvenile officers, for example) to these matters.

Case III: Police-Invoked Order Maintenance

In this instance the police, on their own authority and initiative, intervene in situations of actual or potential disorder. The most common charges are drunkenness, disorderly conduct, or breach of the peace. Not all drunk or disorderly arrests, of course, result from a police-invoked response—some, to be discussed below, are police ways of handling disorderly situations to which the police have been called by the citizen. Because the police invoke the law, the administrator has some control over patrolmen's discretion. He can urge them to "keep things quiet" but he cannot, as in traffic enforcement, judge each officer's "production" by how many arrests he makes on the assumption that there is an almost inexhaustible supply of disturbances to go around. Nor can he insist, as he might with cases of shoplifting, that an arrest is always the best way to handle the situation. In short, discretion in these cases is more under the control of the patrolman and can be modified only by general incentives to be "more vigorous" or to "take it easy." The administrator can boost drunk arrests but only by ordering his officers to treat drunks as problems of law enforcement rather than order maintenance: arrest on sight a man intoxicated in a public place even if he is bothering no one. In this case, a drunk arrest falls under Case I and accordingly is subject to the same relatively high degree of control.

Case IV: Citizen-Invoked Order Maintenance

In this last case, a citizen calls for police assistance because of a public or private disorder. But for the reasons given in Chapter 2 [not included here], being of assistance is often not an easy matter. In almost every department, such a citizen call must be followed by a police response to avoid the charge of "doing nothing"; however, the way the patrolman handles these situations will depend on his assessment of them and on the extent to which the participants are inclined to be tractable and victims prepared to sign a formal complaint. Thus, although the handling of these situations will vary considerably, that variation will depend more on the personal characteristics of the officer and the citizen participants than on departmental policies. Young college-educated patrolmen in a pleasant suburb may handle these matters in one way; older, working-class officers in a racially mixed central city may handle them in another.

In sum, in Cases I and IV the patrolman has great discretion, but in the former instance it can be brought under departmental control and in the latter it cannot. In Case II the patrolman has the least discretion except when the suspects are juveniles and then the discretion is substantial and can be affected by general departmental policies and organization. Case III is intermediate in both the degree of discretion and the possibility of departmental control....

NOTES

1. Property crimes—burglary, larceny of items valued over $50, and auto theft—accounted in 1965 for 82 percent of the major crimes ("Index Crimes") reported to the FBI and 84 percent of the causes of victimization reported by respondents in the Crime Commission household survey. About 21 percent of these three crimes were, according to police reports to the FBI, "cleared by arrest." About 57 percent of those arrested for these offenses (and those arrested, of course, may not be representative sample of those who committed the crimes) were under the age of 18. *See* President's Commission on Law Enforcement and Administration of Justice, *Crime and Its Impact—An Assessment* (Washington: Government Printing Office, 1967), p. 17; and Federal Bureau of Investigation, *Uniform Crime Reports, 1965* (Washington:

Government Printing Office, 1965), pp. 97, 112. A study by the Oakland Police Department in 1963 showed that 74.6 percent of all persons processed by the police for shoplifting were juveniles, that is, under the age of 18. Most of these cases came from retail stores with security guards and only a few stores accounted for most of the arrests. Between January 1962 and October 1963, 2,394 shoplifting cases were reported by 453 stores; over half came from 57 stores, 29 percent came from only four stores, and 10 percent came from just one store. Oakland Police Department, "An Analysis of the Shoplifting Problem in Oakland, 1962 and 1963," (mimeograph, November 1963). *See also* Walter B. Miller, "Theft Behavior in City Gangs," in Malcolm W. Klein, *Juvenile Gangs in Context* (Englewood Cliffs: Prentice-Hall, Inc., 1967), pp. 25-37.

The Philosophy of Police Discretion

Thomas F. Adams

INTRODUCTION

In our search for a meaningful study in criminal justice administration we focused on the important but not often discussed topic of discretionary decision making by the field police officer. As a police academy instructor in this specific subject, I found the study most relevant to my needs for course background. As pointed out in the President's Commission on Law Enforcement[1] and various other sources, there is considerable variance in police practices, particularly in tactical and arrest situations. The consensus of the many sideline observers of law enforcement seems to be that law enforcement agencies provide little or no control for their officers in the form of guidelines; they leave most decision making to the discretion of the individual officer.

In this study we agreed upon an hypothesis and tested it through a questionnaire survey. Hopefully, our initial study will lead to a valid and reliable instrument to survey random samples of law enforcement officers of various rank, tenure, experience, and educational background. I believe that the questionnaire led to significant inferences, which I used to prepare my course outline.

PART A. THE HYPOTHESIS

The personal value systems of individual police officers determine the parameters of law enforcement practices by the police.

Within the organized structure of law enforcement agencies in the United States we have nearly one-half million police officers. They operate as

From an unpublished paper prepared for graduate study at California State College at Long Beach, 1969.

independent agents in both routine and extraordinary "infield" situations that affect the lives of the millions of people with whom they come in contact during the performance of their duties. In developing our hypothesis, it was our considered opinion that the broad discretionary powers of the individual policeman and policewoman include such actions as dealing with traffic law violators, disturbances of the peace involving single violators or hundreds, criminal law enforcement, apprehension and detention of juvenile delinquents, regulation of public and private morals through vice enforcement, and a myriad of other duties. He functions with virtually no direction or guidance in many agencies, and with only minor supervisory control in others. A survey form was designed and administered to 288 persons to test both the hypothesis and the instrument itself. Inferences drawn from evaluations of the survey will be discussed later in this paper.

PART B. WHAT THE CRITICS AND EXPERTS SAY

In an excerpt from a 1969 issue of the *Michigan Law Review*,[2] Wisconsin law professor Herman Goldstein made the following observations:

> The police must exercise great discretion in their authority. They must decide which laws to enforce, select from among the available techniques for investigating crime, decide whom to arrest, and determine how to process a criminal offender.
>
> The policeman's primary authority does not involve arresting a person to prosecute him for crime. For every time that a police officer arrests a person he also disposes of scores of incidents by employing a lesser form of authority, such as ordering people to move on, turning children over to their parents, or separating combatants.
>
> While there have been some efforts by police to provide guidance for day-to-day decisions, the overall picture reflects a reluctance on the part of police administrators to establish policies to fill the existing void.
>
> The individual officer either develops his own informal criteria for disposing of matters which come to his attention or employs informal criteria which have, over a period of years, developed within the agency of which he is a part.
>
> Functioning in this way, individual policemen often succeed to an amazing degree in muddling their way through, but unfortunately, the results are often less satisfactory, primarily because the criteria that are employed emerge largely in response to a variety of pressures to which the police are exposed and are therefore not carefully developed.
>
> Police are now accustomed to looking toward the legislatures and the courts for their guidance, but should be made responsible for formulating their own policies subject to challenge if they were not consistent with the general legislative purpose.

In his *Justice Without Trial*,[3] Jerome Skolnick surveyed how the police conceive the meaning of law and order and how these conceptions develop and are implemented by the police. He summarized his findings about the issues and suggested that the dilemma of the police in a democratic society arises out of the conflict between the extent of initiative contemplated by the officers' nontotalitarian norms. He also discussed the concept of police professionalization and its limitations in terms of material efficiency. His study was then directed to a discussion of how the policeman's self-concept is compared with the expectations of the community. He stated: "... the focus is upon the relation between the policeman's conception of his work and his capacity to contribute to the development of a society based upon the rule of law as its master ideal."

Skolnick points out that there are five features of the policeman's environment that weaken the rule of law as a primary objective of police conduct.

1. Social psychology—that is the relation between occupational environment, working personality, and the rule of law.
2. The policeman's stake in maintaining his authoritarian role and his interest in bolstering accepted patterns of enforcement.
3. Police socialization, especially as it influences the policeman's administrative bias.
4. Pressure put on the policeman to "produce"—to be efficient rather than legal when the two norms are in conflict.
5. The policeman's opportunity to behave inconsistently with the rule of law as a result of the low visibility of much of his conduct.

Skolnick opined that these factors seem more closely joined to the concept of policemen as *craftsmen* rather than as *legal actors*, as skilled workers rather than civil servants obliged to subscribe to the rule of the law. They are not professional humanitarians, whose goal it is to look upon various situations differently than craftsmen. He stated that professionalism may be good or bad, depending on one's perspective, explaining that professionalism tends to produce uniformity of ideals, values, and technical competence.

According to Skolnick, Emile Durkheim stated in *Professional Ethics and Civic Morals* that professional groups not only have high status, high skill, and a distinctive structure of control over work, but—more important—that a profession is an infusion of work and collective organization with moral values, plus the use of sanctions to insure that these moral values are upheld.

Another of Skolnick's concepts of professionalism is that the professional takes on the personage of a "bureaucrat, almost as a machine calculating alternative courses of action by a stated program of rules, and possessing the technical ability to carry out decisions irrespective of personal feelings."

Max Weber, sometimes referred to as the "father of bureaucracy," has said:

> ... bureaucratization offers the optimal possibility for the realization of the principle of division of labor in administration according to purely technical considerations, allocating individual tasks to functionaries who are trained as specialists and who continuously add to their experience by constant practice.

Professional execution in this case means primarily execution "without regard to person in accordance with calculable rules."

In his article, Skolnick pointed out that in an effort to overcome police corruption and political favoritism, critics of the police have attempted to introduce fairness, calculability, and impersonality into American administration of criminal justice. Such a marginal concept of professionalism as expounded by O. W. Wilson and William Parker, said Skolnick, has been professed by Wayne LaFave in his book *Arrest: The Decision to Take A Suspect Into Custody.*[4]

Skolnick quotes LaFave:

> The development of police expertness should be encouraged, and its existence should be recognized when appropriate. . . . There is need, and ample precedent in other fields, for the development of methods of communicating the existence of police expertness to trial or appellate courts which are called upon to decide arrest issues. . . .

Following are a few additional comments by Skolnick:

> There are . . . costs in developing a professional code based upon the model of administrative efficiency. Such a conception of professionalism not only fails to bridge the gap between the maintainance of order and the rule of law; in addition it comes to serve as an ideology undermining the capacity of police to be accountable to the rule of law. The idea of organization based on principles of administrative efficiency is often misunderstood by officials who are themselves responsible for administering such organizations. In practice, standardized rules and procedures are frequently molded to facilitate the tasks of acting officials. The materials of this study have clearly demonstrated that the policeman is an especially "non-mechanical official."
>
> The needed philosophy of professionalism must rest on a set of values conveying the idea that the police are as much an institution dedicated to the achievement of legality in society as they are an official social organization designed to control misconduct through the invocation of punitive sanctions. . . . What must occur is a significant alteration in the ideology of the police, so that police professionalization rests on the values of a democratic legal order, rather than on technological proficiency.

Skolnick states that legal professionalism, *not* managerial professionalism, may succeed only if the community demands compliance with the *rule of law* by rewarding the police for each compliance, instead of holding the police solely responsible for controlling crime. Unfortunately, the police professionalism concept, says Skolnick, is usually regarded by the public as the managerial professional concept. He continues in *Justice Without Trial:*

> Under the circumstances of mass administration of criminal justice, presumptions necessarily run to regularity and administrative efficiency. The negative of the presumption of innocence permeates the entire system of justice without trial. All involved in the system—the defense attorneys and judges, as well as the prosecutors and policemen—operate according to the working presumption of the guilt of persons accused of crime. As

accusal after accusal is processed through the system, participants are prone to develop a routinized callousness, akin to the absence of emotional involvement characterizing the physician's attitude toward illness and disease.

An order perspective based on managerial efficiency also tends to be supported by the civic community. The so-called power structure of the community . . . often stresses to the police the importance of "keeping the streets clear of crime."

Warren Bennis, in "Beyond Bureaucracy,"[5] lists the limitations of bureaucracy which Skolnick believes are similarly limitations on large urban police forces. They are:

1. Bureaucracy does not adequately allow for personal growth and development of mature personalities.
2. It develops conformity and "group think."
3. It does not take into account the "informal organizations" and the emergent and unanticipated problems.
4. Its systems of controls and authority are hopelessly outdated.
5. It has no adequate judicial process.
6. It does not possess adequate means for resolving differences and conflicts between ranks, and most particularly, between functional groups.
7. Communication (and innovative ideas) are thwarted or distorted due to hierarchical division.

In the March 1969 issue of *The Atlantic Monthly,* Paul Chevigney, author of "Police Power"[6] made these observations concerning police use of discretionary power:

The consensus among the authorities who have studied the problem (of police abuse) is that the police do sometimes try to provoke violence in order to make an arrest. It is logical to think that policemen will try such things with outcasts, whom they fear and dislike and would prefer to see in jail.

The root problem is the abuse of power, the fact that the police not only hit a man but arrest him. Once they have arrested him, . . . lying becomes an inevitable part of the procedure of making the quarrel look like a crime. . . .

In writing about a routine police matter which he defines in the category of "order maintenance," James Q. Wilson[7] discusses the dilemma of the police officer in citizen quarrels and similar situations.

Because an arrest cannot be made in most disorderly cases, the officer is expected to handle the situation by other means and on the spot, but the law gives him almost no guidelines on how he is to do this; indeed, the law often denies him the right to do anything at all other than make an arrest. No judge will ever see the case, and thus no judge can decide the case for the officer. Alone, unsupervised, with no policies to guide him and little sympathy from onlookers to support him, the officer must "administer justice" on the curbstone.

Wayne LaFave, author of *Arrest: The Decision to Take a Suspect Into Custody,*[8] made these observations:

> The exercise of discretion by the police, which seems inevitable in current criminal justice administration, continues unrecognized. In practice, policies to guide the individual officer whether to make an arrest or not formally developed within the police agency, and no sustained effort is made to subject existing practices to reevaluation. This being so, the first step toward better understanding of the problem is identification and analysis of the criteria presently employed in practice.

Following are selected excerpts from the President's Crime Commission, *Task Force Report: The Police,* published in 1967:

> In view of the importance, complexity, and delicacy of police work, it is curious that police administrators have seldom attempted to develop and articulate clear policies aimed at guiding or governing the way policemen exercise their discretion on the street. Many police departments have published "general order" or "duty" or "rules," regulations, and procedures manuals running to several hundred pages. They deal extensively, and quite properly, with the personal conduct of officers on and off duty, with uniform and firearms regulations, with the use of departmental property, with court appearances by officers, with the correct techniques of approaching a building in which a burglary may be in progress. They instruct an officer about taking a suspect into custody and transporting him to the station, or about dealing with sick or injured persons, or about handling stray dogs, or about cooperating with the fire department, or about towing away abandoned automobiles—with, in short, dozens of situations in which policemen commonly, or uncommonly find themselves. What such manuals almost never discuss are the hard choices policemen must make every day: whether or not to break up a sidewalk gathering, whether or not to intervene in a domestic dispute, whether or not to silence a street-corner speaker, whether or not to stop and frisk, whether or not to arrest. Yet these decisions are the heart of police work. How they are made determines to a large degree the safety of the community, the attitude of the public toward the police and the substance of court rulings on police procedures.
>
> Reasons advanced for this lack of policy guidelines are usually:
>
> 1. That is an extremely hard thing to do.
> 2. That if stated, they would be highly controversial.
> 3. That the police do not realize that they make policy informally every day.

The Commission report continues: "Not only should policemen be guided by departmental policy in making such delicate decisions, but the people who will be affected by these decisions—the public—have a right to be appraised in advance, rather than ex post facto, what police policy is."

The Commission recommended:

> Police departments should develop and enunciate policies that give police personnel specific guidance for the common situations requiring exercise of police discretion. Policies should cover such matters, among others, as the issuance of orders to citizens regarding their movements or activities, the handling of minor disputes, the safeguarding of the rights of free speech and free assembly, the selection and use of investigative methods, and the decision whether or not to arrest in specific situations involving specific crimes.
>
> ... but while the Commission believes strongly that it is not only appropriate, but necessary, for policemen to exercise discretion about arrests, it also believes that it is both inappropriate and unnecessary for the entire burden of exercising this discretion to be placed on individual policemen in tumultuous situations. It is incumbent on police departments to define as precisely as possible when arrest is a proper action and when it is not.

The Commission also listed some of the potential benefits that might be gained by such action:

> Restoration of decision making to Chief's level, where it should be.
> A body of standards to make police work consistent.
> An understanding by the courts of police procedures.
> Compulsion for departments to delve more deeply into the social and technical aspects of police work.
> Police contemplation of deterrence methods.
> Experiments with patrol and investigative methods.
> Experiments with equipment and management systems.
> A computerized bank of data that could be queried from the field for instant policy statements to aid the officer in making his decisions.
> Standardized training programs.
> An end to police isolation and encouragement for professionalization.

In summarizing the critiques by the "experts," we may make the following statements:

> The police lack guidelines.
> Administrators do not now provide sufficient guidelines.
> The police must and do exercise great discretion in virtually every duty they perform.
> Individual officers seem to succeed by "muddling through" the maze of decisions. They sometimes react to pressures, resulting in incompletely developed decisions.
> Police look toward legislature and the courts for guidance but should formulate their own policies.
> "Professionalism" movement of law enforcement as we may now conceive it is inconsistent with society's expectations. Occupational norms value an impersonal uniform application of the law with technological proficiency, rather than a "domestic legal order," according to Skolnick.
> All persons in the system of criminal justice are prone to develop an

emotionally uninvolved callousness, which may be detrimental to the fair treatment of the accused.

Some critics state that some policemen actually provoke violence to make an arrest, then perjure themselves to justify their "defense" against attack by persons under arrest.

Judicial review and guidance is no more possible than legislative guidance because in some discretionary actions the decision involves taking only informal action. The officer must administer "curbstone justice" on his own with no supervision, no policies to guide him, and little sympathy from onlookers to support him, according to James Q. Wilson.

It appears that the critics, students, and other experts agree on at least two points:

1. The police exercise individual discretion.
2. A system of guidelines for police discretionary action is needed.

THE SURVEY

We prepared and administered the survey discussed in the following pages to ascertain if the people involved in the policing process and students who are preparing to go into law enforcement and allied occupations were aware of these two points. The form and statistical information will be followed in this paper by a discussion of the results of the survey.

THE QUESTIONNAIRE FORMAT

Instructions: Please respond to the questions below with whatever statement most logically—in your opinion—addresses the questions and reflects your sincere judgment.

Your age   Sex   Rank   Time in Service

1. What are your most important duties as a police officer?
2. What do you in fact spend most of your time doing as an officer?
3. How do you feel a police officer decreases the crime rate?
4. To what extent do you have the authority to arrest?
5. What are the factors that influence you to make an arrest?
6. What do you believe to be the objectives (goals) of an arrest?
7. What are the limitations placed upon your authority to arrest?
8. Are there any offenses for which you just will not make an arrest?
9. If you have a choice, for which crimes would you make the most arrests?
10. If you had a choice, for which crimes would you make the least arrests?

EMPIRICAL EVALUATION OF THE SURVEY

This instrument has provided us with sufficient data that we should be able to prepare a workable "forced-choice" type questionnaire that would lend itself to factor analysis and reliable testing on a larger scale than our pilot survey.

Of the 288 individuals queried during the survey, and the statistically recorded responses (made the subject of another report by a fellow researcher), we have taken for this report only two groups: (1) middle management (MM), consisting of an MM class including 2 captains, 19 lieutenants, and 2 sergeants; (2) field officers (FO), consisting of 112 policemen and 5 sergeants with field assignments.

Percentages of responses will not total 100 percent because of irregular numbers of people. Also, some questions were answered with more than one answer.

Questions and Response Categories		FO	MM
Q. 1.	What are your most important duties as a police officer?		
	ORGANIZATIONAL RESPONSE (Protect life and property, enforce laws, prevention and suppression, in-view patrol, supervision)	89.0	85.7
	SOCIAL RESPONSE (Public service, public relations, public peace, and welfare)	19.6	17.3
	INDIVIDUAL RESPONSE (Not included in other two categories)		8.7
Q. 2.	What do you, in fact, spend most of your time doing? Not relevant. Excluded from study.		
Q. 3.	How do you feel a police officer decreases crime?		
	ORGANIZATIONAL (Patrol, in-view, apprehension, deterrent, convictions, enforcing laws, good arrests)	85.9	64.0
	SOCIAL (Public relations, punitive, plainclothes)	3.1	8.0
	INDIVIDUAL (Professional knowledge, being impartial, being aggressive)	8.6	20.0
	DOES NOT	0.8	4.0
Q. 4.	To what extent do you have the authority to make an arrest?		
	PROBABLE CAUSE	62.2	56.7
	STATUTES, LAWS	10.8	21.7
	ALL OTHERS	29.7	21.6
Q. 5.	What are the factors which influence you to make an arrest?		
	ORGANIZATIONAL (Reasonable cause, penal code, departmental, warrant, knowledge of law, experience, patience)	39.3	38.0
	SOCIAL (Public welfare)	4.1	7.6
	INDIVIDUAL (Seriousness, type, circumstances, situation, attitude,		

Questions and Response Categories		FO	MM
	appearance, intent of the individual, intent of legislature)	54.0	51.8
	NO ANSWER	2.8	3.8
Q. 6.	What do you believe to be the objectives (goals) of an arrest?		
	ORGANIZATIONAL (Conviction, prosecution, court appearance, apprehension, deterrence, suppression, law enforcement, presentation of evidence in court, corpus delicti, solving crime)	67.0	62.8
	SOCIAL (Rehabilitation, protection of society, fairness)	31.1	38.2
	OVERTIME PAY	0.8	
	NO ANSWER	2.3	
Q. 7.	What are the limitations placed upon your authority to arrest?		
	ORGANIZATIONAL (Penal code, courts, legal, decision, departmental, warrants, knowledge of law, jurisdiction, vehicle code)	67.8	76.6
	SOCIAL (Societal, fairness)	6.4	2.9
	INDIVIDUAL (Reasonable cause, elements none, no unnecessary force, seriousness, excessive force, verbal, common sense)	24.0	17.6
	UNKNOWN	11.2	2.9
Q. 8.	Are there any offenses for which you will just *not* make an arrest?		
	UNKNOWN, OR NO RESPONSE	7.2	8.7
	NO	48.4	56.6
	YES	9.2	13.0
	SITUATION, CIRCUMSTANCES	13.6	17.4
	ANTIQUATED LAWS	5.9	4.3
	UNREASONABLE LAW	2.7	
	ELEMENTS	2.7	
	DISTRICT ATTY REFUSAL TO PROSECUTE	0.9	
	DRUNK DRIVER	0.9	
	DRUNK IN PUBLIC	0.9	
	CIVIL DISPUTE	0.9	
	PAPER BOYS IN STREET	0.9	
	ADULTERY	2.7	
	RAPE (Both consenting, but female under age)	0.9	
	SPITTING ON SIDEWALK	0.9	
	TRAFFIC VIOLATIONS	0.9	
	LOW FLYING AIRCRAFT	0.9	

Questions and Response Categories		FO	MM
Q. 9.	For which crimes would you make the *most* arrests, if you had a choice?		
	NARCOTICS, DRUGS	16.2	11.5
	PERSONS, VIOLENCE	14.1	34.9
	BURGLARY	9.2	7.7
	FELONY, GENERAL	7.2	3.8
	DRUNK DRIVING	8.6	
	SEX OFFENSES	6.5	
	ROBBERY	6.5	3.8
	CHILD VICTIM	6.5	11.5
	DRUNK IN PUBLIC	3.2	
	RECKLESS DRIVING	1.3	
	INDECENT EXPOSURE		3.8
	THEFTS	2.1	7.7
	VEHICLE CODE, MOVING	2.1	
	HIT-RUN	0.6	
	STOLEN AUTO	0.6	
	ORGANIZED CRIME	0.6	
	MISC. RESPONSE (Life, property, impartial mala en se, supervision, seriousness)	8.0	7.6
	DISCRETION (No explanation of terms)		7.7
	NO RESPONSE	6.5	
Q. 10.	For which crimes would you make the *fewest* arrests, if you had a choice?		
	UNKNOWN, OR NO RESPONSE	15.7	
	CIRCUMSTANCES	5.6	21.85
	ANTIQUATED LAWS	4.8	
	CRIMES THAT HAVE NO EFFECT ON SOCIETY	5.6	
	NONE	6.4	21.85
	CIVIL DISPUTES	11.2	13.0
	DRUNK IN PUBLIC	10.0	13.0
	DISTURBING THE PEACE	10.4	4.3
	VEHICLE CODE, MOVING VIOLATIONS	1.8	
	JUVENILES (Curfew, drinking)	3.4	
	STATUTORY RAPE	4.2	
	PETTY THEFT	1.8	4.3
	BETWEEN GANGS, FIGHTS	1.8	
	MARIJUANA POSSESSION	2.5	
	VEHICLE CODE, MINOR VIOLATIONS	5.7	
	MUNICIPAL CODES		8.7
	MALA PROHIBITA	0.9	4.3
	GENERAL MISDEMEANOR	3.4	8.7
	MISCELLANEOUS–NON RELATED RESPONSES	9.0	

INFERENCE GAINED FROM THE SURVEY

It appears that the hypothesis is correct from the questionnaire evaluation. Although it will be necessary to design another questionnaire for an objective evaluation and factor analysis, there is ample evidence to show that the individual police officers do in fact set the parameters for law enforcement. To what extent we do not know, but it is abundantly clear that the field officer has broad discretionary powers and is aware of those powers. How he exercises those powers is the point of contention among many critics and observers of law enforcement.

Although the need for considerable further study is indicated, the respondents seem to hold three types of views about law enforcement: organizational, social, and individual; yet they are not necessarily separable. In our opinion, the police officer is not the "organization man" that some might choose to believe. He functions as he thinks—*as an individual.*

Of what significance is such a study, one may ask. It is essential that the progressive police administrator acknowledge that his officers have broad discretionary powers and develop guidelines for the new officer to follow within the framework of the law. At the same time, he must give them discretion to assure the people that they will be served and protected as individuals with the bureaucratic system. The law enforcement educator must assume the responsibility for instilling in the new police officer an awareness of his discretionary powers, help him articulate appreciation for certain ethical standards, and then provide a learning environment in which he may practice the judicious use of those powers. A law enforcement philosophy must include the intent of the legislators, special circumstances, and a thorough knowledge of the letter of the law.

INSTRUCTIONAL GUIDELINES FOR DISCRETIONARY DECISION MAKING

Instruction in this important topic has been prescribed by the California Commission on Peace Officers Standards and Training as a part of the basic course for recruits. Following are some of the key points that should be covered in the academy when instructing this topic:

Laws

The California system of criminal justice abundantly provides for broad use of discretion by its law enforcement officers and all others similarly involved in the system. At the time the new penal code was introduced (February 14, 1872), the legislature had provided for such discretion by the wording of Section 4:

> The rule of the common law, that penal statutes are to be strictly construed, has no application to this code. All its provisions are to be construed according to the fair import of their terms, with a view to effect its objects and to promote justice.

A leading case that further elucidates the intent of law and those who enforce it has been described in the California Supreme Court's ruling in *The People* v. *Alotis,* 60 Cal. 2d 698 (1964):

> When language reasonably susceptible to two constructions is used in a penal law, that construction which is more favorable to the defendant will be adopted. The defendant is entitled to the benefit of every reasonable doubt as to the true interpretation of words or the construction of language used in a statute.

A police officer has the responsibility and the authority within our existing criminal justice system to act or react in a variety of ways when he encounters what in his opinion constitutes a violation of the law or some other incident calling for his official response: The officer may contact the suspected violator and admonish with no arrest. The policeman may arrest and release with no further action because of what he believes to be lack of sufficient evidence or cause for further action. He may issue a citation and release the violator from custody when he signs a promise to appear in court at some later designated time and place. As another alternative, the officer may take the accused into custody and lodge him in jail for induction into the criminal justice system. Once introduced, the case is adjudicated according to the system's established procedure with other individuals exercising the discretion. In a large percentage of cases, the officer will act informally, which means that the people dealt with on this basis are never introduced to the rest of the system beyond the individual police officer. This is the area in which the officer must be most judicious in the use of his power.

Specific sections of the California Penal Code involving discretion include the following:

Sec. 833   Search for weapons on reasonable cause.
Sec. 835   Reasonable restraint when making an arrest.
Sec. 835a Reasonable force to effect an arrest, prevent escape, or overcome resistance.
Sec. 836   Discretionary power to arrest on reasonable cause.
Sec. 196   Justifiable homicide by peace officers.

Certain words in various sections of the code indicate the use of discretion involving value judgments. Examples of those words are "intent," "reasonable or probable cause," "malicious," "unsafe," "too close," "unfit," "unnecessary," and "reliable," to mention a few.

Discretionary Decisions

In addition to decisions whether to arrest, the officer must determine if and when to shoot, if at all; when to pursue and when to abandon a pursuit; when to use force and how much force to use; and when not to take action. These cover only a few of the many discretionary decisions to be made by the police officer, but they should be sufficient to illustrate the necessity for wise instruction in this tremendously important area.

CONCLUSION

The use of discretionary prerogatives by individual police officers is a positive and on-going practice that exists in modern law enforcement. The novice officer must become as aware of this process as his senior counterparts are; he must be guided throughout his career by fair-minded and socially aware administrators and educators who are conversant with the mores of society, the intent of the law, and the letter of the law. The officer must perform his job in such a manner that his performance will later be judged by others to have been correct under the circumstances.

BIBLIOGRAPHY

Bennis, Warren. "Beyond Bureaucracy." **Trans**-*action* (July-August 1965), p. 32.

Chevigny, Paul. *Police Power: Police Abuses in New York City.* New York: Pantheon Books, 1969.

Goldstein, Herman. *Sacramento Legal Press,* 27 July 1967. News item excerpting statements from *Michigan Law Review.*

LaFave, Wayne R. *Arrest: The Decision to Take a Suspect into Custody.* Boston: Little, Brown and Company, 1964.

Skolnick, Jerome H. *Justice Without Trial: Law Enforcement In Democratic Society.* New York: John Wiley & Sons, 1966.

Task Force Report: The Police. Washington, D.C.: The President's Commission on Law Enforcement and the Administration of Justice, 1967.

Wilson, James Q. "What Makes a Better Policeman?" *The Atlantic Monthly,* March 1969.

NOTES

1. *Report of the President's Commission on Law Enforcement and the Administration of Justice* (Washington, D.C.: U.S. Government Printing Office, 1967).
2. Recounted in the 27 July 1969 issue of the *Sacramento Legal Press.*
3. *Justice Without Trial: Law Enforcement In Democratic Society,* (New York: John Wiley & Sons, 1966).
4. Boston: Little, Brown, and Company, 1964.
5. **Trans**-*action* (July-August 1965), p.32.
6. *Police Power: Police Abuses in New York City,* (New York: Pantheon Books, 1969).
7. "What Makes a Better Policemen?" *The Atlantic Monthly* (March 1969).
8. Boston: Little, Brown, and Company, 1964.

SECTION SIX

Critical Issues in Criminal Justice

Overview

A JUSTICE SPEAKS ON LAW AND ORDER. Charles E. Whittaker of the United States Supreme Court (retired) discusses his views on law and order and the jeopardy he believes the nation is in at the present. Under the guise of so-called "civil disobedience," certain self-appointed leaders have caused many of their followers to act with lawless and wanton disregard for the health and safety of their fellow Americans. An editorial on the need for restoration of strict law enforcement and an end to permissiveness, this is the full text of an address Justice Whittaker made before a Bar Association meeting in Nashville, Tenn., June 7, 1965.

BILL OF RIGHTS IN SPOTLIGHT DURING THE 1960s, COURT RULINGS TRY TO INSURE FAIR TRIALS, MIRANDA CASE ESTABLISHES CLEAR INTERROGATION GUIDE LINES. These are three of a series of stories concerning court decisions written by Harry M. Humphreys originally written for the *Van Nuys News.* These well-written articles unfold the historical development of the many landmark decisions that have so directly affected the criminal justice system for the past few years that some of them have stimulated lively dialogue and pointed criticism from the pros whose work has changed considerably as a result of those decisions.

NEEDED: ORDER IN THE COURTS. The U.S. Chamber of Commerce details the many problems of court *dis*organization: crowded calendars, trial scheduling problems, inefficient judges and other court officials versus the competent ones, and their methods of selection. The article also presents many recommendations of the American Bar Association concerning the problems. The situation is critical, according to the writers, but not hopeless. The solution lies in the identification of the problems and their systematic correction.

WHERE THE CORRECTIONAL SYSTEM REQUIRES CORRECTING. The U.S. Chamber of Commerce describes the corrections system as one fragmented, uncoordinated amalgam. It is referred to as a series of federal, state, and local agencies and programs with no rhyme or reason in their management. A profile of the average prisoner reminds the reader that the prisoners are humans with real problems that they are bringing back to their communities with them in an average of two years. Rehabilitation of convicted persons so far has generally been ineffective, according to this article, but at least one program described seems to have promise, according to the authors. The article is stimulating and presents a challenge to professionals.

CURRENT ISSUES IN LAW ENFORCEMENT. California State Senator George Deukmejian, speaker at a police academy graduation ceremony, discussed some of the current issues involving the police, such as crime on the streets, public support of the police, and recruitment of police personnel. An interesting comment from a legislator, it seems, was ". . . we don't need more laws, we just need to enforce the laws we now have on the books."

MAKING LAW AND ORDER WORK. Mayor John Lindsay of New York City addressed an American Bar Association meeting in August, 1970, and spoke of some of his reflections on the problem of "order maintenance" in one of the country's metropolitan centers. His thesis is that the only way to rebuild criminal justice as a workable system is through ". . . tedious, systematic, nuts and bolts work . . . ." Mayor Lindsay delineates some of that work as including a redefinition of crime to lessen the burden on the police, the courts, and correctional agencies. Another problem that must be solved is that of keeping the policeman out from under the burden of paperwork and out on the street. He compares the nation's expenditures on defense and war abroad with the amount of money spent on the war against crime at home.

THE POLICE AND SOCIETY. This chapter from Paul Chevigny's book *Police Power: Police Abuses in New York City* discusses a specific city police department from the viewpoint of an attorney who represented many people who claimed victimization of police abuses. The chapter provokes thought and should lead to some lively discussion on the topic.

AN OPEN LETTER ON POLICE REVIEW BOARDS. Editor William H. Hewitt most adequately introduces his topic, which deals with a process of review of police practices that is vehemently opposed by many police administrators; and just as vehemently proposed by some critics of law enforcement who believe there is a crying need for such a process. The open letter was written by the Police Commissioner of New York City to Mayor John Lindsay. His term of office expired on February 21, 1966 and he was replaced by Commissioner Howard R. Leary.

POLICE BRUTALITY—FACT OR FANTASY? The author discusses the phenomenon from the philosophical viewpoint of a police practitioner. A topic that was the subject of frequent speaking engagements, this article is condensed from several of those presentations.

LAWMEN INSIST ONLY MORE MEN CAN CURB STREET CRIME. This article reflects the views of many police administrators that sophisticated equipment and modern technology are great aids to modern law enforcement, but they may never replace the need for more manpower.

IMPACT—DETROIT. This is a program initiated by that large city to cope with an impossible situation: lack of manpower. Confronted with providing mediocre service for all the calls for help that have been traditionally delegated to the police, Detroit police administrators took a hard look at their system and made many changes.

A Justice Speaks on Law and Order

Charles E. Whittaker

No doubt you, just as I, have noticed in the news media an ever-increasing number of items and articles that show with unmistakable clarity a rapid spread of lawlessness in our land that seems to be thoroughly planned, and also to be designed to destroy, and that seriously threatens to destroy, law, order and all vestiges of decency in our land.

Recently, while sitting in my library meditating upon that subject and upon appropriate remarks here today, and also listening to the beautiful music of "My Fair Lady"—and being, perhaps, thereby lulled into a satirical mood—it occurred to me: Why not speak on "Old-fashioned Law and Order—Wouldn't That Be Loverley?"

One of the recent articles that had deeply impressed me was by a

This is the full text of an address by Charles E. Whittaker, associate justice of the Supreme Court (retired), before a meeting of the Tennessee Bar Association, Nashville, Tenn., on June 17, 1965.

husband-and-wife team of eminent criminologists of the Harvard Law School. It dealt with the rapid increase and spread of crime, and concluded with the statement that "unless much is done to check [current] vicious cycles, we are in for a period of violence beyond anything we have yet seen."

Another recent and impressive article contained the theme—which I think is fundamental—of the recent presidentially proclaimed Law Day, 1965, which was: "Uphold the law—a citizen's first duty."

Believing that this theme states an indisputable truth, yet, having read and heard many recent open and direct preachments of disrespect for and disobedience of our laws, and, also having seen the destructive effects of those preachments upon the good order and morality of our society, I am moved to speak out in demand for an immediate end to such conduct by the vigorous and evenhanded enforcement of our laws.

While I do not claim that all of our crime is due to any one cause, it seems rather clear that a large part of the current rash and rapid spread of lawlessness in our land has been, at least, fostered and inflamed by the preachments of self-appointed leaders of minority groups to "obey the good laws, but to violate the bad ones"—which, of course, simply advocates violation of the laws they do not like, or, in other words, the taking of the law into their own hands.

And this is precisely what their followers have done and are doing—all under the banner of "peaceable civil disobedience," which they have claimed to be protected by the peaceable-assembly-and-petition provision of the First Amendment to the United States Constitution.

Although such preachments and practices have become far more vocal and widespread in our recent racial strife, they did not have their origin in that strife, but, rather, in the labor strife, sit-ins and lie-downs of an earlier era.

More recently, certain self-appointed racial leaders, doubtless recalling the appeasements and, hence, successes of that earlier conduct, have simply adopted and used those techniques in fomenting and waging their lawless campaigns which they have called "demonstrations."

They have recently used these techniques to incite their followers to assemble, from far and wide—often, unfortunately, with the encouragement and at the expense of well meaning but misguided church organizations—into large and loosely assembled groups, which many have regarded as mobs, to wage what they have called "demonstrations" to force the grant of "rights" in defiance of the law, the courts and all constituted authority.

At the beginning, those "demonstrations" consisted of episodic group invasions and appropriation of private stores, first by sitting down and later by lying down therein, and, eventually, by blocking the entrances thereto with their bodies.

Seeing that those trespasses were often applauded in high places, were generally not punished, but, rather, were compelled to be appeased and rewarded, those racial leaders and their groups quickly enlarged the scope of their activities by massing and marching their followers on the sidewalks, streets and highways—frequently blocking and appropriating them to a degree that precluded their intended public uses.

And that conduct, too, being nearly always appeased, the process spread areawise, as might have been expected, from one Southern city to another, and then into many Northern cities, including St. Louis, Chicago, Pittsburgh, Philadelphia, Washington, New York, Brooklyn, Syracuse and Rochester, and, eventually, pretty generally throughout the land.

"Crime," says Webster, means "an act or omission forbidden by law and punishable upon conviction." It cannot be denied that each of those trespasses violated, at least, the criminal-trespass laws of the local jurisdiction involved, nor that those laws impose penalties for their violation, nor, hence, that those trespasses constituted crimes.

In the first place, that conduct cannot properly be termed "peaceable," for we all know from experience that the assembly of large groups for the avowed purpose of forcing direct action outside the law amounts to the creation of a mob bent on lawlessness, and inherently disturbs the peace of all others.

One could hardly deny the truth of the statement written by Mr. Justice Black, joined by two other Justices, in June, 1964, that "force leads to violence, violence to mob conflicts, and these to rule by the strongest groups with control of the most deadly weapons."

Nor can this conduct even be termed "civil disobedience," for conduct violating criminal laws is not "civil" but "criminal" disobedience. And, lastly, that conduct is not protected by the peaceable-assembly-and-petition provision of the First Amendment.

That provision says: "Congress shall make no law... abridging... the right of the people peaceably to assemble and to petition the Government for a redress of grievances."

Nothing in that language grants a license to any man, acting either singly or in a group, to violate State criminal laws—including those laws which prohibit trespass upon, and appropriation of, private property, and those laws prohibiting the willful obstruction of the public walks, streets and highways.

Rather, as Mr. Justice Roberts wrote upon the subject in 1939, "The privilege of a citizen of the United States to use the streets and parks for communication of views on national questions must be regulated in the interest of all; it is not absolute, but is relative, and must be exercised in subordination to the general comfort and convenience, and in consonance with peace and good order...."

Surely, no thoughtful person will disagree with that statement, nor with the statement made very recently by the president of Yale University in a speech at Detroit, that the current rash of "demonstrations" make "a ludicrous mockery of the democratic debating process."

The philosophy of "obeying only the laws you like," and of openly defying and breaking the ones you do not like, has given rise to mobs and mob actions that have proven—as certainly we should have expected—to be tailormade for infiltration, take-over and use by rabble-rousers and Communists who are avowedly bent on the breakdown of law, order and morality in our society and, hence, in its destruction.

And even though those results may not have been contemplated, and surely weren't wished by those Americans who so advocated disobedience of our laws, nevertheless, they did advocate that philosophy and they did put its process into action, and cannot now escape responsibility for its results.

The process has now spread even into the campuses of many, indeed most, of our great universities. A fair example of what is there happening was recently related by the California State superintendant of public instruction, who, in commenting about conditions on the campus at Berkeley, said:

"Demonstrations there provided a vehicle for infiltration by rabble-rousers, red-hots and Communists and resulted in assaults, kidnapings, and imprisonment of police officers, the commandeering of public-address systems, and their use in spewing over the campus the most filthy four-letter words, and the general breakdown of law and order."

A recent national magazine contained an interview with Dr. James M. Nabrit, president of Howard University—the largest Negro university in our country—who finds on his campus "open defiance of law and order," which he characterized as part of a campaign "to bring the university into general disrepute."

"FRAUDS" IN RIGHTS MOVEMENT

Dr. Nabrit cautioned: "We must beware of some people who come to us like the Greeks bearing gifts. They do not believe in civil rights for anyone. They are children of lawlessness and disciples of destruction. They are people who cloak themselves in the roles of civil righters but plot and plan in secret to disrupt our fight for justice and full citizenship. They must be unmasked for the frauds that they are, they must be fought in every arena."

He stated that he had seen known Communists passing out throwaways and helping to deliver placards to pickets on and about his campus.

The Kansas City Times of Wednesday, May 19, published an Associated Press dispatch about the lawless demonstrations in progress on the campus of the University of Wisconsin. It is said that one of the leaders openly espoused, from a public rostrum on the campus, that "the students should band together to bring down the Government by any means."

It also said that the "demonstrations" there had now been infiltrated and were being led by "eight to a dozen" ringleaders who are operating under "pretty good cover"; that at least some of them are known members of the DuBois clubs of America, which Senator Dodd and J. Edgar Hoover have recently described as a "new Communist-oriented youth organization dominated and controlled by the Communists."

These lawless activities, nauseating as they are, can hardly be surprising, for they are, purely and simply, some of the results that we should have known would inevitably come from tolerating open and direct preachments to defy and violate the law.

A very recent issue of *U.S. News & World Report* [May 17, 1965] contains two pertinent articles. One saying that "increased Communist penetration and influence inside some sections of the Negro movement in the United States is a subject of growing concern to the FBI and White House." The other saying, "J. Edgar Hoover, FBI Director, and President Johnson both are increasingly concerned by the growing activity of known Communists on the campuses of colleges around the country. They would like to alert the country to the situation, but are concerned about being considered 'Red-baiters' if they do."

I, for one, would like to lend a voice of encouragement to them to forget those fears and to alert the country fully about the facts, for surely that is their duty and no odium can result from exposing those who are preaching and practicing defiance of our law and, hence, the destruction of our society.

There are, of course, first duties of citizenship, but there are also first duties of government. It is undoubtedly true, as recited in the theme of the presidentially proclaimed Law Day, 1965, that "a citizen's first duty is to uphold the law," but it is also a first duty of government to enforce the law to do so by prosecuting and punishing those who violate our criminal laws.

In no other way can our people be secure from assaults and trespasses upon their persons and property, or maintain an ordered and moral society.

Because some of our citizens will not voluntarily perform their "first duty" to uphold the law, our governments, State and federal, have the paramount duty of, at least, making them obey it.

We have all along been told, and many of us have preached, that crime does not pay, but the recent rash and spread of law defiance, and the successes—however tenuous and temporary—of that philosophy in attaining goals, seems to compel a reappraisal of that concept, for, from what we see currently happening, one could reasonable believe that certain types of crimes are being permitted to pay.

PUBLIC APATHY AND LAWLESSNESS

Probably because of a rather widespread recognition that, at times and in certain sectors, some of our colored brethren have suffered unconstitutional discriminations, and because many of us have been sympathetic to the ends they seek—and have not, therefore, thought very much about destructive means they have embarked upon to attain those ends—there has been a rather general public apathy toward their preachments to violate, and their practices in violating, our laws.

Indeed, one of those who first advised, and was most successful in inducing, his followers to take the law into their own hands—and, who, now that their conduct has led to widespread disorder, attempts to excuse his responsibility for it with the doubtless-true statement:"I cannot control then"—parenthetically, an excuse quite reminiscent of the one given by the man who lighted the squib and threw it into the crowd—was rather recently twice honored. Once by an old and respected American university by conferring upon him an honorary degree—not in some new political science—but in law, and, second, by an honored foreign cultural group by awarding him a prize for, of all things, his contributions to peace.

What, I would like to ask, has happened to our sense of values?

But a recent article in the May 3, 1965, issue of *U.S. News & World Report* hints at a new and different appraisal of this conduct, and indicates some official impatience with this gentleman's apparent insatiable appetite for power, and some displeasure at his recently voiced criticism of the Administration's foreign policies in Vietnam and elsewhere—concluding with the statement that "some Washington observers profess to see an attempt [by this gentleman] to 'escalate' his status as a national figure—perhaps with political goals in view."

This is heartening, as it indicates a new awareness of the inevitable destruction of ordered liberty that must be expected if we continue to allow any of our citizens to incite others to disobey the law—to take it into their own hands, and to get away with it.

Whatever may have been the provocations—and, doubtless, there have been some—no man, or any group or race of men, can be permitted, in a government of laws, to take the law, or what they think ought to be the law, into their own hands, for that is anarchy, and sure to result in chaos.

The fact that the provocations may have been themselves constitutionally unlawful cannot justify unlawful means for their resolution.

Both types of conduct are wrong—constitutionally wrong, the one as much as the other. And, obviously, two wrongs cannot make a right.

All discriminations that violate the Constitution and laws of the United States are readily redressable in our courts, which have always been open to all citizens. And no one has any room to doubt that, if he will resort to those courts, and have the patience to await their processes—as we all must do, in an ordered society—all his constitutional and legal rights will be vouchsafed to him, whatever his creed or color.

But there has been impatience with the judicial processes, manifested by the recent hue and cry for "action now—not the delays of the law."

Certainly this cliche, too, advocates such direct action as amounts to a clear call for disobedience of the laws, the judgments of the courts and of all constituted authority and lawful processes.

It is true that legal processes, being refined and deliberative processes, are slow.

But like the mills of the gods, though they grind slowly, they grind exceedingly fine, and their judgments are most likely to be just.

In all events, there is no other fair and orderly way to decide the issues that arise among us, and to have an ordered liberty.

Every ordered society in history has found it necessary to establish laws, and courts fairly to interpret and enforce them; and the same history makes clear, too, that the first evidences of a society's decay may be seen in its toleration of disrespect for, and disobedience of, its laws and the judgments of its courts.

HOW MINORITY GROUPS CAN LOSE OUT

The great pity here is that these minority groups, in preaching and practicing defiance of the law, are, in fact, advocating erosion and destruction of the only structure that can ever assure to them, or permanently maintain for them, due process of law and the equal protection of the laws, and that can, thus, protect them from discriminations and abuses by majorities.

In May, 1965, Mr. Lewis F. Powell, president of the American Bar Association, in a speech dedicating the new Missouri Bar Center at Jefferson City, said, "Many centuries of human misery show that once a society departs from the rule of law, and every man becomes the judge of which laws he will obey, only the strongest remain free," and also that "those who break the great tradition of respect and tolerance for the differing views of others by resorting to coercion, whether 'violent' or 'nonviolent,' menace the spirit of responsible inquiry essential to [our] institutions." "No 'end,' " he said, "however worthy [can ever] justify resort to unlawful means."

He concluded with the statement that "America needs a genuine revival of respect for law and orderly processes, a reawakening of individual responsibility, a new impatience with those who violate and circumvent laws, and a determined insistence that laws be enforced, courts respected and due process followed." To this, I say amen.

Surely we must always strive to eliminate injustice and discrimination, but we must do so by orderly processes in the legislatures and the courts, and not by defying their processes and actions, nor by taking the laws into our own hands.

We must take the laws into our hearts rather than into our hands, and seek redress in the courts rather than in the streets.

A very recent issue of *The Kansas City Star* contained several articles about the general breakdown of law and order on our college campuses.

One of them fairly puts the finger on the cause. It did so through quoting one of the "demonstrating" students. He was asked why some students had abandoned historical "panty raids" and similar college pranks for open and riotous rebellion. "Why," he said, "you could get kicked out of school for conducting a panty raid and things of that kind, but no one is ever kicked out or punished for demonstrating for something like civil rights."

It is thus plain that the students, knowing just as everyone else knows, that open and riotous rebellion in the name of "civil rights" is not being punished, but is being tolerated, have been thus encouraged to wage and spread rebellion.

Another of these articles quoted some comments of J. Edgar Hoover about the effects of spreading crime upon the peace and safety of our citizens. He said: "There is too much concern in this country...for the 'rights' of an individual who commits a crime."

"I think he is entitled to his [legal rights], but I think the citizens of this country ought to be able to walk all the streets of our cities without being mugged, raped or robbed." But, he said, we can't do so today, and he added: "All through the country, almost without exception, this condition prevails."

The April 10, 1965, issue of the magazine *America* contained an article on the imperative need for certain and severe punishment of crime, which made many pertinent observations, including this one:

"[Government] has no right to turn the cheek of its citizens. Instead, it is gravely obligated—by the very purpose of its existence—to see to their protection.

"Sure and swift punishment [is our only way] to guarantee that protection....We stand in need of sure, swift, tough punishment if we expect to decrease the crime rate, and to protect the great mass of our upright citizens."

To this, too, I can only say amen.

The causes are plain. We have, in high places, tolerated and even encouraged preachments to break the law—such as: "Obey the good laws but break the bad ones," which, of course, means to obey only the laws you like; and such as: "Action now, not the delays of the law," which is, of course, a call for direct action outside the law and the courts.

And we have also tolerated and in some high places have even encouraged, the actual defiances of the law which those preachments have advocated and brought into existence, and which have now spread to all areas of the nation, and seriously threaten the breakdown of law, order and morality.

REMEDY: DEMAND RESPECT FOR LAW

The remedy is equally plain. It is simply to insist that our governments, State and federal, reassume and discharge their first duty of protecting the people against lawless invasions of their persons and property and from assaults upon their liberties by demanding and commanding respect for law and legal processes through the impartial, evenhanded, vigorous, swift and certain enforcement of our criminal laws and the real and substantial punishment there under of all conduct that violates those laws.

These are not platitudes, but are fundamentals and vital, as every thinking man should see, to the survival of our nation.

In no other way can we orderly resolve the issues that confront and divide us, or live together in peace and harmony as a civilized nation of brothers under the fatherhood of God.

Bill of Rights in Spotlight during the 1960s

Harry M. Humphreys

JUDICIARY SYSTEM REVISES APPROACH TO CRIMINAL LAW

Historically the Bill of Rights, or first ten amendments of the United States Constitution, was adopted as something of a sop to the Jeffersonian, anti-Federalist forces for needed help in ratifying a constitution with many conservative and aristocratic features.

But even though the amendments had been incorporated into the charter of national life for some 170 years, it wasn't until the decade just passed that the attention of the American Judiciary was focused most heavily on the Bill of Rights and corollary issues, especially in the police procedures and criminal law context.

Moved to Center

This is not to say that the protections of the Bill of Rights were disregarded by courts in past eras nor that the guarantees of liberties lay dormant. Rather other issues, frequently economic ones, held the center of the judicial stage, although the First Amendment (freedom of religion, press, assembly, etc.), the Fifth Amendment (the right against self-incrimination in cases involving national security), and Amendment 10 (states' rights) had increasingly come under judicial scrutiny.

In the 1960s the Fourth and Sixth Amendments moved toward center stage, and the Fifth Amendment was scrutinized for relevance to confessions in criminal cases.

Cite Article IV

Article IV provides, "The right of the people to be secure in their persons, houses, papers and effects, against unreasonable searches and seizures, shall not

---

Reprinted with permission of the author from Harry M. Humphreys, "Criminal Courts and the Law," P.O. Box 2524, Toluca Lake Station, North Hollywood, California 91602. Copyright ©1970 by Harry M. Humphrey.

be violated, and no warrants shall issue, but upon probable cause, supported by oath or affirmation, and particularly describing the place to be searched, and the persons or things to be seized."

Article VI provides, "In all criminal prosecutions, the accused shall enjoy the right to a speedy and public trial...and to be informed of the nature and cause of the accusation; to be confronted with the witnesses against him; to have compulsory process for obtaining witnesses in his favor, and to have the assistance of counsel for his defense."

The substance of these amendments was applied to the states almost invariably through the Fourteenth Amendment's guarantee that no person be deprived of "life, liberty or property" without "due process of law."

The dawning of the new age, prior to which most courts had confined their rulings in criminal trials only to the merit of the evidence presented and not how it had been obtained for purposes of prosecution, was to be seen in the 1950s.

Not surprisingly, California, which has enjoyed a reputation for being a "progressive" state, was at the forefront in much of litigation leading up to nationwide application of the so-called "exclusionary rule" of evidence.

Doctrine Weakened

Although it had been held in 1914 that evidence obtained by federal officers in violation of a defendant's constitutional rights was inadmissible in federal prosecutions, the Supreme Court explicitly held that the exclusionary rule did not apply to state proceedings as late as 1949 when the nation's highest tribunal refused to reverse a state court conviction which had been based on evidence unlawfully seized by state officers. However, a small minority of the states, not including California, did choose to abide by the rule.

The doctrine of inapplicability to the states was weakened, however, in *Rochin* v. *California* (342 U.S. 165) a Los Angeles case, when the United States Supreme Court ruled in 1952 that narcotics which had been pumped out of the defendant's stomach and then used to obtain a conviction was "too close to rack and screw methods" and violated the Fourteenth Amendment's mandate that no state "deprive any person of life, liberty or property without due process of law."

In *Irvine* v. *California* (347 U.S. 128) in 1954 the Supreme Court rejected an argument that the Fourteenth Amendment required states to reverse convictions based on what was an unlawful search and seizure by federal standards. However the court suggested that California should reconsider its rules of evidence.

Opinion Reversed

"A San Francisco bookmaker was convicted; the U.S. Supreme Court sustained the conviction but asked the U.S. attorney to investigate the police department up there for improprieties of search and seizure," Los Angeles City Atty. Roger Arnebergh recalled. "The court put pressure on California and other states to adopt the exclusionary rule."

Pressure or not, adopt it California did in 1955 in *People* v. *Cahan* (44 Cal 2d 434), an opinion written by Justice Roger J. Traynor, reversing a horse racing bookmaking decision by a Los Angeles Superior Court judge.

In this important case an officer attached to the Los Angeles Police Dept. intelligence unit testified that he had installed a recording device at two places occupied by the defendants after getting permission from the Chief of Police as a section of the Penal Code then provided when "such use and installation are necessary in the performance of their (police) duties in detecting crime and in the apprehension of criminals."

"Principles Violated"

Justice Traynor noted near the beginning of his opinion that the case was analogous in several ways to *Irvine* and wrote that "such methods of getting evidence have been caustically censured by the United States Supreme Court."

"That officers of the law would break and enter a home, secrete such a device even in a bedroom and listen to the conversations of the occupants for over a month would be almost incredible if it were not admitted," he quoted from the *Irvine* decision.

"Few police measures have come to our attention that more flagrantly, deliberately and persistently violate the fundamental principle declared by the Fourth Amendment," he added.

Justice Traynor next looked at the section of the Penal Code the Los Angeles police had argued permitted installation of the recording devices, and said the provision "does not and could not authorize violations of the Constitution."

Held Inadmissable

"The proviso under which the officers purported to act at most prevents their conduct from constituting a violation of that section itself," Justice Traynor went on, noting that "the evidence obtained from the microphones was not the only unconstitutionally obtained evidence" as "there was a mass of evidence obtained by numerous forcible entries and seizures without search warrants."

Justice Traynor held that "evidence obtained in violation of constitutional guarantees is inadmissible," adding that "when, as in the present case, the very purpose of an illegal search and seizure is to get evidence to introduce at a trial, the success of the lawless venture depends entirely on the court's lending its aid by allowing the evidence to be introduced.

"It is no answer (to the question of admitting illegally seized evidence for trial) to say that a distinction should be drawn between the government acting as law enforcer and the gatherer of evidence and the government acting as judge," Justice Traynor added, anticipating the arguments of critics of the exclusionary rule.

These critics were and still are quick to cite Justice Traynor's opinion 13 years before in *People* v. *Gonzales* (20 Cal 2d 165), a theft case in which the Justice declined to apply the exclusionary rule.

Anticipate Argument

"The fact that an officer acted improperly in obtaining evidence presented at trial in no way precluded the court from rendering a fair and impartial judgment," Justice Traynor wrote then.

Also anticipating arguments that criminal and civil remedies were available against officers who violated constitutional rights in obtaining evidence, Justice Traynor wrote, "Reported cases involving civil actions against police officers are rare, and those involving successful criminal prosecutions against officers are nonexistent."

"It is morally incongruous for the state to flout constitutional rights and at the same time demand that its citizens observe the law," Justice Traynor philosophized, "...Crime is contagious. If the government becomes a lawbreaker, it breeds contempt for law, it invites every man to become a law unto himself; it invites anarchy."

In 1961 case, *Mapp* v. *Ohio* (367 U.S. 643), the United States Supreme Court applied the exclusionary rule nationwide.

Not Admissable

In this case, police officers appeared at the home of Miss Mapp waving what they asserted was a warrant. The woman placed the piece of paper in her bra, but officers recovered it after a struggle, then began searching through the house where they discovered the alleged obscene material.

The United States Supreme Court held that evidence obtained in violation of the 4th Amendment was, as a matter of due process, inadmissible in all state as well as federal courts.

"Significantly, among those (states) which now follow the (exclusionary) rule," Justice Tom Clark wrote, "Is California, which, according to its highest court, was 'compelled to reach that conclusion because other remedies have completely failed to secure compliance with the constitutional provisions (against illegal search and seizure).' " He cited the *Cahan* decision, and added that the "experience of other states" had shown "such other (criminal and civil) remedies (against police) to be worthless and futile."

"Poisoned Tree"

In addition the Justice noted that "in nonexclusionary states (such as California before 1955) federal officers, being human, were by it (exclusionary rule application in federal court) invited to and did, as our cases indicate, step across the street to the state's attorney with their unconstitutionally seized evidence."

The nation's highest court extended the exclusionary rule further in a 1963 case, *Wong Sun* v. *United States* (371 U.S. 488), holding it applicable to both direct and indirect products of an unreasonable search.

Under this so-called "fruit of the poisoned tree" doctrine the court ruled as inadmissible evidence such things as personal items, office memos and correspondence obtained during an illegal search or, for example, a confession obtained by police following an illegal arrest.

The increasingly important right of privacy was given the protection of the Fourth Amendment in *U.S.* v. *Katz* (386 U.S. 954) when the Supreme Court in 1967 held inadmissible at trial any evidence obtained without a search warrant by use of electronic eavesdropping devices even though law enforcement agencies don't trespass on a suspect's property.

But probably the most liberalized extension of the exclusionary rule was *Chimel* v. *California* (23 L. Ed. 685), handed down last June 23.

Orange County Case

In that case involving an Orange County man subsequently convicted for burglary in state courts, Justice Potter Stewart sharply limited the right to search incident to a lawful arrest within a suspect's premises without first having obtained a search warrant.

In this landmark case three police officers had arrived at Chimel's Santa Ana home with a warrant authorizing his arrest for the alleged burglary of an Orange coin shop Chimel's wife permitted the officers to come inside where they waited the suspect's return from work.

Coins Seized

When the officers handed Chimel the arrest warrant and asked him if they could "look around," he objected. Although no search warrant had been issued, the officers, nevertheless, told Chimel that they would search "on the basis of the lawful arrest."

Coins were seized during the search, but the case, to use Justice Stewart's explanation, presented the United States Supreme Court directly with the "question whether the warantless search of petitioner's (Chimel's) entire house can be constitutionally justified as incident to that arrest."

Justice Stewart conceded that his court's decisions were "far from consistent," but he held that the search had exceeded constitutional limitations and, therefore, the evidence seized was excluded from being presented in court under the Fourth Amendment.

Of the "proper extent" for a "search incident to arrest," Justice Stewart said, "There is ample justification for a search of the arrestee's person and the area 'within his immediate control'—construing that phrase to mean the area from within which he might gain possession of a weapon or destructible evidence."

Warrant Needed

"There is no comparable justification, however, for routinely searching rooms other than that in which an arrest occurs—or, for that matter, for searching through all the desk drawers or other closed or concealed areas in that room itself," Justice Stewart continued.

"Such searches (out of the arrestee's 'immediate control'), in the absence of well recognized exceptions, may be made only under the authority of a search warrant," he concluded. "The adherence to judicial processes mandated by the Fourth Amendment requires no less."

The "well-recognized exceptions" Justice Stewart speaks about will be explored in subsequent articles as will be the effect of this *Chimel* decision on search warrants which, since June, (1968) have more than tripled in the Valley and throughout the county generally.

COURT RULINGS TRY TO INSURE FAIR TRIALS

Must Tell Suspect Rights, Miranda Decision Declared

If, as is generally believed, the exclusionary rule and its extensions were adopted on the moral premise that the government should not profit by its own wrong through the lawless enforcement of the law against the individual rather than some abstract notion of "fairness" another series of important decisions was aimed clearly at maximizing the chance for fair trials by according procedural protections to the constitutional rights of the individual.

These decisions, buttressed by the Sixth Amendment right to the "assistance of counsel" and the Fifth Amendment privilege against self-incrimination in criminal cases, culminated in the 1966 United States Supreme Court case of *Miranda* v. *Arizona* (384 U.S. 757).

The *Miranda* decision, still one of the most controversial of them all, held simply that prior to police interrogation—when the suspect is "in custody at the station or otherwise deprived of his freedom of action in any significant way"—the suspect must be informed of his right to remain silent.

He must also be told that any statements he makes may be used as evidence against him, and that he has the right to the presence of an attorney, either retained or appointed if he can't afford one, while being questioned.

Furthermore, the opinion by Chief Justice Earl Warren held that these rights could only be given up by a clear, intelligent and voluntary waiver.

The *Miranda* decision was not a spur-of-the-moment ruling, but rather was the culmination of at least a decade of constitutional development, beginning for relevant purposes in 1957 when the United States Supreme Court held a confession inadmissible not so much because it had been obtained by some kind of brute torture, but because it had been a gross violation of a procedural rule effective in Washington, D.C. requiring a suspect be brought promptly before a magistrate.

Subjected to Tests

In that case, *Mallory* v. *United States* (354 U.S. 449) a 19-year-old boy of substandard intelligence was arrested on suspicion that he had commited a fatal rape.

Following his arrest he was interrogated for a lengthy period and subjected to at least two lie detector tests until a confession was signed. He was told nothing of his constitutional rights to remain silent or to have counsel.

The boy was tried in a lower federal court and sentenced to death, but a unanimous United States Supreme Court reversed the conviction and sent the case back for a new trial.

The major reason for the reversal cited by the court was police violation of a provision of the Federal Rules of Criminal Procedure that a suspect be taken before an arraigning magistrate "without unnecessary delay."

Probable Cause

Justice Felix Frankfurter vigorously condemned "those reprehensible police interrogation practices known as the 'third degree' which, though universally rejected as indefensible, still find their way into use."

He also reiterated the legal principle that police must arrest on probable cause (that they have a reasonable basis to believe a crime has been committed by a particular person); and admonished officers that they cannot use an interrogation process after arrest solely for the purpose of eliciting damaging statements to support the arrest.

In federal court, confessions obtained during an unreasonable period of police detention and interrogation had been held inadmissible beginning in 1943 as violating the requirement of prompt arraignment.

Served Notice

However even as late as 1955 in *Rogers* v. *Superior Court* (46 Cal 2d 3), California courts were declining to go along with the federal standards. In the *Rogers* case the State Supreme Court held that illegal detention of a person under arrest for eight days before being taken before a magistrate was not by itself sufficient grounds for excluding statements about the crime made voluntarily.

However, the publicity generated by the *Mallory* case served notice that a new day of tougher procedural standards was dawning, and police and prosecutors across the country, spurred on by state court decisions, began preparing for it.

The next major thrust in the extension of procedural safeguards afforded criminal defendants by the courts came in the early years of the 1960s and was tied in with the right to counsel under the Sixth Amendment.

Provide Counsel

Within the space of about a year the United States Supreme Court handed down decisions giving defendants counsel as a right in state court felony trials, for postindictment questioning and when an investigation has begun to focus on a suspect in police custody.

In *Gideon* v. *Wainwright* (327 U.S. 335), which had little impact in Los Angeles County when it was handed down in 1963 because of the existence of the public defender's office, the Supreme Court saw it as an "obvious truth" that "in our adversary system of criminal justice, any person hauled into court who is too poor to hire a lawyer cannot be assured a fair trial unless counsel is provided for him."

In *Messiah* v. *United States* (377 U.S. 201) in 1964 the same high court held that the postindictment stage was a "critical stage" of proceedings during which the defendant is entitled to the advice of his attorney, and that any incriminatory statements gathered from a defendant then in the absence of his counsel could not be used against him in court.

Admit Evidence

"A constitution which guarantees a defendant the aid of counsel at...trial could surely vouchsafe no less to an indicted defendant under interrogation by the police in a completely extrajudicial proceeding," the *Messiah* opinion noted, "anything less...might deny a defendant 'effective representation by counsel at the only stage when legal aid and advice would help him.'"

In the more noteworthy *Escobedo* v. *Illinois* decision (378 U.S. 478), also in 1964, the state court had admitted into evidence at trial incriminating statements made during police interrogation before the accused was formally indicted.

Without informing the suspect of his right to remain silent, Chicago police had denied Escobedo's request to consult with his attorney (who waited outside the interrogation room), had told Escobedo they had convincing evidence of his firing the fatal shots and urged him to make a statement.

For the court, Justice Arthur Goldberg held that since the police investigation had been "focused on" the accused as a "particular suspect" rather than it being a general investigation into an unsolved crime, ignoring of the accused's request to consult with his counsel denied him his Sixth Amendment rights as applied to the states by the "due process" clause of the Fourteenth Amendment. Statements Escobedo had made at the interrogation were held inadmissible for a new trial.
new trial.

Since what happened at the interrogation could, Goldberg said, "certainly affect the whole trial," it therefore was a "critical stage" in the proceedings and constitutional protections were vital.

Like many of the other cases, *Escobedo* had its detractors on the Supreme Court bench.

Bar from Evidence

Justice Potter Stewart dissented on grounds that the right to counsel shouldn't begin until formal institution of criminal proceedings by indictment, information or arraignment.

Justice Byron White contended that the decision "approaches a goal of barring from evidence all admissions obtained from a person suspected of crime" and would make law enforcement more difficult.

Taking note of these objections, Justice Goldberg penned, "The right to

Soon afterwards, however, the United States Supreme Court in 1965 declared the rule unconstitutional in *Griffin* v. *California* (380 U.S. 609).

California's constitutional provision and practice were held invalid on the grounds that they placed a penalty on a person's right not to be a witness against himself as guaranteed by the Fifth Amendment and made applicable to the states via the Fourteenth Amendment.

Taking Blood

The first significant modification to the strict procedural standards which the Supreme Court had adopted in an effort to assure what it considered a fair trial in *Miranda* and *Griffin* occurred in *Schmerber* v. *California* (348 U.S. 757).

In this 1966 case it was ruled that evidence of a noncommunicative nature, more particularly withdrawal of a blood sample from a suspect, did not come within the scope of the Fifth Amendment privilege against self-incrimination.

"The court held that taking blood from a suspect in a medically approved manner was not a denial of due process. Although it was an incriminating product of compulsion it was neither the accused's testimony nor evidence relating to some communicative act or writing," explained Van Nuys Municipal Judge Edward Davenport who personally argued this Tarzana case before the Supreme Court.

"It was not testimonial compulsion; it was a taking of real or physical evidence by use of reasonable force. There was a lawful search and seizure after a lawful arrest," the Judge added.

Shortly thereafter in *Chapman* v. *California* (386 U.S. 18), the Supreme Court adopted what it called the "harmless error" standard in 1967.

As formulated by Justice Hugo Black, the standard to be applied was as follows:

Before an error involving denial of a federal constitutional right can be held harmless in a state criminal case, the reviewing court must be satisfied "beyond a reasonable doubt" that the error did not contribute to the defendant's conviction.

Following this relatively short period of consolidation, however, the United State Supreme Court was off again on a new tack—applying the right to counsel to police lineups.

Handed down on the same June day in 1967 were decision in *United States* v. *Wade* (388 U.S. 218) and *Gilbert* v. *California* (388 U.S. 263).

In *Wade* the court held the lineup, as it had done a couple years before with the interrogation, to be a "critical stage" in a criminal proceeding necessitating counsel to further promote the possibility of a defendant's receiving a fair trial.

The *Gilbert* case reiterated the *Wade* rule and more cogently established the principle that in-court identifications were inadmissible should they be found to have resulted from a postindictment lineup presented without notice to and in the absence of defendant's counsel.

These two decisions were tempered somewhat by a third one, *Stovall* v.

"At this point," he added, "he (suspect) has shown that he intends to exercise his Fifth Amendment privilege; any statement taken after the person invokes his privilege cannot be other than the product of compulsion, subtle or otherwise."

"If the individual (suspect) states that he wants an attorney, the interrogation must cease until an attorney is present," it was added.

He also pointed out the *Miranda* rights could be "intelligently" and "knowingly" waived, albeit emphasizing the waiver must be "demonstrated by the prosecution at trial."

"There is no requirement that police stop a person who enters a police station and states that he wishes to confess to a crime, or a person who calls the police to offer a confession or any other statement he desires to make," the Chief Justice went on.

"...Our decision does not in any way preclude police from carrying out their traditional investigatory functions," he stated, noting further that "although confessions may play an important role in some convictions, the cases before us present graphic examples of the overstatement of the (need) for confessions."

Miranda, charged with kidnaping and rape, had been identified by eyewitnesses, the Chief Justice pointed out.

In a corollary Los Angeles case, *California* v. *Stewart,* handed down at the same time as *Miranda,* the Chief Justice noted articles stolen from the victim as well as from several other robbery victims had been found at Stewart's home at the "outset of the investigation."

And marked bills from the robbed bank were found in another defendant's car in a third case handed down that day in 1966.

In an important footnote to the *Miranda* opinion, the Chief Justice warned "In accord with our decision today, it is impermissible to penalize an individual for exercising his Fifth Amendment privilege when he is under police custodial interrogation."

"The prosecution may not, therefore, use at trial the fact that he stood mute or claimed his privilege in the face of accusation," it was elaborated further.

State Provision Upheld

This in effect marked the beginning of an extension of what the nation's highest tribunal had conceived to be Fifth Amendment violations permitted by many states allowing, to use California Chief Justice Roger Traynor's words in a recent address to the Los Angeles County Bar Association, "comment on the defendant's failure to take the stand to explain or deny facts when he could reasonably be expected to do so."

Despite a 1964 United States Supreme Court decision moving toward overturning such comment rules, the California Supreme Court a year later was still reaffirming the validity of a state constitutional provision which allowed restricted comment on the silence of a criminal defendant.

counsel would indeed be hollow if it began at a period when few confessions were obtained."

". . .Nothing we have said today affects the powers of the police to investigate an unsolved crime by gathering information from witnesses and by other proper investigative efforts," he added.

Request for Counsel

The *Escobedo* doctrine was developed a bit further on the California scene a year later in the 1965 case of *People* v. *Dorado* (62 Cal 2d 338).

In *Dorado* the State Supreme Court emphasized that the request for counsel is unnecessary, and that the police should inform suspects about this right.

"To require the request would be to favor the defendant whose sophistication or status had fortuitously prompted him to make it," the opinion said.

Next on the federal level came *Miranda,* where the court held inadmissible a confession because the defendant was not told of his right to counsel, even though he had signed a confession containing a typed paragraph stating that the confession was made voluntarily with full knowledge of his legal rights and with understanding that any confession he might make could be used against him.

Placed in Cell

In a corollary case, *California* v. *Stewart,* handed down at the same time as *Miranda* on the same principles, the United States Supreme Court upheld the California Supreme Court's reversal of a Los Angeles Superior Court conviction based in part on the defendant's confession.

Stewart had been placed in a cell at University station for five days and interrogated on nine separate occasions before making his confession. Although this suspect had denied the alleged offenses during the first eight attempts to get him to talk, Chief Justice Warren held that the court would not presume that Stewart had been advised of his rights to remain silent and to have a lawyer in the absence of a record showing these rights had been given.

Citing the California *Dorado* ruling that the suspect need not make a preinterrogation request for a lawyer, Chief Justice Warren wrote, "While the authorities are not required to relieve the accused of his poverty, they have the obligation not to take advantage of indigence in the administration of justice."

In handing down the lengthy *Miranda* opinion Justice Warren looked at many alleged inadequacies in police work and even made reference to interrogation manuals officers insome places were using.

"The use of physical brutality and violence is not, unfortunately, relegated to the past or (to) any part of the country," he wrote.

Submit To Test

A Kings County, N.Y., incident was cited where "police brutally beat, kicked and placed lighted cigaret butts on the back of a potential witness under interrogation for the purpose of securing a statement incriminating a third party."

Also alleged in the Warren opinion was a 1945 Colorado incident where the "defendant was held in custody over two months, deprived of food for 15 hours, and forced to submit to a lie detector test when he wanted to go to the toilet."

Cited also was a 1959 Los Angeles County case, *People* v. *Matlock* (51 Cal 2d 682), where a suspect was "questioned incessantly over an evening's time, made to lie on a cold board and to answer questions (posed by police) whenever it appeared he was getting sleepy."

Describes Manuals

Most shocking abuse of all alleged perhaps was a 1957 Maryland case where, as summarized by the Chief Justice, "a police doctor told an accused who was strapped to a chair completely nude that he proposed to take hair and skin scrapings or anything that looked like blood or sperm from various parts of his body."

Of the manuals, Justice Warren noted, "To highlight the isolation and unfamiliar surroundings of police interrogation, the manuals instruct the police to display an air of confidence in the suspect's guilt and from outward appearance to maintain only an interest in confirming certain details."

"That counsel is present when statements are taken from an individual during interrogation obviously enhances the integrity of the fact-finding processes in court," Justice Warren claimed.

Prediction Fails

Three dissenting justices charged the *Miranda* decision was an example of poor constitutional law and would result in harmful consequences for the country at large.

While opinions differ on the consequences after almost four years of living under the *Miranda* precedent, at least one dire prediction voiced at the time—that it might result in lawyers or public defenders having to ride in every squad car—has certainly not materialized.

Problems of application faced by courts in California, the adjustment of local public defenders' offices to it and extensions of *Miranda* and related doctrines will be looked at subsequently.

MIRANDA CASE ESTABLISHES CLEAR INTERROGATION GUIDES

Although there has been some confusion about and numerous court testings of the Miranda admonitions and how the interrogation process is to be administered, Chief Justice Earl Warren did set out pretty clear and comprehensive guidlines in his opinion.

"If the individual (suspect) indicates in any manner at any time prior to or during questioning that he wishes to remain silent, the interrogation must cease," wrote the former California Governor.

Denno (388 U.S. 293) handed down at the same time.

In essence, this case held that "emergency situations"—for instance, where the victim is not expected to live—may as a practical matter necessitate showing the accused singly and immediately in an effort to obtain possible identification.

Noted in Wade

Exhibiting the accused singly to the victim under such circumstances, it was ruled, rather than in a regular showup, would not be a denial of the Sixth Amendment right to counsel. Still "unnecessarily suggestive" lineups of showups, police were admonished, could constitute a violation of constitutional rights.

Justice William Brennan did, however, note in the *Wade* case that "Legislative or other regulations, such as those of local police departments, which eliminate the risks of abuse and unintentional suggestion at lineup proceedings and the impediments to meaningful confrontation at trial may also remove the basis for regarding the stage as 'critical.' "

In most places, however, the stage has remained "critical," and in California at least the judicial thrust has been toward liberalizing the right to counsel at lineups.

The latest decision of the state Supreme Court was handed down on Dec. 9 in *People* v. *Fowler* (1 Cal 3d 335) a case where an Oakland defendant was not told that if he so desired, an attorney would be appointed to represent him at the lineup.

Although the *Wade* and *Gilbert* cases had, on the face of the opinions, seemingly been made applicable to only "postindictment" lineups, the highest state court carefully examined those and other decisions and saw "manifest(ed) a conclusion that the protections elucidated in *Wade* are as necessary at the preaccusation state as they are at the postaccusation stage."

"Moreover, we think it manifest that when the right to counsel at lineup has attached, the suspect is entitled to be so notified and to be notified that counsel will be appointed if necessary. Only if he is so notified can his election to proceed in the absence of counsel be deemed an intelligent waiver of the accrued right," the opinion went on.

"It was error of consitutional magnitude," the opinion continued, "to admit evidence of the lineup itself, and under the rules announced by the United States Supreme Court, that error cannot be cured by any showing that the subsequent in-court identification had a source independent of the illegal lineup."

The court then ordered the jury's judgment of first degree robbery reversed "unless the People can show 'beyond a reasonable doubt that the error complained of did not contribute to the verdict obtained.' " The reference here was to the "harmless error" rule of *Chapman*.

"We specifically do not here decide the extent to which the *Wade-Gilbert* rules are applicable to pretrial confrontations occurring our of the context of a formal lineup," the court noted, making reference to the *Stoval* decision.

In *Simmons* v. *U.S.* (390 U.S. 377), the high court declined to apply the requirement of having an attorney present when FBI officers used photographs which enabled witnesses to a robbery to identify the criminal.

"We hold that each case must be considered on its own facts and that convictions based on eyewitness identification at trial following a pretrial identification by photograph will be set aside on that ground only if the photo identification procedure was so impermissibly suggestive as to give rise to a very substantial likelihood of irreparable misidentification," Justice John Harlan wrote.

He cited for authority the *Stovall* case and *People* v. *Evans* (39 Cal 2d 242).

As with the lineup cases, so with *Miranda* during the past couple years have lower courts had some difficulties in arriving at viable applications in all circumstances.

In *People* v. *Fioritto* (68 Cal 2d 714), decided by the California Supreme Court in June 1968, it was held that once a suspect refuses to talk or confess, the police couldn't interrogate him later and use a confession made then.

In this case two accomplices of Fioritto confessed to a burglary when questioned by a Riverside sheriff's deputy, but Fioritto refused to talk. Shortly afterward, when brought together with his two cohorts and told they had confessed, Fioritto admitted his part in the crime.

Ruling Cited

The high court reversed his conviction and held the confession inadmissible, ruling, in essence, that a suspect who refuses to talk, then changes his mind, can talk to interrogating officers only if his attorney agrees.

The most significant recent word perhaps from thy United States Supreme Court itself on *Miranda* is a ruling handed down last term (1969) that the decision is not restricted to police questioning at the station house.

In *Orozco* v. *Texas* (22 L.Ed. 2d 311) the suspect was questioned in his bedroom shortly after a man had been killed in a tavern brawl. The officers questioning Orozco did not tell him of his *Miranda* rights even though they admitted that from the moment the suspect gave his name to them he was under arrest.

An opinion by Justice Black noted that *Miranda* "iterated and reiterated the absolute necessity for officers interrogating people 'in custody' to give the described warnings" whether the person be at the station house or otherwise deprived of his freedom in any significant way.

A dissent by Justice Byron White argued that the *Miranda* warnings should be limited to applying at the station house, where the setting may be unfamiliar to the suspect and police pressure (to confess) could be intimidating.

Although California appellate courts have held recently that the police need not advise an accused of his rights at each questioning and that confessions that are subsequently voluntarily initiated after a knowing and intelligent waiver of *Miranda* are admissible, some readers might well be forewarned that it has been repeatedly held that no right to counsel exists, for example, before required submission to a blood, breath, or urine test under the state's so-called "implied consent" law following drunk driving arrests.

Nor have the results of such tests been held inadmissible at trial as being in violation of the Fifth Amendment provision against self-incrimination.

Not only have adult suspects benefited from the *Miranda* decision, but in a landmark 1967 case *In re Gault* (387 U.S. 1), the United States Supreme Court held that juveniles also must be warned of the same rights and given most of the same procedural protections now accorded adults.

Needed: Order in the Courts

U. S. Chamber of Commerce

The cornerstone of the criminal justice system—the criminal courts—is in various stages of disintegration. What should be the system's linchpin is, in many localities, worn to within a hairbreadth of the breaking point. In short, the criminal court is beset with organizational fragmentation and rigidity, managerial and administrative anachronisms, and undertrained and poorly supported personnel who are frequently of less than mediocre caliber.

This, then, is the state of the institution around which the police and corrections have evolved and to which they are responsible in large measure. The court's rules, procedures, and decisions limit, expand, or otherwise shape the activities of the police. Through the prosecutor, the court determines who of those arrested will or will not be subject to judicial action. By the type and length of its sentences and by the extent of foot-dragging inefficiency, the court determines the work of the correctional system. Indeed, the court is charged by law to monitor the very legality of the correctional process.

In far too many jurisdictions, the hallmark of today's criminal court is delay ad nauseam. The scar that undue delay leaves upon the criminal justice system is indicated by these effects of clogged courts:

From *Marshalling Citizen Power Against Crime* (Washington, D.C.: U.S. Chamber of Commerce, 1970), pp. 38-60. Copyright © 1970 by the U.S. Chamber of Commerce. Reprinted by permission of the publisher.

Almost 60 percent of the estimated 14,000 individuals housed in the local jails of a major city were prisoners awaiting their day in court. Of the 60 percent about 12 percent were imprisoned because they could not raise bail of $500 or less, which is unrelated to whether they would be a danger to the community if freed but directly related to the many millions the city spends on pretrial detention and welfare recipients each year.

Many detained prior to trial see charges against them dropped. In effect, they served time though innocent. Some of those who are found guilty are freed because they have served their sentence before being judged.

Many of those genuinely dangerous to the comunity make bail and wait months, even years, for trial. The longer the wait, the greater the likelihood of the person becoming a fugitive or commiting additional crimes.

Despairing after numerous canceled court appearances, witnesses drop by the wayside and police and prosecutors wind up with countless wasted hours instead of convictions.

Victims and witnesses fail to continue appearing in courts because of numerous adjournments and interminable delays.

Evidence stales; memories fade; reasonable doubt leading to acquittal grows.

Prosecutors are mesmerized into moving the tremendous volume of cases, not administering justice. In one lower court, this was a significant factor in an understaffed prosecutor's office dropping outright nearly half the intake of criminal cases, prosecuting only one in six felony arrests as a felony, agreeing to reduce the charges against a defendant in return for a guilty plea, and allowing a defendant who pleads guilty to select any amenable judge. This helps to explain reports that while felony arrests in a large city were increasing to a yearly rate of 75,000, only 608 felony trials were completed.

Yet, as every informed observer realizes, delay is merely a symptom—monstrous as it is—of a number of deep-rooted maladies afflicting the judicial system. To blame delay on the crushing volume of cases entering court is not as simplistic or superficial a judgment as it may first appear. As noted earlier, many maintain that the courts would be relieved of a great burden if the thousands of offenders whose troubles are rooted in alcoholism, narcotics addiction, mental illness, and the like were diverted to appropriate social, medical, or psychiatric services for treatment instead of being routed through the criminal courts for a judicial processing whose cures do not fit the disease.

Nonetheless, volume alone is not the culprit, particularly for those courts whose backlog is minimal; if it were, more judges and facilities would be the answer. But such is not the complete answer, just as additional personnel and equipment are not the entire solution to police problems—and for many of the same reasons: fragmented and uncoordinated operations and organization; deficient selection, training, and utilization of personnel; and a disinclination, hostile resistance, or inability to employ managerial and administrative methods of the twentieth century.

FEDERAL PROBLEMS ARE THE TIP OF THE JUDICIAL ICEBERG

Referring to the federal courts, Chief Justice Warren E. Burger commented, "In the supermarket age we are like a merchant trying to operate a cracker barrel corner grocery store with methods and equipment vintage 1900." He also noted the following ironies:

1. A single C-5A military plane costs $200-million, whereas the current budget for the entire federal judiciary is $128-million.
2. The nation has trained more astronauts to explore space than it has court administrators to hack a path through the judicial thicket.
3. Additional judges required in 1965 were authorized in 1970.
4. A 10 percent decrease in guilty pleas requires a 100 percent increase in manpower and facilities, because the federal courts operate on the premise that 90 percent of defendants will plead guilty. In some courts, only 65 percent plead guilty.
5. New laws have been demanded and enacted, but no provision was made for federal courts to handle the additional workload.
6. Desirable as they may be, federal outlays to fund the defense of the poor represent close to half the budget for all federal courts.
7. In an age when sophisticated management methods are available, they are not applied to the courts—in part because the courts have little or no staff to devote to managerial matters.
8. Whereas the swift and certain application of justice is the goal, antiquated court procedures not only permit delay but also encourage it.
9. Regarding the deterrent effect of criminal justice on crimes that trouble Americans most, "whatever deterrent effect may have existed in the past has now virtually vanished as to such crimes."

The Chief Justice observed that what is needed is primarily better management, better methods, and better trained personnel—not just more judges. What afflicts the federal courts is magnified enormously—both in breadth and depth, as one proceeds down the judicial ladder into judicial processes of the states—particularly the operation of the lower criminal courts, where 90 percent of the nation's criminal cases are heard.

UNIFICATION TO ELIMINATE DUPLICATION AND PROMOTE QUALITY

The President's Commission concluded that the court structure of many states reflects that of an earlier age. "There is a multiplicity of trial courts without coherent and centralized administrative management. Jurisdictional lines are unnecessarily complex and confusing. Each court and each judge within the court constitute a distinct administrative unit, moving at its own pace and in its own way." Thus, modern management and efficiency "can be promoted by putting all courts and judges within a state under a single, central administration with provision for the shifting and allocation of judicial and administrative manpower to meet changing requirements." In short, integrate all courts in a state into a single state court system that consolidates courts at the same level.

The impact on the criminal courts of such a solution to the fragmentation problem is major. In most states, there are at least two court "systems" for criminal cases: the felony courts and the lower criminal courts. The latter are "lower" in the sense they handle misdemeanors, petty offenses, and perhaps preliminary hearings for felony cases. Each system has its own judges, court personnel, and procedures, facilities, prosecutors, public defenders, and probation services.

In one metropolitan area, prior to court reform there were three completely separate court systems with criminal jurisdiction, two separate prosecutors offices, three probation offices, and two separate criminal bars.

Within the lower courts, structural disorganization "is often seen in its worst form," asserts a task force report to the President's Commission.

> In a number of cities an offender may be charged . . . in any one of three or more courts: a city or municipal police court, a county court, or a state trial court of general jurisdiction. Each of these courts may have different rules and policies resulting from differences in judges, prosecutors, and traditions. One court may be overloaded with cases, while the docket of another is current. . . . In one set of courts the judges may be nonlawyers, the cases may be prosecuted by police officers, and probation services may be unknown. In other courts there may be judges trained in the law, professional prosecutors, and probation officers, but great disparities still may exist in the quality of personnel. . . . An arbitrary choice by the arresting officer of the court to which he will bring a defendant may determine the offender's final disposition, the type of treatment he will receive, or his chances for eventual reintegration into the community.

From the standpoints of sound organizational principles, financial sanity, and uniform dispensation of justice—not to mention "the scandal of the lower criminal courts," discussed below—unification of the felony courts and lower courts is more than justified. The President's Commission agrees with prior conclusions about the lower courts; namely, "the best solution to the problem would be the abolition of these courts." Specifically, "Felony and misdemeanor courts and their ancillary agencies—prosecutors, defenders, and probation services—should be unified."

THE LOWER COURTS: WHERE THE BIGGEST PROBLEM IS

Though many judges, prosecutors, defense attorneys, and other lower court officials are as capable as their counterparts in felony courts, the descriptions generally applicable to lower court personnel are "least capable," "most inexperienced," "lowest paid," "unprepared," "poorly qualified." Sometimes lower court judges and prosecutors are not even lawyers.

A judge of one lower court is reported as referring regularly to defendants as bums or liars and interrupting them to interject that no matter what they say, he will not believe them. In another lower court, a judge sentenced a defendant to one year in prison for a misdemeanor and based his decision on the defendant's prior conviction for rape. The defendant's legal aid lawyer remained silent, but the court clerk ultimately advised the judge he was reading from another defendant's criminal record. Another judge admitted he did not know whom to believe; to be safe, however, he would find the defendant guilty.

Ironically a felon is accorded many more elements of due process than is someone charged with a less serious offense in a lower court; better representation, more care in disposition, and better facilities for rehabilitation.

Despite all this, millions of arrested persons are brought before the lower criminal court, which is usually their court of last resort. For example, of over 108,000 nontraffic cases heard and disposed of in one lower court, only 23 were appealed.

Though these courts are often inept and fraught with delay, the implications of the work for which they are responsible are even more important than those of the felony courts, according to one authority interviewed for this report. First, lower courts are often *de facto* felony courts. When so many felonies are reduced to misdemeanors through plea bargaining induced by clogged calendars, when the difference between a felony and a misdemeanor is determined by the number of stitches the plaintiff required, when a misdemeanor in one state is a felony in another, the distinction between the two offenses somehow fades.

Second, when a felon is processed through the lower courts as a misdemeanant, he often receives a sentence that denies him access to the rehabilitative facilities that higher courts could tap.

Third, to the extent that lower court defendants are at an early stage in their criminal careers, appropriate correctional treatment should be available; yet, this is often not available to lower courts.

Fourth, the finality that lower court decisions hold for so many combined with frequent lack of fairness administered in noisy and cramped courtrooms by badly trained personnel employing undignified, perfunctory, and sometimes illegal procedures creates a critical lack of respect for law and the administration of justice. As a task force report to the President's Commission asserts, "No program of crime prevention will be effective without a massive overhaul of the lower criminal courts." Some of the problems this overhaul must address are discussed below; many pertain to the higher criminal courts as well.

THE QUALITY OF JUSTICE REFLECTS THE QUALITY OF JUDGES

The President's Commission declared that the "quality of the judiciary in large measure determines the quality of justice.... No procedural or administrative reforms will help the courts, and no reorganizational plan will avail unless judges have the highest qualifications, are fully trained and competent, and have high standards of performance."

Highlighting the problem of selecting well-qualified individuals as judges is this observation by a local chamber of commerce: "Contributing to the decline in respect for the legal profession is the discreditable opinion among the public that 'party support' appears to be a more important quality than 'professional competence' for appointment to a judicial position." States the President's Commission, "A recent survey showed that only about one-half of newly elected judges have any prior courtroom experience and that few of them have any background in criminal cases." Also: "Selection of candidates tends to be dictated to an excessive degree by party considerations and other factors unrelated to the candidates qualifications for office, and the electoral process gives voters little opportunity to weigh the relative abilities of the candidates. . . .Indeed there is reason to believe that the elective method discourages the candidacy of good potential judges. . . ."

One disgusted lawyer in a major city flatly asserted that local judges "are political hacks, each an island unto himself. All that judges do is fool around with calendars." Another lawyer interviewed for this publication commented, "Judges like the present chaos because it puts a cloak on their own inefficiency."

The President's Commission "believes the best selection system for judges is a merit selection plan generally of the type used successfully in Missouri. . . ." The basics of the Missouri plan are as follows:

1. A nonpartisan commission of qualified laymen and lawyers nominates a panel of judicial candidates.
2. Appointments are made from the panel only.
3. Voters review judicial appointments after judges serve a short probationary term of service; the voters decide whether the record of the incumbent warrants his or her retention. If his record satisfies the public, he remains on the bench; if not, he is removed and the governor or mayor appoints another judge from the panel of candidates and the process begins anew.
4. After approving a judge's probationary service, the voters periodically review his subsequent record and determine whether he should be retained.

Desirable as such a plan is, its success is hardly automatic. A great deal depends on the actions of those on the nominating commission. In a major city, a Missouri-like judicial screening commission is staffed by men of stature but, according to a frank observer, they have no idea of how the criminal court operates and they do little more than "play a game with the mayor." The game is called "we give him one and he gives us one," the end result being that 50 percent of the appointments are political payoffs owed by the mayor. Some of these judges have been so incompetent that a good portion of the court-delay problem is caused by them. Ironically, the mayor recently castigated the city's court delay problem as contributing to the overcrowding at a pretrial detention facility in which prisoners staged a major protest.

Because lengthy tenure is one way of removing judges from political influence, a problem presents itself of how, prior to the end of their terms, judges may be removed if they are no longer fit to serve because of mental, moral, physical, or professional deficiencies. Impeachment proceedings, recall by voter referendum, or legislative resolution are considered too time consuming, cumbersome, and expensive for practical application. History proves this.

Some states, therefore, have established removal commissions, whose staffs investigate all complaints not patently absurd. Frequently, only a letter from the commission to a judge is enough to remedy the situation. Often, resignations result before investigations are complete; within four years, 26 judges in one state voluntarily left the bench because they were being investigated. In a recent case, a commission's action calling for the removal of a judge grew out of charges against him for obscenity, solicitation for prostitution, and resisting arrest. Action against other judges are being taken for their ties with the organized underworld.

Early in 1970, the American Bar Association went on record in support of legislation establishing a commission for the removal of federal judges because of disabilities or misconduct.

Court unification and commissions for selection and removal will provide great impetus in phasing out those nonlawyer, part-time, fee-paid judges called justice of the peace, who man the anachronistic and unsupervised rural counterpart of urban lower criminal courts. A President's Commission task force states that one justice reportedly tried a case while repairing a car; another did so while sitting on a tractor. The Commission recommended abolishment of the justice-of-the-peace system.

The hours that some judges put in have come under criticism; as one lawyer remarked, "You might as well forget about Fridays." Vacations of four months are not unheard of.

Lack of training, of opportunities for training, and of requirements mandating training for judges represents another problem area. "After election or appointment, judges might well be required to spend their first months in full-time formal training programs and in sitting with experienced judges," asserts the President's Commission.

Regarding juvenile court judges, the Commission found that 50 percent did not hold an undergraduate degree; 20 percent received no college education at all; and 20 percent were not members of the bar. About 75 percent devoted less than one-quarter of their time to juvenile and family matters, and judicial hearings frequently are little more than 15-minute interviews.

THE PROSECUTOR'S OFFICE AND ITS BURDEN

The power of the prosecutor is awesome. Without doubt he is the most influential court official, except for the judge.

Prosecutors determine whether an alleged offender will be charged. About 50 percent of those arrested are dismissed by the police, prosecutor, or magistrate early in the case. Many of these dismissals are desirable. For example, because police can arrest on "probable cause" and conviction requires proof beyond a reasonable doubt, the prosecution of many arrested on justifiable grounds would almost certainly not lead to convictions but merely contribute to overcrowded courts.

Also dismissals often result when prosecutors feel that an alleged offender's conduct can be better dealt with outside the criminal process than within it. This can result in "the early elimination of many cases . . . and thus relieve the system from some of its caseload burden without sacrificing the proper administration of justice," states the President's Commission.

The Commission regards this "exercise of discretion by prosecutors as necessary and desirable." However, "it has found that more often than not prosecutors exercise their discretion under circumstances and in ways that make unwise decisions all too likely." For instance, because of a work overload, inadequate information, an absence of standards or procedures to guide inexperienced assistants, a prosecutor may release those who are really guilty or dismiss or prosecute a case that might better be referred to an agency outside the justice system.

Prosecutors also have the power to determine whether a conviction should be attempted through guilty plea negotiations: in some jurisdictions, 95 percent of convicted defendants are not tried but plead guilty, often after negotiations with the prosecutor. The negotiated plea of guilty may result from a reduced charge or sentence or from a promise that the case will come before a lenient judge. Such a plea may result because the prosecutor is ill-prepared, ill-equipped, ill-trained, or afraid of losing a case based on the original charge.

The negotiated plea has a legitimate role: to assure that an offender against whom the prosecutor has a weak felony case will at least receive judicial action as a misdemeanant (this may happen when, to improve their records, police arrest persons as felons); to gear punishment more closely to the facts of the case than otherwise would be possible under inadequate penal codes; to receive information, assistance, or testimony about other serious offenders. The American Bar Association (ABA), through its project on minimum standards for criminal justice, has drafted standards relating to pleas of guilty.

Though plea bargaining, or "trading out," is frequently appropriate, its abuse is widespread. Too often in hard-pressed courts it is merely a device to cope with crushing volume instead of an instrument with which to administer justice. As the President's Commission notes, "dangerous offenders may be able to manipulate the system to obtain unjustifiably lenient treatment."

When cases do go to trial, the prosecutor's skill, or lack of it, can be a major factor in the conviction rate. And the extent to which many cases are even prosecutable hinges on the prosecutor's investigative ability. Finally, the prosecutor has substantial influence on police procedures, for he advocates their position in the courts.

In short, the prosecutor's decisions affect police practices, the volume of cases in the courts, and the number of offenders referred to the correctional system. Yet many, if not most, prosecutors work parttime, are understaffed, receive low pay, are not trained for their job, are selected and elected on a partisan political basis, and serve short terms. Under such conditions, talented attorneys are not induced to serve as prosecutors for long periods. Frequently, the office is regarded merely as a steppingstone to higher political office or the bench.

To make matters worse, the prosecutorial function in a state is fragmented among a number of independent agencies. Each of these prosecutors' offices is autonomous, often with little or no coordination among them. Thus a strict enforcement policy in one county may simply drive criminals into neighboring areas. And fragmentation hinders application of uniform minimum standards or rules and impedes the temporary assignment of personnel from other jurisdictions to meet the demands of peak caseloads.

TRIAL LAWYERS—THEIR SUPPLY AND QUALITY

In the words of an eminent jurist "I am convinced that as an indispensable part of our long-range planning we must give due recognition to the importance of developing competent trial lawyers and the necessity of shoring up the trial bar to optimum strength and efficiency. All of us, no doubt, have had the embarrassing experience of watching an inexperienced or inept attorney plead a case in court. The results of such cases frequently are not only disastrous for that attorney's client but also impede efficient court administration in general."

A task force of the President's Commission noted that "there are not enough competent criminal lawyers available to serve even those defendants who can afford to retain counsel." The impact of competent counsel is often felt far beyond the cases they handle. "They ask questions and put pressure on everyone in the system to examine what he is doing and why. They organize reform and become a powerful force for change." This is precisely what happened when "uptown" lawyers of a major city volunteered to help defend arrested rioters after a large-scale disturbance. For most counsel this was their first look at a lower criminal court—and they were appalled. As a result of action they initiated, today those courts are reorganized and procedures altered.

Nonetheless many defense attorneys are less than forthright about protesting improper action in the criminal courts. A study by a local chamber of commerce quoted a lawyer as saying, "I could probably argue the point and win the case, but it is obvious that the judge already has his mind made up. If I question his decision and prove him wrong, I may win this case and lose the next three." Also, regarding questionable court practices, "the committee structure of the local bar does not lend itself to objectivity . . . [it] is almost entirely staffed by judges, active on various benches. Few, if any, could find their own court to be free of criticisms made."

Worse still, some criminal lawyers are on retainer and are actually house counsel for groups in the organized underworld and advise on criminal enterprises. And in many cities, asserts a President's Commission task force, "there is a distinct criminal bar of low legal and dubious ethical quality. These lawyers haunt the vicinity of the criminal courts seeking out clients who can pay a modest fee ... They negotiate guilty pleas and try cases without investigation, preparation, or concern for the particular needs of their clients." One authority interviewed for this report severely criticized what he termed the ineffective and secretive efforts of the organized bar to weed out those members who are incorrigibly incompetent and unethical.

The provision of counsel for defendants unable to obtain adequate representation is another area of concern. Whether an assigned counsel or public defender system is employed, problems exist relating to competency, supervision, and compensation. The ABA's draft on minimum standards relating to the provision of defense services deserves careful study. This report notes that our system of justice produces the best results when prosecutor and defense counsel are of substantially equal skill and experience. Therefore, both from the viewpoint of the defendant and of society, what is important is that "the system for providing counsel and facilities for the defense be as good as the system which society provides for the prosecution." The draft states that the problem of providing defense services is not necessarily a matter of adoption of a particular formula but of the implementation of a plan suited to local conditions. Underscoring the financial implications to state and local governments, the President's Commission asserted that a "moderate estimate of what counsel services may soon cost nationwide might well run in excess of $100 million a year."

COURT ADMINISTRATION AND MANAGEMENT

The goal of efficient, competent court administration and management is, as one jurist commented, "not to set a record for dispatching court business," but to assure that neither offenders nor the law-abiding public "is injured because of deficiencies in court administration which, in the aggregate, truly are tantamount to a denial of justice itself." There is plenty of room for short-cutting the system without short-cutting justice.

Most courts in the nation are not well run; most do not have effective management capability. One of the fundamental reasons for "the administrative morass which entangles the judicial system," as one local chamber of commerce put it, is contained in this statement of a court administrator: "Nobody designed the system. It just grew that way."

All too often, court management—a full-time job in itself—is left in the laps of judges, who already have what should be the full-time job of adjudication. Management tools "are not acquired in law school or from the private practice of law," a report to the National Commission notes. Thus judges try to cope with administrative matters which they are ill-equipped to handle and which preempt to a significant degree the time available for adjudication.

The job of managing today's courts is formidable; yet its procedures, sometimes referred to as "displaced rural," are geared to less complex and demanding times. Among the many managerial facets of the courts are the following:

Projecting costs and preparing budgets.
Training of judiciary, prosecutors, and court personnel.
Handling personnel and their problems.
Allocating space and manpower.
Making purchases.
Conducting research.
Keeping records and statistics.
Maintaining facilities.
Planning facilities—in one city, there are 17 courtrooms to process 1,000 cases daily.
Building sound relationships with the legislature, police, corrections, and community agencies.
Deciding on computerization.
Overseeing collection of fines.
Scheduling cases.
Monitoring performance and meting out discipline.

The effects of poor administration are varied. Judges fail to appear or sit for only part of the day. Vacation periods are not staggered. There are no procedures for shifting judges when one falls ill, goes on vacation, or is facing an abnormal backlog. Defendants are "lost" and cannot be located. Independence in rendering decisions is carried over to administration, which results in "a lack of administrative control unparalleled in other segments of government or in industry," states a task force report to the President's Commission. In effect, no one and everyone is in charge. Records are so incomplete or irretrievable that a judge may not realize that the defendant before him has also been recently arrested for another alleged offense and is scheduled for trial before another judge. Uncollected delinquent fines and court costs pile up. A local study by a midwest chamber of commerce indicated over 260 persons owed delinquent fines totalling $30,000. In one case, the $500 fine of a defendant convicted for the possession of gambling equipment in 1963 had not been paid as of March 1970. Statistics helpful to pinpoint the nature and extent of problems are woefully inadequate; one court administrator said the figures he receives could be "as much as 10,000 off." Some court facilities are almost unusable during the summer because of a lack of air conditioning.

Perhaps the greatest managerial failure of the courts is in the area of scheduling and monitoring the progress of cases. One court study reported that despite a half-million case backlog in a local court system, some judges spend only two hours daily on the bench and are in their robing rooms the balance of the day waiting for more cases to emerge from a blocked judicial pipeline.

Frequently, there is not an effective mechanism to assure the coordinated appearance of the parties to the case. A defense lawyer, witness, arresting officer, complainant, or even the defendant himself may be missing from court. Many times this results from one judge sending cases to another judge's courtroom without knowing the case schedule of that judge (as when a lower court judge conducts a felony preliminary hearing and then transfers the case to a felony court—a situation that could be avoided in a unified court system). Thus there are continuances ad infinitum.

When the parties appear in court, something should happen—other than a continuance. A not infrequent event is for the defendant to hand the judge a note from defense counsel, who explains he is tied up in another court. Result: another continuance, another discouraged witness, another frustrated complainant, another wasted appearance for the arresting officer.

Even when a party is sick, for example, often there is no procedure to alert the other trial participants before their appearance in court. Sometimes the names of all parties are not available. Even to schedule a courtroom appearance sufficiently in advance so that the parties can make appropriate plans is frequently a feat beyond the capability of the court. One lawyer told his client, a cab driver, to call in every 30 minutes for word about his next scheduled appearance.

Schedules are sidetracked by the frivolous granting of continuances: the judge simply wants to go home; an inordinate number of adjournments are permitted because the defense attorney has not been paid; or the continuance is granted for no other reason than it was requested.

The early morning scene in many large-city courtrooms is like the end result of an effort to cram 20 people in a phone booth: witnesses, defendants, complainants, police, lawyers, and friends thereof—all milling about awaiting the call of their cases. One lawyer interviewed for this report asked, "Has no one thought of staggered calendar calls?"

When cases are called, there is usually no selectivity in scheduling them for future judicial action. Often the serious cases—presumably the more time-consuming ones—are put off while minor cases are given priority, which is another example of how backlogs warp judicial judgment.

The ABA's draft on minimum standards relating to speedy trial states that "the trial of defendants in custody and defendants whose pretrial liberty is reasonably believed to present unusual risks should be given preference over other criminal cases." Speedy trials are also important for the defendant who is not incarcerated because the facts may show that person is far more dangerous to the community than a person who is detained previous to trial.

In some courts, the judicial process is divided into "parts"—an arraignment part, a hearings part, a continuance part, a trial part, etc. As a defendant goes from part to part he goes to different physical locations, is governed by different rules, and greets a different judge, different prosecutor, and, if the defendant is poor, a different public defender. While by no means impossible to cope with, the scheduling problem usually becomes more complex, as does the monitoring of the progress of the case. "... It results in the loss of an overall view and control of cases," states a President's Commission task force. And, as a lawyer remarked, "This system almost guarantees a successful defense—a defense lawyer who stays with the case has a tremendous advantage over the dozen or so different prosecutors, judges, etc. he faces in the various parts."

A common error of scheduling systems, declares the President's Commission, is that "attention is directed at the single case without consideration of its relation to the entire caseload of the court in terms of priorities, delay, attorney commitments, and the availability of judges and courtrooms." The system catches cases as they come up, one by one, and does not monitor the flow of cases or those that have not met time standards.

One major city has attempted to improve matters by computerizing its present court procedures, much to the disgust of some observers. They point out that when lousy procedures are computerized, all you achieve is to make the real problem—the procedures themselves—more difficult to streamline; that is, the basic problem now becomes technologically locked into the "system."

And when technology is appropriate, observed a Senate committee witness, "the court has no trained personnel who understand the equipment and how to use it...." Also: "There is no career development within the divisions of the court to any great extent. Thus a person who joins a five-man jury commission division can expect that to be the total future growth in that spot—five positions."

Desperately needed by active courts, therefore, are professional court administrators to whom judges can delegate management functions. In what has been termed the most significant step toward modernization of court administration in the past 30 years, an institute for court management has been established in Colorado—the nation's first school for court administrators.

Some administrative functions could be completely taken over by these administrators; other managerial duties could be delegated in part. The administrator would report to a chief judge or administrative judge, who would be given power to monitor the performance of colleagues and to discipline them if necessary—a far cry from many courts today, where each judge is essentially his own boss. As an eminent jurist has written, "Someone must be boss. When a modern court system is established, there should be an administrator at the head of the entire organization."

Illustrative of the needed power that could be invested in a court's chief judge are the provisions of a recently enacted statute of a midwestern state:

> He has broad power to discipline other judges. If necessary he can initiate removal proceedings against his colleagues on the bench for unsatisfactory performance.
> He may assign cases in any manner he desires, thereby leveling the caseloads.

He will maintain adequate records.

He fills in on change of venue cases in compliance with state law seeking to curb change of venue abuse by requiring a special judge—selected from a panel—to hear such requests.

PRETRIAL RELEASE—BAIL AND OTHER PROBLEMS

Legally, bail is set only to assure the defendant's appearance in court. In fact, judges also set bail to detain defendants considered too dangerous to free prior to trial. Yet experience proves that a defendant's ability to afford the bail bond premiums bears little relation to the likelihood of his appearance at trial or his committing future crimes. What bail frequently does accomplish, however, are (1) the imposition of tremendous costs upon the community and (2) the transfer from the criminal justice system to bondsmen of the decision regarding which defendants shall walk the streets prior to trial. As the ABA's draft on minimum standards relating to pretrial release comments, "The bail system as it now generally exists is unsatisfactory from either the public's or the defendant's point of view."

Recent studies prove that the appearance of a defendant in court is related much more to factors concerning his roots in the community than to his ability—or a bondsman's assessment of his ability—to post bail. In one experiment 65 percent of all felony defendants interviewed about their background and community ties were recommended for release without bail. Less than 1 percent failed to appear.

The cost of unnecessary bail requirements to the public and to those so detained is huge. The defendant goes to jail, loses his earning capacity during his detention, and perhaps loses his job permanently. His family may be forced to seek public welfare, for which taxpayers must foot the bill. Taxpayers must also pick up the tab related to costs of detention—perhaps $6 to $9 daily per prisoner. In 1962, this cost the public of one major city $10 million.

In many cases, bail—even in substantial amounts—does not serve to prevent the release of a truly dangerous criminal or, upon his release, the commission of additional crimes prior to his trial. The President's Commission notes that professional criminals or members of organized criminal syndicates "have little difficulty in posting bail, although, since crime is their way of life, they are clearly dangerous." And the National Commission asserts that "a bondsman may consider the worst kind of professional criminal a preferred risk, and may even release him on credit. The bondsman knows that the 'pro' can obtain the money for the premium, and that he will honor his obligation to return to trial or post enough collateral to protect the bondsman in case he should be called upon to forfeit the bond."

Literally, very frequently bondsmen hold the key to the jailhouse. If a judge decides in favor of pretrial release and sets bail in a reasonable amount, the bondsman "may in effect veto the decision of the judge by refusing to provide bail for good reasons, for bad reasons, or for no reasons," as the National

Commission observes. Bondsmen have been guilty of a number of abuses:
1. Bondsmen post the same property, real or otherwise, for many concurrent bonds—in one case, for up to 125 different bonds at a time.
2. When "credit bonds" are outlawed by statute, bondsmen get around the requirement by producing an as yet uncashed check signed by the defendant, who may be counting on pretrial crimes to back up the check.
3. Bondsmen and bonding companies have refused to pay forfeitures, occasioned by the nonappearance of defendants.
4. As a local chamber of commerce puts it, "The arrest of a person on 'suspicion' and his or her forced detention until a 'particular bondsman' or attorney appears before a formal charge is placed, enabling a bond to be 'set,' is a coincidence too remote not to arouse 'suspicion' of more than just the person charged."

Thus as a means to detain dangerous criminals—assuming "dangerousness" can be predicted—the instrument of bail is weak indeed; as an ABA study concluded, "So-called preventive detention should be dealt with openly and on its own merits, not masked behind manipulations of bail amounts."

Nonfinancial conditions of release, such as those permitted by the Federal Bail Reform Act of 1966, may frequently suffice to assure a defendant's court appearance and a clean pretrial record. These conditions may range from assigning a defendant to the custody of a person or organization to supervise him, to restricting his travel and associations, to placing him in pretrial custody so that he may work during the day but is confined at night. Indeed, a speedy trial may turn out to be the best solution of all. For example, one study indicated that 68 percent of crime by those on bail was committed more than 30 days after a defendant's initial release.

MOTIONS, DISCOVERY, APPEALS, AND REMEDIES

Many of the lawyers interviewed for this report pointed to various stages of the case-processing cycle that could be streamlined. One such stage is that of pretrial motions—motions by the defense seeking suppression of evidence, requesting discovery and inspection, challenging the charge, etc. In most courts these motions represent a major source of delay. One recommendation is that instead of filing motions piecemeal, defense counsel should be required to file an omnibus motion; that is, all motions are filed at the same time.

The problem of motions is really part of the larger question of pretrial discovery and procedure. Though common in civil cases, pretrial discovery has received only limited use in criminal cases. Pretrial discovery involves the exchange of certain information between prosecution and defense that would, among other things, minimize unnecessary and repetitious trials by bringing to the surface procedural or constitutional issues and dealing with them before trial and minimize interruptions and complications of trials by identifying issues relating to guilt or innocence prior to trial. In the words of one lawyer, discovery would reduce the likelihood of "sloppy cases, time-consuming fights and motions by defense for information, and subsequent appeals based on constitutional questions that could have been properly resolved during the initial trial."

The ABA draft on minimum standards relating to discovery and procedure before trial notes that the "need for changes in procedures appeared manifest in order to lend more finality to criminal dispositions, to speed up and simplify the process, and to make more economical use of resources."

In addition to the general absence of pretrial discovery, the "criminal law revolution" (caused by U.S. Supreme Court rulings in recent years) and the growth of public defender agencies have contributed to a rising tide of appeals by defendants and of requests by prisoners for post-conviction reviews. There has been concern that many such appeals are frivolous and are overburdening the courts, particularly as defendants of prisoners have nothing to lose.

Noting that many defendants are completely without counsel during the decision to appeal or to secure post-conviction remedies and that significant numbers of defendants do not act contrary to the evaluation of counsel in whom they have confidence, the ABA draft on minimum standards relating to criminal appeals asserts that "the most effective point of attack on frivolous appeals" is to improve the lawyer-client relationship "so that defendants will receive and, having received, will accept competent legal advice." Furthermore, the ABA draft on post-conviction remedies recommends sanctions for "abuse of process"; e.g., the "defendant who deliberately and inexcusably fails to raise a known defense during the prosecution proceedings may be precluded from doing so at the post-conviction stage."

A CLOSER LOOK AT SENTENCING

Mentioned earlier were examples of the absurd legislature-mandated sentences whose severity varies inversely with the seriousness of the crime. Of equal absurdity—and concern—is the imposition, without any reasonable basis, of unequal sentences for offenses of comparable seriousness. In the northern section of a state, the average sentence for forgery was 68 months; in the southern section, 7 months. Over a 20-month period in one court, a judge imposed prison terms upon 75 to 90 percent of the defendants he sentenced; another judge of the same court did so in about 35 percent of his cases.

As a task force report to the President's Commission observes, unjustified sentencing disparity causes problems for correctional administrators. "Prisoners compare their sentences, and a prisoner who is given cause to believe that he is the victim of a judge's prejudices often is a hostile inmate, resistant to correctional treatment as well as discipline." Also sentencing disparities among judges of the same court generates delays caused by defense counsel tactics to secure hearings before the more lenient judges.

Sentences that are too short (98-day sentence for armed robbery) "can deprive the law of its effectiveness and result in the premature release of a dangerous criminal," states an ABA draft on sentencing alternatives and procedures. Sentences that are too severe or improperly conceived (a first-offender gets 11 years for illegally importing parrots) "can reinforce the criminal tendencies of the defendant and lead to a new offense by one who otherwise might not have offended so seriously again," comments the ABA study. Thus, just as no one should want to "coddle criminals" through sentences that are mere "wrist slappings," no one should desire to intensify criminal behavior and to waste correctional resources by demanding inappropriate or overly harsh sentences.

Proper sentencing represents a delicate balancing of the need of protecting the public, the seriousness of the offense, and the rehabilitative needs of the defendant. The ABA draft recommends the minimum amount of custody or confinement consistent with those multiple sentencing goals. In other words, why waste money on correctional overkill? The ABA draft also concludes that correctional programs most likely to deter offenders from committing future crimes are those that "minimize the dislocation of the offender from the community and which make a maximum effort to readjust him to it." This also conforms to the firm opinion of the many corrections officials interviewed for this report.

Research findings bear on the problem of sentencing. Knowledge of penalties does not deter crime. Fear of arrest and imprisonment deters many from crime, but fear of long imprisonment does not. Research to date demonstrates there is no single reason why a person commits crime, and there is no one type of correctional method that fits all offenders. Correction, and thus the sentence, must be tailor-made, not mass-produced. And for some offenders—the true incorrigibles, such as the hierarchy of the organized underworld—the goal of sentencing cannot be offender correction but must be public protection.

Therefore, judges make important correctional decisions, but they receive little training in correctional methods. Judges require information about the defendant in order to fit the sentence to the criminal as well as to the crime, but they frequently do not receive the presentence reports that would contain this information. Excessive, inadequate, and disparate sentences are serious obstacles to criminal justice, yet the majority of states do not provide for appellate review of sentences. As cited by the ABA study on standards relating to appellate review of sentences, a judge has commented that although nine of ten defendants plead guilty without trial, and for them punishment is the only issue, "we repose in a single judge the sole responsibility for this vital function." Judicial training and sentencing institutes, constitute one means of affecting more consistent and rational sentences.

THE JUVENILE COURT—OUTRUNNING REALITY

Observers of juvenile courts must agree with the assessment of the President's Commission: " . . . the great hopes originally held for the juvenile court have not been fulfilled. It has not succeeded significantly in rehabilitating delinquent youth, in reducing or even stemming the tide of delinquency.... To say that juvenile courts have failed to achieve their goals is to say no more than what is true of criminal courts in the United States."

The problem is not that there is separate treatment for children—indeed, to throw them wholesale into the lower courts would only make matters worse. The problem is that the reach of the juvenile court has exceeded its grasp. States the President's Commission,

> The spirit that animated the juvenile court movement was fed in part by a humanitarian compassion for offenders who were children. That willingness to understand and treat people who threaten public safety and security should be nurtured....But neither should it be allowed to outrun reality....Rehabilitation of offenders through individualized handling is one way of providing protection [to the community], and appropriately the primary way in dealing with children. But the guiding consideration for a court of law that deals with threatening conduct is nevertheless protection of the community. The juvenile court, like other courts, is therefore obliged to employ all the means at hand, not excluding incapacitation, for achieving that protection. What should distinguish the juvenile from the criminal court is their greater emphasis on rehabilitation, not their exclusive preoccupation with it.

One of the problems of the juvenile court is that there is not a screening process to filter out those whose conduct—particularly noncriminal conduct—is more appropriately controlled and corrected by means other than court action, which so often only serves to perpetuate delinquency through a process by which a child acts as he is perceived and as he perceives himself—namely, as a deliquent. Unfortunately the necessary community resources to serve as effective alternatives to formal court action are frequently unavailable.

Those cases that would pass through the screening process and fall within the narrowed jurisdiction of the court would pertain to offenders whose adjudication "should no longer be viewed solely as a diagnosis and prescription for cure, but should be frankly recognized as an authoritative court judgment expressing society's claim to protection," asserts the President's Commission. Such adjudicatory hearings should be consistent with the basic principles of due process, which has often been absent in the past.

IN CONCLUSION

Having major implications for action programs directed toward shoring up the sagging performance of the nation's criminal courts, these general observations flow from the discussion above:

1. Though more personnel and facilities are undoubtedly needed lined procedures, increased diversion of certain offenders from the criminal justice system, updated management and administration, and enforced

standards of performance and accountability—all of which will reduce delay, among other things.
2. The courts whose performance has the greatest impact on criminal justice are those that are now in the worst shape and require the most help. These are the lower courts, which handle 90 percent of all criminal cases.
3. The procedures, policies, and decisions of the courts frequently extend beyond the realm of the judicial system and affect—for better or for worse—the jobs of police and correctional officials.
4. The mere application of technology—such as computers—to the judicial system will merely churn out chaos at a faster rate and inhibit true reform unless preceded by a rational restructuring and revamping of current court organization, policies, and procedures.
5. A speedy trial is a much greater deterrent of crime than is the indiscriminate imposition of long prison terms, which frequently represent nothing more than judicial overkill that is a correctional burden to taxpayers and a stimulus promoting intensified criminal behavior by the offender, who will continue to run up the public's crime bill upon release. Cost-benefit considerations, if nothing else, demonstrate the irrationality of public demands for sentences based purely on revenge and retribution. However, this does not deny the need for long-term incarceration of incorrigibles.

Where the the Correctional System Requires Correcting

U. S. Chamber of Commerce

Beyond rational dispute, the nation's correctional system is ineffective. This is a generous assessment. Frequently, the correctional process does more harm than good. Generally, those line and staff personnel who man the parole, probation, and institutional components of the system have never performed—or never have been allowed to perform—their correctional responsibilities in an adequate manner.

A FRAGMENTED, UNCOORDINATED AMALGAM

Reflecting a diverse conglomeration of theories, techniques, and programs is a pyramid of facilities, starting with the 30 or more federal correctional

From *Marshalling Citizen Power Against Crime* (Washington, D.C.: U.S. Chamber of Commerce, 1970), pp. 61-76. Copyright © 1970 by the U.S. Chamber of Commerce. Reprinted by permission of the publisher.

institutions and spreading downward through the 464 or so state institutions and finally encompassing the many thousands of county and municipal jails. At the state and federal levels, about 56 percent of the institutions are for adults, the balance for juveniles.

Typically, each level of government follows its own independent course. Federal authorities have no direct control over state corrections. A state may have responsibility for prison and parole programs, but probation may be tied to court administration as a county or municipal operation. Counties do not have jurisdiction over town and municipal jails. Because parole and probation services frequently hold themselves aloof from jails and prisons, the transition between the manner in which an offender is handled in an institution and the way he is supervised in the community is often irrationally abrupt.

Approximately 111,000 persons are employed by the nation's correctional institutions and agencies, exclusive of jails: 7 percent by the federal system; 73 percent by the states; 20 percent by local governments. About 2 percent of the total work in central offices, 68 percent in institutions, 23 percent in probation and parole, and 7 percent in juvenile detention.

Recruitment of corrections personnel is ordinarily conducted in an uncoordinated and haphazard manner. There is no one established way of entering into correctional work. Candidates are often of the drop-in, write-in, or referred-by variety. Those who are hired often find themselves occupationally immobilized because of the fragmentation of the field, which prevents the crossing of jurisdictional lines. "Promotion is usually confined to the internal structure of a single agency or department, and restrictive hiring practices either discourage or prohibit lateral transfers," concludes the Joint Commission on Correctional Manpower and Training (hereafter referred to as the Joint Commission). Generally, the correctional system is understaffed by undertrained personnel.

WHO IS THE OFFENDER?

The jails, workhouses, penitentiaries, and reformatories of the nation admit, control, and release an estimated 3 million individuals each year. On an average day, approximately 1.3 million people—greater than the 1970 population of any of 15 states—are under correctional authority in the United States, roughly one-third of whom being in institutions and the balance on parole or probation. About two-thirds of all offenders are committed to institutions. If past trends continue, the average daily population in corrections in 1975 is projected at 1.8 million, with 523,000 of that number in confinement.

Correctional officials describe the average state prison inmate this way: 85 percent are school dropouts; 65 percent come from broken homes; the average educational attainment is the fifth or sixth grade; the average I.Q. is 85; 20 percent are mentally retarded, with 5 percent of these severely retarded; 50 percent are under age 25; 18 percent are illiterate; 40 percent are without previous sustained work experience; most have a distorted value system and warped standards; the majority are insecure, exhibit little self-discipline, and possess a low self-image. Most important, 96 percent will again walk the street as free men after an average prison stay of two years.

THE PARADOXES OF CORRECTIONS

Only about 20 percent of the correctional dollar and 25 percent of the manpower are allocated to treat or supervise the two-thirds of the offenders who are in the community. Though we maintain huge maximum security institutions, wardens testify that no more than 50 percent of the prisoners therein require that degree of security.

In some states, observes the General Secretary of the American Correctional Association, supervision of monkeys is assigned greater importance than is the supervision of human beings, inasmuch as the salaries of zookeepers are greater than those of corrections personnel. In another state, game warden candidates must undergo nine months of training; no training is required for those desiring to enter the correctional field. The head of a state corrections department remarked that we have a better idea of how many whooping cranes there are than we do about the number of inmates in local and county jails.

Though employment is crucial to an offender's success after release, frequently we train him—if at all—to operate obsolete equipment or prepare him for jobs whose license requirements bar ex-offenders. And even if an offender receives valid training, what good is it if his Achilles heel is alcoholism? Indeed, the President's Task Force on Prisoner Rehabilitation concluded that in the employment area, "those very entities that are responsible for rehabilitating prisoners, the states and Federal government, set a most unedifying example. Most states either are barred by statute or bar themselves by habit from hiring ex-offenders. The Federal government let down its bars somewhat a few years ago; it will now hire ex-offenders on an individual basis, if the agency that wants their services presents a strong brief, and after an elaborate and time-consuming screening by the Civil Service Commission. In other words, it is a great deal more trouble to hire an ex-offender than somebody else...."

Short-term institutions probably house more inmates than any other type of facility, yet they suffer the most from the adverse effects of political patronage. Thus long-term felons are more likely to receive proper treatment than are short-term misdemeanants.

Whereas the bulk of correctional manpower and money is institution-oriented, alternatives to incarceration are largely unexplored even though many authorities—and experiments—indicate such alternatives could decrease the inmate population by 40 percent and, for the money spent, produce at least as good results.

If a goal of the correctional system is to convert tax-using offenders into tax-paying citizens why is the staff-to-inmate ratio 1 to 2,172 for vocational rehabilitation counselors and why did correctional authorities tell a Senate subcommittee that nothing less than a major overhaul of correctional institutions can protect the public from the dangerous criminals released from today's institutions?

"Seldom does one hear of a zookeeper torturing one of his animals to death. But such things have happened, and still are happening, in our nation's prisons and youth reformatories," asserts the National Commission. And the President's Commission concludes, "Life in many institutions is at best barren and futile, at worst unspeakably brutal and degrading." Among the many examples cited by responsible authorities are these:

> Children not only have been placed in jails unfit for animals, which has resulted in suicides and injuries, but also confined among adults who may be mentally ill or sexual offenders.
> A state criminal justice planning agency noted that its jails "suffer from neglect, often promote unsafe and outright brutal practices and encourage many first offenders to become career criminals." The planning agency of another state reported that in one jail "the plumbing had backed into the cells of prisoners discharging human feces on the floor and walls"; that in another jail prisoners slept on mats on top of welded cages because of overcrowding, a juvenile was held in an isolation cell without a toilet, prisoners kept an open fire burning in the cell block to keep warm, and "conditions were even worse in other places." About 61 adult penal institutions were opened before 1900, 25 of which are now more than 100 years old. Of the dormitories and cell blocks now in use, 31 percent are more than 50 years old.

The focus of corrections is typically on felons and juvenile offenders, but misdemeanants form a far larger group than both of the others combined in terms of number of cases. A 12-state study indicated that 93.5 percent of those arraigned for nontraffic offenses were charged with misdemeanors. As noted, many of these were probably felony arrests reduced to misdemeanors; in addition, though the deeds of misdemeanants may differ from those of felons, the motivation and rehabilitative need is not so dissimilar. Thus the following correctional policies and processes for misdemeanants are self-defeating at best:

> Sentences are frequently suspended.
> Probation is not widely used, and the supervision offered is minimal; the average caseload is a reported 114 probationers.
> Parole is almost nonexistent, with the resultant lack of supervision of offenders upon their release from confinement.
> Institutions for misdemeanants act independently of both higher governmental authority and similar units at their own level; there is virtually no comprehensive planning or conduct of programs nor any pooling or coordination of resources. One state has 150 jails with an average of 1 prisoner each. A major city may have to acquire a fourth institution, although the state has 3,000 empty cells.
> The majority of misdemeanant facilities are old and do not meet minimum standards in sanitation, living space, and segregation by age and type of offense.

Two-thirds of misdemeanant facilities surveyed reported the absence of rehabilitative programs. For misdemeanant institutions as a whole, only 3 percent of the 19,000 or so who staff them perform rehabilitative duties.

Though dangerous criminals must, of course, be confined until they no longer pose a threat to the community, "for the large bulk of offenders, particularly the youthful, the first or the minor offender, institutional commitments can cause more problems than they solve," concludes the President's Commission. But the bulk of correctional resources is spent on incarceration, which tends to isolate offenders from the society that corrections is supposed to reintegrate them into and serves to cut offenders off from schools, families, jobs, and other supportive means found necessary to minimize an offender's return to crime. Though the prevalent body of informed opinion maintains that conservation and enlargement of offenders' contacts and involvements with the community represent the best hope of protecting the community from the today's revolving door cycle of crime-imprisonment-crime, prisons are frequently located in remote areas where contact with society is almost impossible even if it were considered desirable and where very few of the badly needed corrections professionals are willing to work.

Though the public hopes offenders will eventually lead "normal" lives within the community, citizens frequently prefer to reduce the likelihood of such an outcome by more readily accepting a 700-inmate institution on the outskirts of town than a 30-man community-based halfway house in a neighborhood.

Though the goal is to motivate offenders to operate within society—not prey upon it—persons convicted of felonies and certain serious misdemeanors frequently lose for varying periods the right to vote, to hold appointive and elective public office, to serve as a juror, to testify in court, to obtain certain professional, business, and occupational licenses, to enter into contracts, to take or transfer property, and to sue civilly.

If only because of the billions the public is pouring into police and court operations in an attempt to channel offenders to appropriate correctional programs, the paradoxes and monstrous irrationality of corrections are nothing short of criminal—criminal because that is precisely the type of behavior that most correctional efforts either intensify, create, or do nothing about.

HOW THE PUBLIC CAN BE A PROBLEM

Many correctional officials interviewed for this report indicated that the self-contradictory state in which corrections finds itself results from a public that cannot make up its mind. One corrections official declared, "One day we are accused of coddling criminals, and on the next day we are charged with brutalizing inmates." To a significant degree, this is a point well taken. Without a public consensus on what constitutes an effective correctional approach, legislative support will be fragmentary and inconsistent at best.

And, perhaps more important, without such a public consensus, implementation of desirable programs may be thwarted *despite* legislative backing. For example, according to a survey conducted for the Joint Commission, although 72 percent of respondents feel rehabilitation *should* be the major focus of corrections today and although the public expressed disillusionment with penal institutions, support was disappointing for community-based correctional alternatives as a more effective method of rehabilitating offenders. For example, while support was heavy for the concept of the halfway house, only 50 percent would personally favor one being located in their neighborhoods. Any by better than two to one, people thought most of the neighbors would oppose such a facility.

While 60 percent stated that finding employment was a serious problem for offenders and 42 percent saw winning community trust as an obstacle, 22 percent stated they would hesitate in hiring a former bad-check passer as a janitor; 21 percent, as a production worker; 53 percent, as a salesman; 54 percent, as a supervisor; and 68 percent, as a clerk who handled money. Ironically, a state official administering a Labor Department program that bonds ex-offenders declared that nationwide statistics regarding the program's loss experience indicate that its clientele is a better risk than the average company vice president. Finally, only 33 percent said they would support higher taxes in order to pay for correctional rehabilitation programs.

The Joint Commission sums up the situation in this manner: "Increasingly it is recognized that reintegration of offenders into the community can be brought about only with the wholehearted support of the community. It does little good to counsel, educate, and train offenders for meaningful work roles in a community which looks upon them with suspicion, distrust, and prejudice"—particularly as "corrections has been shifting its focus from nearly complete reliance upon treating the offender in isolation from his social environment toward efforts that seek to engage society and social institutions."

THE TASK OF SHIFTING GEARS: CORRECTIONS IN THE COMMUNITY

With reported recidivism rates ranging up to 70 percent or more, this and other evidence "makes it obvious that 'more of the same' will make no appreciable improvement in correctional performance," asserts the Joint Commission. Thus the emergence of a strong shift toward community-based corrections. This simply means that to the maximum degree consistent with the protection of the community, offenders live within the community and tap into such community resources as vocational guidance and training, employment assistance and opportunities, medical services, mental health facilities, religious counseling, educational institutions, etc.—not to mention just plain contact with society. Offenders, therefore, can utilize resources whose cost would be prohibitive for penal institutions to provide. And because the corrections process is occurring within the real world—not in isolation from it—the chances for the offender's successful reintegration are seen as maximized. At the very least, vigorous research has found that a large number of those scheduled for incarceration may instead be retained and treated in the community as safely, as effectively, and at much less expense. Thus a properly executed community-based corrections program is clearly ahead on a cost/benefit basis even if resultant recidivism rates are the same as those resultant from incarceration.

There are many types of community alternatives to incarceration and by no means have all reported success on a cost/benefit basis. Halfway houses—which may be referred to as community correctional centers, community residential centers, community treatment centers, day care or attendance centers, guidance centers, or group homes—may be occupied by those half way in prison (probationers), half way out of prison (inmates still under sentence of imprisonment); by parolees; and by offenders released upon expiration of their sentence. Prerelease programs are directed toward the intensive preparation of inmates to facilitate their transition from a state of near-total dependence to one of social and economic independence. Work release programs permit inmates to engage in outside employment during the day.

To date, community-based corrections has been applied primarily to youths. Perhaps the most notable, enlightened, and promising community-based approach to delinquents is embodied in California's Community Treatment Project (CTP). Instead of the normal procedure of institutionalizing delinquents for eight to ten months and then returning them to their communities on parole status, CTP youths are paroled directly back into their community (after a number of weeks at a reception center) where they immediately begin the CTP program of intensive supervision and treatment, within the environment into which they will eventually have to be reintegrated or reinstated or with which they must satisfactorily cope. Both the normal institutional approach and the CTP program generally take from two and a half to three years. About 65 percent of all males and 83 percent of the females normally committed by juvenile courts to institutions are eligible for the CTP program. Ineligibility reflects in part the judgment that the delinquent is too dangerous for treatment in the community.

The eligibles are randomly assigned to either experimental or control status. The experimentals receive intensive supervision and treatment in the community. Those in the control group were either directly paroled without intensive care or sent through the eight- to ten-month institutional program prior to parole.

The average recidivism rate for the control group was 52 percent after 15 months; the experimentals recorded a 32 percent failure rate. After 24 months the recidivism rate was 62 percent and 41 percent for controls and experimentals, respectively.

These and other findings "suggest the relevance of this type of program both to the medium- and perhaps longer-range interests of individual clients, and to the concerns for protection on the part of the larger society," concluded a CTP official. In addition, he notes that "as a result of community programs, the state has saved several million dollars in capital outlay. When a correctional system is capable of handling many hundreds of offenders by means of intensive programs within the community proper, expensive institutions do not have to be built.... An additional cost factor is that of *maintaining* a youth. This comes to $5,800 per year within an institution and $2,300 in CTP."

Obviously, on a cost/benefit basis, CTP appears extremely successful. Though a community setting for correction efforts certainly contributed to the highly favorable cost outcome, such a setting per se seems to contribute "little if anything to the experimental-control differences in parole success." What does appear to have a major impact on the benefit side of the cost/benefit yardstick is the degree to which the community setting is taken advantage of. CTP research has singled out five factors as having made the most significant contribution to the benefits—i.e., parole successes—of the program:

1. Certain types of parole agents are matched with certain types of youth.
2. Parole agents selected for the program must meet certain criteria regarding ability and perceptiveness.
3. Low caseloads permit intensive and/or extensive intervention by parole agents with regard to several areas of the youth's life (family, school, employment, etc.).
4. There is an emphasis on "the working-through of the parole agent/ youth relationship as a major vehicle of treatment."
5. A procedure that classifies youths into various types permits the treatment to be tailored to each youth—"a relatively individualized plan of intervention can be developed for each youth."

Properly executed probation programs—as well as well-conceived parole efforts, such as CTP—can also serve as an effective vehicle by which to execute community-based corrections. Again, California must be singled out as an outstanding example of how corrections can be made less costly and more effective. That state's probation subsidy plan pays a maximum of $4,000 to counties for every offender—juvenile as well as adult—who is not committed to a state correctional institution but whose incarceration would have been expected on the basis of past performance (in terms of commitments per 100,000 population). In essence the state is buying local service, based on performance not promise, in lieu of state correctional service.

The $4,000 state payment to counties provides better local probation service not only for the one new admission the county does not commit to the state but also for several eligible cases already under local probation supervision. "Experience during the first two years suggests that the county can give improved service to five or six probationers for every new uncommitted case held at the county level," comments a probation subsidy report.

Also during the first two years, 3,814 offenders were treated locally who might otherwise have entered state institutions. This represented a gross savings of $15.2-million for the state; after subsidy payments, the state saved $9.8-million. Such an "eat your cake and have it too" outcome resulted from the indefinite postponement of the scheduled construction of several state correctional institutions and from the much lower (up to 14 times lower) outlays needed to provide probation service than required to incarcerate.

Nor has the $9.8-million state savings merely shifted state institutional costs to the county or city facilities. Indeed, the rate of local incarceration slowed significantly. "Probation is being used more and revoked less," concludes an official report. "This finding supports the original premise that good probation practices can reduce commitments to state institutions while offering substantially increased protection to local taxpayers through improved supervision of probationers."

The apparent California success with community-based corrections that relies directly on beefed up probation and parole procedures could well portend increased nationwide use of those tools. Indeed, from a cost/benefit standpoint, many are questioning whether many offenders now residing in community-based facilities or working in the community under released-time programs might not just as well be placed directly on parole or probation.

For correctional officials to explore fully the promise of the community-based approach requires the wide support of local citizens, as noted earlier. To secure that support is one of the major tasks facing correctional officials today. The recent report of the President's Task Force on Prisoner Rehabilitation concluded that "perhaps the greatest obstacle to improvement in the correctional system always has been the tendency of much of the public to regard it and treat it as a rug under which to sweep difficult and disagreeable people and problems. The myopia of this attitude scarcely requires demonstration. After all, the overwhelming majority of offenders do not stay under the correctional rug...as a matter of fact, the two-thirds of the correctional population who are on probation or parole are in the community right now in body, if not in spirit. 'Community-based corrections' is no visionary slogan but a hard contemporary fact."

PROBATION AND PAROLE—
THE OBSTACLES TO OVERCOME

In addition to their traditional duties of conducting presentence investigations for the courts and of supervising probationers, modern probation departments may be involved in the operation of detention facilities, treatment clinics, halfway-in houses, group counseling programs, and the like. Likewise, the traditional supervisory function of parole departments has expanded to the operation of community-based facilities, which are designed to help the parolee to bridge the gap between penal institution and complete freedom.

Though the promise of properly implemented parole and probation programs has been demonstrated many times, their full cost/benefit potential is yet to be fulfilled on a nationwide basis. The President's Commission notes that "probation and parole services are characteristically poorly staffed and often poorly administered." Of 250 counties surveyed by the Commission, one-third provided no probation service at all. And most misdemeanants are released from local institutions and jails without parole. Many juvenile courts rely primarily on release with suspended sentence instead of probation supervision. On the basis of an average caseload of 35 offenders per officer, additional manpower is needed desperately, states the Commission: 6,100 more probation and parole officers for the juvenile field; three times the number of such officers currently employed to handle adult felons; an additional 15,400 officers for misdemeanants.

In one major state, only 98 of 254 counties have any kind of adult probation service. Felony caseloads range from 80 to 400 per officer. In many of the counties with probation services, probation is nothing more than release without any form of supervision. Presentence investigations and reports are almost nonexistent in the state. In another state, only 84 percent of the full-time probation officers met minimal educational standards.

A task force of the President's Commission notes that although the "best data available indicate that probation offers one of the most significant prospects for effective programs in corrections," in most jurisdictions two requisites for effective probation are missing: a system that facilitates effective decision-making as to who should receive probation; the existence of good community programs to which offenders can be assigned. The task force also reports that further work is needed to specify with greater accuracy the levels of service required for various kinds of cases.

Also mentioned are the difficulties that can arise when a probation department is subject to detailed administrative direction by both a judge and chief probation officer. The task force observes that to manage a widely dispersed probation operation is "almost impossible for a judge whose career investment is not in administration." Interviewed for this publication, a chief probation officer of a major city lamented that "No administrator has charge of the whole operation for which he is held accountable. The judges run it; the politicians run it; the probationers run it." Another administrator complained about overly restrictive civil service regulations that severly limit who can be hired, fired, and disciplined. One probation administrator described the contempt in which one of his probation officers held probationers; yet under current administrative restrictions he is powerless to take appropriate action.

While estimates indicate that slightly over half of the offenders sentenced to corrections are placed on probation, more than 60 percent of adult felons are released on parole prior to the expiration of the maximum term of their sentences. But, as with most statistics, the 60 percent figure masks wide variations: some states release 100 percent of inmates on parole; other states parole less than 15 percent.

Many times deservedly, parole—or, more accurately, its improper execution—has been attacked as "leniency" or "coddling criminals." However, parole—and probation—when properly implemented is essentially a method of public protection, for it seeks to maximize the chances of a crime-free future for offenders. In reality, asserts a task force of the President's Commission, "prisoners serve as much time in confinement in jurisdictions where parole is widely used as in those where it is not. No consistent or significant relationship exists between the proportion of prisoners who are released on parole in a state and the average time served for felonies before release."

Although the parole board decision of whether to grant parole should be based on such factors as the prisoner's prior history, his progress in the institution, his readiness for release, his need for supervision and assistance in the community, and his attitude and general conduct during a hearing before board members who are qualified by experience and training, reality most often corresponds to something quite different:

> Information is supplied to parole boards by overworked case-workers, who gather data through brief interviews with prisoners and from meager institutional records.
> This information is frequently compressed into an excessively stereotyped format and written with a sameness of reporting style and jargon that hinders comprehension of the individual aspects of the case.
> Members of parole boards are often ill-suited by experience, training, or even basic intelligence to assess what available information there is in order to reach reasonable conclusions regarding release. Some members are part-time only.
> Hearings at which offenders are present are omitted in several states. Where hearings are conducted, in some states they are heard by only one or two members of the board, who report to the full board. An interviewed official commented that one parole board member literally falls asleep during hearings.
> Decisions regarding release are frequently determined primarily by an assessment of how docile a prisoner has been during confinement.
> Board membership may be a political plum at best, a matter of corruption at worst.

Once released, inmates may be subjected to overly stringent and self-defeating conditions of parole governing his employment, mobility, associations, etc. Or, equally self-defeating, reasonable conditions may not be enforced. Parolees may be under a well-meaning but overworked, undertrained parole officer with few, if any, community resources available to him.

Despite the far-from-ideal qualitative and quantitative conditions existing in the parole and probation fields, studies indicate that roughly 55 to 65 percent of parolees are not returned to prison (of those that are, about two-thirds are returned for parole violations, not for new crimes) and 60 to 90 percent of probationers complete their probation term without revocation.

THE DRIVE FOR QUALITY

Just as in the other facets of the criminal justice system, quality personnel, not mere quantity, are the key to effective corrections. Yet there are many barriers to the attainment of this goal.

Reports the Joint Commission, "There are still far too many employees in institutions, probation departments, and parole agencies who are there not because they were educated or trained for particular jobs but because their appointments satisfied political needs."

And too many correctional workers moonlight or leave the field in order to earn a decent living. Low pay is the principal reason offered by those who leave corrections; lack of advancement is next. Those who wish to enter and remain in corrections find too few educational or training resources by which to further their knowledge.

That corrections recruitment has been flagging is indicated by findings that only 16 percent of those now employed in corrections came directly from classrooms and 50 percent of today's correctional employees were 30 years of age or older when they entered the field. Minimum-age requirements for entering corrections are considered too high; maximum-age limits are too low.

Ironically, although the Joint Commission believes there are "many potential uses for ex-offenders in corrections," it finds that "agency or civil service policies and practices, rather than laws, are the major roadblocks to the hiring of offenders or ex-offenders for work in corrections." Indeed, "fully half of all correctional personnel interviewed in the Joint Commission's survey objected to the hiring of ex-offenders as full-time correctional workers."

Despite an education and work experience that have not necessarily prepared today's correctional administrators for mamagerial roles, neither time nor resources are generally available for the development of personnel showing promise of becoming effective managers. Heavy pressure for unionization, for example, indicates the desirability of labor relations training.

As reported by a task force of the President's Commission, a number of studies have concluded that "most correctional institutions and agencies are clearly understaffed, deprived of essential professional services, and manned by personnel with little or no educational preparation for correctional work." Even more concisely, the task force sums up by saying, "There are gaps in the quantity and, perhaps even more significantly, in the quality of available manpower."

The many highly competent professionals in corrections are keenly aware of the task ahead. Through the American Correctional Association, they are in the final stages of implementing a corrections accreditation plan—based on the Association's *Manual of Correctional Standards*—for institutions and services.

Just as the problems facing the police and courts are severe in both breadth and depth so also are those confronting corrections. Though not all obstacles hindering an effective correctional process have been discussed, nonetheless several conclusions bearing implications for remedial action are warranted:

1. Corrections must be viewed as a system whose effectiveness will never approach full potential unless its many interrelated components are of uniformly high caliber. If there is no probation officer to prepare a presentence report that enables a judge to arrive at an informed sentence, an offender may be committed to an excellent but inappropriate correctional facility; as a result, the correctional process fails before it begins. If a prison is operated on the basis that inmates are little more than human rubbish, the best parole program imaginable is unlikely to succeed. And even if probation, incarceration, and parole are all appropriate and well administered, little will be accomplished for an offender unless community resources and attitudes are supportive.
2. "Rehabilitation" and "reintegration" should be interpreted not merely as "the offender must be treated so he can return to the community" but as "both the offender and the community must take appropriate steps to adjust to one another."
3. Whether a particular correctional method is tantamount to "coddling" an offender is irrelevant if that method is an effective means of making the community safer by minimizing the likelihood of future crimes by that offender.
4. Since correctional funds are not, and will never be, unlimited, a rational way of defining "effective means" as used above is in cost/benefit terms—that is, apply those correctional methods that will yield the maximum amount of long-range community safety per dollar spent. If this calls for probation in one case, so be it; if a lengthy prison term is appropriate in another case, so be it. Those who clamor for stiff sentences across the board not only will intensify criminal behavior for many types of offenders but also will be selecting a very expensive correctional tool; in cost/benefit terms, a large expense is incurred that in many cases will produce a negative benefit.
5. A principle of management that applies equally well to corrections is that responsibility should be delegated to the lowest organizational level consistent with effective decision making. The probation subsidy program in California, where counties are handling cases previously referred to the state, is a good example of how the principle might be applied.
6. The corrections system needs more personnel and more qualified personnel. But upgrading quality and quantity will fall short of the mark if the pervasive inefficiency and ineffectiveness due to jurisdictional fragmentation is not substantially reduced through regionalizing, coordinating, and/or pooling facilities and services.
7. The impact that an effective correctional process would have on the police and courts is obvious. Corrections can and should be regarded as potentially a major, if not the major, method of crime prevention.

Current Issues in Law Enforcement

George Deukmejian

It is not often that I have the opportunity to speak to future police officers, and while I have the chance, I want to issue a complaint about the recent Supreme Court decisions. I think it is unfair that the constitutional rights you will be reciting to persons in the next few years apply only to criminals and not to politicians. Lately, it seems, the political issues of the day have become more and more controversial, and I can assure you that on more than one occasion I wish that *I* had the right to remain silent. And to make it worse, for the seven years that I have been in public office my opponents have violated my constitutional rights by telling me that everything I say will be held against me!

The issues of the 1970 campaigns will certainly include, among others, in intense discussion and debate on the quality of education, campus unrest, high government spending and high taxes, air and water pollution control, transportation and housing in urban areas and the increase in crime.

I believe we would agree that each of us wishes to accomplish improvements in each of these areas. If we are to achieve the progress and advancements most of us desire, it will be due in large part to our reliance upon the rule of law as the cornerstone of our government and our society.

The central issue today is whether change can be accomplished through the rule of law or *must be brought* about only in defiance of law. It is our laws which serve to protect each citizen from injustice. It is our laws which maintain order. It is our laws which guarantee to each American the freedom to seek out his own individual destiny. It is our laws which are the avenues of progress. Today our rule of law is threatened *by those* who are contributing to the staggering increase in crime, and by those who are fomenting political lawlessness in the streets and on the campuses of our State and nation.

It is essential that we recognize this danger and do all that we can to eradicate it. As the immediate past president of the American Bar Association, William Gossett said, "...the rule of law can be wiped out in one misguided—however well-intentioned—generation."

From an address by California State Senator George Deukmejian delivered to the graduates of the Golden West College Police Academy at Huntington Beach, November 14, 1969. Reprinted by permission of the author.

These are times when fear creates extremists of the left, demanding complete license and on the other hand, creates extremists of the right, demanding absolute repression of the rights of some of our citizens. Throughout the history of this country, political protest and criticism have not only been protected; they have been encouraged. One need not be a learned political scientist to realize that, without the protection of the freedom of speech, press and assembly, our system of government would have failed long ago. In recent years, however, dissident elements in our society have increasingly turned away from the traditional—and Constitutionally justified—means of protest, and have instead embarked on a course of violence, disruption, intimidation, and coercion.

Those who would justify "crime for a cause" have promulgated the view that people who violate the law ought not to be arrested and punished if their violation has protest as its purpose. By calling criminal acts "civil disobedience," they seek to persuade us that offenses against public order should be immune from punishment and even commended. Those who have brought bloodshed and destruction of property to our cities and campuses justify their actions in the sacred names of "academic freedom," or "equal opportunity," or "Constitutional rights."

There is no academic freedom when young toughs enter a classroom and, under threat of violence, tell a teacher and his students that they cannot hold their class. There is no equal opportunity when a minority of students, ostensibly in protest of a just cause, force the closing down of a public educational institution. Indeed, there is no opportunity at all for anyone. There is no section of the Constitution which says that the right to protest includes a right to block a public street, set fire to university buildings or kill a United States Senator. It is time to tell the perpetrators of violence and disruption: If there are conditions and/or regulations with which you cannot abide, by all means seek redress of your grievances—but do so through legitimate channels and by legitimate means. You can even be "militant," so long as your militance denotes a peaceful persistence and *not* a state of war. It is time that they were told "We will not—we cannot—allow you, in the supposed expression of *your rights* and *your freedom,* to trample on *our rights* and *our freedom.*" Just as we must now take a stand against "crime for cause," so must we take decisive action to halt the spiraling increase in the more "traditional" forms of crime.

Rampant crime is like a plague. Its costs, whether economic, physical, or psychological, are felt in every home on every street in every neighborhood. It creates a climate in which people make choices, not freely and out of confidence, but out of fear.

The President's Crime Commission revealed that 43 percent of the people say they are afraid to go out at night, alone, in their own neighborhood. A recent national survey revealed that people living in so-called ghetto areas say they are even afraid to remain in their own homes alone at night. Such action must involve a critical assessment of our entire criminal justice system—law enforcement, courts, corrections—followed by efforts to make any necessary improvements in that system.

Here in California, Governor Reagan has sought to develop a systematic, all-out attack on crime in the state. I am happy to say that law enforcement in California has a brighter future by virtue of the establishment in 1967 of the California Council on Criminal Justice. Prior to my authorship of the legislation which established the Council, our state had long had a basically fragmented governmental structure in the field of criminal justice. This legislation cleared the path for new and modern approaches to problems which cut across the whole field of law enforcement and the administration of justice.

As a member of the Council I am proud to say that it has now begun to rectify the shortcomings of our old policies. Through the Council, persons representing all facets of the administration of justice are brought together in an effort to coordinate current efforts and to develop master plans for the prevention, detection, and control of crime. The Council's major thrust is the evaluation of state and local programs associated with the prevention of crime, law enforcement, and the administration of justice, and to encourage the preparation of comprehensive plans for the improvement and coordination of all aspects of law enforcement and criminal justice.

If we look at the areas on which work is being done, we can see that the Council has already begun to make significant progress. These efforts include:

1. Providing for a superior protective service to the public by determining local police agency deficiencies that hinder the effective control and suppression of crime.
2. Enhancing the police agencies' capacity to deal with crime by building confidence in and support of the police through local programs aimed at increasing police community relations.
3. Involving the total community in a variety of anticrime programs through communication and planning with cooperative citizens and nonpolice agencies of local government.
4. Coordinating local government functions in the prevention and control of crime.
5. Identifying methods by which police agencies can better recruit, more effectively test, and more rapidly select and promote personnel.

By working on these projects the Council is taking an important first step. If we are going to make any headway against rising crime, we must work tirelessly to come up with new answers to old questions. Police officers are daily asked to put their lives and safety on the line in order to protect the public. Yet, we must work to assure that their efforts are not made in vain; that the sacrifice of law enforcement officers is not crippled in the criminal justice system. We can do no less.

I fervently believe that the efforts of such farsighted programs as the Council will have the byproduct of developing in society's cynics a greater respect for the police officer and—just as important—greater respect for the rule of law. Much depends on the willingness of all facets of criminal justice to work together in the solution of common problems. But the potential for innovation and achievement is great. And if we are dedicated and diligent in our task, we shall realize that potential to the fullest.

Legislation, coordination and plans are needed. But let's be realistic. Whatever laws are passed, whatever plans are laid by government, they will all be irrelevant unless several other factors come into play in the struggle against crime.

If there is one thing I have learned in my 7 years in Sacramento, it is that we don't need more laws, we just need to enforce the laws we now have on the books. Enforcement of the law includes not only arrest; it also means adequate prosecution and proper decision and sentencing by judges. The courts are not responsible for the increase in crime and disorder but some judges refuse to sentence convicted criminals in accordance with the intent of the law as passed by the Legislature; and other judges make decisions which make the job of law enforcement more difficult and which result in keeping the truth away from the jury.

Some say they can live with these decisions. Maybe they can, but I don't believe the individual law-abiding citizen should have to be exposed to the danger of having known guilty men turned loose in the community.

To those who might object to my criticism of some judges let me say this, my criticism is not based on a lack of respect for the court, rather my criticism is based on my deep regard for the law and a belief that the court must restrain its exercise of power. The judicial system is but one-third of our governmental system and the suggestion that it is above scrutiny or criticism is to relinquish one's rights as provided by law. As Supreme Court Justice Frankfurter once said, "Judges as persons, or courts as institutions, are entitled to no greater immunity from criticism than other persons or institutions. Judges must be kept mindful of their limitations and of their ultimate public responsibility by a vigorous stream of criticism expressed with candor, however blunt."

Secondly, the individual citizen simply *must* lend his interest, his concern, and yes, even his dollars to the fight against crime. For the real and final answer to our crime problem lies within the realm of the individual.

The police cannot solve crimes that are not reported to them; the courts cannot solve crimes that are not reported to them; the courts cannot administer justice fairly and surely if citizens will not serve as witnesses and jurors. We will turn out generation after generation of juvenile delinquents who will mature into hardened adult criminals unless concerned citizens take part in intensified delinquency prevention programs in their local communities. Ex-convict after ex-convict will return to crime unless concerned citizens organize to help them regain their dignity, find a job, and become responsible participants in society. These things cannot be bought with phrases, or with good intentions. A bumper sticker which says "support your local police" simply will not suffice any longer.

Thirdly, it is fundamentally important that we realign some of the attitudes in this country. We must seek, we must achieve, a reaffirmation of those moral and legal precepts which have always been basic to our system of laws. We are witnessing the decay of the moral fiber upon which this country was built. We are seeing permissiveness in the attitudes of right and wrong.

In my opinion, government has two equal primary responsibilities—one is to provide the best possible educational system for our young people and the other is to provide protection for all citizens so that they may study, work, and live in peace and safety. With crime increasing at a much faster pace than the growth in population, we are obviously failing in that latter responsibility.

There are those who say that the only way to save America is to first destroy it—I say America does not need that kind of bloody salvation. I didn't come to public office to destroy anything, I came to build—to build a better society for all who live in our State and Nation.

A lawful society is not only the best society, but the only hope for mankind. *As far as I am concerned, there remains no higher calling and no higher responsibility than the commitment of one's life to the maintenance and the advancement of the rule of law.*

I said earlier that the law is being sorely tested. I believe it is the responsibility of every citizen to see that the law meets the test. It is our responsibility to see that the law is upheld.

Making Law and Order Work

John Lindsay

No lawyer, no politician—and especially those of us who are both—can afford to neglect the principles and procedures of the law. For if the machinery of the law fails to work swiftly and justly, Americans will abandon faith in the Rule of Law.

That faith is already profoundly shaken.

As a lawyer and a Mayor, I hear about it from eight million clients.

A cabdriver in the Bronx complains: "I'm afraid to drive anymore. I don't know whether my next customer will tip me or kill me."

The Honorable John Lindsay is Mayor of the City of New York. This article is from an address to the American Bar Association convention in August 1970.

From John Lindsay, "Making Law and Order Work," *Trial* (August-September 1970), pp. 20, 21, 28. (Publication of the American Trial Lawyers' Association.) Reprinted by permission of the publisher.

A businessman in Queens despairs: "They steal from my car. They steal from my store. When will it stop?"

An old woman in Brooklyn tells me: "I'm scared to go to the market at night. Does anyone care?"

A mother in Harlem wonders: "How can I raise my son? The junkies are everywhere."

And on Staten Island, they say: "We moved here because it was safe. Will it stay that way?"

The Mayors of Chicago and Cleveland, Boston and Seattle—the Mayors of every city and increasingly every suburb—could tell you that they hear the same from their own citizens.

In some way, distant or intimate, real or remote, 160 million metropolitan Americans now sense the stark human implications of crime in the streets. We are living with fear. Rising crime threatens all.

What good will it do to recover prosperity, if crime endangers our livelihood and our lives?

What good will it do to end the war in Indochina, if crime converts our streets into combat zones?

For all our hopes and all our boasts, we cannot fashion a decent society unless we fashion an orderly society.

And whether we are lawyers or politicians or both, our task is to reclaim the streets from crime and return them to peaceful citizens. We must make our streets once again places to enjoy together instead of to fear alone.

We are told that "strict construction" and talking tough will do the job. But that's not what it's all about in the streets. The issues are:

Whether people feel free to walk to the newsstand after dark.
Whether police arrest criminals.
Whether courts convict the guilty.
Whether correctional systems really rehabilitate.

By those standards, no one—on any side of the crime issue—has proved equal to the task of assuring safer streets in a more secure society. Our people are learning in some very painful ways that the system of criminal justice is collapsing.

The signs of a breakdown are all around us. Ask any victim or any defendant. Ask the Chief Justice of the United States. Ask the grief-stricken family and friends of Judge Haley.

From San Rafael to Scarsdale, crime in America is now everywhere. Crime rates have risen by hundreds of percentage points in a single decade.

The courts are institutional cripples, stumbling along in the pattern of an outworn tradition, compiling a record of incredible inefficiency.

While defendants languish in jail, some prosecutors and lawyers multiply continuances—and some judges work hours that would shame a retired banker. Of New York's 14,000 inmates, 8,000 are awaiting trial. They are sleeping three in a cell, with one on the floor. This August, their rage almost sparked a riot in a city prison too aptly named the Tombs. And because speedy trial is a phrase, not a reality, some defendants released on bail repeat crimes over and over again.

If, at the end of it all, there is a conviction, the serious offender usually does his time in a prison that is a school for crime. He is finally released with nothing more than a free bus ride back to the slum he came from. It is almost assured that he will return to a life of crime.

No wonder we are losing faith in law enforcement. No wonder our doubts have spawned a host of new proposals for crime control.

But, in a very real sense, most of the proposals are anything but new.

In 1931, the Wickersham Commission made sweeping recommendations for police, judicial, and correctional reforms. Because the recommendations were largely ignored, the National Crime Commission repeated them in 1967. And in 1968, the Kerner Report on Civil Disorders echoed the Crime Commission. As Vice-Chairman of the Kerner Commission, I know how much we borrowed from earlier efforts. I also know how much the Violence Commission's 1970 Report borrowed from us.

The route to safe streets has been mapped out over and over again in the last 40 years. But no one has really followed it.

Despite all the experts and all the advice and all the commissions, there is still too little reform and too much pretense. Waging an effective war on crime, the Violence Commission warned, would cost an additional six billion dollars. Six billion dollars for more police and better courts, more rehabilitation and better corrections, more safety and less crime. But lawyers in high places—men who should surely know better—are engaged in a futile attempt to combat crime on the cheap.

Washington talks about unsafe streets and juvenile crime and drug abuse. Then it requests far less money than Congress has authorized for the Safe Streets Act, for the Juvenile Delinquency Prevention Act, and for the Narcotics Prevention and Treatment Act.

Washington talks about more police, better trained and better paid. Then it ignores Congressman Cowger's bill to provide federal funds for additional police protection.

Washington talks about the dangers of recidivism. Then it proposes a system of preventive detention that, according to its studies, will not work.

There is a vast distance between anti-crime rhetoric and the reality of crime control. Talking tough may satisfy some psychic longing—it may permit us to vent our anger and our frustration—but it will win no victories over crime on a dimly lit Wichita street on in a deserted Tulsa park. It will win no victories for Rule of Law.

But criticism alone wins no victories either. Critics of current law enforcement have an obligation to transform their criticism into a constructive program to secure law and order.

Law and order is often denounced as a code word. But we cannot abandon the English language because it has been turned into code words. And no responsible lawyer or politician can abandon the fight to make law and order the Rule of Law that works instead of a code word that doesn't.

Law and order in your town or mine is not preventive detention or "no knock" or repression.

Law and order works when you open a new narcotics center in New York City, when you hire more policemen in Los Angeles, when you computerize court calendars in Pittsburgh.

It's not as dramatic as talking tough. It may not be good political gamesmanship. But tedious, systematic, nuts and bolts work is the only way to rebuild criminal justice.

It is time to begin. With what we have learned from the commissions and in our own communities, with a good lawyer's instincts, we can create a just and peaceful society.

We must ask some uncomfortable questions. And we must venture some unorthodox answers.

The most basic question concerns the definition of crime. For too long, we have reacted to major social problems by trying to outlaw them. When we shove drunkenness and addiction and similar offenses into the criminal process, we impose a fantastic burden on the police, the courts, and correctional agencies. Busy with the tasks psychiatrists and social workers could do better, law enforcement cannot do the best job of protecting people and property.

For example, six years ago, one-third of all arrests in New York City were for common drunkenness. Policemen were preoccupied arresting the same offenders night after night. Judges heard the same sad excuse and the same desperate pleas day after day. Now, with special medical facilities and innovative treatment methods, we have moved drunkenness out of the criminal process. Similar steps in other areas might free enforcement agencies to enforce laws that really count.

And any citizen on the streets of any American city could tell you how much that would mean.

But rethinking the definition of crime will actually mean little unless we reform the machinery of justice. Look at the dismal state of police and judicial management.

A policeman's place is in the streets, not in the stationhouse. But today, policemen spend too little time as peace officers and too much time on petty bureaucratic tasks. A recent study in a medium size city reported that the local police allocated less than 17 percent of their working hours to crimes against persons and property. Over 50 percent of their time was consumed by administrative assignments. The result: In many police departments only one-tenth of the men are on the streets at any hour, day or night. The rest are often locked behind typewriters, turning out the 15th copy of a report that may become just another testament to another unsolved crime.

We must reexamine the police role. We must radically reallocate police manpower. We must hire civilian personnel to take over clerical and administrative tasks. We must build flexibility and openness into police structures. Then, perhaps, policemen can abandon the typewriters and the triplicate forms and focus on fighting crime—the job they signed up for.

If we must repair police structures we must virtually revolutionize the judicial system. The archaic machinery of justice has not taken off the green eyeshades of a century ago. If Charles Dickens could see our courts now, he would feel the contempt only familiarity can breed: contempt for the delays, anachronisms, and inequities.

In my own city, the recent addition of 20 new Criminal Court judges has made no appreciable dent in calendar delays. So we must recognize how desperately our courts need new management techniques.

If computers can keep tabs on millions of airline tickets, they can surely do the job of calendaring. Judges should cede their administrative powers to professional administrators. No Criminal Court judge can still indulge the luxury of outmoded prerogatives that divert him from the work of justice. And no city or state can still afford to clog up the courts with petty offenses. That's why New York City has just transferred four and a half million parking cases a year from the Criminal Courts to a new Parking Violations Bureau.

Management reforms could make our courts effective and efficient in dealing with the street crimes that threaten us most. If a potential mugger knows that justice is swift and sure, not a year or three away, he may decide that crime really does not pay. Moreover, a modern court system would combine thoroughness with speed. Speed would sharply curtail criminal activity by defendants released on bail. Thoroughness would increase the probability that dangerous criminals would be put where they belong—in jail.

And any citizen on the streets of any American city could tell you how much that would mean.

But all the work of reform and all the reshaped structures will still fail unless we alter the correctional system. Rehabilitation deserves more than verbal tribute and a paltry 3 percent of our criminal justice funds.

We must spend what it takes to make correctional structures responsive and open—responsive to the need for training and educational opportunities; open to paraprofessionals, who can communicate with released offenders and who cannot be fooled or conned by their clients; open to every person, every government agency, and every private institution that can aid down and out individuals. Then we can turn more first-time criminals into productive citizens rather than repeat offenders.

And any citizen on the streets of any American city could tell you how much that would mean.

The essential struggle for law and order in America is a struggle to reform the machinery of criminal justice. And beyond the criminal process, there is so much we must do.

Some of it involves the basic social reforms that will add up to a just society, where destitution and despair do not drive each succeeding generation to crime and disorder.

Some of it involves apparently small changes that may have large consequences. We know, for example, that a busy street is a safe street. So New York City is trying to revive the street life that television killed two decades ago. Experiments like pedestrial malls and street bands are recreating the streets as peopled places. And there *is* safety in numbers.

Police reorganization, efficient courts, effective corrections, social reform—in naming our goals, we number our deficiencies.

And these deficiencies are breeding not only crime, but a dangerous decline in our people's traditional faith in the law. Ask why there are more guns than people in America, and think upon how crucial the Rule of Law is for civility and survival and peace.

We must summon new resources and new talent to the war against crime.

For the blunt, hard truth is that reform in American criminal justice is stymied. Though we think New York City has the nation's finest police department, we know it could be better if we could afford to give it more financial support. We are proud of our efforts in the neighborhoods and with narcotics. We have made a good start on court reform. But the major tasks remain undone. And we do not have enough money to do them. No city does.

While Houston can talk to the moon, police stations often cannot talk to a patrolman a few blocks away. A missile can span continents in thirty minutes—but it takes St. Louis days to trace a fingerprint from Chicago. We have developed sophisticated and expensive equipment to sense an enemy in an Asian swamp. But a housing policeman in Newark lacks even a simple television monitor to check the hallways he must walk alone.

The real victims of all this are the men and women and children who have placed their trust in someone else to enforce the law. That trust is precious. We are on the verge of losing it.

The real villain is our nation's priorities. Eighty billion dollars for defense and war abroad—less than five hundred million dollars for safety in our streets at home.

Like every Mayor in every city, I am now practiced in pleading the case for new priorities. As a Mayor, I am used to asking for money.

Today, I want to ask for something beyond that. For my city and for other cities, for the suburbs and for the towns, for every citizen in America who feels the threat of crime, I am asking for your help.

You must work for reform in your own cities and states. And you must pressure Washington to put its priorities where the problems are: in the streets of America.

You must serve as a lobby for law and order—as a check on those who hope to fight crime on the cheap—as advocates of new structures to strengthen criminal justice.

Your voices will be heard. You are expert and influential.

Your views count. In the final analysis, they may determine whether our citizens can live in peace, with justice, under law.

The legal system has been good to every lawyer. It has given us much. In return, it now asks for our concern and our commitment.

There is abroad in our nation an intense passion for social order. It will never be satisfied until lawyers ignite their own passion for order within the legal system. Tolerance and understanding and patient discussion are no longer enough. Lawyers must act.

Police Brutality or Public Brutality?

Robert C. Byrd

Law enforcement in America is in trouble.

To me, this situation reflects that our entire country is in trouble, because when our law enforcers are weakened and made impotent, then the laws which govern our Nation are in danger of collapsing.

For any number of reasons and alleged lofty causes the men and women of the law enforcement establishment are being made ineffectual. Alarmingly, a long parade of individuals with odious tactics are straining the tolerance of our Constitution to the breaking point. At the same time, this small cadre of confused idealists and irresponsible extremists are seeking to tear down respect for law and for the law enforcement officer.

The American public is more and more being subjected and exposed to every conceivable kind of outrage by hordes of rag-tag beatniks, agitators and professional troublemakers who insist upon lying down in the streets, blocking traffic, forming human walls in front of business establishments, swarming over private property, and staging noisy sit-ins and demonstrations. All of this is supposedly being done in order to "dramatize" grievances against our society and against the policies of the American Government at home and abroad.

This small band of demonstrators have so successfully cloaked themselves in the mantle of martyrdom that few people have dared to voice an objection for

The Honorable Robert C. Byrd is a U.S. Senator from West Virginia.

From Robert C. Byrd, "Police Brutality or Public Brutality," *The Police Chief* 33, no. 2 (February 1966): 8-10. Reprinted by permission of the publisher.

fear of being labeled "bigot." They have succeeded in mesmerizing large segments of our population to the extent that representatives of law and order have become pictured as the villains while lawless marchers and sit-downers have become the figures for compassion.

One of the unfortunate byproducts of this curious public attitude is the denigration of the law enforcement officer. There is a great deal of furor these days over discrimination against Negroes and other minorities. Few stop to think, however, that a group most discriminated against today is the law enforcement officer. He is constantly the subject of usually unsubstantiated charges of police brutality. His will and his morale are being shattered because the clamor of such charges is not counteracted by support from law-abiding, decent citizens. He is being psychologically assailed and physically assaulted, and few responsible individuals have come to his aid. In 1964, one out of every ten police officers was attacked as he attempted to carry out his duties. There is every reason to believe that when the figures for 1965 are compiled they will show an increase in such attacks.

It seems everyone is concerned with police brutality and yet no one is concerned over what I like to term "public brutality"; that is, the maltreatment of our officers of the law by citizens of every type. Until the American public realizes the brutality which is being inflicted upon our police officers, the law, which is the cornerstone of our Republic, will continue to be flaunted and diluted.

I am appalled at the lengths to which some charlatans are going as they take advantage of sometimes legitimate civil rights protests. Piteously, they cry of persecution by police who use what they term, of all things, "oral brutality." At the same time, however, they themselves delight in using the same type of brutality against police officers by characterizing them as gestapo, fuzz and in terms too opprobrious to be printed. It is truly amazing that as far as these insincere street marchers are concerned, there is only one side to the coin. They are the only ones persecuted; the policeman wears the uniform of authority—which, in itself, is anathema to the hoodlum element—and, as an officer, he becomes a ready target for oral abuse, vituperation, and, yes, physical assaults. To overly militant leaders, a Negro policeman should not wince when he is called an "Uncle Tom" or a "handkerchief head," because he is on the side of the law.

To the exploiters of the strife which America is enduring, the only victims are the rioters, the looters, the arsonists, the snipers, the thieves, and the murderers who commit vicious crimes while falsely wrapping themselves in the banner of the civil rights movement. I do not mean to imply that Negroes and other minorities in this country have not been discriminated against nor that they have escaped injustices at the hands of the majority. As Mr. Quinn Tamm, Executive Director of the International Association of Chiefs of Police, has said, however, "We are tired of the cry that because one segment of our population has been deprived for 100 years the balance of society must accept 100 years of anarchy." The majority happens to have some rights also, and it, too, has suffered some injustices.

In the last several years, the law has been made to work quite effectively for the benefit of the downtrodden. It seems, however, that the more the workable processes of democratic justice have been applied to right grievous wrongs, the more greedy and impatient some factions in our society have become. Not satisfied with what the law has done for them, they seem bent upon destroying the only truly effective safeguard they have.

This incongruous philosophy is also apparent in the activities of those who protest the overseas policies and activities of the U.S. Government. Again, the police are the prime targets of weird individuals who have infiltrated groups sincerely concerned about our involvement in Vietnam and elsewhere. We have seen these ideologically confused individuals storm the White House, the very ramparts of our country's dignity; we have seen them, in effect, pledging allegiance to the Government of Hanoi by holding aloft Vietcong flags and promoting blood banks for the enemy; we have seen attempts in Oakland, California, at thwarting the movement of military goods to our fighting men in Vietnam; we have seen police officers assaulted, cursed, spat upon, and bitten by so-called nonviolent demonstrators allegedly seeking academic and political freedom on the campus of the University of California in Berkeley.

In these situations, the police have stolidly suffered the unjustified charge of "brutality" and "gestapo." To my way of thinking, the police in all of these incidents have handled their responsibilities with restraint, patience and a gentleness which would be unknown in most any other country in the world. Meanwhile, however, pseudoliberal organizations continue to harp upon the necessity that it is the duty of the police to insure that both protesters and counterprotesters each have the opportunity to express their views. The galling aspect of this admonition is that the police are already aware of this. They are men of the law and know more about their responsibilities than many of their detractors.

I wish to reiterate that the police have done an outstanding job of protecting all factions. Of course, there have been exceptions, and there will always be. Police are supposed to be impartial; yes, but at the same time, they are not automatons. They are men of emotions who happen to be wearing uniforms. It takes a man of steel to ignore a Vietcong flag on America's streets. It takes an imperturbable man to calmly witness bearded idiots trampling the Constitution and Bill of Rights. It takes a strong man to hold his temper as he is spat upon and reviled by unwashed, scraggly-haired revolutionaries and uncouth, insolent, irresponsible hoodlums.

When it is borne in mind that the police are a military-like organization, it is surprising that they are able to maintain any degree of composure in the face of such senseless rebellion. Many of them have sons and brothers in Vietnam, and a draft card burner to them is anathema—but they are not allowed to show it. Police also have a great deal of sympathy with the troops in Vietnam because they fight a similar type of dirty war in which the enemy is forever striking from the shadows. The police know guerrilla warfare because they fight it day in and day out with criminals in America's streets. They also know that among the chief goals of communism and other un-American ideologies is that public faith in the police must be destroyed in order for the seeds of dissension to be planted.

The police also know that the campaigns against them are not reckless ones. They are well planned, and there are pamphlets written to educate militant demonstrators in ways of skirmishing with police in order to make the law enforcement officer appear to be the brutal aggressor.

The police accept this. They also accept the fact that it is their sworn duty to uphold the law and that they cannot be dissuaded from their responsibilities by the fact that they are made to *look* bad in the eyes of the public.

Since the beginning days of the modern sit-ins, wade-ins and sleep-ins, the police have worked through their professional organization, the International Association of Chiefs of Police, to devise means of counteracting these despicable tactics. Of course, the simple answer would be retaliation, but the police officer of today is more professional, and, through conferences, research and study, he is getting closer to devising means of nullifying these tactics; that is, carrying out the letter of the law with as little violence as possible despite the efforts made to place him in an untenable position.

So-called civil disobedience cannot be countenanced by the law enforcement officer. Under our legal system, when there is an intent to break a law the act which follows the intent constitutes a crime and the individual should be punished. Unfortunately, those who seek martyrdom do not wish to understand this. They prefer to violate the law and then receive amnesty. Civil disobedience and lawlessness cannot be excused. We cannot allow one American to blithely burn his draft card while another bravely gives his live for the honor of his country in Vietnam.

The enigma surrounding the exhibitionists who seek martyrdom is compounded by the fact that some well-intentioned souls, understandably worried about the dangers present in an age of nuclear energy and a day when injustice to minorities still exists, will continue to demonstrate as they have in the past. To people who act in a mature and sincere manner, I say it is their Constitutional right to peaceably and lawfully assemble and to petition the government, but laws must be obeyed and police officers respected by all. With regard to those who counsel and perpetrate unlawful acts, the majority of Americans must react with vigilance, sternness, and speed in the dispensing of just and legal desserts for the offenders.

I am appalled when I hear or read statements to the effect that this gang of hirsute ragmuffins is so small and their impact so negligible that they should be ignored. That this is not so is the reason this type of lawlessness must be stopped. The morale of our troops in Vietnam is obviously affected. The North Vietnamese concept of the American will is without question a misconstruction since the Hanoi Government believed such attitudes to be so widespread that it issued commemorative stamps depicting Americans picketing against the war and even went so far as to picture the grisly self-immolation by that unfortunate man on the grounds of the Pentagon as an indication of American beliefs.

Persons responsible for aiding our enemies and destroying Americans' faith in other Americans must be punished. Not the least among the reasons for this is the fact that our police who bear the first brunt of these activities must be supported by their community officials, by the press, and by the public. What does it avail a police officer, moreover, to risk life and limb in arresting rioters and unlawful protesters if they are freed, and even lauded, by the courts and when our Constitution and Bill of Rights are twisted well beyond any meaning that our forefathers attempted to convey?

Recent events have emphasized that there has been a violent breach of two cardinal principles of our American society—the respect for law and order and the recourse to orderly process of law to seek redress of wrongs. There is a great cry that the police of this nation must hew to the letter of the law, whereas others who do not agree with it have the right to break the law with impunity. The vast majority of the 300,000 men and women of the police service in this country are remaining within the framework of the law in the face of great provocation daily. When we reach the stage that the other side can break the law without punishment while the police must continue to use Marquis of Queensbury rules, then it is obvious which will be the loser. The loser will be John Q. Citizen—you and me, our wives and children, old and young, black and white, in city and hamlet all over America.

Our country cannot stand firm upon laws that are manipulated like clay. American can endure only so long as it has as its foundation solid bedrock. And, that bedrock is the law and the men and women who enforce it.

If the police of this nation are not supported now, the law will perish, and this Republic cannot endure long thereafter.

The Police and Society

Paul Chevigny

Previous chapters have shown that the anatomy of street-corner abuses is unchanging. The policeman on the beat sees his job to be one of maintaining tranquillity and perpetuating the established routine. Any person out of the ordinary is suspicious; if he is recognizably deviant, then he is potentially criminal. Potentially criminal also, and a severe threat to good order, is any challenge to the policeman's authority. A challenge may come either from the deviant, simply by his failure to respond to an officer's order, or from the ordinary citizen who is openly defiant. In either case, the challenge will be met by anger and one or more weapons out of the arsenal of legal sanctions, from a summons up through summary corporal punishment. Criminal charges, beginning with disorderly conduct and ranging up to felonious assault, are commonly laid to cover the actions of the policeman and to punish the offender. In the eyes of the police, arrest is practically tantamount to guilt, and the police will supply the allegations necessary for conviction; the courts are treated as a mere adjunct to their purpose. Distortion of the facts becomes the most pervasive and the most significant of abuses. The police ethic justifies any action which is intended to maintain order or to convict any wrongdoer (i.e., anyone actually or potentially guilty of crime). In studying search and seizure, for example, we found that the police tend to justify a search made "in good faith"—really looking for a crime—regardless of whether it is a lawful search or not. Once again, the facts are distorted so as to justify the search in the eyes of the courts, although there is less distortion in connection with house searches than with searches of persons on the street.

We have seen that some abuses do not precisely fit our conception of the tendencies in police behavior that give rise to abuses—those, for example, which are committed for personal reasons like family revenge or professional advancement. Although it is significant that these are the abuses which are generally condemned by policemen themselves, it is important to observe that

From Paul Chevigny, "The Police and Society," in *Police Power: Abuses in New York City* (New York: Pantheon Books, 1969), pp. 276-83. Copyright ©1969 by Paul Chevigny. Reprinted by permission of Pantheon Books, a Division of Random House, Inc.

such actions shade off subtly into duty-oriented abuses, because the department encourages the man to identify himself with his authority. Other abuses, such as those that occur during mass police action, seem to be similar in origin to ordinary street abuses, but are distorted out of all recognition by mass frenzy. Finally, a few abuses are chronic because they are systematically encouraged by the department. In condoning systematic abuses, the department itself acts upon much the same rationale that the individual policeman uses to justify isolated street abuses. When the Department authorizes an action in violation of due process, such as a roundup of prostitutes, it does so to preserve order ("a clean city") and to harass a group of people who are considered undesirable. The chief difference between isolated and systematic abuses is that there is less distortion of the facts about the latter, because the individual officers find it unnecessary and thus make no attempt to cover their own actions. Except in the case of systematic harassment, then, distortion of fact is the thread that runs through all abuses, however different they may seem. The distortion of fact, and indeed every abuse, is rationalized by the need to maintain authority and catch wrong-doers.

The tendencies in police behavior which give rise to abuses do form a sort of "police character": a man, suspicious of outsiders, who is concerned with order, reacts aggressively to threats to his authority, and regards every attempt to control that authority with cynicism. Other authors have attempted to mold this character, or a similar one, into a sociological or psychological framework. Neiderhoffer, for example, has analyzed the policemen according to the characteristics of an "authoritarian personality." For our purposes, terms like this are tautological; the word "authoritarian" either reiterates what we know already about policemen, or else it is irrelevant. To get at the roots of police behavior, I should have to go to a deeper psychological level, and the fragmentary nature of the evidence collected here, together with the fragmentary nature of the available psychological studies, prevents me from performing the task adequately. It is enough here for us to know that the characteristic police reactions are a logical product of the police role (e.g. maintaining order) and the traditions of the department (e.g. secrecy).

The important point for us here is that police abuses *do* form a pattern, and that they reveal one aspect of police character. Police abuses are a set of consistent responses in similar situations, and not very surprising responses at that. The policeman identifies with the office with which he is vested, and considers a threat to that office the most serious of threats to good order. It is misleading to say that his views are unlawful or unethical. They may participate in a different ethic, and perhaps even in a somewhat different law from the criminal law of the modern, liberal state, but unquestionably there are ethics and law at work here. It is a "good guys versus bad guys" ethic, free of the strictures of procedure: the person who is "wise to a cop" has no respect for authority and deserves to be punished. Deviants are undesirable, and the police should ride herd on them to keep them from intruding on the rest of society. A criminal ought to be caught and put in jail the quickest way that one can get him there.

Is this really such an unfamiliar cannon of ethics? Doesn't it rather ring of the opinion reflected in most of our newspaper editorials and shared by thousands of citizens? We should realize that the appeals courts ask an extraordinary act of will from the policeman. They ask him to be concerned solely with "enforcing law," not with simply catching wrongdoers. It is an abstract distinction that most of us treat with the same suspicion as does the policeman, and the policeman continues to ignore it partly because we encourage him to do so.

Max Weber distinguished between the substantive rationality and the formal rationality of legal systems. A substantively rational system obeys generally consistent, if poorly articulated, norms of ethics and law. The formally rational legal system is more coherent and logically consistent. It is the typical system of a society governed by an impersonal bureaucracy dealing at arm's length with citizens. Our criminal law is becoming increasingly rational in the formal sense, as economic and political relations become more abstract, while the police continue to adhere to a kind of substantive rationality. Formal rationality is increasing partly because the rough rules of the police are simply inadequate to the social changes taking place in our society, and to the ideal of equal justice. The conflict in which the police are placed—between their own code and the formal code—is the conflict of modern city administration, and indeed of the people who live in the cities. The question which the citizens of New York, and of every city which pretends to a liberal administration, must ask themselves is whether they would rather have the police follow their old-fashioned rules, or whether they really want the police to adhere to the formally rational (and substantively different) rules of due process of law. It is clear that there is something in most of us that does not want the police to change; the landslide vote against a civilian review board demonstrated that, if nothing else. We want efficiency, quick work, order above all, though we claim to want due process and equal justice as well. Without basic changes to eliminate the obvious injustices in our society, we cannot expect to have all these, but if all else fails, we think we would like to preserve at least the appearance of order ("peace and quiet"). It is for the police to play the tough, no-nonsense half of this conflict. The enlightened feel a little guilty about their own impulse to coerce respect by force, and it is easier for them to turn the police into a whipping boy than to admit to such instincts themselves. The police do all the "wrong" things—club people who are outcasts or defiant of authority—but the unfortunate truth is that much public disapproval of their actions is sheer hypocrisy. Many, perhaps most, citizens feel that it is desirable for a policeman to coerce adherence to his code by punching a "wise kid" or ransacking an apartment without a warrant. They hide from themselves the fact that every act which coerces obedience from a man by unlawful means is by definition an act of oppression. For people who accept such practices, much as they may recoil from the consistency with which they are applied by the police, virtually no abuses are recorded in this book.

For legislators and judges the police are a godsend, because all the acts of oppression that must be performed in this society to keep it running smoothly are pushed upon the police. The police get the blame, and the officials stay free of the stigma of approving their highhanded acts. The police have become the repository of all the illiberal impulses in this liberal society; they are under heavy fire because most of us no longer admit so readily to our illiberal impulses as we once did.

The welter of statutes intended to control morality by penalizing the possession of some contraband, or the act of vagrancy or loitering, pointedly reveals the hypocrisy in the administration of our laws. The legislature passes such statutes, knowing quite well that their enforcement encourages a host of police abuses, including unlawful searches, dragnet arrests, and systematic harassment. The links between these abuses and morals legislation is no accident; the impulse in each is the same. It is the drive to legislate the lives of others and to force them to adhere to an accepted mode of life; that impulse cannot be enforced without abusing the rights of citizens.

Viewed in this light, the distortions of fact by policemen, which we have pronounced at once the most dangerous and the most pervasive of abuses, do not seem quite so shocking or unnatural. Lying is a bridge between the substantively rational rules of the police and the formally rational ones of the criminal law, by which the first are made to appear to conform to the second.

The actions of the police probably embody a natural tendency of any group of bureaucrats, working out in the field where their decisions have low visibility, to avoid the effect of restrictive regulations that conflict with existing practices. A book similar to this could perhaps be written about welfare workers or even public school administrators. The effects of the conflict between rule and practice are more dramatic in the case of the police than of other bureaucrats because the victims of their practices wind up in jail, and more prolonged and exaggerated because of the traditional solidarity and secrecy of the police. Like many other minor bureaucrats before them, however, the police continue to adhere to their old customs because they know that their superiors and much of the rest of society approves. They have no motive to change.

Up to this point, I have made little effort to choose between the substantively rational rules of the police and the formally rational rules of the courts. Even without a choice between the two, the distortion of facts by the police is an inherently dangerous practice. In our society, law enforcement officers are expected to respond to civilian legal directives, and if they fail to do so, then the power of society to change its laws is significantly decreased, and the police in effect control the criminal law. But the covert adherence to another set of laws is not nearly so serious if in fact those laws are superior to, or just as good as, the stated laws. If the formally rational rules are unworkable or unnecessary, to avoid them is a relatively minor failing, because in the long run the laws themselves will probably change. It is not the function of this book to make value judgments about the effectiveness of the formal rules, but the problem cannot be ignored entirely if we are to understand the effect of police abuses.

We must at least look a little more deeply into the formal rules.

Let us consider, as an example, the requirements of "probable cause" for an arrest and search. The limitations of probable cause are established to make sure that the police arrest only people whom a neutral and rational observer would suppose to be guilty. A system of dragnet arrest and search would probably catch more persons carrying contraband than the application of probable cause, but the courts attempt to make a prior judgment so that those who are obviously or probably innocent will not be harassed. Any rule that relaxes the requirements of probable cause necessarily lowers the standards of suspicion and tends to include more innocent persons. As we have seen, police methods, when they depart from probable cause, do tend to punish innocent people together with the guilty. The point for use here is that the courts have made a policy judgment to exclude as many arrests of the innocent as possible, consistent with catching the obvious criminal. The rule of the courts, apart from being formally rational, also embodies a substantively rational rule *different* from that of the police, and the formal nature of the rule is intended to control police action and enforce the underlying substantive principle. The substantively rational police rule favors investigation so long as it is done in good faith, a policy judgment which is properly for the courts are better equipped to strike the balance between investigation and freedom. The police rule inevitably favors investigation—favors the authorities, in short. It is apparent, then, that the rule of the courts is not dryly logical or lacking in practical effectiveness, but is simply based on a judgment different from that of the police about the needs of society.

There are two principles underlying such procedural rules: first, that the elaboration of legal rules is properly a matter for the courts, and second, that the balance is properly struck on the side of personal liberty. Our society is suspicious of both these principles; it finds the police rules easier to grasp than the court rules. Though the incidence of police abuses may be reduced by institutional reforms, the police rules cannot change finally until society decides to disapprove of them. More citizens must come to accept the principle that the term "law enforcement" refers to enforcement of the laws and not to the arrest or harassment of defiant or deviant citizens. More citizens must come to accept the principle that all police abuses constitute the enforcement of a private code by unlawful means and that, as such, they are inherently oppressive. Too many people, in fact, understand this already and yet secretly (or openly) approve the acts of the police because they fear the defiance of others as much as do the police. They recognize that nearly every form of defiance of an authority, whether it be from a "wise" teen-ager, from the hippie way of life, or finally, from an open revolt by students or black people, is a demand for a new way of life both social and economic. They fear that demand for change enough to use force to oppose it, and unless that fear disappears, they will continue to condone police acts of oppression, and police rules will not change.

The saddest aspect of police abuses is that they defeat their avowed purposes.

The rationalization for street abuses is that they create or at least maintain respect for authority. Punishment for the wise guy is supposed to "teach him a lesson," but the system of police abuses creates only contempt for authority. A man, and especially the already defiant black man in this country, does not feel respect when he is clubbed, when he is charged with a crime, and when he loses his only job because he has been convicted. Words cannot convey the despair, the hatred, induced by a system which injures a man and then brands him as a criminal. It is not enough to say that the behavior of all the administrators involved—the officer, his superiors, the prosecutor, the judge—is understandable. The system within which the police work is evil, for the simplest of reasons: because it injures people and destroys their respect for the legal process. It is not for nothing that ghetto people have chosen police abuses as the symbol of oppression; it is because they actually *are* acts of oppression.

This brings us back to the importance of police abuses and the urgency of the problem they present. They are hardly the only acts of oppression in our cities, but they are the easiest to recognize. The anger they instill is part of the fuel for the violent uprisings in our cities during the past five years. As an indispensable condition for ending those uprisings, the police must change their allegiance from a private code to a publicly recognized rule of law, and it is only when society itself demands this change that it will take place.

An Open Letter on Police Review Boards

Edited by William H. Hewitt

EDITOR'S NOTE

The issue over police civilian review boards for America's municipal police forces is being heard in an ever-increasing volume. One of the major struggles in this dilemma is now occurring in New York City. The problem is so noteworthy and significant to our times that the editor thought the New York situation and, in particular, Commissioner Vincent L. Broderick's letter of February 9, 1966,

Professor William H. Hewit is with the Center for Law Enforcement and Corrections, The Pennsylvania State University, University Park, Pennsylvania 16802.

From William H. Hewitt, "An Open Letter on Police Review Boards," *Police* 10, no. 5 (May-June 1966): 33-35. Reprinted by permission of the author and the publisher, Charles C Thomas.

to Mayor John V. Lindsay should be made available to all serious students of professional police administration.

New York City is one of three American cities in the East which possess a civilian review board. The other two communities are Philadelphia and Rochester, New York. Commissioner Broderick himself advocates, as you will note from his following letter, a civilian review board. New York's present civilian review board consists of three civilians who are appointed Deputy Police Commissioners, none of whom has ever been a police officer. Two are lawyers and one is a former newspaperman. Their job is to deal with complaints from the public against the police.

The record of New York's Civilian Review Board for last year is very impressive. The Board heard 324 complaints, of which twelve resulted in formal charges by the department, seven policemen were reprimanded, and four other cases were referred to other public agencies. Ninety-six other complaints were thrown out as unsubstantiated and the remainder were pending at the end of the year. According to a recent New York Times editorial, "... persons claim it insulates the police from effective public protests and permits the department to sit in judgment on itself. Critics maintain that communication and trust between citizens and the 27,000 police has broken down, and that there have been increased incidents of police brutality, particularly against minority groups who are afraid to complain through exclusively police channels."

Mayor Lindsay's recently appointed "Law Enforcement Task Force," headed by former Federal Judge Lawrence E. Walsh, also recently advocated, in its written report, a civilian review board to adjudicate complaints. Because of this issue, Mayor Lindsay was not expected to reappoint Commissioner Broderick on February 21, 1966, when his term expires.

The distressing part is that the gap between the Commissioner and the Mayor never should have evolved in the first place. If one reads between the lines of the Task Force Report and the Commissioner's rebuttal, one senses that most of the Task Force proposals could have been readily reconciled with departmental procedure. The report, when studied closely, is not, in fact, a personal criticism of either the police or the Commissioner, but a series of recommendations for improving methods and practices that are the accumulation of decades. Most of the recommendations are certainly in concert with professional police administration. Note is taken in certain instances of improvements already made or in the making, and the department is commended for what it has accomplished.

The principal surface difference is over adding civilians to the present civilian review board. The present board is merely an advisory body. Under present procedure, civilian complaints are investigated by plainclothesmen and passed upon by a board of three deputy commissioners. Both the Mayor and the Task Force propose the addition of four civilians to the present three-man board. The New York Times, also in a recent editorial, came out in full support of this proposal.

Certainly there is no place for a civilian type review board in a police department. However, to let an issue gain momentum where a civilian board is already functioning without police personnel complaining and to possibly damage morale is in bad taste. If review boards are permitted to gain a foothold here, then who will investigate complaints against the Military Police, FBI, state police, sheriffs' departments, Treasury Department law enforcement agencies, Postal Inspectors, etc.

Following is the letter of the Commissioner of February 9, 1966, to Mayor John V. Lindsay. This letter was composed and presented by Mr. Broderick before his replacement as Police Commissioner by Howard R. Leary.

Dear Mr. Mayor:

We in the Police Department have carefully reviewed the report to you dated December 31, 1965 of the Law Enforcement Task Force, copies of which you made available to me on January 21, 1966. I enclose, herewith, a memorandum incorporating my specific comments thereon.

The task force has performed a distinctive public service in drawing to the attention of the citizens of New York various projects within the Police Department; in effect, in process or in the planning stage, which have thus far escaped public view.

The fact that the task force has set forth these projects as, in the main, its own proposals, without reference to the Police Department's role in developing them, is possible attributable to the haste with which the report was prepared, or perhaps to the expectation that in releasing the report you would make clear the extent to which so much of the sound thinking contained in the report has emanated from the department.

The fact of the matter is, Mr. Mayor, that most of the vital ideas contained in the task force report have been developed and explored within the department itself; that many of them have already been implemented and some are in the process of being implemented; that some of those not yet in effect require further planning or the availability of funds.

A strength of the report is, in fact, that it consolidates much of the original and imaginative thinking that has been done in the department in recent years. The vice is that it combines this with the bromides of the past. Because the task force was unwilling, or unable, to separate valid criticism and suggestions from undocumented folklore, the report will not, in my judgment, be a useful blueprint for the future.

Some of the ideas put forth in the task force report, and particularly some of the underlying assumptions, are simply wrong. It is important to underline, now, the extent to which they are wrong, before the report becomes a bible to which the uninformed turn for information.

If an informed member of this department had served on the task force, or as a consultant to the task force, I am quite sure that some of the clearly erroneous ideas and assumptions in the task force report could have been avoided. It is surprising, at best, that a task force dealing with the large problem of crime and the administration of justice in the City of New York had, on the committee itself and on its staff, no member of the New York City Police Department.

One of the basic premises of the report, that there is "a lack of strong public support for the police in the performance of their duties" is manifestly wrong. Never in the history of the city has public confidence in the Police Department been so high, or public support for the police been more vigorous. Your own experience in the transit shutdown must persuade you of this.

The remarkable feature of the task force report is what it does not say. Thus, it says nothing of the continuing successful effort which has been made in the past twelve years to divorce the Police Department from political interference and political control.

The Police Department of the City of New York has solidly advanced, in many areas, in the past twelve years; the first step in that advance, and a hallmark of its progress since, was the establishment in 1954 of the policy that politics was to be kept out of the Police Department and the Police Department was to be kept out of politics.

The Chicago Police Department has made remarkable progress under O. W. Wilson; but the first step in its progress was the establishment of the principle that O. W. Wilson, and not the political establishment, was to direct and control the Police Department.

Nor does the report say—and this is the fact, and hence a remarkable omission—that New York City has today the finest force in the world. I am sure that you realize this, Mr. Mayor, and I am sure that you realize it has only become such because it has been led, at every level of command, by imaginative, dedicated, forward-looking men.

You had occasion, during the recent campaign, to speak in laudatory terms of the Chicago Police Department under Superintendent Wilson, particularly in terms of its fight against violent crime.

I am sure that you realized then, as you must realize now, that the New York City Police Department does a more effective job, on a comparative basis, of containing violent crime than does Chicago or any other major city in this country; that we have less murder, rape, or felonious assaults in proportion to population than do Chicago or the other major cities.

I noted one other very significant omission in the task force report. Nowhere did I see any discussion of the importance of a strong, dedicated, and independent police commissioner in the administration of the Police Department. Yet, in my judgment, the police commissioner, his attitudes, and his policies, are the core of the effectiveness of this department.

If he will tolerate lax discipline, there will be lack of direction. If he will tolerate corruption, there will be corruption. If he will tolerate bias or prejudice in the enforcement of law, there will be such bias and prejudice. If he will tolerate laxity in the investigation of complaints, there will be such laxity.

If he will condone political interference on any level, in the administrative or operational processes of the department, then promotions and assignments will be made on the basis of political consideration rather than merit and need, and police officers will be deployed on the basis of relative political pressures rather than on the bases of balancing the needs of all areas and all peoples in the city.

If on the other hand, the police commissioner insists on a free hand to run the department in the interest of all the people of the city; if he insists upon vigorous discipline at all levels of command; if he makes it perfectly clear that corruption, bias, and prejudice will not be tolerated; and if he insists upon vigorous and effective investigation of all complaints, New York will continue to have, as it does today, a police force with an extraordinary level of morale, which has confidence in its leadership and a dedication to the public it serves, and the citizens of New York will continue to have, as they have today, a high confidence in and a great affection for their police.

The task force report is critical, I note, of the methods of selecting and advancing detectives. This criticism is not, in my judgment, well grounded. Merit—only merit—has been the touchstone which has determined, during my administration, which men serve as detectives and superior officers in the ranks above captain. Among the criteria considered have been integrity, experience, capacity, seniority, and evaluations by superior officers.

When a request was recently made to me by the office of the Deputy Mayor to hold open six first-grade detective positions for the Mayor, you swiftly made it very clear that you would brook no political interference with the Police Department.

I was gratified that you saw so promptly the importance, from the point of view of effective administration of justice and the integrity of the Police Department service, to subscribe publicly to such a policy. For 12 years no one but the Police Commissioner has selected and appointed deputy commissioners, superior officers, and detectives in this department.

This policy must continue and be rigidly adhered to. I was perturbed that the task force did not deem this question of the insulation of the Police Department from political interference sufficiently important to merit treatment.

And Now, Mr. Mayor, to the subject of an independent civilian complaint review board.

Mr. Mayor, there are many thousands of people in our city who desperately need our help. Many of our fellow citizens, Negro and Spanish-speaking, have been deprived of their full rights as citizens; they have been and are being discriminated against in housing and forced to live in ghetto areas; they have been and are being discriminated against in employment opportunities; many of them are forced to live today in a poverty so devastating that it is a trap from which they cannot escape. This is a municipal problem and it is a national problem. It is the pressing issue of our time.

Mr. Mayor, is it not about time that we as responsible leaders of the community, started to focus upon this problem and deal with it realistically? Is it not about time that we started to accord our fellow citizens a full measure of the human dignity which is theirs of right as children of God?

Is it not time that we commenced to marshal all the resources of this municipality, and to demand the marshaling of all of the resources of the state and federal governments, to help these, our fellow citizens, to help themselves?

And is it not time, Mr. Mayor, for responsible leaders such as yourself, to renounce this cruel hoax, this bromide, this palliative, of an independent civilian review board? Is it not time for us to stand up and say that we intend to deal with substance and not with shadow?

Is it not time for you as Mayor to say that you know that a civilian review board is shadow and not substance; that you realize the establishment of an independent board to review complaints against police officers will solve no problems and may create new problems?

Is it not time, Mr. Mayor, for you to say that you renounce political expediency; that you realize that the principal effect of an independent civilian review board will be to depress the morale of your Police Department and hence to impair its capacity to prevent crime?

Is it not time, Mr. Mayor, for you to say you have confidence in the capacity of your police commissioner effectively to administer and to discipline his department, and that you are aware of your obligation to replace him if he does not administer it and discipline it effectively?

You certainly must be aware, Mr. Mayor, that a police commissioner who does not take swift and effective action against a police officer who abuses his authority, or who uses undue force, is an incompetent police commissioner who must be replaced.

You must also know, Mr. Mayor, as the chief administrative officer of the greatest city in the world, that the question of who reviews complaints means very little if there is not an adequate investigation; that the obligation to see to it that there is a full, fair, and vigorous investigation is a function of command, and that if the police commissioner requires such an investigation with respect to any complaint, he will also see to it that the investigative report receives a full and fair review.

I oppose outside civilian review, Mr. Mayor, but not because I think it is unfair to police officers. I oppose it because it is an administrative travesty and is unfair to the public.

I oppose it because I am convinced that the effect of outside civilian review will be to lower the morale of the Police Department, and hence to dilute the nature and the quality of the protection which it will render to the public.

I am very much aware, Mr. Mayor, as I know you are, of the need, in our city, for sympathetic communication between our citizens and the police who serve them. I have done everything in my power to develop channels for such communication. I am certain that no Police Department has better relations with the public it serves than does our own.

And I am also certain, Mr. Mayor, that the public of this city wants police officers who will be alert and vigorous to act when the occasion demands. And this is perhaps more true, Mr. Mayor, of the citizens who live in the deprived areas of our city than those who live elsewhere. One of the sobering facts of urban life is that the crime rate tends to be highest in the most deprived areas, and the victims of this crime are the residents of those areas.

Require your police commissioner to maintain a vigorous and alert discipline, Mr. Mayor; be certain that he is committed to relentless investigation of claims made by citizens against the police and to fair and impartial disposition of those complaints. If he is not so committed, replace him forthwith. But do not, Mr. Mayor, dilute the police service of the city by undermining the administrative authority of the commissioner.

I advocate civilian review of complaints against police officers, Mr. Mayor. It is available today. The Police Department has a civilian complaint review board composed of three deputy commissioners, which painstakingly reviews the investigation of all complaints made by civilians against police officers and, where warranted, directs that disciplinary action be taken.

Each of these deputy commissioners is a civilian and has never been a police officer: two are lawyers, one a member of a minority group; one is a former newspaperman. Each of them is sophisticated in Police Department matters and knows when an investigative report, however carefully composed, is inadequate and should be sent back for further investigative work.

Each shares my commitment to a Police Department in which the abuse, verbal or physical, of a citizen by a police officer will not be tolerated. In my judgment, this department's civilian complaint review board is more thorough, more competent, more objective, and more conscientious than is any review board in any police department in the land.

There are, today, several other avenues of civilian review of complaints against police officers open to the citizen. The complaining citizen may apply to Criminal Court for a warrant; he may bring the matter to the District Attorney for presentation to a grand jury; he may seek financial redress in Civil Court; or he may complain to the Commissioner of Investigation.

An outside civilian complaint review board has become a rallying cry, Mr. Mayor, with some deceptive political appeal. But it is, I repeat, a cruel hoax. It has drained off energies which should be dealing, realistically, with basic problems of human relations, and, more deeply, with the underlying problems of poverty, discrimination, slums, inadequate schooling, and unemployment which beset our deprived communities today. Let us deal with these basic problems and not with shadows.

Assure yourself, Mr. Mayor, that your police commissioner shares your dedication to basic human liberty and basic human dignity, or else replace him with one who does. Then mandate him to administer and discipline the Police Department without interference from anyone.

Respectfully yours,
VINCENT L. BRODERICK

Police Brutality—Fact or Fantasy?

Thomas F. Adams

In view of considerable publicity on the subject, particularly during recent months, let us consider the problem of police brutality. Does it really occur as frequently and with such fervor as some of the more vociferous of our critics would have the general public believe? The fact that it has occurred cannot be denied. However, in most instances when a policeman's abuse of authority comes to the attention of a professional police administrator, the incident is thoroughly investigated and proper disciplinary action taken. We in the police service have just as much, if not far more, desire to keep sadists and emotionally unstable misfits and hotheads out of our departments. If a man is able to slip past his psychological testing and screening by a qualified psychiatrist and secure a position, and then later identifies himself as an individual of intolerance and abusive vocal or physical actions, he is positively not wanted and will be separated from the service.

In our modern society, let us look at the people who make up our community structure. There are the apathetic, the passive, the aggressive, the bigoted, the tolerant, the sympathetic, and the emotionally unstable. They have their longstanding likes, dislikes, prejudices, moral and ethical standards, and all of their other human strengths and weaknesses. From this same society are chosen the members of our police and other law enforcement agencies.

Once appointed, the new officer is properly advised by his chief and supervisors that the nature of his role in society requires that he maintain and display a neutral and impartial attitude while performing his official duties. He represents law and order in the entire community, and can no longer publicly identify himself with one small segment from whence he originated, or to which he belongs as a private individual. The truly professional police officer continues to think his personal thoughts as he chooses, but his actions reflect none of his private likes, prejudices, jealousies, or hatreds. No one can deprive him of his right to dislike green people who drive red sports cars, but if he should ever

From a speech presented to various service clubs during 1967-68 while the author was employed by the Santa Ana Police Department.

arrest one, it must be obvious that the arrest is precipitated by a violation of the law and not the personal bias of the officer.

Most charges of police brutality are accompanied by charges that the officer's actions were the result of personal motives, such as racial or political prejudice. Accusers imply that the officer entered into the combat situation with a preconceived hatred or dislike for his adversaries and a premeditated intention to cause the "opponents" some harm and even the deprivation of their personal liberty. It appears, then that police brutality can best be defined as an identifiable state of mind rather than specific acts of physical violence upon the person of another during incidents of physical conflict.

It is self-evident that someone will sustain injuries whenever a squad of police officers moves to quell a disturbance in which the participants are fighting each other and then turn on the police with knives, sticks, bricks, fire bombs, guns, stones, and bottles. It is the duty of the police to restore order by persuasion when possible, and by whatever force as is necessary. There can be no compromise with lawlessness on the streets of America; law and order must prevail. The officers are armed with firearms, night-sticks, sometimes tear gas, and whatever other special weapons that are necessary to get the job done as efficiently and effectively as possible. A well-trained officer must advance into such a situation with nothing more—or less—in mind than to preserve life and property with a minimum of injuries and property loss. His weapons are for defense, and are not weapons of aggression.

Let us look into the type of situations out of which charges of police brutality issue. There are daily complaints of police abuse for a variety of reasons, most of them baseless bids for sympathy or publicity, arising out of incidents involving single individuals or small groups; but the more serious charges arise during major incidents which receive nationwide, if not international, publicity.

A crowd composed of many individual persons is always watched by the police with some anticipation and apprehension, for it takes a crowd to make a mob, and in turn, an unlawful assembly or riot. If the crowd maintains its casual character there is little cause for concern and preservation of the peace is a routine assignment. The crowd is a collection of individuals, each with his own thoughts, emotions, needs, desires, moral and ethical standards, and self-control. Each is ruled by his own inhibitions and conscience. There is no overall organization in the crowd, nor is there any central leadership; each person is his own master.

With a few changes, the crowd can be transformed into a mob and incited to participate in a riot (some may have been planned) or the reaction may be spontaneous. The crowd may be gathered together for some common purpose, such as an accident, a sports event, or a demonstration. It may be a heterogeneous spontaneous crowd, or homogeneous as the crowd of young people at a football game. There may have been some preconditioning, such as rumors that two rival factions were going to be present and that they were going to "settle their differences"; or press coverage on racial, political or labor-management strife may have indicated impending trouble; then the preconditioning transforms the current situation, such as the actual meeting of opposing factions. The crowd may find itself drawn together into an emotionally responsive volatile mob.

The mob, which started as a crowd composed of individuals, now becomes characterized by its homogeneity (perhaps not original, but now its goal to become unruly, to cause injury to each other, and damage to property), emotionality (tempers are lost beyond reason), and its irrationality. The individuals comprising the crowd are no longer individuals—they are merely parts of a seething grossly unruly mass of humanity caught up into the web of collective hypnosis. The mob is unresponsive to reason, there are no inhibitions or earlier training habits of respect for authority to which one may appeal. The many subjects are anonymous and take advantage of their desire to release repressed passions and emotions with the delirium of their new-found unexplained euphoria. Along with the formation of the mob evolves leadership—imported or spontaneous—by one or many persons who stimulate action by words and by example, who organize the many individuals into a single responsive unit. They gain a motive for action—such as defiance to authority, wresting an arrestee from the custody of a police officer, killing or maiming an innocent victim—which may have been suggested by someone with a real motive of retaining his own anonymity by using the mob to accomplish his own insidious purpose. There is only one way to render the mob ineffective and restore the individuals to their senses—some sort of dramatic action, a task usually left to the devices of the police.

The action taken by the police during the first few minutes following their arrival at the scene of a riot or unlawful gathering often determines the course of events for the remainder of the situation. At the time of initial contact, talk is oftentimes ineffective, it goes unheard and unheeded. Order must be restored, so an organized team of officers with a show of force and strength must be utilized if the situation is to be handled with dispatch with a minimum amount of casualties and property loss. The moment of initial contact by the police with the mob is the moment of truth: will it be later touted and applauded as a necessary and successful police tactical maneuver, or will it be tagged with a label of police brutality?

Two elements are essential to assure a favorable verdict in the eyes of the beholders when such dramatic crowd control tactics are necessarily employed by the police. They are *professional impartial attitude* of the officers, and *objective and unbiased acceptance* by the public. The first element is primarily the responsibility of police administrators in proper selection of new members for the police service, and in framing professional attitudes of the officers once selected. The latter element is the mutual responsibility of the police and the public in reaching a common understanding of the purposes of the police in preserving the peace and protecting life and property by persuasion when possible, and by force whenever necessary. Law and order must prevail if we are to preserve our American way of life.

Lawmen Insist Only More Men Can Curb Street Crime

John Dreyfuss

It was a normal Tuesday in Los Angeles.

Two thugs shoved a 61-year-old man into the shade of a phone booth, hit him on the head with a hard object and threw him face down on the sidewalk. The would-be robbers, each half their victim's age, were scared off by the man's screams. They left him bleeding from gashes in his head.

A 59-year-old waiter was accosted in daylight by two young men and a girl. "If you don't give me any money I'll hit you on the head," one youth said, displaying a heavy iron bar.

The waiter gave him 75 cents, and the trio walked to a car and drove off.

A single purse-snatcher grabbed three purses at one intersection. It was a normal Tuesday. A Tuesday on which the list of unprovoked street crimes in Los Angeles County continued to grow at an alarming rate.

Often crimes against pedestrians lead to more than a gashed head, the loss of 75 cents or stolen purses. Last month a 48-year-old transient was knocked unconscious, then his throat was slit with his own pocket knife. The murder was committed in daylight in a Compton alley. Three teen-age boys were held on suspicion of murder. One reportedly told a policeman, "One of us did it for no reason at all."

In a middle-class Los Angeles neighborhood, Sidney Raycraft was brutally knifed to death near his home for no apparent reason. He had a wife and nine children. Who slugs, robs and murders pedestrians? The street criminal is usually a young man—often a teen-ager. His victim is usually elderly—often a woman. The robber is most often someone who has nothing to lose. He may get 25 cents for a robbery, and getting caught can mean prison. But in jail the offender may find himself better off than he was on the outside. At least he gets clean sheets and three meals a day.

From John Dreyfuss, "Lawmen Insist Only More Men Can Curb Street Crime: But New Ways Tried in Attempt to Halt Violence," *Los Angeles Times* 9 July 1967, p. 1, Sec. C. Copyright ©1967 by the *Los Angeles Times*. Reprinted by permission of the publisher.

Putting the street robber in jail is not easy. He is an elusive culprit. It takes only five seconds to scan the street for a police car, club a victim, rob him and run. On whom does the street criminal prey? On everyone, police say. The incidence of street crime is highest in the low socio-economic areas. But the mugger, purse-snatcher, street robber and murderer roam even the finest neighborhoods.

Many victims of crime in the streets never see their assailant. Others catch only a glimpse of a fleeing figure. Older persons who do see their attacker often have trouble remembering his appearance. Regardless of age, a street robbery victim seldom takes methodical note of his assailant's looks. Most street robbers escape.

RATE HERE SOARS

Reported street robberies in Los Angeles have soared in the past 10 years from 1,711 to 3,073 annually. The same story, more or less, is told by police departments from New York to San Diego, from Seattle to Miami.

In Los Angeles city and county, Police Chief Tom Reddin and Sheriff Peter J. Pitchess agree on how to solve the skyrocketing street crime problem— hire more men to patrol the streets.

Reddin wants to build his force from 5,329 to 11,200 officers. Pitchess says he needs 1,200 more deputies, for a total of 4,843 to police the county and 29 cities who contract for Sheriff's Department services.

But neither man is waiting for more officers to help make the streets safe. Both have developed methods to make life a little harder for the street thug.

Pitchess' deputies search from the air for street criminals. Seven nights a week, and much of every day, two deputies in a helicopter criss-cross the 34-square mile Lakewood area south of Los Angeles. The mere presence of the chopper has cut crime in Lakewood.

Not long ago, deputies Jim Pierce and Richard West were aloft on a predawn patrol when they spied a man struggling to force a woman into his car. The officers landed in a nearby intersection. When the amazed suspect roared away in his car, the deputies took off and swooped after him. He was quickly apprehended by a patrol car directed from the air.

Financial problems have slowed to a crawl two other sheriff's department operations against street crimes: Operation Crime Free and a sheriff's anti-robbery platoon, both aimed at saturating high-crime areas with peace officers.

Tried three times, the operations were termed successful by Sheriff Pitchess. But their futures are uncertain. "We'd like to use both operations more often," the sheriff said, "but we're kept tied up with day-to-day operations. Our acute shortage of manpower makes it impossible to field the deputies necessary for Operation Crime Free and the anti-robbery platoon."

The sheriff also maintains a 40-man Special Enforcement Bureau to deploy in trouble areas. When the rate of crime against pedestrians climbs in a district, bureau members can be assigned to patrol the streets.

In the Los Angeles Police Department, Capt. Joseph Stephens heads an elite 82-man squad similar to the Special Enforcement Bureau. It has successfully slowed street crime.

The Metropolitan Squad goes where it's needed. It answers no standard calls and concentrates exclusively on specific trouble spots.

Although they often wear uniforms, Capt. Stephens' officers are likely to be seen in any sort of clothing, ranging from tuxedos to swimming trunks.

Recently, 23 Metro Squad men spent two weeks patrolling four square miles in a high-crime district. They cut street crime by 17 percent.

During the patrol period two Metro Squad men spotted a husky, 17-year-old boy meandering along the sidewalk behind a couple in their 50s. The patrol car spotlight revealed a kitchen knife gleaming in the boy's left hand. Jumping from their car, the policemen arrested the youth and almost certainly saved the couple from a violent robbery.

When the crime situation demands it, any police division will saturate areas under its jurisdiction with unusually large numbers of officers.

Explorer Posts have been organized to train teen-agers in police methods, encouraging young men to become officers.

Pamphlets on crime prevention are published. Community relations officers maintain close contact with neighborhoods offering help and advice where needed.

PLAN STUDY GROUP

Still in the planning stages is the Tactical Operations Planning Group. Chief Reddin described the group's primary objective as "determining the most efficient method of using the Los Angeles Police Department's total resources to prevent street crime."

The group's experiments may include increasing motorcycle patrols in high-crime areas, using bicycles, increasing walking patrols, varying the number of men in cars and using more plainclothes officers. "In fact," Reddin said, "the Tactical Operations Planning Group will try just about any crime prevention method one can think of."

With so much effort being expended to cut street crime, why is it soaring? "There are more people and relatively fewer policemen in the street, that's the crux of it," Chief Reddin said.

While the chief's answer is correct, it is incomplete, according to Dr. Edward Stainbrook, chairman of the psychiatry department at USC and chief psychiatrist at Los Angeles County General Hospital.

"People in the lower socio-economic classes see the affluent society around them," the psychiatrist told *The Times,* "so they are stimulated to get the same kind of power and resources the other people appear to have. They develop an aggressive attitude in order to get what they want the only way they believe they can get it." The solution, as Dr. Stainbrook sees it, lies in education and employment for street criminals and potential street criminals.

Los Angeles area peace officers are trying to curtail current street crime as well as seeking long-range solutions—and they are joined by law enforcement agenices in every major city across the nation.

New York City's 27,834-man police force uses 130 radio-equipped motor scooters. Officers on scooters do the same job as foot patrolmen, but cover more ground and are seen by more persons, said Dep. Commissioner Jacques Nevard. Plans call for more than doubling the number of police scooters in New York next year. In the past year, the New York City Police Department has increased its patrol cars by more than 50 percent. More than 500 officers have been pulled off clerical jobs to go on street duty.

A 1954 experiment in New York proved that doubling police manpower in a Harlem precinct cut street crimes by 70 percent in a four-month period. A similar experiment, seeking simultaneously to put more men in uniform and give them the latest communications equipment, is under way in New York.

Chicago police have enlisted the aid of drivers of radio-equipped taxis and trucks. They radio their employers if they see any thing suspicious, and the employers immediately report to the police. Chicago also has instituted a community relations program to ferret out trouble spots, developed a computer system to help assign officers to high-crime areas, and raised patrolmen's pay from $410 to $556 a month since 1960. (Corresponding Los Angeles Police Department salaries have increased since 1960 from $464 to $677. Deputy sheriffs' pay has jumped from $489 to $677).

Street crime increases in San Francisco cannot be attributed to any single factor, according to that city's Police Chief Thomas Cahill. But one factor he cited was "social change" in his city. He said the change requires valuable police manpower to control demonstrations, rallies and marches. In Washington, D.C., Police Chief John B. Layton deploys a tactical force of 250 officers who work on their days off for extra pay.

DOGS FIND ROLE

Washington police also use scooters, and Layton said a canine corps has been effective in helping to apprehend and deter street criminals. Detroit's police department recently created two new details to fight crime in the streets.

The Youth Investigation Bureau surveys the behavior of established delinquents in an effort to learn their motivation. The bureau uses its information to help prevent other youngsters from becoming criminals.

A Police Precinct Support Unit in Detroit keeps men and cars ready to move into any precinct where a crime has occurred. Philadelphia has developed Tactical Foot Patrols. They consist of three to five policemen who park their car in a high crime area and then patrol on foot.

When will the street crime problem be solved in Los Angeles? Considering the bleak outlook for putting more policemen and deputies on the streets, Sheriff

Pitchess and Chief Reddin gave the same answer to that question. "The Los Angeles area street crime problem will not be solved."

Impact—Detroit

Detroit Police Department

Obviously strained beyond operational capabilities, this program reflects one department's effort to provide professional services under extreme hardships of demands far exceeding the limits of manpower and equipment.

RE: YOUR LETTER OF OCTOBER 6, 1970; SCREENING OF TELEPHONE REQUESTS FOR POLICE SERVICE. (GENERAL ORDER NO. 2145)

In 1965 the department formed a Communications and Procedures (CAP) Committee. The Committee was composed of executive, line, and staff officers. One of the prime objectives of the committee was to provide a method of separating incoming emergency calls from thousands of routine administrative calls handled by a single switchboard. During the past few years the department experienced an average of nearly 50,000 additional requests for service (runs) annually. The committee examined the areas in which the patrol force was committed to certain nonpolice responses. A recommendation was made to carefully screen certain types of calls in order to insure that vital police service was available when needed. Acting on the recommendations of the CAP Committee, on March 29, 1966, the Deputy Superintendent issued an order to all members of the department prescribing screening procedures.

On April 1, 1966, this department launched Project IMPACT, the introduction of a new two-number telephone system. At this time we received full coverage from the news media.

On two separate occasions the department has issued guidelines for the screening of telephone requests for police services. The first issue, March 29, 1966 (Addendum I), was primarily developed for Communications Division personnel. The second issue, August 19, 1968 (Addendum II), was a refined restatement in order to insure department-wide uniformity of screening procedures. Addendum III is the first page of General Order #2145 after necessary revisions. The two graphs depict the actual "runs dispatched" since the

This letter and General Order were received from the Commissioner of the Detroit Police Department and are reprinted with the permission of that department.

inauguration of IMPACT as opposed to projected runs that would have been dispatched without IMPACT screening.

Citizen complaints have been minimal compared to the total volume of requests for service. The majority of complaints from the public in this area are generally based on "no service or slow response" due to the unavailability of patrol cars.

DETROIT POLICE DEPARTMENT
Office of the Commissioner

General Order No. 2145
August 19, 1968

TO ALL MEMBERS OF THE DEPARTMENT:

Subject: The Screening of Telephone Request for Police Service

To insure that vital police service will be available when needed, the following guidelines have been developed for screening telephone requests for police service.

Effective immediately, officers receiving telephone requests for police service shall use the following steps:

1. To determine whether a scout car is needed, officers shall adhere to the guidelines set forth in General Order No. 2145.
2. If the situation warrants police service, the officer shall inform the caller that a scout car will be sent as soon as one is available; he will promptly relay the necessary information to the IMPACT Board or by direct line to the concerned dispatcher.

The objective of the screening is to determine whether or not an officer is needed at the scene. Before denying or granting a request for police service, the guides outlined should be closely considered as well as the complainant's ability to make an in-person report without great inconvenience.

If an officer cannot determine whether a car should be dispatched or if the caller is insistent although his request is not within the guidelines, the call may be referred to a supervisory officer for disposition.

When extenuating circumstances are present and an officer feels a car should be dispatched although the guidelines preclude it, a request may be made to the supervisor in charge of the IMPACT Center by the supervisor in charge where the call emanated.

I. ASSAULTS

A. *Misdemeanor Assaults and Threats of Assault*

When all three factors below are present, advise the complainant to report the incident to any precinct station. If he wishes to prosecute, he shall apply in person to the detectives in the precinct where the assault took place at 8:00 A.M. weekdays.

1. There is no injury or there is an injury but immediate medical attention is not required.
2. It appears reasonable that no further assault is imminent.
3. The identity of the assailant is known to the victim.

B. *Felonious Assaults*

Scout cars will normally be dispatched on felonious assault complaints unless:
1. the assault was not promptly reported and the complainant is not in need of medical attention; and
2. the reporting delay will not hinder the apprehension of the defendant.

When both of these factors are present, the complainant should be advised as noted above for simple assaults.

II. LARCENIES

Generally, a car shall not be dispatched to the scene of a larceny when:
1. it is not reported promptly after discovery; or
2. if the report is being made only to meet insurance requirements; or
3. if the property taken is not readily identifiable and the possibility of apprehending the perpetrator by an immediate response is remote.

In these instances, advise the caller to report the larceny at any precinct at any time.

III. MALICIOUS DESTRUCTION OF PROPERTY

Generally, cars shall not be dispatched to answer complaints of MDP if:
1. the incident is not promptly reported after discovery; or
2. the report is being made only to meet insurance requirements; or
3. the value of the property is small and the possibility of an immediate apprehension is remote or if the perpetrator is known to the complainant.

In these instances, advise the caller to report the incident to any precinct station.

IV. FAMILY TROUBLE

Family trouble is basically a civil matter. It is not a police function to arbitrate or undertake negotiations in marital difficulties. If the complaint constitutes an assault, advise the party as in other assault cases. If the caller does not wish to prosecute, other referrals may be made depending on the nature of the complaint.

Alcoholics—refer to Alcoholics Anonymous (WO 1-6982)

Mentally disturbed—refer to City Physician's Office, Detroit General Hospital (861-3381)

Needing legal advice—refer to private attorney or the Legal Aid Society (833-2980)

Spiritual counseling—refer to a clergyman

Family counseling—refer to the Family Service Association of America (831-1300)

A. *Return of Personal Effects*
   The department cannot provide an escort for persons securing their personal effects. This is a civil matter.
B. *Trouble with Son or Daughter*
   Complainants of noncriminal misbehavior of juveniles should be referred to the Women's Division or the Youth Bureau whichever is appropriate. If the son or daughter is an adult, refer the caller to one of the agencies noted above.
C. *Nonsupport*
   Nonsupport complaints should be referred to:
   Recorder's Court (Enforcement Division)
   1321 St. Antoine, room 330
   phone: 963-7440
   If a valid warrant is outstanding, a vehicle shall be dispatched.

V. NEIGHBOR TROUBLE
   A. *Property Disputes*
      Disputes over property lines, overhanging tree limbs, shrubbery and fences, etc., are civil matters. Advise the caller to consult an attorney.
   B. *Children Complaints*
      Unless children have clearly violated laws or ordinances, advise the complainant to seek satisfaction with the children's parents or to contact the precinct Youth Bureau or the Women's Division, as applicable.

VI. LANDLORD-TENANT TROUBLE
   Landlord complaints such as nonpayment of rent, eviction, tenant's carelessness with landlord's property, and similar complaints are civil matters. Complaints of inadequate heating, or withdrawal of other utility services and unsanitary building conditions shall be referred to the Board of Health, Substandard Housing Division, phone 965-4200, ext. 444.

VII. SICK OR INJURY CALLS
   A. *Private Dwellings*
      If the caller describes the illness or condition as a cut finger, headache, toothache, doctor or hospital appointment, trip to drugstore, fever and chills and similar minor conditions, advise the caller that the Police Department provides transportation in emergency cases only and suggest the following course of action:
      1. call a friend, relative or neighbor for transportation;
      2. call a taxi or utilize other public transporation;
      3. call a private ambulance service; or
      4. call the City Physician's Office if the caller indicates no funds are available.
      When from the conversation with the caller, it appears that the victim is suffering a stroke, severe difficulty in breathing or a heart attack, a Detroit Fire Department Rescue Squad or a police vehicle will be sent.

If the caller indicates other serious illness or miscellaneous injury, i.e., serious bleeding, hysteria, miscarriage, etc., or the caller is alone and cannot respond to adequate questioning, a vehicle shall be dispatched. Attempt to determine if a station wagon is required.

B. *Public Place*

Generally, when a person suffers illness or injury in a public place that requires medical attention, a vehicle shall be dispatched.

VIII. MATERNITY CASES

When a caller requests transportation for an expectant mother experiencing ordinary childbirth, advise the caller of the alternatives listed under Sick and Injury Calls.

IX. MENTAL ILLNESS

When a physician has prepared a written order that a person is mentally ill, Michigan State Law demands that the police convey the subject to a hospital or other place of confinement.

In cases where a caller describes a person as "crazy," "insane," or "psychotic" the caller shall be advised to contact the City Physician's Office. If the caller indicates that the party has homicidal or other dangerous tendencies, a car shall be dispatched and action may be taken as directed by Chapter 9, Section 71, of the Police Manual.

X. ANIMALS

A. *Animal bites*

It is not normally a police function to treat or convey persons bitten by an animal. A car will not be sent unless:

1. the victim was bitten by an unknown dog or other animal that is still at large; or
2. when the victim is bitten on the head or face; or
3. when the injuries from the bite are serious enough to require immediate medical attention.

If the above factors are not present, the caller shall be advised to take the victim (or go himself shall he be the victim) to a doctor. He shall report the animal bite to the Department of Health before or after treatment. Telephone no. 872-3334, between the hours of 8:00 A.M. and 11:00 P.M. daily, seven days per week.

Note: The Department of Health recommends medical attention to an animal bite within 72 hours. In the interest of public safety, recommend treatment within 24 hours.

B. *Dead or Injured*

In the event of an injured animal, advise the caller to contact one of the following:

Dog Pound	825-5770
Michigan Humane Society	872-3400
Anti-Cruelty Association	891-7188 (24 hours)

In the event of a dead animal, the caller shall be advised to contact the Department of Public Works.

East Side   921-1679
West Side   825-0981

Large injured animals that constitute a danger to public safety or constitute a traffic hazard, and cannot be removed due to a lack of equipment of above agencies shall be given police attention.

XI. ACCIDENTS—VEHICULAR

When a call is received for police services at the scene of an automobile accident, determine the following:
1. Was anyone injured?
2. Was there damage to city property?
3. Was either driver under the influence of liquor or narcotics?
4. Was this a hit-run accident?
5. Can the car move under its own power?

If the answer is NO to questions 1 through 4, and YES to question 5, the caller shall be advised to report the accident at any precinct station.

Police shall be dispatched in noninjury type accidents described above only when extreme extenuating circumstances demand police service.

XII. STREET DEFECTS

Advise the caller to telephone the Street Maintenance and Construction Division of the Department of Public Works, 826-5900, during normal business hours. Police shall be dispatched only when the street defect is a hazard to public safety and temporary traffic control is required until the affected city department can get a crew to the site. (Patrolling officers will continue to report such defects when encountered.)

XIII. RUBBISH COMPLAINTS

If the caller is complaining that his own rubbish is involved, he shall be advised to telephone the Sanitation Division of the Department of Public Works, 832-2400, during normal business hours of 8:00 A.M. to 4:00 P.M. If the caller is complaining that the rubbish of others is a problem, he shall be advised to telephone the enforcement officers of the Department of Health Sanitation, 871-1922.

Requests for general information are often received by phone. Replies to these inquiries shall be courteous and to the point. Care should be taken that no misinformation be given. If the correct information is not available, it is better to reply that this is not a police matter and that the answer to the query is not known. If possible, the party should be referred to any department having jurisdiction or any public or social agency concerned.

Requests for police service not requiring an immediate police response, i. e., report of vacant homes, traffic complaints, abandoned cars and other complaints or conditions that require precinct or special unit attention shall be handled by the precinct or unit concerned.

JOHANNES F. SPREEN
Commissioner

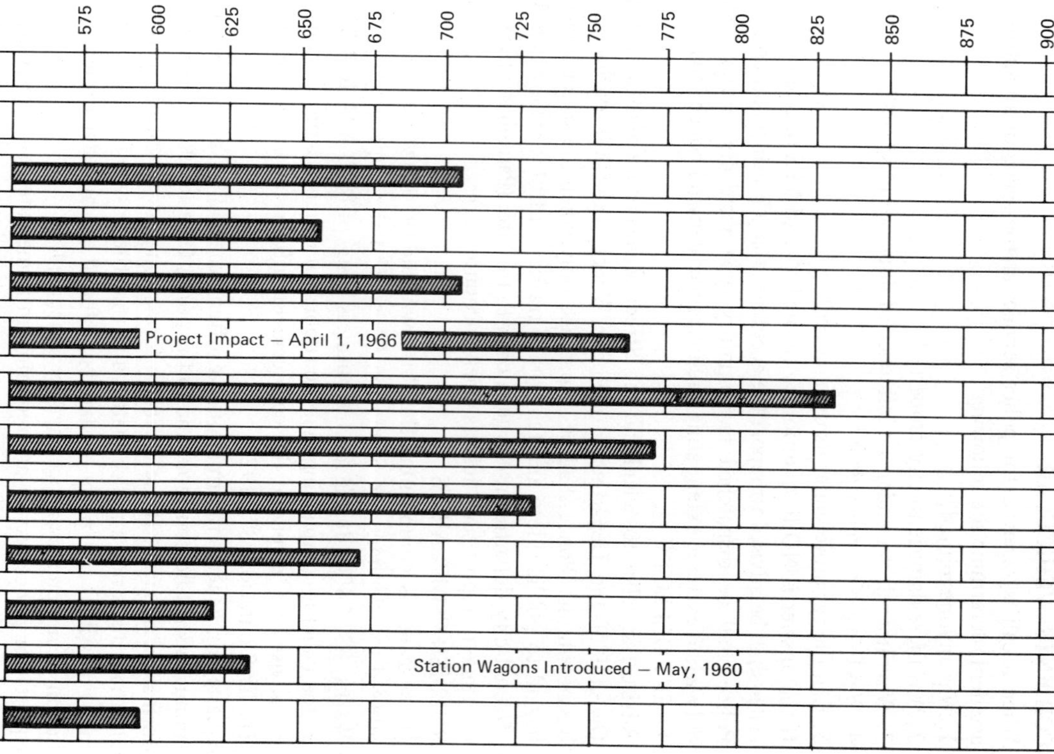

DISPATCH RUNS-11 YEAR PERIOD WITH IMPACT SCREENING

Year	Total Runs	+Increase −Decrease Over Prev. Yr.
1971		
1970		
1969	704,105	+46,823
1968	657,282	−49,225
1967	706,507	−48,634
1966	755,141	−70,110
1965	825,251	+54,672
1964	770,579	+40,468
1963	730,111	+56,225
1962	673,886	+50,614
1961	623,272	−11,845
1960	635,117	+43,541
1959	591,576	−11,962

Project Impact — April 1, 1966

Station Wagons Introduced — May, 1960

328

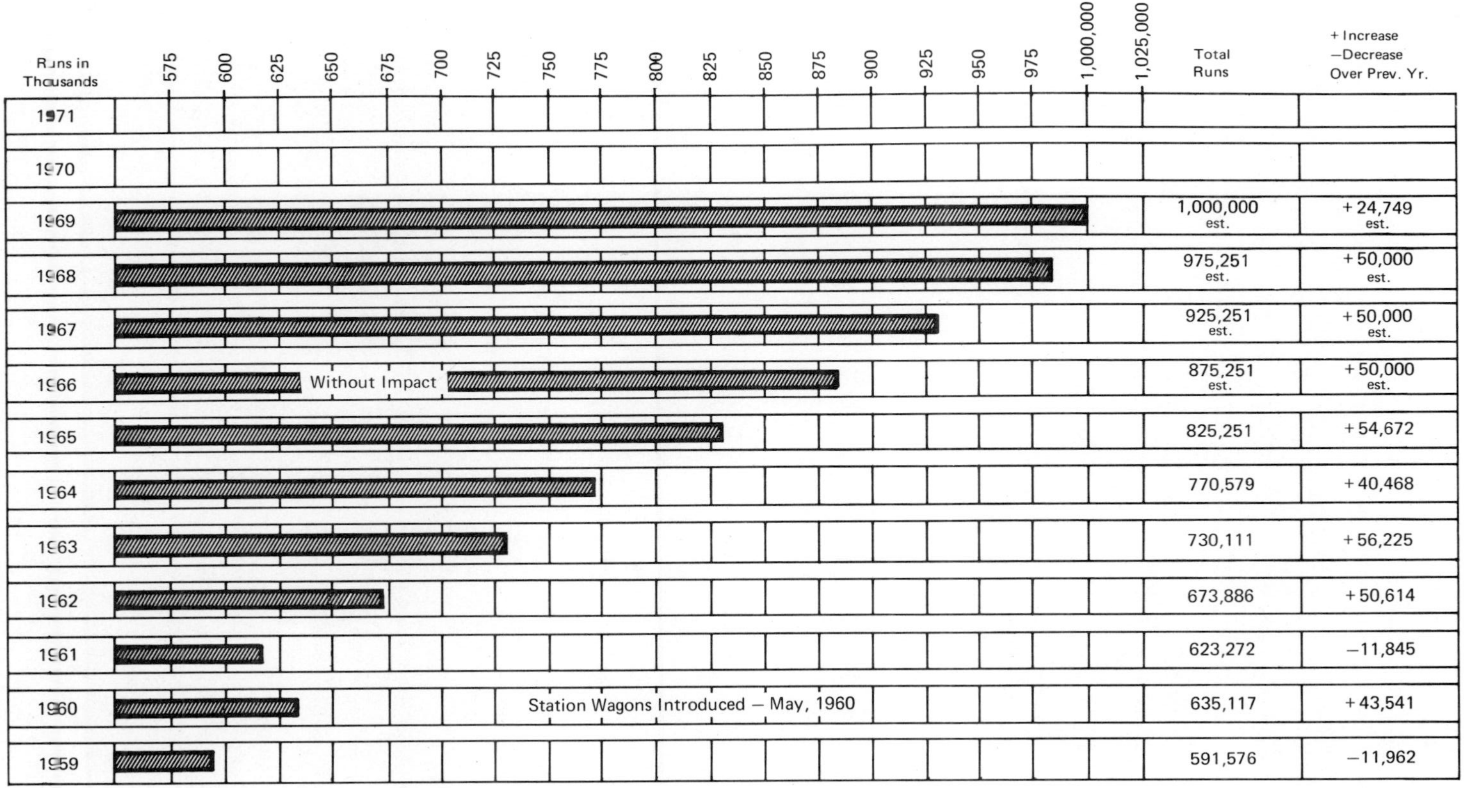

Runs in Thousands	Total Runs	+Increase −Decrease Over Prev. Yr.
1971		
1970		
1969	1,000,000 est.	+24,749 est.
1968	975,251 est.	+50,000 est.
1967	925,251 est.	+50,000 est.
1966	875,251 est.	+50,000 est.
1965	825,251	+54,672
1964	770,579	+40,468
1963	730,111	+56,225
1962	673,886	+50,614
1961	623,272	−11,845
1960	635,117	+43,541
1959	591,576	−11,962

Without Impact (1966)

Station Wagons Introduced — May, 1960

DISPATCH RUNS-11 YEAR PERIOD Projected Increase—NO SCREENING

329

SECTION SEVEN

Community Relations

Overview

THE POLICE ROLE IN COMMUNITY RELATIONS. This is an address by the late Chief William H. Parker of Los Angeles. For several years that department has been an aggressive leader in community relations. Chief Parker's address in 1955 reflected an overview of his department's community relations philosophy at that time, which is still considered a "lighthouse" on the uncharted and unpredictable sea of community realtions. Equality of law enforcement was Chief Parker's central theme.

THE FRINGES OF POLICE-COMMUNITY RELATIONS—EXTREMISM. Nelson A. Watson of the International Association of Chiefs of Police addresses the increasing problem of extremism as it affects law enforcement activities—a critical problem that calls for intelligent action. This article discusses a wide variety of extremist organizations representing a broad spectrum of political and social philosophies. Not only is the article well written, but it offers some suggestions for at least addressing—if not solving—the problem.

POLICE AND POLITICS: SPEAK OUT ON THE ISSUES. This is a refreshing approach to an often-debated problem—police involvement in politics. In *LAW ENFORCEMENT: An Introduction to the Police Role in the Community*, it is recognized that policemen should not become publicly involved in partisan politics, thereby taking on the posture of hyphenated and politically tainted policemen. In this article, Mark H. Furstenberg suggests a different type of nonpartisan political participation by the police. Is it appropriate for the police officer to speak out on the issues that involve law enforcement? Read this provocative article and form your own opinion, then speak out at least on Furstenberg's proposal.

COMMUNITY INDIFFERENCE AND THE GROWTH OF CRIME. Professor Frank D. Day of Michigan State University candidly discusses the problem of public apathy and noninvolvement in the relevant context of the growing crime rates in the United States. Day's indifferent community includes some police officers—who are similarly indifferent to the problem of doing something about indifference. The alternative to the indifference—of course—is meaningful involvement.

COMMUNITY ORGANIZATION AS A SOLUTION TO POLICE-COMMUNITY RELATIONS. Dr. Oscar Handlin, distinguished Professor of History at Harvard University proposes that both the police and the citizens in our community seek a way to develop a relationship with each other based on a mutual trust and understanding. Distrust and misunderstanding of the police role is a condition that has existed for more than 150 years. Dr. Handlin points out that the solution to the problem will require considerable effort on the part of all persons involved.

The Police Role in Community Relations

William H. Parker

Within a few hundred miles of this point, a group of scientists are devising what they call "an improved nuclear device." We do not know its range of total destruction or its date of completion. But this much we do know—its power is such that its designers live in dread and apprehension of the forces they have created. And across the seas, other scientists, using other languages, race to surpass our weapons. The power of total destruction may lie within our immediate future. Each second which passes brings man nearer the moment of awesome and irrevocable decision.

As this moment of supreme crisis draws near, we have gathered to discuss community affairs. And I think it is only right to ask whether our subject is rendered meaningless by the uncertain future; whether our preoccupation with simple day-to-day matters, is really very important.

In answering this question, I believe we approach the true import of this Institute. The small problems, the seemingly petty issues we discuss today, are in reality neither small nor petty. Our subject is not overshadowed by the great

From William H. Parker, "The Police Role in Community Relations," in *Parker on Police,* ed. O. W. Wilson (Springfield, Ill.: Charles C Thomas, 1957), pp. 135-46. Reprinted by permission of the author and the publisher, Charles C Thomas.

international disputes and their deadly consequences. Rather, the reverse is true. The great crisis which compels our attention was born in the inequities, the blind passions, and the senseless conflicts which furnish our subject. Conflicts begin not between nations or blocs of nations, but between men. If there is an absolute and enduring solution to conflict it will not be found at levels where ministers of state propound compromises. It will be found at the everyday level of social intercourse—in our homes, or on our streets, and in our individual consciences.

My initial premise, then, is that community relations problems are not an unrealistic and relatively unimportant concern, but a vital issue—a question of human weakness and society's failure to control that weakness.

You will note I did not say "correct" human weakness. Let me repeat. Community relations is a question of human weakness and society's failure to control that weakness. If social equity and tranquility were dependent upon perfection of the species, then despair might well keynote this conference. If our discussions are to produce results, there is one fact which must dominate all our thinking—we have not solved the human equation. Lacking a solution to human imperfection, we must learn to live with it. The only way I know of safely living with it is to control it.

When one man assaults another or one group violently flaunts the rights of another group, the immediate and pressing issue is the conflict, not the beliefs which incited it. We have not yet learned to control what men believe, but we can control what men do. I do not deny for a moment that the final solution is the perfection of human conscience. But in the interim, and it may be a long interim, we must have order.

My second premise, then, is that social order is the first concern of those interested in improved community relations. It provides, not a perfectly equitable pattern of life, but at least a peaceful arena in which those inequities can ultimately be solved. Community order works another advantage which, to my mind, has never been properly assessed. Man is a creature of habit, not of hate. Order, even though it is enforced order—nonviolent conduct, despite intolerant and discriminatory beliefs—creates among the peoples of the community habitual patterns of conduct. I suspect that this habit of order, like any other habit, can be so ingrained into the human mind that it will displace baser instincts.

Let me make it abundantly clear at this point, I do not recommend and will never support a police state. My interest is not in more regulation or tighter restrictions on human liberty. I have no interest in broadening police powers. I am concerned that existing police responsibilities, those vital to a peaceful productive society, be professionally and effectively discharged.

Our laws are far from perfect, but even so they are sufficient for the maintenance of human intercourse without violent conflict. That these laws have not prevented violence is not the fault of the laws but of the manner in which they are construed and enforced. I intend to outline here, a realistic and immediately practical program for securing and maintaining social order within the limits of existing legislation.

Some will question the confinement of the discussion to the bare limits of legal propriety. I would like to dispose of those questions now. What of freedom of economic opportunity? What of effective de-segregation in business and professions, as well as in schools? What of the multitude of "gentlemen's agreements," the harmful, though not actually illegal actions, which relegate some groups to second-class citizenship? Are these not also important questions, some of them as damaging and painful as actual physical violence? The answer must be in the affirmative. But these evils will never be eliminated, so long as conflict keeps alive the beliefs that created them. In the ruins of mob action, in the pain of physical assault, and in the renewed and intensified hates and fears which follow violence—there are no solutions. Conflict does not beget peace. But where people can walk together and live together and do business together without violence, an affirmative step has been taken.

Under our system of government, any discussion of enforced order is necessarily a discussion of local police agencies. We have no national police; legislative and judicial branches of government are prohibited from usurping police powers; our armed forces can be used civilly only under the gravest and most extraordinary emergencies. Our rich and complex economic system, our political freedom, the very conduct of our way of life, is made possible because of the security provided by local police agencies. Indeed, the entire social structure is balanced upon patterns of order created by community law enforcement.

This is quite a balancing act. Historically, it is a rare concept; few nations have rested so much on so slender a foundation. Recognizing this, it would appear that excellence of the police would be a principal and constant concern of community leaders. Their selection, their training, their morale would seem to be of critical importance. Understanding all this, certainly our leaders should have provided the police with the finest young men, the most capable leaders, the wisest counsel. That we have not done these things is as obvious as it is regrettable. The disorder and violence which troubles us as we meet here today, is part of the price we pay for our neglect.

There is in existence today a community which has decided that the price is too high. It is a case study in the successful application of enforced order to the problem of community relations. I have had the good fortune of taking an active part in the experiment. I have watched it mature during 28 years of service as a professional police officer.

I refer your attention to Los Angeles. That city is, today, characterized by a quality of inter-group cooperation which renders it almost unique among our great cities. It is not a model city. It has intolerant citizens; it has incidents of conflict. But those factors have not been permitted to accumulate into mass disorder. Los Angeles has not experienced an instance of organized group violence in the past twelve years.

If organized violence occurred anywhere, it should, by all socio-economic standards, have been in Los Angeles. In the last decade, the city has nearly doubled in size; it suffered the intense dislocation of adjustment to an industrial economy; it has been and still is the focus of one of the greatest migrations in this nation's history. Its two million, two hundred thousand people, the hub of a five-million person metropolitan area, is a melting pot of races, colors, creeds, and ideas.

Let me cite some examples. Los Angeles is the home of nearly one-quarter million Negroes, an increase of 168 percent since World War II. It has the largest Japanese group in the nation; the third largest Chinese group. The number of persons of the Jewish faith at least equals the urban average. The city is a cross section of the races, colors, and creeds which make up our nation. And, for reasons no one has ever explained to my satisfaction, we are somehow a Mecca for not only strange religious cults, but also for every brand of zealot, bigot, and fanatic that our society breeds.

This is Los Angeles—not the city colorfully depicted on travel posters—but the one which interests us here today. It has, like other great metropolitan centers, nearly every element which creates community tensions. But its peoples of different background are learning to live together.

The story of that city's freedom from strife is largely the story of the professionalization of its police department. In this respect, I do not discount the efforts of other agencies, particularly those working for community and group betterment. Their progress in the fields of human understanding, education, and welfare, has been remarkable. It holds great promise for the future. But they made one additional contribution. They recognized that there was one thing which would make social tranquility immediately possible. They gave dynamic and unflagging support to police improvement.

I want to approach the subject of police improvement in a bluntly realistic manner. There has been a great deal of discussion about it at this Institute, and I am anxious that one serious error be avoided.

As I left Los Angeles yesterday, I was introduced to a feature writer from another city's metropolitan newspaper. He is a capable man. His task was to analyze the Los Angeles Police Department, study its techniques and procedures, and take the story back home. This is good journalism—the type which justifies our faith in the Fourth Estate. I hope he won't make the error I'm concerned about. If he doesn't, it will be a rare instance. Since Los Angeles has achieved its eminence in law enforcement, dozens of citizen groups, city officials, and journalists have studied our methods. The usual result is a storm of bitter criticism of their department, and a demand that their police adopt Los Angeles' professionalism.

How simple that sounds. And how dangerous it is to assume that a city's so-called police problem stems from the police themselves. These people who demand that their police be more efficient, more honest, more impartial—I invite them to join me in an exercise in realism. Who actually runs a police department? The mayor, the police commission, the chief? The people do! They set its policies, establish its standards, furnish its man-power, and supply its budget. The police department is not a private endeavor; it has no funds of its own. It is not a legal entity; it has no rights, no vested interests. It is merely a group of citizens employed to exercise certain functions. It is created by the public, shaped by the public, and operated by the public. And if it operates badly, the responsibility cannot be disowned by the public.

I have often heard the complaint that the police organization is all right, but the officers just are not producing. And if an employee isn't producing—whose fault is it? The public selected that man—did they select the wrong man? The public furnished the training—was it bad training—or did they neglect to provide funds for training of any sort? What about the supervisors and commanders? Were they selected by competitive examination on a merit basis—or were they promoted on a political basis? If so, whose politics? If there is a machine in town—a few police votes don't keep it running. But the public vote does!

A recent news report tells of widespread police graft in a southern city. Officers are "squeezing" merchandise from businessmen, parking fees from truckers, gratuities from other citizens. The good citizens there, horrified at the expose, might do well to accept some personal responsibility. The basic salary of their police officer is $220.00 per month. On the six-day week, that runs about a dollar per hour. Carpenter's helpers in the same town earn nearly double that scale. What kind of policemen do they expect to get for a dollar an hour? Their police department costs less than a million dollars per year. Of course, the crime bill, the disorder, the under-the-table pay-offs run 15 million dollars per year. A shrewd bargain these good citizens have driven. Of course, they are going to solve their problem. They're replacing the chief, the seventh in six years.

If a journalist or a citizens' group from that city calls upon Los Angeles for assistance, what should we tell them? They'll want to study our organization, inspect our Planning and Research and Intelligence Divisions, our strong disciplinary program, observe our cadet school, our continuous in-service training. There are no secrets about these things. They are merely adaptions of sound administrative technique. They are available and understandable to qualified police officials everywhere. But they cannot be put into effect until competent personnel are attracted by decent job benefits, until an adequate operating budget is furnished; until public cooperation replaces disinterest, shallow-interest, and special-interest. Professional police work will come into being only when the public takes a long hard look at their police, and instead of disowning what they themselves have created, accept full responsibility for the errors of generations.

Returning, then, to the Los Angeles experiment—the thing which made police progress and social order there a reality was a public acceptance of these very basic facts. At first, it was understood by only a small group—community leaders such as those represented at this conference. The job of selling this concept was a difficult one. Not that it was a particularly new concept—but at some community levels it is an ugly one. Los Angeles members of the groups represented at this Institute were key factors in that sales job.

Assuming a community is ready to support the professionalism of its police agency, there are certain techniques which the Los Angeles experiment has proved necessary. The first step is the attraction of proper recruits. Los Angeles policemen draw $440.00 monthly at the end of three years' service. This is probably a minimum figure. Below that, the possibility of attracting sufficiently educated and capable persons is almost nil. I am of the opinion that the base salary for an experienced line officer should be in the neighborhood of $600.00 monthly, at present living costs. The first city to adopt such a scale will attract high quality personel who now select other professions. At the present time, I am trying to convince Los Angeles that we would save money by paying more. Our attrition rate among the most qualified officers is too high. I had the pleasure of meeting our former staff researcher here today—a former Los Angeles policeman, now Professor Albert Germann of Michigan State University.

There must be minimum recruiting standards—and these minimums must be held even though the department operates below strength. Far better to have to increase unit output than to corrupt your police future with substandard men. In Los Angeles, less than 4 percent of all applicants meet our rigid police standards. We have been considerably under authorized strength for five years, at one time ten percent under an allowed figure which was itself nearly 40 percent under the recommended population, square mile ratio. We have managed to do the job only because personnel quality allowed us to steadily improve efficiency. We were told by administrative experts we might improve 2 percent per year with much planning and labor. We upped work output 15 percent last year and we are going to do better in 1955.

Recruit selection must be made solely on a merit basis, preferably by an independent civil service department. If a ward boss, an alderman, or a councilman can influence selection in any manner, tear up your plans and start over. As a matter of fact, if he can interfere in any way other than through official channels, the police improvement plan is doomed. Categorically, professional police work and politics do not mix—and there are no shades of gray to that philosophy.

A psychiatric test must be included in the recruit selection program. This bears directly on the problem of community relations. The finest training, direction, and discipline cannot correct or control serious emotional defects.

Our Cadet Training School runs 13 weeks at present. Again, this should be considered a minimum and then only if the recruit has an educational equivalent of two college years. I am personally in favor of a six-month training period, plus a six-month additional field probation under strict supervision. This should be followed up with in-service and advanced officers' schools, specialist aand command schools such as are provided in Los Angeles. This is, of course, only a sketch of recruiting and training considerations. With it in mind, I would like to consider in more detail some of the training which bears directly on the subject of community relations.

Once the police cadet has received basic technical information, the direction of training pivots to the consideration of human relations. The cadet must be taught to translate his technical background into solutions of field situations—problems which involve people.

In these courses, sociology is stressed more than ethnology. Applied human relations is stressed more than theoretical psychology. The purpose of the training is to provide, immediately, useable knowledge. Training schedules do not allow time for building the broad base of theoretical knowledge necessary in university training. The police administrators should not attempt that impossible task under present training time minimums. The advantages of a college education requirement for police applicants is readily apparent here. Lacking this, colleges do provide upper level courses, and officers should be encouraged to take advantage of these facilities. In a recent survey, we found that 40 percent of our officers were engaged in such training.

The cadet learns that people differ—by race, religion, politics, economic status, occupation, and in a thousand other ways. He learns they have a right to be different. He learns that we are all minority group members—that each of us belongs to many groups, any one of which can be and often has been discriminated against.

In other classes, statistical diagrams of the composition of the city are studied. The various peoples are discussed, the movements of groups are traced, the tensions resulting from these movements are pin-pointed and analyzed in detail. The racial composition of police districts are an important lesson here because it must be made clear that there are no "Jim Crow" areas, no "Ghettos." Every police division has everything found in all other divisions, differing only in proportion. The aim here is to correct stereotyped impressions that the city is divided into clearly defined groups and areas, and that law enforcement differs accordingly. The police department's policy of one class of citizenship, one standard of police technique, then becomes readily understandable.

Another class expands this policy. The officer now understands the composition of the community, he has learned how people differ. He is now taught that these variations cannot influence him in the discharge of his duties. His department handles the people involved in incidents only according to the degree of their involvement. There is no other measurement. Existing laws are enforced and nothing else. We do not enforce beliefs or prejudices—including the officer's. During his hours of duty, he is a composite of the entire community.

Typical course titles are Police Sociological Problems, Human Relations, Ethics, Professionalism, Civil Disturbances, and Public Relations. Course titles do not reveal the full scope of the 520-hour program. For example, although the Human Relations class lasts two hours, that subject is a principal concern in courses such as Interrogation, Patrol Tactics, and Investigation. The firearms' class gives more time to "when not to shoot" than it does to "how to shoot." The entire training staff is constantly alert in the classroom, on the exercise field, and in the locker room, to discover signs of disabling prejudice which might make the cadet a poor risk. Conditions of tension are artificially created so that the man's reaction can be studied—and he may never know that the situation was contrived to test him.

At this point, let us consider the subject of racial and religious prejudice. The cadets, of course, reflect a broad cross section of society and bring to us the intolerant attitudes to which they have previously been exposed. The question—what to do about these beliefs?

Recently, a chief of police from a mid-western city made an inspection tour of our department. He was particularly interested in the extremely low percentage of citizen complaints received alleging prejudicial treatment of minority group members. He was also interested in case studies where so-called minority group organizations defended the police department against accusations of such misconduct. One of these instances involved a metropolitan Los Angeles daily newspaper which began a series of articles with the caption: "Cops Lay Heavy Hands on Minorities." You have all seen such articles and, in many cases, they represent good journalism—accurate coverage. In this instance, the facts were patently incorrect. The writer, a new resident, was securing information from old newspaper clippings and from certain special interest groups. He was committing the cardinal reportorial sin of not checking current facts. The article shook police morale and public confidence. Assuming the facts had been true, it offered no solutions other than a vague recommendation that the police ought to do something about this mess! Fortunately, certain community organizations recognized where the "mess" really was. A coordinating group representing 60 social service agencies contacted the publisher of that paper. He was told, and in no uncertain terms, that the story was untrue, that it was inciting lunatic fringe-elements into disorderly conduct, and was playing directly into the hands of subversive groups. The result—that particular series was discontinued and, to the credit of that publisher, a new series of articles underscoring police-public cooperation was instituted in its place.

The visiting chief of police was understandably impressed. In most jurisdictions the police fight lonely battles. He assumed that such overwhelming public support meant we had somehow erased prejudicial and intolerant beliefs held by police officers. He was wrong. Those of you who work in the field of education recognize we do not and can not accomplish this miracle. Of course, we will not accept an applicant whose intolerance is so high it is a disabling factor. Where it is not too deep-seated, we can erase it, or at least diminish it. In the majority of cases, we must learn to operate equitably despite it. We do that by controlling the results of these beliefs. With policemen, as with society in general, our immediate concern is not in what the man thinks but what he does Los Angeles police policy recognizes only one class of citizenship—first class citizenship. Any incident of police action which deviates from this policy is met with swift and certain discipline.

A police department's community relations program begins with a training, a firm human relations policy, and strong disciplinary machinery to enforce it. It is a departmental application of my second premise—that the immediate issue is conduct and the immediate solution is enforced order.

For those who question whether that degree of discipline is possible, I have an example. I am thinking of a certain Los Angeles police officer who walks a foot beat in the old section of the city. The street is a racial melting pot. I know the officer personally; he is one of the "old school," recruited long before psychiatric examinations were instituted. If there is a maximum number of racial and religious prejudices that one mind can hold, I am certain he represents it. This officer has been exposed to the complete range of police human relations training. He has memorized every maxim, every scientific fact, every theory relating to human equality. He knows all the accepted answers. Of course, he doesn't believe a word of it.

This may surprise you—the officer's eight-hour duty tour is characterized by tolerance, applied human relations, and equitable treatment of all persons. Both his division commander and myself have watched his work closely, a little wary that his deep-seated convictions might win out over discipline in moments of stress.

This has not happened during the five years he has patrolled this highly critical district. We are very near an opinion that his intolerance has become a victim of enforced order—habit has won out over belief.

Discipline, enforced compliance with police policy, is a key which is available to every police administrator. If it works in Los Angeles, it will work elsewhere. The entire community relations program is at stake on every officer in the field. It is here that the police department proves itself, or is found wanting.

The second-line community relations effort is handled by specialized police units. One of the most successful of these is our Community Relations Detail working out of the Public Information office. Its mission is to establish and maintain communication between police and the so-called minority segments of the community press serving them, and key individuals in the human relations field. These officers are members of 60 organizations representing a cross section of specialized community interests. Few police details pierce so deeply into the stratifications of our complex society or maintain so many privileged sources of information.

Their first task was at the community press level. Certain of these newspapers were parlaying instances of law enforcement against minority group members into sensational accounts of police prejudice and brutality. Many of these articles were written solely from the unsubstantiated account given by the arrestee. The accumulated result was the fomenting of an hysterical "cop-hating" attitude which rendered suspect every police action involving non-Caucasian persons.

The Community Relations officers went to these publishers and laid their cards on the table. Sensationalism was selling newspapers, but it was hurting the community. They pointed out that sensationalism was actually manufacturing new incidents—feeding upon itself. They offered, with the full backing of the office of the chief, to provide the publisher with exact and complete facts on every inquiry, whether the police action was right or wrong; whether the facts helped us or hurt us.

The confidence I have in the men who publish the nation's newspapers was justified. Community interest won out over self-interest.

The Community Relations Detail is, *first,* a public information activity, acquainting community groups with police policies, procedures, and tactics. Where necessary, it interprets specific police actions, explaining why they were necessary and how they were taken. *Secondly,* the detail transmits information in the other direction, keeping the police staff informed about minority and inter-group problems and activities. We have found the police are sometimes overly suspicious of a group's militant efforts, seeing in it a threat to order which does not actually exist. The two-way communication furnished by the detail brings the facts to both sides. *Thirdly,* the detail reports any police activities which are discriminatory, or may appear to the community to be discriminatory. The police staff does not operate under the assumption that it is infallible. Critical comment from this specialized unit often prevents more dangerous and expensive criticism from the public at large. *Lastly,* the detail operates as an advance listening post, alert for rumors which might prelude violent conflict. In a recent instance, these officers were informed that racial violence was brewing at a school. A quick investigation indicated the situation was critical. The detail flashed the word to citizen groups organized to combat just such emergencies. Affected police field units were placed on a stand-by basis. The result—this detail, working with citizen groups, contained the situation.

It is profitable to assign to these specialized units officers belonging to minority groups. They are often more sensitive to the problem, have previously established contacts in those communities, and encounter few barriers. However, it must be emphasized that the officer's competency, and not his ancestry, is the overriding consideration in making the assignment. Community relations details are not "window-dressing"—they are not publicity gags designed to display non-Caucasians in key positions.

A similar detail works out of the Juvenile Division. In this case, the principal concern is with actual offenders. One of this unit's primary values is its detailed knowledge of gang members, leaders, and methods. They know their homes, their meeting places, their territories. They deal with what the law recognizes as children, but do not be mistaken—this is intelligence activity of the highest order. The disheartening message of our crime statistics is all too clear—today's delinquent is often a dangerous criminal—an immediate threat to community order. He is sometimes the innocent tool of intolerant adults, but he can also be a moving force behind community violence. We are sympathetic with the ideals of juvenile correction—of rehabilitation over punishment. Here, as with other community problems, we invite welfare agencies to work to eliminate causes. Meanwhile, we ask them to remember that the police is not a social agency. We are bound to read the message in police records and employ protective tactics accordingly. In Los Angeles, as in other cities, we have a juvenile problem. We do not have a problem in mass juvenile disorder, because we face facts, and on the basis of these facts, employ units such as the ones I have described.

Three factors compose the Los Angeles Police Department's community relations program: Training of officers—including training through discipline, public information activity, and efficient line police work. Unless they are all in existence and interworking, a community relations program does not exist. Training provides a base, but public information and line officers must forward to training that information which keys it to current needs. Public information is a useless activity unless it is backed up with competent line officers who are enforcing the laws equitably. And the most dedicated line commanders can accomplish little unless training provides well-schooled personnel and public information creates a co-operative public.

I would rather have brought to this Institute a simple and revolutionary device—some easy way to an effective program. I know of no such device. I can promise that, to a mutually cooperating public and police department, no problem in community order is beyond solution. The methods are known, they are proving themselves in the Los Angeles experiment—all that is needed is dedicated citizens who will put them into effect.

To this point, this has been a progress report. The Los Angeles experiment seems to justify the philosophy of enforced order as the first step toward improved community relations. Progress of this type can be reported objectively, without seeming to seek praise because law enforcement is absolutely dependent upon the public for any successes it may have. The credit for Los Angeles progress must go primarily to Los Angeles citizens.

I would not want to close, however, leaving the impression that the experiment is concluded. It does not represent the ultimate in community equity and tranquility. Certain factors now at work could bring all the progress crashing down into rubble and violence. I have pledged forthrightness and honesty in this report, and it requires some critical comments, perhaps touching upon activities and attitudes or organizations represented here.

The first comment concerns minority dixcrimination against the public as a whole. Reaction to police deployment furnishes a good example of this danger. Every department worth its salt deploys field forces on the basis of crime experience. Deployment is often heaviest in so-called minority sections of the city. The reason is statistical—it is a fact that certain racial groups, at the present time, commit a disproportionate share of the total crime. Let me make one point clear in that regard—a competent police administrator is fully aware of the multiple conditions which create this problem. There is no inherent physical or mental weakness in any racial stock which tends it toward crime. But—and this is a "but" which must be borne constantly in mind—police field deployment is not social agency activity. In deploying to supress crime, we are not interested in why a certain group tends toward crime, we are interested in maintaining order. The fact that the group would not be a crime problem under different socio-economic conditions and might not be a crime problem tomorrow, does not alter today's tactical necessities. Police deployment is concerned with effect, not cause.

When I am told that intense police activity in a given area is psychologically disturbing to its residents, I am forced to agree. And I agree that it can add weight to discriminatory beliefs held by some who witness it, and that it can create a sense of persecution among those who receive it. Is the police administrator, then, to discard crime occurrence statistics and deploy his men on the basis of social inoffensiveness? This would be discrimination indeed!

Every citizen has the right to police protection on the basis of need. The police have the duty of providing that protection, and of employing whatever legal devices are necessary to accomplish it. At the present time, race, color, and creed are useful statistical and tactical devices. So are age groupings, sex, and employment. If persons of one occupation, for some reason commit more theft than average, then increased police attention is given to persons of that occupation. Discrimination is not a factor there. If persons of Mexican, Negro, of Anglo-Saxon ancestry, for some reason, contribute heavily to other forms of crime, police deployment must take that into account. From an ethnological point-of-view, Negro, Mexican, and Anglo-Saxon are unscientific breakdowns; they are a fiction. From a police point-of-view, they are a useful fiction and should be used as long as they remain useful.

The demand that the police cease to consider race, color, and creed is an unrealistic demand. Identification is a police tool, not a police attitude. If traffic violations run heavily in favor of lavender colored automobiles, you may be certain, whatever the sociological reasons for that condition, we would give lavender automobiles more than average attention. And if those vehicles were predominantly found in one area of the city, we would give that area more than average attention. You may be certain that any pressure brought to bear by the lavender manufacturer's association would not alter our professional stand—it would only react to their disadvantage by making the police job more difficult. Such demands are a form of discrimination against the public as a whole.

For a moment, let us consider this entire problem of group identification. It is one thing for the police to employ it for statistical and descriptive purposes; it is quite another if it is employed to set a group apart from the rest of society. The question must be brought out into the open and discussed because it represents a conflict of opinion within the physically-identifiable minority groups. Some of these citizens object strenuously to being identified with their background. Others publicly announce it by joining organizations bearing that stamp of identity. Either attitude can be supported by argument. But I humbly submit that the man, or the group which changes identification at different times and under different conditions, confuses and impedes the social assimilation process. There is no place for dual status in our society, and it is incongruous that the groups with the keenest interest in eliminating dual status should create conditions which perpetuate it. Organizations which publicly identify themselves with a certain racial group are keeping alive the phantasy that the group is diferent. By setting it apart from the whole, they help keep it apart. We need such organizations; they fill a vital role in our changing system; I heartily endorse their good works. I suggest that if a single class of citizenship is the key to social assimilation, then practices and titles which contradict it, must be examined and resolved.

Another problem which plagues the police administrator is organized group pressure to promote officers and make command assignments on the basis of race, color, or creed. Before a recent Los Angeles election, I encountered tremendous pressure to replace an Anglo-Saxon commander of a detective division with another commander belonging to a certain minority group. I refused to engage in racial discrimination against the Anglo-Saxon commander. He was the most qualified man for the job and, as such, he retained the job. Neither do I consider ancestry a factor in making promotional appointments. The Los Angeles policy is to take the top man from the list. Racial background should not hinder advancement; neither should it help it. Shortly before I left Los Angeles, I had the pleasure of pinning a Lieutenant's badge on a young officer born in Mexico. He got that badge because he was the top man, not because accidents of conquest created a national border between our places of birth.

No one is more critical of the American police service than myself. For 28 years I have outspokenly expressed that criticism and have sat in meetings and applauded others who have criticized constructively. Certainly, few other organizations in history have been so unanimously castigated. I have no complaints to make—it is part of the painful process of growth and improvement. There is one danger inherent in this process—a point of group-masochism is reached where all other groups become wise and faultless and self-reproach becomes the total answer. I caution the police against this danger.

I have made the point that discrimination is a two-way street. Those who are most active in combating it are sometimes guilty of advocating that the police practice it. There is nothing shocking in this critical observation—no group is characterized by omniscience. The fact that minorities have received intolerant and discriminatory treatment does not automatically lend justice to all of their demands. They are as prone to error as majority groups, and the wiser and calmer citizens within those groups recognize this fact. Thoughtful citizens expect the police to stand their ground when they believe they are right. They expect the police to criticize as well as be criticized.

I have tried to steer a course between these extremes tonight. I have assessed the situation as forthrightly as I know how. There is always a temptation when speaking on a subject so emotion-laden as this, to skirt issues, to woo friends, rather than court truth. In my experience with the National Conference of Christians and Jews, I have never felt it necessary to compromise my honest convictions, and I did not intend to dishonor this Institute by doing so tonight.

I would like to close by expressing my philosophy of citizenship, a philosophy which I humbly believe embodies the convictions of all persons and groups represented at this gathering.

Good citizenship is expressed in many ways. It consists not only of bearing arms for one's country, but also of bearing truth for it. It consists not only of facing spiritual enemies: Intolerance, Bigotry, and Hate. It consists not only of holding high the regimental banners, but also of holding high the banners of Duty, Faith, and Love. Although not all citizens can prove themselves on a battlefield, all can do it by the quiet and devoted living of the spirit of our country. It is sometimes more difficult to live ideals than to shed blood for them.

The Fringes of Police-Community Relations— Extremism

Nelson A. Watson

In the past three days we have been focusing our attention on ways and means of improving the police function in our respective communities. Our principal emphasis has been on developing or opening communications channels so that more people in all walks of life will understand the problems their police have in protecting them. It is our hope that out community relations programs will involve many citizens in a successful effort to reduce crime and promote order. We want people to feel free to approach us knowing they will be respected. Only in a well-ordered society can each individual hope to realize his dreams and enjoy the fruits of his labors.

Unfortunately, there are always some who are at the bottom of the social ladder. This is understandable when we look at the whole population in terms of individual differences. People succeed or fail depending on how they measure up

Dr. Nelson A. Watson is project director of the IACP Research and Development Division in Washington, D.C. This paper was originally presented at the IACP Police Administrators Conference in 1966.

From Nelson A. Watson, "The Fringes of Police Community Relations Extremism," *The Police Chief* 33, no. 8 (August 1966): 8-9, 64-68. Reprinted by permission of the publisher.

on a great array of factors. Those who have great drive and energy do better, on the whole, than those who are lazy. Those who are smart do better, as a rule, than those who are dull. Naturally, therefore, we would expect the lazy and stupid persons to be somewhere down the scale. But to be strictly honest and realistic about it, we must all admit that it doesn't always work that way. Sometimes the bosses' son who was born with a silver spoon in his mouth and is just an idle play boy has a much bigger share of his world's goods than he earned. Sometimes, too, a young man of great intellect and ambition is held back by conditions over which he has no control.

Let's cast the play in personal terms. Suppose your son is an officer in your department. Suppose he has worked his way up to a lieutenant's rank—strictly on his own merit. In fact, because you are the chief he had to be demonstrably better than the other candidates so there could be no charges of favoritism when he was promoted. Incidentally, I am sure you all understand that such charges are going to be made anyway by some of those who didn't get the promotion even though most people don't believe them. But, now, let's say a captaincy opens up and your son again is clearly the best qualified—highest grade on the promotional examination, best service record, far and away the best educational background, etc., etc. Still, in spite of all this, someone else gets the promotion—not because he is better, but for some reason unrelated to his qualifications. Maybe the powers that be fix things so that the other fellow gets the job because he is Catholic and you are Protestant or he is a Democrat and you are Republican or he is from the north side and you are from the south side or vice versa on all of these. Or, maybe the powers that be chose the other fellow because he is white and you are Negro or vice versa again. I am sure we all see the point. The real reasons for the choice have nothing to do with the man's qualifications for the job. Now, let's assume this happens three times in a row so that your son or you, for that matter, are passed over unfairly by people who are of a different religion or politics or color of skin. Would you feel bitter? Fight back? How—assuming you had no power? Resign yourself to a second or third rate role? Suppose instead of getting to be a lieutenant your son was *forever* relegated to a patrolman's rank—not because he wasn't able, but because he was the "wrong kind" so they wouldn't even let him take the exams or they "conveniently" lost his papers or disqualified his papers for some flimsy technical reason. Would you then perhaps become a candidate for some kind of extremist views—some extremist movement—a group that held out even a faint hope of changing things—or of at least getting even?

This brings me to the main subject I want to talk about—extremism. We as law enforcement officers have a responsibility to all of our constituents of whatever creed, color, or political persuasion to be aware of, well informed about, and prepared to deal with the dangers presented by the extremists of all types. Extremism can lead to a Harlem or a Watts just as extremism produces church bombings, cross burnings, and murders.

I do not want to give the impression that I regard extremism as the heart and core of the police-community relations problem. It is only part of the problem. Extremist groups, when sufficiently aroused and militantly oriented, are certainly dangerous. They can set off holocausts of social devastation. Their propaganda and activities keep things stirred up. All of this is true, but we must realize that, in terms of sheer volume, it is the thousands upon thousands of contacts made every day by police with people on the streets that provide at one and the same time a potential for bad feeling and a potential for improvement in the way people feel about their police and their willingness to cooperate. Nevertheless, we would be derelict in our duty if we did not keep alert to the activities of the extremists both in our own jurisdiction and elsewhere. For, remember, the spirit is contagious. An incident like the shooting of James Meredith could well trigger a riot in some far away city and a speech by a fiery Negro extremist could well inspire violence against Negro marchers somewhere across the country. Echoes from Philadelphia, Mississippi, may well be heard on Columbia Avenue in Philadelphia, Pennsylvania.

In the great cities of our nation, in the small towns, at the state, county, and federal levels, police forces are responsible for law and order. Jurisdictions differ in many ways but the one thing common to all law enforcement agencies is the promotion and maintenance of order in society. This means that every law enforcement agency, within the scope of its jurisdiction as defined by law, must fight crime and disorder on behalf of the people. As we are all sadly aware, this job is becoming more and more difficult. It is becoming increasingly complex and police problems are being aggravated by confusion and dissension among various groups.

We are in the midst of a social upheaval in which old, settled, and cherished values are being upset and displaced. The result is bitter conflict. Our American philosophy of government calls for equality of opportunity for everyone. This is a settled policy which nearly everyone would consider one of the cornerstones of our freedom. Yet, there is much disagreement as to what this means and how it should be implemented. To many, the only measure of equality of opportunity is equality of results. In the view of some, the only way to overcome our failure to achieve equality of results is through reverse discrimination. In other words, make up for lack of equality in opportunity by discriminating in favor of those previously denied. In this view, both the protagonists and the antagonists find the road to extremism and in extremism police find the seeds of disorder.

Like everything else, extremism is a relative matter. What is extreme to some may seem mild or even conservative to others. Some may see the NAACP as a group of revolutionary fanatics, but others may look upon them as a bunch of stodgy, pedestrian slowpokes. You gentlemen, of all people in this country, must be aware that there are many citizens who are convinced that anyone advocating racial equality is a Communist or at least a Communist pawn. If those who advocate eliminating race as a factor in voting, housing, education, and jobs are extremists, then those who advocate "keeping the nigger in his place" are extremists at the other pole. If those who are chanting "black power" are extremists, then those who are chanting "white power," are also. There are extremists who are seeking the lead discontented minorities into explosions of violence and there are extremists who are seeking to keep them subjugated through violence.

What is extremism so far as the police are concerned? When we attempt to define such a term we run into practical difficulties because of its relativity—because people do not agree. There is no clearly discernible line of distinction beyond which everything is extreme. Yet, we have the responsibility for maintaining order and controlling extremists. Yes, in a very practical sense, police are expected to contain extremism. Thus, for our working definition of extremism, we must look to the law. For us, any act which violates the law is sufficiently extreme to require action. In order for us to exercise police power, the factors constituting the violation are both sufficient and necessary conditions. There must be a violation and, when there is, that is enough.

Part of the difficulty we run into these days—no small part—arises from police actions taken for the purpose of *preventing* violations. As a practical illustration, when a crowd gathers at the scene of a routine arrest, an order from an officer to move along is resented as an infringement on personal liberty. Those ordered to move do not see themselves as subject to police authority because they are not violating any law. They question the officer's right to order them away. When they react, they sometimes react violently. Then there is a violation of the law for which they hold the officer responsible—they believe he provoked it, and they feel they are blameless. Some officers can handle these situations better than others and when they do, it is because they persuade rather than order.

We all recognize that there is an urgent need for communication, communication that is both meaningful and productive. We know it is important that our officers show respect for persons as individuals. We are aware of the need for police officers to give people decent, courteous, common-sense treatment. We fully appreciate the need for chiefs of police and other police executives to concern themselves with the broad community problems out of which police difficulties grow. All of these areas are important and deserve our urgent attention. But, lest we be lulled into letting down our guard—lest we be seduced by our sincere desire to be helpful, fair, and impartial—lest we be caught unaware by some with ulterior motives, let us, *with respect to potential violence,* be more than ever alert and in a constant state of preparedness so that explosions instigated by extremists can be handled with dispatch.

If we are to cope successfully with extremism—which I predict will increase rather than subside—we can and must take positive action in several fields and the sooner the better. Why this is so should be obvious, but, for the record, we should state our belief that domestic peace and social order serve the best interests of all people in the long run. It should also be made clear that police are not solely concerned with extremism on the part of Negroes, Puerto Ricans, or other minority groups. Police interest and concern extends to any group—students, strikers, sports fans—having a potential for violating the law. This potential is present just as surely in conditions leading to murders such as those of Evers, Penn, and Liuzzo as it is in conditions that produce riots in our major cities. All such events contain elements of extremism and as such must receive the same careful and vigorous police attention.

The tools and trappings of extremism constitute a formidable arsenal: Molotov cocktails, rifles, side arms, rocks, bottles, and all the rest. Words and slogans, more words and songs, the printed word, the shouted word, the threat, the imprecation. Prayer and profanity, cruel jest and prejudice, propaganda and living slang. Fear and frustration, hatred and anger, and the determination of despair. And above all ACTION. Do something! Plot and plan, get ready, recruit, train, fire-up tempers, prepare the people through propaganda. Of these weapons, words are by far the most powerful. A gun can destroy but a few; words are by far the most powerful. A gun can destroy but a few; words can activate triggers to kill thousands.

People may think of extremists as the lunatic fringe and may have a tendency to shrug off their mouthings. But you and I know we must take them seriously. A small band of self-styled Nazis swaggering around with arm bands and swastikas may not pose much of a physical problem by themselves, but the reaction to them by others can be disastrous.

There have been reports of various radical or revolutionary groups from time to time: Black Muslims, Minutemen, Revolutionary Action Movement, Deacons for Defense, and others. They may be local and limited, relatively new and unorganized, or they may have a long history and widespread influence like the Ku Klux Klan. Whatever their origin, nature, and propaganda, they are dangerous for many reasons. First, there may be small and as yet relatively uninfluential groups in your city which would try to get something started so as not to be outdone by others. Second, there are enough angry and frustrated people, including armies of kids, who, though not allied with any group, will swell the ranks once disorder starts. Third, many people feel they have little to lose anyway so why not shoot, loot, and burn? Fourth, some spokesmen, whether for minority groups or radical white groups are becoming more openly dedicated by violence. Stokley Carmichael, appearing on national television, refused to disavow violence as a tactic even though he heads the Student Nonviolent Coordinating Committee. One of Washington, D. C.'s spokesmen recently openly advocated violence as the only means left to Negroes.

Life magazine on June 10 of this year quoted from The Crusade, a pamphlet published in Cuba by a self-exiled Negro as follows: "The weapons of defense employed by Afro-American freedom fighters must consist of a poor man's arsenal. Gasoline fire bombs, lye or acid bombs . . . can be used extensively. During the night hours such weapons, thrown from roof tops, will make the streets impossible for racist cops to patrol . . . gas tanks on public vehicles can be choked up with sand . . . long nails driven through boards, and tacks with large heads are effective to slow the movement of traffic on congested roads at night.

Derailing of trains causes panic. Explosive booby traps on police telephone boxes can be employed. High-powered sniper rifles are readily available. Armor-piercing bullets will penetrate oil-storage tanks from a distance... Flamethrowers can be manufactured at home...."

On the other hand, listen to this from a publication of the Minutemen called "On Target." "You Need the Minutemen—if you are captured or held prisoner, it will be important for you to know that others are aware of your situation and that they will help you to escape if at all possible.

"To defeat your enemies you must know all you can about them. It is not enough simply to say the enemies are Communists. We must know what kind of cars they drive. Where they live, their physical appearance, their strong and weak points, their habits and travel patterns. The Minutemen organization has already compiled more information in its files than any one of us could accumulate in a lifetime.

"Each member is expected to own his own gun, ammunition and other combat gear. These things are just the beginning of what an underground resistance fighter must have. The time may come that your life will depend on counterfeit identification papers. The lives of your family may depend on counterfeit food ration stamps. Few individual members have the equipment necessary to engrave and print such documents.

"Suppose you succeed in capturing a number of enemy demolition charges but your band does not include an expert that knows how to use them safely. There will be many times that your individual group will need the help of outside specialists which the organization can supply."

Another revealing glimpse comes from a statement by the Reverend Connie Lynch of the National States Rights Party, an anti-Negro, anti-Semitic militant organization. At a meeting in St. Louis last October, he told an audience that a racial war is in the making in the United States, "and when it is over, there isn't going to be a black face to be seen anywhere." At the same meeting, a Klan leader said, "I didn't join the Klan. I was born a Klansman and I will die a Klansman. They say they're going to stamp out the Klan. They've been trying for a hundred years and they haven't done it yet. If we had a few hangings in St. Louis, we would stop all this raping and murdering by Negroes. Buy a gun. Arm yourself. The Klan is in St. Louis and we're here to stay. We mean business."

Life magazine also published what purports to be a conversation with a member of RAM. It is frightening.

"Question: How far do you suppose the brothers might go if the next big riot were to take place, say in Harlem?

"Answer: Well, let's see...hmm. What's that first big commuter train to Connecticut after it gets good and dark? The 7:05? Yeah, well what do you suppose all those big Madison Avenue men would do if that train was to be derailed at 125th Street, or just before it came out of the ground at 91st? Stay there in line in the bar car waiting for that drink in a paper cup? Hah! How? Man, wouldn't they make some hostages?

"Question: Where would the police be while all this is going on?

"Answer: Don't you suppose like the police might be busy several other places just then? Like putting down a big fuss over on Lenox Avenue, yeah, or trying to unsnarl the world's biggest traffic jam on the East River Drive. Maybe the lights might all go out about now. . . ." Unquote.

Ominous? Of course! Extreme? You bet!

How about this? A group of students at a well-known university distributed a leaflet in which the following appears: "When in the course of human events it becomes necessary to abolish the Negro race, proper methods should be used. Among them are guns, bows and arrows, sling shots and knives. We hold these truths to bo self-evident: that all whites are created with certain rights; among these are life, liberty, and the pursuit of dead niggers."[1]

Unless our country, our states, our cities can do something toward changing these extreme, violent, poisonous views, I am afraid the social dynamite which educator Dr. Conant talked about some years ago will explode. And if it does, you know who the number one target will be—the police. Many of our cities have tinderbox areas which a spark can set off. The spark can come from many quarters, it is possible that it may be provided by police action. One of your officers, in a thoughtless moment by a rash act, by an ill-conceived remark, by losing his temper in exasperation, even when making a perfectly legal arrest, can provide that spark. Of course, as has been said here many times, the fundamental conditions out of which these bitter feelings grow are not within the primary responsibility of the police. That is small comfort, however, when snipers are shooting at you, when police cars are being stoned and burned and overturned, when building after building goes up in flame.

It is to prevent outbreaks like this that we are trying to reach out to the people through our police-community relations programs. It is to cut down on violent crime. It is to make the jobs of our officers less dangerous and more effective. It is to take a good, hard, self-critical look at what police are doing so we will not provide the spark that starts the conflagration.

So far as police *action* is concerned, there are things that come to my attention on that, too. I hear of incidents from police and from civil rights workers. I read about them in the press, in magazines, and books. I cannot vouch for the accuracy of these reports because we all know how easily things can get distorted and misinterpreted. But, accurate or not, it is vitally important that we all remember that people form opinions and take action on the basis of what they hear and what they believe without checking its accuracy. Things like the following illustrate what people are saying, what they believe, and what is back of the way they behave:

CASE NO. 1

"The cops pulled us over and came up to the car with guns in their hands. This one cop (incidentally, the officer was a Negro) told me to show him my license and registration. When I asked him why, he told me to do as I was told and not get smart. Then they made us all get out of the car while the other guy looked inside. When they couldn't find anything wrong, they told us we could go. I asked them what it was all about and the one cop said they had a lot of stolen cars around there lately so they had to check up."

CASE NO. 2

A newspaper reported that a man had complained about the actions of an officer which he felt were uncalled for. It was reported the officer had arrested a man and had handcuffed him. For some reason, the man fell to the ground and the complainant said the officer then put his foot on the man's neck. The complainant said the arrested man was not fighting the officer and, after all, he was handcuffed. He cited this as an example of police brutality.

CASE NO. 3

An officer patrolling a beach where kids had caused trouble approached a teenaged boy who was sitting by himself on a bench drinking from a bottle. Drinking liquor by minors was forbidden by law. The officer asked the boy what he was drinking and the boy replied it was Coke. The officer took the bottle and smelled the contents. Finding that it contained no liquor so that he had no basis for arrest, the officer poured the remainder of the drink onto the sand and ordered the boy to move along.

CASE NO. 4

A man reported a fight in progress and said some shots had been fired. He later complained that it took the police nearly an hour to respond and charged that the same report from a white neighborhood would have brought them on the double.

CASE NO. 5

A Negro who witnessed a robbery was asked by two officers to come with them to see whether he could identify a suspect who was working in a gas station. The place was miles away across town. When they got there, the suspect had left. The officers put the witness out of the car saying they were too busy to take him back home.

CASE NO. 6

A Negro was observed walking in a white neighborhood one evening about 10:00 o'clock. Two officers stopped and asked him to explain his presence there. He told them it was none of their business, that he had a right to walk on any street any time he felt like it. He refused to answer questions so they took him to headquarters for further interrogation. It turned out he was a minister who was very active in the civil rights movement. He had no criminal record and had done nothing to sustain any charge in this instance. He complained that the officers' action was indicative of the attitude of police toward all Negroes.

CASE NO. 7

With respect to the Puerto Rican disturbances in Chicago recently, the *Christian Science Monitor* reported as follows: "There was little doubt that the presence of police—and their handling of Puerto Ricans over a period of several years—was the center of the controversy in this conflict. We heard no other argument or issue in the seven hours we worked the streets. . . . Despite careful guidelines, police tactics were not uniformly discreet. One instance took place before we began breaking up the congestion at Division and California. Most of the young men had gone, and we had been thanked by the sergeant on the corner. Suddenly a police captain with a dozen blue-helmeted men stormed across the street. I was standing inside a restaurant at the time because the street was virtually clear. The captain and three men pushed into the restaurant where more than 50 people, in family groups, were quietly eating their evening meal. In a loud voice, he demanded to see the owner. Moving to the kitchen he demanded that she clear the place and close up. Then he stalked out, shaking his fist and shouting: 'I'll give you 15 minutes to get everybody out of here, you understand. Fifteen minutes.' Then he slammed the door with such force the storefront windows rattled. In less than a minute, he had changed quietness into anger. . . . A spokesman for the police department said it was only one of several complaints about the same captain. At 10:50 p.m., only a handful of people were left on the street. A lieutenant and a group of policemen raced to the upper floor of a three-story building on Division Street and hauled out two men who someone said had been seen with crude antipolice signs in a window. Then the police closed a restaurant below where there were a number of Puerto Ricans. Those in the restaurant scattered as ordered. But two youths, walking slowly a block away, were spotted by a sergeant who cursed them, saying to the lieutenant. 'Those guys were in the restaurant. Let's go get them.' At this point, the only incident of undue physical roughness I observed during the entire night took place. Two police searched one of the youths, and then gave him a hard shove that sent him sprawling toward the police wagon. The lieutenant and sergeant stood on the curb discussing what they could charge the two youths with since they had only been walking down the street. . . . "

Now, as I said, I cannot vouch for the accuracy of these reports. I suspect there is a considerable bias in them. I also realize that when they are shaved down in the retelling, there may be significant facts omitted. *But the point is that these are the kinds of things people hear and it is on the basis of such stories they form their opinions about police.* Then, when approached by an officer, they expect rough, inconsiderate, impolite treatment.

I know, and so do you, that it sometimes takes pretty strong talk and forceful action to get the police job done. However, I am sure we can agree that an officer who uses profanity is definitely out of line. So is one who is so prejudiced that he cannot treat the objects of his prejudice as ordinary human beings. An officer who generates resentment, who makes people rise up in anger by the things he says or does or the way he acts toward them is a source of trouble. An officer who would stand by and watch someone being beaten is violating his oath. One of the things that we must attend to in our effort to improve relations with the people in our communities, therefore, is the way our officers are doing their job on the street day in and day out. This is not to say that all the fault lies in police behavior, but, to the extent that *any* of the fault lies there, we must accept the blame and correct it.

The article in *Life* reports the following statement by one of the extremist leaders in Los Angeles: "I want a *unity* in this town, so that man—that cop—is not going to come down here and snatch *nobody.* I try to tell The Beast, and I'll tell him once more: You're pushin' too hard. We're *with* the brother on the street. Even when the guy's *wrong* we're gonna be with him. This has got to be understood. If nothing's done. I'm sure not going to tell these fellows—ah—not to defend themselves."

Anyone who believes in law and order cannot buy that extreme view. When someone is "wrong" to the extent of violating the law, the police have no choice but to take affirmative action. We have no choice but to arrest people who violate the law. If the law is bad, then those who have responsibility for legislation should change it. No individual can disregard the law with impunity no matter how strong his belief that the law is bad. If he violates the law he must accept arrest. This is what is meant by a government of laws not men.

In our system of government, people have a right to protest what they think is wrong. That right, however, carries with it certain responsibilities. President Johnson put it this way. "No American, young or old, must ever be denied the right of dissent. No minority must ever be muzzled. Opinion and protest are the life breath of democracy—even when it blows heavy. But I urge you never to dissent merely because someone asks you to, or because someone else does. Know why you protest. Know what it is you dissent from. Dissent and protest must be the recourse of men, who challenging the existing order, reason their way to a better order."

Our police-community relations programs are methods we use to help us reason our way to a better order. It is going to take more than talk, though. It is going to require a clear demonstration of sincerity. A friend of mine who is a school superintendent in a large city participated recently in a program designed to do something for high school dropouts to help fit them for employment. The program was successful in the main, but he told me that the young people involved—mostly Negroes—were convinced that teachers, preachers, and police—white or Negro—were phonies. "They give you a lot of high sounding talk which they don't believe themselves and when you turn your back they kick you back downstairs." In other words, word and deed do not match so far as they can see. Promises are not fulfilled in performance.

Let us bear in mind that today's triumph may be tomorrow's tragedy, for tragedy and triumph are but points of view. The pinnacle of success can be the beginning of the road to disaster for the unwary. The lesson we can take from this is that community relations programs which offer nothing but talk just won't accomplish anything. It is going to take action—action which demonstrates we mean it when we say we will not tolerate brutality, action which demonstrates we mean it when we say our Negro officers are just as much policemen as our white officers, action which demonstrates we mean it when we say we are going to enforce the law fairly and impartially, and we mean it when we say we shall enforce the law.

Our community relations programs must be geared to these kinds of action. Mobilize the people on the side of law and order. Let them see that policing in their city is done for their benefit. Show them that the law offers neither condemnation nor deference based on color, creed, or class.

NOTES

1. Mark Sherwin, *The Extremists* (New York: St. Martin's Press, 1963), p. 189.

Police and Politics: Speak Out on the Issues

Mark H. Furstenberg

That politics and the police are incompatible is an unquestioned article of the professional policemen's faith. And to raise it again may seem trivial. Is there any more accepted truism than that the police must be above politics? You who are concerned with professionalization certainly wouldn't reconsider *that* question.

I am going to be doubly presumptuous. Not only am I, who have never been a

At the time this article was written, Mark H. Furstenberg was assistant to the Honorable Joseph D. Tydings, U.S. Senator from Maryland.

From Mark H. Furstenberg, "Police and Politics: Speak Out on the Issues," *The Police Chief* 33, no. 8 (August 1968): 12-18. Reprinted by permission of the publisher.

policeman, going to comment on the police role; but in addition, I am going to challenge that universally accepted truism about police and politics. I am going to suggest that the police get into politics. But I do not mean that old-fashioned kind of political involvement in police affairs, and vice versa. And I do not mean partisan politics.

When police think about politics, they react viscerally: "Take the police out of politics!" It means to you an order from the mayor to promote his friends. It means a request to forget about a traffic citation. It means the transfer or demotion of a too-vigorous vice squad captain. You wisely resist that kind of political interference.

But in its external operations, there is practically nothing the police do which is not political. At every point of public contact, you are in politics. The question of political inhibition of criminal justice—the question of taking the police out of politics—is meaningless. There is nothing you can do to remove yourselves. You may as well accept it, because it's the nature of your job. Let me cite some examples:

1. Your city is concerned about crime. The city council is floundering under public pressure. It passes a couple of "get tough with criminals" resolutions, and expresses its devotion to the "lonely policeman on his beat." But the public isn't satisfied. So the Council summons your commissioner to discuss ways of reducing crime. He knows that if he goes, he and the force will be humiliated by the Council before the television cameras. He knows that Councilmen will compete with each other to display to the public their toughness on crime, and that they will do so by taking it out on him. On the other hand, he knows that if he refuses to go, tries to remain aloof, the Council will be offended, and will proceed to show him who is the boss.

2. A ghetto neighborhood blows up, and your force is confronted with a riot. The mayor orders all police to be restrained, and to sacrifice property to avoid killing. Your commissioner interprets this as an order not to use guns, a strategy with which he agrees. He sends you out on the streets to face bricks, bottles, stones, epithets, and, at all times, to keep your revolvers holstered. There is not a single incident of police error, and you and your colleagues are proud. But then, two days after the end of the disorder, your mayor goes on television, and publicly humiliates the commissioner and the force by saying that you should have shot those "hoodlums and scavengers."

3. You take into custody a suspect in a routine burglary case. You offer him a lawyer, and he says that he doesn't want one. You hope that he will confess; but you know that if he does, you may face a searching court of inquiry into the way in which that confession was obtained. What do you do? Do you interrogate him? For how long? How can you make the correct judgment? How can you keep your interrogation free of intimidation?

4. For some months your vice squad has been conducting a broad gambling investigation. A number of leads point to the same man—a prominent member of the state legislature. You know that to pursue this investigation will bring down

the roof. You face the decision of dropping the investigation or pursuing it. (Both courses are political.)

The police are involved in politics. If you avoid all political choices, you cannot do your job. The only question is *how* you are going to be involved. You can be passive, and be buffetted from one force to another—always everybody's scapegoat. Or you can, for the good of the community and the profession, take a stand on issues—*knowing* that you are engaging in politics.

Make no mistake. There are only two choices: Active involvement or *in*active involvement. You cannot be uninvolved. Pretending that the problem does not exist is a decision—a decision to be passively involved. And you must face the probability that for the next few years the problem is going to be intense.

Crime is the major political issue of the year. The public is worried about crime. Congress must pass legislation. The President must have legislation. People are frightened. They are demanding that something be done. And, whatever your past habits, you cannot now hide from public view.

The question you must answer is: Should you not help the political community to define what will be done about crime? Who has a greater stake than you in the programs being considered? Who should be more concerned than you that we create good law enforcement programs, rather than shams?

Crime is a new issue, and people are terribly unsophisticated about it. On the one side are those who make their contribution to the debate by putting "Support your local police" bumper stickers on their cars. On the other are those who believe that standard police equipment includes rubber hoses for beating confessions out of suspects.

Of course, there is a lack of police understanding, appreciation, and sophistication about your work. Are you helping to correct this?

It is up to *you* to teach police issues to the public. *You* must explain to the public what goes on in the stationhouse during an interrogation, and why interrogation is an indispensable part of investigation.

Do you feel handcuffed by Supreme Court decisions? A majority of the United States Senate thinks you are. Do you? How have Supreme Court decisions inhibited you? How have they changed your behavior? Tell us.

How do you feel about the wide range of social services you are required to perform? Do you feel qualified to be youth workers, family counsellors, legal advisors, recreation instructors? Is your training adequate for the task? If you need more training and more funds to conduct it, that too is an issue of public concern.

You see welfare families, juvenile delinquents, alcoholics, addicts, hippies, and all other kinds of people from a perspective entirely different from that of the public. The public needs to know that perspective. If you must provide services to so many people, do you not have the right to comment on their problems?

What about professional issues? Do you need a new communications system, more patrol cars, higher salaries, more research funds? Why don't you share your needs with the public? If you ever dared to make legislative stinginess a public issue, you might be able to mobilize public pressure to force political leaders to help you.

The public should understand the discretion a policeman is asked to exercise. Many people think your job consists of getting a call, rushing with siren screaming to the site, asking questions, dusting for fingerprints, getting leads, following them, and catching (or not catching) the suspect.

This simplistic view of the police role—far more widely held than you think—is one of the reasons the public feels entitled to criticize the police. People just really do not understand the complexity of the police profession. They see police work as a simple straight line beginning at a crime, and ending at arrest. They do not understand how wide a range of choices policeman have, and how many decisions you must make for nearly every act you perform.

Why do you suppose the public fails to understand you? Because they are not interested in you? Nonsense. The public is devoted to two American folk heroes—the cowboy and the cop. But you have never been able to translate that devotion to the radio-television cop into understanding of, and support for your work.

The reason, I believe, is that for too many years you have been a close fraternity—trying to do your job, believing that nobody understands the policeman, withdrawing more and more from meaningful public contact, declining to communicate your problems, uncertainties, and angers.

One consequence is that: in the whole range of public-contact areas, you have been reluctant to develop clear, specific guidelines for police behavior, and then communicate them. You do this in questions of internal management, which you do not have to share with the public. But you do not do so for those areas in which the public is affected.

You argue, quite correctly, that you must have flexibility. You say that you cannot make complicated decisions by rigid procedures. Moreover, many people believe that some good police practices cannot be reconciled with constitutional legal standards. If that is true, should the public not know about it? Tell them. Then you use your flexibility as a mandate to develop policies as specific as possible: Confide in the public your perfectly proper need to maintain flexibility.

You have tried to maintain flexibility by inaction. And in declining to talk about your problems, you have alienated everybody—those concerned primarily with more police protection, and those who are worried more about civil liberty.

So the courts have moved in to do what you have not done—develop clear guidelines. The *Miranda* case is a good example. There was no good reason for the Supreme Court to tell *you* that suspects have rights. You knew it. But the failure of some to develop proper policies, and the failure of all to communicate forced the Court to act. And where were you when the Court was considering this and other cases which affect police? Are you not as entitled as the ACLU to file *amicus curiae* briefs?

So as the need for a dialogue between the police and other institutions increases, so does your avoidance of it. Many of you now have only the most professional dealings with the public. Your colleagues are policemen. Your friends are policemen. When do you see civilians? I must say—I believe that the gap between the police and the public is growing, bumper stickers to the contrary notwithstanding. I don't know how you feel about it; but in my opinion, it is terribly dangerous.

I think you must take the first step to reach out and initate a dialogue with the public. Those who care to speak and write should do so—for the public. You should all begin talking to civilians. Perhaps, you should bring residents of the neighborhoods you serve into the stationhouse to watch and help you. You may not like that notion. But you have nothing to fear from the public. I am certain that public observation and assistance can only help you. It may not at first be too pleasant. It may force you to reexamine some notions.

You might start with the issue of consolidation. When you mix with the public, you may find it difficult to persuade them that we really need 40,000 separate agencies to enforce the laws of this country.

And while you are considering that, perhaps you will move on to consider the whole notion of local autonomy. We take it for granted that local control of police is a great bulwark of freedom. But is it? Are we certain that it is the best method of administration?

Then how about lateral entry? That issue was settled years ago in other professions. But you are still debating it. You want to be treated like a profession, which is what you are; and you cannot behave like a union.

Finally, perhaps you can then begin to move into issues which are not exclusively yours, but on which society needs your contribution. You might begin by asking whether police can really control crime. You believe you can; and you have encouraged the public to judge you by your ability to control the crime rates.

This belief is beginning to get you into trouble. For a while longer you will be able to blame rising crime on our failure to invest more money in the police. But when you begin to receive large amounts of supplementary federal money, and crime continues to rise, people are going to start asking why.

To forestall the consequences, you might want to begin admitting that police action—no matter how good—has a limited effect on incidence. That does not not make you any less important. After all, can diagnosticians prevent all diseases all the time? You are the diagnosticians of society.

So the first step, I believe, is for you to initiate new forms of public contact. And the second is to put your traditional beliefs and notions to new tests. Try to imagine how the public sees you and your ideas, remembering that to open the minds of the public, you must approach the public with an open mind.

The third step is to organize your extra-curricular activities. When you have begun to speak on more issues, you may want to speak through your organizations. Why not? Other professions do it. Lawyers have their bar associations, doctors their medical societies. And you too must have organizations responsive to your professional views, and eager to advocate your causes.

Through your organizations, I hope you will begin to speak on issues *external* to your profession. How about beginning with your role in riots?

You are now being asked to hold society together. You are being asked to do it quietly, nonviolently, and without complaint. In return, do you not have the right to say to political leaders, "All right. If you want us to be society's last defense, tell us what *you* are prepared to do about the *causes* of urban disorders?"

Who has more of a right to ask this than you who are on the front lines?

Then, perhaps, you might want to say something about gun control. You know that we have no effective gun control in this nation; and not a single bill seriously considered by the Congress would really *control* firearms. *You* are the people hurt most by our firearms anarchy. Haven't you something to say about it? it?

Then, I think you should begin addressing problems like poverty, welfare, middle-class delinquency. Why shouldn't you? You have a unique perspective. You have to deal with society's failures. Are you not entitled to contribute to our knowledge of these people?

Pick your issues carefully. I am not suggesting that you get involved in all issues. I do not believe that you ought to be commenting in your professional capacity about Vietnam or water pollution. And I certainly am not advocating that you get engaged in partisan activity, like supporting candidates for public office. But I think you should speak out on the issues which affect you as police.

Finally, I think you should translate your ideas into activity. Choose your strategies carefully. On some issues you may want to initiate. If the probation department is not doing its job, and you know it and remain silent, your own burdens are likely to mount. On this issue you may want to speak first, without waiting for the crisis.

On other issues, it might be wiser to respond—waiting first for the issue to ripen, and then, at the point when the mayor or city council is considering action, stepping in with your views.

You will also want to use inside and outside strategies, depending on the issue. You may, for example, want to discuss quietly with state legislators salary incentives for higher education. But on another kind of issue—for example, an unrealistic state censorship law which you are required to enforce—you may want to speak out publicly to get support.

Whatever strategies you choose, whatever issues you pick, whatever activity you undertake, you must understand that as crime becomes of public concern, so do the police. As the police become of concern, they find themselves more and more the subjects of political debate.

You have no choice but to be involved. If you choose the involvement of splendid isolation, you risk a great deal. You risk further alienation, less public understanding and sympathy, and legislative action based on inadequate information.

The alternative is to get into the public debate as active participants, share your knowledge and experience with legislatures and courts, and help the public to appreciate you—always remembering what Mark Twain said: "We can secure other people's approval if we do right and try hard; but our own is worth a hundred of it, and no way has been found out of securing that."

Community Indifference and the Growth of Crime

Frank D. Day

Community indifference and the growth of crime in the United States reached serious proportions long ago. They reached record heights in 1964. Because "Crime," as J. Edgar Hoover summed it up in his 1964 crime reports, "continued to outpace population with an increase since 1958 of six times the growth of the national population."

In the war on crime, in 1964, there were 57 officers murdered in the line of duty. Thirty-one others died in accidents, and one of every ten officers was assaulted. Community indifference to crime was evidenced by the fact that hardly a week passed—perhaps not even a day—when the nation's press was without a sensational story of man's failure to measure up to his moral or legal obligations, or both, to his fellow man or his community.

Thus crime and indifference to crime in the United States are facts about which there is little room for serious disagreement. Why the two problems have reached such proportions and how to go about solving them are widely debated topics, but most of it seems to end up in blind alleys. On the other hand, the problems, the day-to-day-happenings, can be brought out in the open and subjected to scrutiny.

CRIME IN THE UNITED STATES

Long strides are being made in interplanetary space exploration. America is concerned with national and international problems. One problem, however, is always with us and steadily grows larger. It is the year-after-year, relentless climb

Frank D. Day is Professor of Police Administration and Public Safety in the School of Criminal Justice at Michigan State University.
From Frank D. Day, "Community Indifference and the Growth of Crime," *Police* 10, no. 3 (January-February 1966): 25-30. Reprinted by permission of the author and the publisher, Charles C Thomas.

of crime in the United States. Crime in the United States is more prevalent than ever. Current statistics on crime—despite the fallibility attributed to them by some critics—should remove any doubt about that.

Since 1940, the crime rate in the United States has doubled. Crime reached an all-time high in the United States in 1964. All previous annual crime rates in the United States will be broken in 1965, if the rate of increase for the remainder of the year follows that of the first six months.

Juvenile crime is a national disgrace, with more than 40 percent of *all* arrests made in 1964 involving persons under eighteen years of age. Arrests in this age group, excluding traffic offenses, increased by 17 percent over 1963. For the country as a whole, these young people comprised 48 percent of all police arrests in 1964 for *serious* offenses. There are people who hold the juvenile crime picture is not nearly as bad as it appears. Figures tend to support their assertion (depending on one's point of view), as only about 1 percent of the youngsters in the United States are arrested for serious crime and less than 3 percent for any kind of offense.

Many people are more or less familiar with the crime statistics for 1964. It is information, nonetheless, that merits being repeated over and over, if for no other reason than that it may make more people think about crime and, in turn, motivate more people to assume responsibility for law enforcement in their communities.

The FBI says serious crimes increased 13 percent across the United States in 1964 over 1963. More than 2.6 million serious crimes were reported to the police in 1964—the total was up more than a quarter of a million over 1963. The increase was most marked in the suburbs, with a rise of 17 percent—a fact that should spark more sociological reflection about crime than ever. The crime rate rose 11 percent in cities with more than 100,000 inhabitants, and 9 percent in the rural areas.

Projections in the future are even more disconcerting. It has been suggested that, if present trends continue, we could see an 80 percent increase in crime in the United States by 1975.

Small wonder that President Johnson in his March 8 crime message to Congress called for stepped-up efforts to "arrest and reverse the trend toward lawlessness" which, he said, is costing the country "tens of billions of dollars annually" plus a frightening toll in death, injury, and heartbreaks. Every American has reason to share both the concern expressed by the President over the growing crime problem and his desire to "arrest and reverse the trend."

The President proposed needed legislation to strengthen the hands of law enforcement. As he declared, however, that is not enough. That is why he put the role of the individual citizen as the first ingredient of progress. "The starting point," he said, "is the individual citizen . . . the people will get observance of law and enforcement of law if they want it, insist on it, and participate in it." No doubt he had these thoughts in mind in setting up "The President's

Commission on Law Enforcement and Administration of Justice" on July 23, 1965.

COMMUNITY INDIFFERENCE AND MORALITY

It would be a mistake to take the position that listlessness toward crime and other social problems on the part of some Americans is a blanket indictment of the moral values of the present generation. Because the inescapable truth is that we are, in 1965, a more moral people than ever before. The Honorable Edith Green, Congresswoman from Oregon, was perhaps more than half right when she said in a speech in the House of Representatives on January 11, 1965, that "The United States of the 1960s is not necessarily a less moral society than the United States of the 1770s. In fact, the general level of moral and ethical behavior may well be far higher. The problem is rather that our citizens today face a more complex world in a more crowded country with more laws and more opportunities to violate laws."

There is less dishonesty in government, local and national, than in the days of the "Spoils System" and the "Boss Tweeds." Our cities are much healthier and less violent than they were in the 1880s. "We do not now have areas in our cities into which the police are afraid to go. That such areas flourished long after the Civil War is a part of our history. Nor do we have vast acreages given over to prostitution and associated vices," as Ralph McGill declared in his syndicated column of November 29, last year.

"We are," he continued, "trying to do what is moral and right in race relations. We are beginning to look coldly at the slum landlord. We are admitting that while we have had public housing for more than thirty years, we have done almost nothing at all about housing for the really poor. We are also aware of our failures in education and the ugly discrimination of our society.... No reasonable person can deny that the nation is more moral and compassionate than ever in its history."

Events like the mother's march on polio, or the march on Selma, clearly show compassion for worthy causes on the part of people who participate in these kinds of activities. It is a kind of morality, nevertheless, that characterizes group action to achieve broad goals with an element of personal recognition threaded into the picture. A sociologist friend of mine describes it as a materialistic or humanistic form of morality that partakes very little of morality rooted in concepts of personal responsibility. This does not mean that people who will take up the cudgel for a worthy cause feel no compassion for individuals who need help.

From their ranks may have come the people who did give a hand when someone needed help, and the ones who did come to the aid of police officers at personal danger to themselves. A mob overpowered a policeman twice and freed his prisoner. Someone plunged an ice pick into the back of the neighborhood grocer who came to the policeman's assistance. A witness to a murder gave the police a description of the killers and the license number of their automobile. He identified them after the arrest. A train rolled over him a few days later after he refused to heed the threat of one of two thugs who accosted him and said: "Forget what you saw."

Americans have been debating the Good Samaritan issue since the national conscience was shocked in 1963 by the fatal stabbing of Kitty Genovese. How to go about getting a person to help another person who needs help is a knotty problem. Some voices speak up for legislation that would punish the bad Samaritan. Others say it is impossible to legislate conscience. A few countries do try to legislate it—with inconsistent results.

California's so-called "Good Samaritan Law," which Governor Edmund G. Brown signed in July, 1965, allows the state to pay private citizens who get hurt while attempting to prevent crime. It is doubtful, however, whether such legislation will do much to change the "I don't care to get involved" attitude of people who feel this way.

COMMUNITY INDIFFERENCE TO COMMUNITY PROBLEMS

Community Indifference to People

Stories of noninvolvement range from shunning jury duty to incidents when no compassion whatsoever was shown to another human being in trouble. Its seriousness was brought out most dramatically when a man attacked 28-year-old Catherine Genovese on March 13, 1963, as she was returning to her home from work. He stabbed her. She screamed for help, and he fled. Repeatedly, she called to her neighbors for help. At least 38 of them heard her, but none of them helped her, and she died. They did not want to "become involved," they said. Many like episodes have been reported without, apparently, making much of an imprint in the minds of a lot of readers. The stories have differed, but the attitude of the principals has been just about the same: "I did not want to get involved."

A nude, ravished girl fled screaming from her attacker. She begged onlookers to help her. Some 40 of them did nothing. Three persons stood by while a man weighing only 100 pounds assaulted a young woman. A hold-up victim, stabbed 22 times, bled to death while more than twenty bystanders made no effort to help him. A crowd yelled, "Jump, Jump" to a confused man on a building ledge.

Such apathy by adults toward others who need assistance is a factor in the growth of crime. It seems reasonable to believe that it may encourage many evildoers to greater boldness, and that it may help to recruit newcomers to their ranks. Apathy of that character, moreover, is but one of several attitudes in a community that tend, together, to promote crime—*as a social product.*

Community Indifference to Authority

There are thousands of persons who have determined to subject themselves to no law but their own, and who flaunt, in every way, their disrespect for both moral and statute law. In this group are found many law enforcement headaches like the "hostile person," the "repeater offender," and the "irresponsible citizen." They have made the headlines many times.

Firemen attempted to reach a burning house. A group of 60 heckling youths refused to move out of the street. Police finally dispersed them. Firemen, who were then able to enter into the building, found the limp form of a two-year-old boy. But it was too late. The child was pronounced dead on arrival at the hospital. Firemen said when they tried to revive the baby on the lawn, several youths ran up and "tried to stomp on the dead body." A woman and two men, part of the growing crowd of 400 persons, were arrested. A brick-throwing crowd of some 300 persons injured three policemen and damaged two squad cars when police tried to give a motorist a "ticket" for a traffic code violation. Eleven of them were charged with resisting and obstructing a police officer, inciting to riot, and aggravated assault. Beer-drinking, carousing youths staged riots and disturbances in five resort towns the past Fourth of July weekend. They battled officers with fists, bottles, and rocks. More than 700 of them were arrested.

Another more subtle form of disrespect for authority, by far, are organized and deliberate acts of civil disobedience. Civil disobedience—the deliberate violation of a law, with every expectation of arrest, as a protest on the grounds that the law, or more social condition which it sustains, is unjust—is not a new problem. It has existed as a law enforcement problem in one form or another down through the centuries. It has taken on some new dimensions, however.

The Supreme Court of the United States upheld a will which limited the student body of a college founded by the testator to "poor, white, male orphans." Pickets march around the college day-after-day demanding that the will be stricken down as discriminatory while other demonstrators picket the pickets. Police are continually on guard to preserve the peace and protect individual rights while other areas of the city go without adequate police protection. City officials debated the adoption of an open occupancy housing ordinance. A number of persons, most of them university students, staged a sit-down demonstration in the street in front of the City Hall to protest nonaction on the bill. The demonstrators rejected all appeals to disperse made to them. They disrupted traffic for nearly three hours. The mayor finally read the city ordinance to them covering blocking of free passage of the public, and gave them five minutes to end their sit-down. Police arrested 59 persons when the demonstrators refused to disperse.

"No individual or group at any time, for any reason has a right to exact self-determined retribution. Grievances must be settled in the courts; not in the streets," as Morris I. Liebman points out in the July, 1965 issue of the *American Bar Association Journal.*

Community Indifference to Law Enforcement

Anyone familiar with law enforcement activities knows that the starting point of any war on crime rests with the individual, who must help law enforcement, rather than merely criticize it. An apathetic attitude by people to that simple proposition, in conjunction with unfounded criticism of law enforcement, are principal factors in the growth of crime.

Law enforcement officers alone cannot contain crime. Crime control is not just their responsibility. It is the responsibility of all citizens. Police officers are simply private persons in uniform who are paid to do what all citizens are supposed to do. The police do not expect their unpaid helpers to risk personal danger. What they do expect, however, is citizen cooperation that rarely need involve any personal risk at all.

The stabbing of Kitty Genovese was a striking example. She was within sight and hearing of 38 people while her attacker leisurely finished her off. A nude young woman pleaded with more than 40 onlookers for help as she fought off her attacker, but they did nothing. None of the witnesses, in either case, would even pick up a telephone to call the police.

More than 100 persons were in the immediate area when a narcotic peddler was shot to death by a rival mobster. At least seven persons saw a three-car crash which cost the lives of two persons. None of the witnesses, in either case, would give the police any information about the incidents.

The tendency to shy away from reporting crimes is a common one. The reluctance of people to give information to the police that could involve them as a witness is even more prevalent. Crime in the United States feeds on such evasions of personal responsibility. "I am my brother's keeper," in a very real way, is a part of good citizenship.

Almost two centuries ago, Edmund Burke said: "The only thing necessary for the triumph of evil is that good men do nothing." Good men and competent law enforcement officers, working together, could reduce crime extensively.

LAW ENFORCEMENT INDIFFERENCE TO COMMUNITY EXPECTATIONS

Competent law enforcement officers are not indifferent to what is expected of them by the people of the communities they serve. But just as there are many citizens, who are either almost totally unaware of their responsibilities to law enforcement, or prefer to ignore them, so there are many police officers who are apathetic and vegetative to their responsibilities to the people they serve.

Officers in that category tend to forget that today's police officer should get along with people, command their respect, and earn their cooperation. It is imperative then, that they "take inventory" of their personalities as it were, to discover whether what they do, or do not do, encourages or diminishes community participation in law enforcement activities.

Law Enforcement Indifference to People

That the average police officer is a pretty suspicious person is a well-known fact. A police officer without this trait would probably be a rather poor officer. But if he allows this quality to dominate his thinking too much, it tends to isolate him from nonpolice people. Some officers seem to take an extreme position, so much so, that they look at most private persons as "friendly" enemies. This has been brought home to me at various times since my active law enforcement career ended.

Recently, for example, the director of a community relations unit of a large metropolitan city invited me to take part in a three-month training program for police on police and community relations. The program was sponsored jointly by the police department and community relations people. The word got around, apparently, that it would be a "brainwashing" kind of experience for the several groups of police officers who had volunteered to take part in the program. That was reflected by the indifferent attitude of many of them—almost to the point of hostility—for the first 15 to 20 minutes of a lecture session.

Police officers must learn to distinguish between their real friends, who want to help them, and others who may have different motives. Some of their best friends come from the ranks of the people who, at times, are the most articulate in their demands that individual rights be protected.

Law Enforcement Indifference to Police Review Boards

Perhaps opposition to police review boards would be more descriptive of the attitude of police personnel, generally, whenever the topic comes up. The indifference visualized here is indifference on the part of most police officers to the fact that people in a community have a legitimate interest in any proposal, yes, even a police review board, that may upgrade the quality of law enforcement services. There is, understandably, confusion relative to the "police review board" concept on the part of both police and citizens.

Police opposition to any review board format is justified when that board would take responsibility for personnel management, along with the authority and power to discipline, away from the law enforcement administrator. The police, however, should not categorically reject the review board concept. A police review board may be established, if one needs to be set up, that would be acceptable to both the police and the citizens of a community. What many police officers fail to understand is that a police review board, properly constituted, may work more for them than against them.

As we point out in *Introduction to Law Enforcement:* "Every effort must be made to end the current tension whereby citizens pressing for review boards assume that police resistance is solely due to a desire to whitewash deficiencies, and whereby police resisting the review board proposal assume that citizen pressure is solely due to a Kremlin-hatched plot. Americans owe more than that to each other."

Law Enforcement Indifference to Law

A police officer takes an oath to enforce all laws. The people invest him with awesome powers to carry out that mission. They expect him to exercise those powers impartially and in a common-sense way.

One of the quickest ways for a police officer to bring public disrepute upon himself and alienate public support for his agency, is to show indifference to what people expect of their police. Competent and conscientious officers are ever mindful of that. Nevertheless, just as all men do not act rationally at all times, so it is with police officers. Some officers, either through ignorance or indifference to the rights of people, sometime enforce the law in a very uncommon sense way.

They are the ones who may believe that a rule like the prompt arraignment rule—taking a prisoner before a court without unnecessary delay—serves no purpose other than to set up a road block to effective law enforcement. They are the ones who would probably make an illegal raid on a gambling place instead of arming themselves with a search warrant and doing it the right way. They are the ones who may forget or disregard the fact that such practices only build a wall of separation, higher and higher, between them and the community they serve.

Many police administrators have adopted positive measures to control illegal or unreasonable police practices. They know that a single complaint of alleged police brutality on the part of any police officer is one too many. They know that a reasonable effort must be made to obey court decisions even though they may disagree with a court's making, or interpretation, of a law. Nor do they stand alone when they voice disagreement with certain court decisions.

Justices of Supreme Court of the United States disagree sharply with one another as is shown by numerous 5-4 opinions wherein one man's judgment made the law. No one, therefore, should question the right of any person to disagree with a decision. But there are affirmative ways and negative ways of doing it.

It is a common practice for many police officers to range too far in their criticism. This is where the danger lies. Police officers must never become indifferent to the fact that a decision is the law until it is modified or overruled. Neither can they ever afford to become indifferent to the fact that the American judicial system is the people's staunchest bulwark against totalitarianism.

Law Enforcement Indifference to Professional Police Work

The rank and file in law enforcement remain indifferent to the fact that a changing society imposes new demands on police education, as well as methods. A quarter-century ago, most policemen would have sneered at the idea that a policeman should know as much about people, or more, than he knows about the tools of his trade. This is still characteristic of many officers today.

However, a small percentage of professional-minded police officers have responded to the challenges that face modern law enforcement in a changing society. They are working with community leaders and educators, for example, to provide in-service training programs for police in human relations. This is a relatively new concept in police work. It means that police officers must know how to get along with people, how to work with people, and how to help people to get along together. Many police officers, however, remain indifferent to a "why-you-do-it" approach to police work. They are somewhat suspicious of any person who says modern police work involves much more than the protection of life and property.

Such officers tend to regard scornfully anyone who is so rash as to suggest that the demands made on police officers in a complex modern world warrant the highest educational standards. They tend to regard the college-trained man or woman who joins their ranks with a certain amount of cynicism.

They tend to be indifferent to the fact that law enforcement officers are a most important part of the administration of criminal justice, and high qualifications of character and educational background contribute materially to the effectiveness of their work. They tend to find it hard to believe that in July, 1965, the Multnomah County (Oregon) Civil Service Commission established the educational requirement of a bachelor's degree for an appointment as a County Sheriff's Deputy. Their indifference to changes and problems create many of the problems that confront many American law enforcement agencies.

BALANCE THE SCALES

They are not indifferent, however, to the idea that there must be laws and laws must be enforced. They are aware, as Oxford historian Charles Reith concludes in *The Blind Eye of History,* that "every civilization throughout the course of human history has perished that has failed to enforce its laws." This is the view taken by most police officers toward nonenforcement of criminal laws. They know that many forces are at work today that make the enforcement of criminal laws a most difficult task for them.

Police officers have much on their side to sustain their belief that today's criminal law is so much out of balance that criminals are being protected at the expense of the law-abiding citizen. Many private citizens are of like mind. Their views find ample support in a story like "Crime Runs Wild—Will It Be Halted?" August 9, 1965, *U.S. News and World Report.*

Of greater concern to the police officers that the crime picture is the idea that society can give its citizens the "right" to break the law as is implied in the concept of righteous, civil disobedience. They feel there can be no law to which obedience is optional, when the law is not static and effective channels for change constantly available.

Civil disobedience, by definition, is an unlawful activity. Prefixing the term by euphemisms like "legal," "non-violent," and "peaceable," does not change that. "Let us beware of pat expressions, such as: 'Justice delayed is justice denied. Justice delayed cannot serve as an excuse for antijustice,' " as Morris Liebman emphasizes in the July, 1965 issue of *American Bar Association Journal.*

Let us understand that police officers are not responsible for the social ills that afflict their communities. Let us understand that for them to be effective they must understand these problems, and that they must understand the motivations of their fellow citizens who are beset by these problems. Let us understand that citizens, by their apathy toward crime and by their failure to shoulder their moral and legal responsibilities to help enforce criminal laws, are far more blameworthy for the alleged breakdown of law and order in the United States than their police.

There are promising signs on the horizon that partial solutions, at least, to some of the crime issues will soon be forthcoming. One of them is a 2.5 million dollar national campaign directed at public safety and apathy to crime that is being undertaken by the National Council on Crime and Delinquency. Another is the National Center on Police and Community Relations which is being established as a result of a $100,000 grant from the Field Foundation. This Center is operative now under the aegis of the School of Police Administration and Public Safety, College of Social Science, Michigan State University.

Such programs should have far-reaching effects in helping police officers to learn to distinguish between "what is" and "what should be" and to assume some responsibility in the task of bringing American law enforcement to the highest possible level of efficiency. It is a responsibility and task that will demand the utmost intelligence, moral character, motivation, and courage. It is a responsibility and a task that cannot be overlooked in any approach to law enforcement.

Such programs should have far-reaching effects in helping private persons from all walks of life to become better informed about their police and to gain a better understanding of their responsibilities.

More than anything else, perhaps, the American people must be made to understand, as Mr. Justice Clark declared, in his 1965 Law Day address at the University of Maryland Law School, that: "The image of the law and the integrity of our system of justice are irrevocably interwoven in the police officer's uniform: every community in America should develop programs toward upgrading and professionalizing law enforcement. That, in the main, is the answer to the ever-increasing incidence of crime."

Community Organizations as a Solution to Police-Community Problems

Oscar Handlin

I am going to talk to you about some of the problems of law and order in our society, in a way that is perhaps more meaningful than the terms in which that issue has entered into the current political campaign. [1] If you can bear with me, I would like to explore some of the problems in the relationships of the police to the community that lie behind these surface manifestations of difficulty which are basic to the attitude of Americans and particularly of Americans in our metropolitan centers toward the problems of law and order.

If we look at this issue on the surface we see an apparent contradiction. On the one hand, substantial parts of the population show deep concern about the need for order and safety in the confused and turbulent condition of the modern city. Everybody in a sense is against crime, that goes without say.ng, but, in addition, everybody feels that something ought to be done about law and order. And yet at the same time we don't feel a corresponding growth of confidence or a corresponding sense of obligation or indebtedness to the police force.

In some cities there is evident a perpetual kind of running hositilty between the citizen, the community and the police who are, after all, the guardians of its safety and its security. That hostility expresses itself not simply in such bread and butter issues as the unwillingness to raise police salaries which is particularly an issue in the part of the country from which I come, but also in the desire in some parts of the country to strengthen civilian authority in ways that would reduce the authority of the police. The demand in some places for review boards of one kind or another shows fundamental suspiciousness of what the police are up to and, most important of all, in many parts of the country there is a sense of non-involvement as if the individual citizen and even groups of citizens do not have any personal concern and personal necessity for assisting the police or for taking positive action to reduce or impede the criminality which we know is endemic in our cities. We are all shocked about occasional dramatic stories of the by-standers who just stand by while crimes are committed. But those exceptional incidents are

Dr. Oscar Handlin is the director of the Center for the Study of the History of Liberty in America, and Winthrop Professor of History at Harvard University.
From Oscar Handlin, "Community Organization as a Solution to Police-Community Problems," *The Police Chief* 32, no. 3 (March 1965): 16-22. Reprinted by permission of the publisher.

simply reflections of a deeper attitude that is worth understanding. In exploring this apparent paradox, I think it is necessary to begin with the recognition of the fact that effective police work depends on more than the use of force, particularly in a free, democratic society.

I suppose that even in a totalitarian dictatorship force alone is an inadequate way of establishing order in the whole society. But certainly in our own communities in which we live by the rule of law, thus preserving important guarantees to the individual, effective police work cannot depend simply on the use of night sticks or the threat of force. It demands the active collaboration of the citizens and of their communital organization and it's a serious question to speculate about why, in our society, that collaboration has not been closer than it has been in the past.

This question is the subject of my comments. I would like to examine some of the reasons why there is a problem of police-community relationships; spend most of my time explaining why, with the hope that the practical people among you will be able to come up with a solution to these difficulties, or, if I can, at least illuminate the nature of the problem itself.

HISTORICAL DISTRUST OF POLICE POWER

At this point, I will inject a little bit of history. I don't mean to pull you back too far in the past and yet I have an occupational stake in this. I am a historian. I do like to talk about the past and I'd like to convince you that the past is important. The past, in this case, is important because part of our problem at least, comes out of the history of the way police forces developed in our communities and the relationship those forces had to community organizations as our great cities took form. The interesting point, I think, is how recent the police system is in the experience of the United States. We think of police as always having been there. And yet, the kind of professionally trained police force that we know is a very recent development in the American experience.

Part of our problem lies in the fact that the police force is so recent and has developed under somewhat exceptional circumstances. I go back for my test, as it were, quite a long way to a magazine article that was printed some 150 years ago in Boston, by a prominent merchant and respected politician in the city, who was writing about the subject of police forces. This was about 1815. He said, "If ever there comes a time when Americans have to have in their cities a paid professional police force that will be the end of freedom and democracy as we have known it." Now, this is a significant statement because it shows a certain underlying attitude on the part of Americans toward police which goes far back in our history. This attitude was partly shaped by what they knew in a vague way about European police who all seemed to be the agents of tyranny and oppression, an agency by which czars and emperors kept their people down. But it was partly also an attitude towards professional governmental employees of any kind.

The dominant assumption for a long part of our history was that nobody really worked for the government as a permanent thing. It was believed that there ought to be a constant turnover and that the tenure in any kind of office ought to be for a limited term. So the conception of having a permanent professional police force seemed then, and for a long time continued to seem somehow exceptional and even un-American. It is necessary to remember this as we consider the problems of dealing with this force when it did appear.

There is a second factor which I think important in our history: the exeptional diffusion of violence in our society. From the very beginning our society was a much more violent society than that of most European countries. People were accustomed to carrying guns, to bearing arms. The Constitution meant it seriously when it said that no person should be deprived of the right to bear arms and the primary way people thought of to protect themselves was by self-defense. There is a long history of violence that runs through our experience and I think still remains characteristic of many elements of our society.

Suppose you look, then, at fairly large cities in, say, 1820. New York perhaps had 150,000 people, Boston, 70- or 80,000 people. Try to imagine what it was like in places like that where you didn't have a police force and where people were accustomed to using violence, to carrying arms and to protecting themselves on their own as it were. Law was still supposed to be enforced by the citizens themselves. The law enforcement officer was the sheriff and when he needed help, he rounded up a posse. This is an idea we associate with the western on television, but it applied almost equally well in the nineteenth century to the largest cities in the United States. So we start with the rather peculiar situation in which there is a violent society which doesn't like the idea of a police force and which depends on its own resources, its own citizens, who are untrained but accustomed to violence, to enforce law to the extent that it is enforced.

Actually, the police force in the sense that we know it wasn't developed until about 120 years ago, around the 1840s. It developed almost by imitation of what was going on in other parts of the world. Actually, the London police force was reorganized first in a way that attracted attention here, then Boston and New York copied it and the interior cities copied those of Boston and New York.

This is a very slow and inefficient kind of development. You don't have the police force appearing in significant size, organization and capacity to act, until these cities reached the range of 300- or 400,000 population.

There are some important characteristics that emerge as this development takes form. First, the police force had a low status. The best way of measuring it was their salaries. They were paid very little. They were not very highly respected. Immigrants of various origins entered the police force because nobody else would. They were not particularly skilled and the whole idea of professional work had not as yet been conceived.

One way of judging the low esteem of the police force came in New York

City, in about 1865, when the suggestion was made that the police wear uniforms. The police didn't want to do it because they felt it would be dangerous if they could be recognized as policemen and thus become the objects of attack by gangs and rowdies. The preferred not to be identified for what they were.

The police force had also, in the beginning, undifferentiated functions. By that I mean that they were public servants who were responsible for health, the cleanliness of the streets and all sorts of odds and ends rather than focusing primarily on the repression of disorder and the apprehension of criminals. And there was a tendency to make the police the scapegoats of every difficulty, since in a way they were regarded as public servants. It was easy for politicians to blame them when anything went wrong and conversely it was easy for people to attack them when they wished to attack the political order.

It is significant that down to the very end of the nineteenth century, that is until around 1900, the most important parts of police work, as we would now interpret it, were not performed by the police force. They were primarily carried out by private agencies of various sorts. This fitted in with the general conception of the cop as a rather backward, dumb character who did not have the force and intelligence of or respect given to the private operator who was capable of solving the crimes and performing the functions that the constituted police could not.

This history paints the background of the modern problem. The police in our past seemed like a foreign invention imported from abroad, un-American, and generally held in low status in the society. The police force was frequently the scapegoat for all sorts of other difficulties and it did not seem to be the best agency by which the community could make its will for the respect of law felt.

TWENTIETH CENTURY BRINGS CHANGING CONCEPTS

Now in our own times this situation became impossible. It is important to take cognizance of the changes in community life and in the structure of our cities that made this primitive conception of the police force anachronistic. It is equally important to realize that although the problems change, the conditions change, the police change, parts of that old conception still linger and still affect the relationships of the police to the public.

What are the characteristics of a modern community that most directly affect this problem? The first is simply its size and complexity. It was probably all right to depend on sheriffs or a cluster of untrained policemen to keep order in the city of 200,000 but it certainly is not all right to do so in a city of 2,000,000. As the cities grew in size, the problem of maintaining order grew more complex. It became obvious even to the most prejudiced and perversive authorities that more was necessary to maintain order than the sheriff and his posse or a group of politically appointed and untrained police officers. So the simple increase in size in the communities of our society made some change essential. Further, this increase was accompanied by the growing complexity of organization of these communities.

There was a time in a fairly large city when neighborhoods were cut off from one another to such a considerable extent it was possible to think of the individual neighborhood as a kind of small village and to depend on it more or less to regulate itself. But as the neighborhoods, the internal divisions within the cities grew larger, they became more heterogenous. Even these smaller units lost their rustic quality and became large and highly complex, full of different kinds of people who could not be depended on to regulate the lives of one another as the older kind of community had, and who needed the formal presence of the law to protect them against one another and against outsiders. This problem was the more complex because a large part of the population was drawn from diverse sources and reflected differences in immigrant background or in racial background that created cleavages within the society. Again, a single community could not be depended upon to regulate itself and instead needed the services of the impartial outsider—a police force.

This complexity, of course, created a very difficult problem of identification that required professional services also. One of the reasons a smaller and less complicated community could take care of itself was that most of the people in it would be presumed to know one another, be able to keep an eye on one another and to exercise a kind of continuing running surveillance of one another. But in the large city, in the complex metropolitan center, anonymity was a characteristic of a large part of the population and particularly of the large part of the population inclined toward criminality. It was only through the techniques of recognizing and identifying individuals out of the mass (requiring professional techniques) that the law breaker could be apprehended and brought to justice. So this again increased the dependence upon the professional police and put a greater value on professional police forces.

Finally, I think I only need to remind you of the big technological changes as they are in our own time, the invention of the automobile and the extent to which it transformed criminality, and the appearance of new forms of weapons and their diffusion in the population which also put pressure on the communities to depend on a professional force at the beginning of this century.

From these changes came a persistent drive to raise the professional quality of a police force, to separate it from politics insofar as possible; to recognize the special skills that enter into police work and to organize it on the basis that would reflect merit and build up heightened professional competence. But this development has gone on against the background of the older patterns that I've tried to describe earlier—a kind of mistrust, which has deep popular sources, of the emergence of the police that has resulted in the kind of ambiguous attitude that we find characteristic of the situation in many metropolitan centers. On the one hand, we have this recognition that the police force is essential to the preservation of an orderly existence in this kind of special situation; recognition that it is desirable to stregthen and to improve the police force as much as possible. And yet, side by side with that, we have a popular distrust of the kind of power that is being lodged in the hands of these people lest they have a kind of control not susceptible to the popular will.

It is my belief that this ambiguity, this mixed attitude, this paradoxical desire to secure more protection from the police and yet fear the power that will make that protection possible can only be resolved by establishing new kinds of links between the police and the community that will make the police seem to the critical elements of the community but an agent of the community that is acting on its own behalf.

Now the means of making the police the agents of the community depend upon the character of the community itself. In a sense the police force is an instrument of the polity, it depends on the political system, it is appointed, and presumably controlled, by the elected officials and you might say this political connection is adequate to give the people a sense of confidence in the work of the police. But, however exciting an election may be, it comes at infrequent intervals and the political leaders are not the only important elements in the community structure nor are they the ones that are closest to the continuing deep interests of the population. If we look at a modern metropolis, its community life is more than that of the municipality, more than that of just the political system; its community life is composed of a medley of different kinds of institutions forming an intricate web of associations that hold people together in their day to day existence and provide them with the regular patterns of organization throughout the year.

When we speak of the community meaningfully then, we cannot limit ourselves to the political community, or to the municipality which represents one; and not, perhaps, even the most important of the organizations of the community as a whole. If we think realistically of the community, we think also of the religious associations and professional organizations, the labor unions, the fraternal and cultural groups through which people actually carry on their lives and through which people do associate on a regular basis. The police as a force is conceived of primarily as an instrument of the municipality, as a political organization, and it is insofar as it functions to maintain the law. But the work of the police also intercepts the work of all these other associations. The work of the police should bring them into contact with these other organized aspects of the life of a community because it is through these other associations that much more intimate relationships can develop with the citizenry as a whole than in its political role. Through that association a relationship of greater confidence and involvement may develop.

I'm not speaking of St. Louis in this connection for it obviously is a special case. But I think it is fair to say if one thinks of the large municipalities as a whole, the links between the police and the communal organizations have not been strengthened in the last quarter of a century and in some ways have been weakened. In an earlier period the policeman walking his beat at least had a certain familiarity with the institutions of his own immediate district. I'm not putting too much emphasis on that nor do I wish to romanticize that gallant figure; but nevertheless he knew something about the actual people and the actual organizations in the district of the beat which he walked. It's a serious question to consider: Do the links between the police force and the associations of the community as a whole adequately compensate for the disappearance of that older and perhaps more primitive kind of relationship—the foot patrolman? In any case there certainly is a long way to go before we can feel that there is an adequate rapport between the police of the community and the whole associational life of the community.

There is a need for an adequate recognition of the mutual interdependence of the police and the community for the common purposes they both serve. In establishing these links, I think it's important, however, to remember one other characteristic of the police developments in the past half century. If this association between the police and community works well there is also a danger that it might work too well—the police may become too consciously an agency of the community and, in a sense perhaps, over-reach itself in acting on behalf of the community. A very simple example will give you an indication of what I mean. I can conceive of a police force in the state of Mississippi being so thoroughly associated with the dominant agencies of the dominant elements of the community and so thoroughly the agents of the community that it actually frustrates the law instead of enforcing it. I can conceive of, even outside of Mississippi, other kinds of situations where the police may become too deliberately a part of the apparatus of the dominant elements in the community and so may become disrespectful of certain features of the law that the community itself at certain times does not respect. The safeguard here is the professional quality of the police. The safeguard here is precisely in the recognition that while the police force is an agency of the community it has obligations and standards of its own. Its obligations are to enforce the law. Its standards are those like other professions of competence, of how you do it despite any immediate local pressures, so that there may well be times in which the largest interest of the community would demand that the police force stand up against the community itself when it acts in ways that run counter to the law and that infringe upon the ultimate obligation of the police as a professional group.

What we need, then, is a development away from our past and its mixed traditions, into which the concept of a professional police force arrived as something extraneous; something that developed out of necessity rather than from any genuine roots in our society; something that developed almost against the will of the dominant elements in our society. What we need is: recognition by our citizens that in the kind of complex world in which our life is organized a professionally competent, skilled police force is essential to the welfare of the community; and recognition by our police that they can be professionally competent and skilled only when they stand apart from, yet through adequate links are vitally associated with, the community.

With these reciprocal sets of relationships firmly established, some of the paradoxes and ambiguities which have troubled us in the past decades may be resolved.

NOTES

1. The 1964 presidential campaign.